NEW YORK LITERARY LIGHTS

NEW

YORK

LITERARY

LIGHTS

WILLIAM CORBETT

 GRAYWOLF PRESS
SAINT PAUL
MINNESOTA

Publication of this volume is made possible in part by a grant provided by the
Minnesota State Arts Board through an appropriation by the Minnesota State
Legislature, and by a grant from the National Endowment for the Arts. Significant support has also been provided by Dayton's, Mervyn's, and Target stores
through the Dayton Hudson Foundation, the Andrew W. Mellon Foundation,
the McKnight Foundation, the General Mills Foundation, the St. Paul Companies, and other generous contributions from foundations, corporations, and individuals. To these organizations and individuals we offer our heartfelt thanks.

Additional support for this publication was provided by the Lannan Foundation and Furthermore, the publication program of The J. M. Kaplan Fund.

Published by Graywolf Press
2402 University Avenue, Suite 203
Saint Paul, Minnesota 55114
All rights reserved.

www.graywolfpress.org

Published in the United States of America

ISBN 1-55597-272-1

2 4 6 8 9 7 5 3 1
First Graywolf Printing, 1998

Library of Congress Catalog Card Number: 97-80077

Map (p. 306): Patricia Isaacs, Parrot Graphics

Cover photograph: Rudy Burckhardt, "Broadway toward Union Square,"
ca. 1947. Courtesy Tibor de Nagy Gallery, New York.

Cover design: Julie Metz

WILLIAM CORBETT
lives in Boston's South End
and is Writer in Residence
at MIT. He edits poetry for
Grand Street. His most
recent books, all published
by Zoland Books, are *Philip
Guston's Late Work: A
Memoir, New & Selected
Poems*, and *Furthering My
Education*.

In Memory of Joe Brainard
(1942–1994)

I happen to like New York.
I happen to like this burg,
And when I have to give the world
A last farewell
And the undertaker
Starts to ring my funeral bell,
I don't want to go to heaven,
Don't want to go to hell.
I happen to like New York.
I happen to like New York.

COLE PORTER

Introduction

The present in New York is so powerful that the past is lost.
JOHN JAY CHAPMAN

Native son Chapman saw in New York City, what the ancient Greek philosopher Heraclitus divined to be the case, that change alone is constant and life's only certainty. Today New York City, Manhattan in particular but the other four boroughs, the Bronx, Queens, Staten Island, and Brooklyn as well, embodies this perception.

This has not always been so. The city, founded as New Amsterdam six years after the Pilgrims landed at Plymouth Rock, developed slowly. As you will see it did not become the first city in America until late in the nineteenth century and became a capital of the world, the "Imperial City," only after World War II.

But beginning on some impossible-to-determine day as early, perhaps, as the 1840s, New York City achieved a rhythm that pulses in it this very minute. All that natives or visitors need do is step onto a city sidewalk and they feel it, relentless and exhilarating. It is the rhythm of unceasing change.

Since New York *never* stands still, this means that the city of the 1980s, of Yuppies, arbitrageurs, Michael Milken, and Jay McInerney's novel *Bright Lights, Big City* is as long gone as Frank O'Hara's city of the 1950s, Ralph Ellison's of the 1940s, and back to the Old New York of Edith Wharton, and before her to that of the first great New York writer, Walt Whitman.

As the first fact about the city, change has dictated the arrangement of this book. Those who wish to encounter Whitman's New York cannot do so by visiting Pfaff's, the saloon he frequented, nor can they go to the 5 Spot where Frank O'Hara "leaned on the john door" listening to Billie Holiday. To walk the downtown streets where these places once stood, readers need a degree of information to orient and prime their imaginations. Thus, this book opens with a short essay that presents the big picture, the broad flow of New York City literary life from the city's beginnings as a Dutch colony to yesterday. This essay also sketches the growth of the city from trading post to metropolis.

Following this comes, in effect, an encyclopedia. A to Z, Auchincloss to Zukofsky, covering not only New York City's writers but publishers, agents, magazines, bookstores, libraries, neighborhoods, institutions from the American Academy of Arts and Letters on 156th Street to the

Poetry Project at St. Mark's-in-the-Bowery, and a miscellany of other information that will enlarge the reader's sense of what creates literary life in the city.

In writing these entries I have followed the principle of honoring the past while serving the present and near present. A book like this ought to speak not only to but for its time. Condemn the canon as we might, history will decide what in the past fifty or seventy-five years is of lasting importance. Here and now we know that the literary life of a great city comes out of a congeries of forces and attitudes and not out of caring about what will last. Oh, we may care or say we do about the eternal, but we cannot really know what will endure, so why start keeping a list? The aim of this book is to inform and delight, and this can best be done by setting the table for a banquet. Reader, begin anywhere.

Literary New York City

The English Puritans who landed in the New World in 1620 were people of the book, the Bible; people who came with the dream of creating a society based on their religious beliefs. The Dutchmen who discovered what was to become New Amsterdam brought with them an account book. Henry Hudson, an Englishman who accompanied the first of them, hoped the river that today bears his name might lead him to the wealth of the Indies. Adraien Block and those who followed saw the possibilities for trade as a soon as they entered New York's commodious harbor. Peter Minuit bought the twenty-two square miles of the isle of Manhattan from the Indians he found there for twenty-four dollars in trade goods. New York City began in commerce and commerce remains its heart today. It is because of this that the city became America's literary capital, but it did not happen overnight. New York City grew slowly into itself. Its literary life did not dominate the nation until well into the twentieth century.

While New England began with a more or less common vision held by people who spoke the same language, New Amsterdam, as befits a city that looks outward, spoke many languages, at least eighteen within decades of its founding. An even more illuminating contrast can be seen in where the different colonists put their energy. By 1638, study being crucial to the practice and propagation of their faith, the Puritans had established Harvard. There would not be a college in New York City until 1754. Clearly, the Dutch and the English, who conquered New Amsterdam in 1664, did not consider study vital to their enterprise. Trade and the pleasures that flowed from wealth were what interested New Yorkers.

New York prospered under the Dutch and their English conquerors, but it remained more an outpost than a bona fide city. The English, for example, never established free schools. While there were many rich merchants living on large estates, New York's population did not swell as did that of Massachusetts and Connecticut. It was not until 1693 that the first printing press came to the city. This was brought by the Philadelphian William Bradford, who had run afoul of the authorities in his native city. He became the city's royal printer, but one printing press cannot create a literary life.

Bradford remained active in the city for more than thirty years and published New York's first newspaper, the *New York Gazette,* in 1725.

More important, he had John Peter Zenger as an apprentice. After learning his trade, Zenger, a German immigrant, began publishing his own newspaper. His trial in 1735 for libel and sedition made the city's first significant literary news and had consequences far beyond New York.

Zenger's paper, the *Weekly Journal,* made rude and raucous fun of the British colonial government until the government lost its patience and threw him in jail under the charge of seditious libel. At the time common law held, as Edward Robb Ellis writes in *The Epic of New York City,* that "the greater the truth, the greater the libel." Zenger's lawyer, Andrew Hamilton of Philadelphia, the most famous lawyer in the colonies, argued, "It is not the bare printing and publishing of the paper that will make it libel. The words themselves must be libelous— that is false, scandalous and seditious—or else my client is not guilty." In other words, Hamilton argued that if what the *Weekly Journal* reported was true then it could not be libel, an argument that the jury accepted in acquitting Zenger.

This verdict did not in itself guarantee freedom of the press, but it was the first step, not just in the colonies, but in the world, toward the free press we have in the United States today. That this happened in New York suggests both the rough-and-ready character of the place and the freedom that was already in the air there—freedom, not in the sense of articulated ideas and legislative acts, but in spirit. The city had a lack of respect for authority that came, perhaps, from the desire of its citizens to go about their business in their own way.

In the eighteenth century there is Zenger and then . . . well, the poet Philip Freneau is born in the city in 1752, but, really, there is very little literary news of note until the end of the century. ("Thrice happy Dryden," Freneau lamented, "could meet some rival bard on every street.")

By 1763 New York's population had reached 12,000, which put it behind both Boston and Philadelphia. The city was, not surprisingly, in the forefront of the fight against the British government's imposition of the Stamp Act. Delegates from throughout the colonies convened in the city in 1765 what has been called the Stamp Act Congress. They joined the cry of "No taxation without representation."

At the outbreak of the Revolutionary War in 1776, the British captured New York from the patriots and did not evacuate the city until war's end in 1783. In 1785 New York City became the nation's temporary capital. New York City was then solely the island of Manhattan and would remain so until 1874. Two years later, in 1787, Royall

Tyler's play *The Contrast* had its premiere in the city. This deserves mention because it was the first comedy written by an American, and because New York had a theater in which it could be performed. Boston, which was about to become the home of the transcendentalists, abolition, and the Hub of the Solar System for at least seventy-five years, did not permit theater.

George Washington was sworn in as president of the United States in New York's Federal Hall in April 1789. When, in October 1790, the capital was moved to Philadelphia, Washington departed the city, never to return. Unlike Paris, London, or Rome, New York was thus left to become a capital in everything but name.

"It takes a great deal of history," native son Henry James once pointed out, "to produce a little literature." In the 1820s, with New York's population at 120,000, making it the nation's largest city, that literature began to be produced by Washington Irving, James Fenimore Cooper, Fitz-Greene Halleck, and others. These writers labored under one handicap that had nothing to do with the length of their city's history. Since there existed no international copyright law cheap editions of British books printed by American publishers flooded the New York markets. Acting on the principle that it made no sense to pay for what you could get for free, publishers kept American writers, who would have to be paid for their work, out in the cold. The success of several James Fenimore Cooper novels, which demonstrated that American books could make money, and the refusal of several publishers to pirate books helped nurse American writing through its infancy.

By 1846 Herman Melville, Edgar Allan Poe, Walter Whitman (he did not name himself Walt until *Leaves of Grass* appeared in 1855), William Cullen Bryant, and Washington Irving were all active in the city of nearly 500,000. While some of these writers certainly knew of one another, they moved in different circles. Part of this is explained by their different generations and, in Whitman's case, the relative little he had published. But it is also true that then, just as today, New York contained multitudes. An establishment literary culture represented by Irving and Bryant was already in place, but there would always be room in New York City for several circles spinning at once and a number of outsiders, *isolatos,* as well.

What kind of city was it as the Civil War drew near? We have a wealth of eyewitness testimony, even that of Charles Dickens. It portrays a loud and filthy city, certainly much louder than today on main thoroughfares such as Broadway. The noise came from the mass of

people, the careening omnibuses that transported passengers in what
were often races up- and downtown, the many carts, wagons, and all
manner of horse-drawn vehicles, and the cows and pigs in the streets. In
the heart of the city on what is now lower Broadway it was busy to the
point of chaos. The dung of the city's animals lay in the streets, open
sewers ran throughout the city, and garbage, which was not systemati-
cally collected until the end of the nineteenth century, was everywhere
underfoot. New York was a boom town, and its government simply
could not keep up with its growth.

Amid this rawness and squalor there was great wealth, for following
the opening of the Erie Canal in 1825 New York stood as the gateway
not only to America but to the west. The economy could and did go
from boom to bust—nineteenth-century American capitalism was a
ruthless state without any of the controls we know today—and the
city's chaos mirrored the drive of its citizens toward what would one
day be called the American Dream. Side by side with this wealth there
also existed terrible poverty. The immigration of Irish and Germans to
the city meant cheap, unskilled labor and the invention of the tenement,
cheap, airless housing that bred disease and crime. The city was then, as
it remains today, a fabulous mixture of the dizzyingly high and the
crushingly low. Exhilarating, absolutely, and already like nowhere else
on earth.

It is significant that when Walt Whitman wanted his *Leaves of Grass*
recognized, he sent it outside the city, to Ralph Waldo Emerson in Concord, Massachusetts. Whitman knew that there was no writer of Emerson's stature in New York. Indeed, New York's intellectual culture
before the Civil War did not have the coherence of New England's.
Nothing there resembled transcendentalism, and no cause, certainly not
abolition, unified New York's thinkers, politicians, and writers. Whitman wanted the respect and blessing of the nation's dominant literary
culture, and he knew it was not in his own city.

The Civil War changed everything in America. Above and beyond
the impact of steel mill growth, the mechanization of agriculture, the
changeover from whale oil to petroleum, and the concentration in the
victorious North of great fortunes, there were the dead men, more than
six hundred thousand of them. How could a void of such proportion be
measured? How could a nation revive itself after such devastation?

Not only did the war deplete and exhaust the nation, but for the victor it provided, as war always does, a high degree of organization.
Whitman, who hardly returned to the city after the war, knew that his

wild, vulgar, and powerfully alive New York had been tamed by the war, its energy sent inward. And then came what Lewis Mumford called the "Brown Decades," 1870 to the turn of the century. Mumford chose the color to emphasize the drabness of the nation's literary and plastic arts. He pointed out that the period's greatest writer was Emily Dickinson, who was next to unknown during the time. In Mumford's words, "The laval flow of industrialism after the war had swept over all the cities of the spirit."

And yet during these decades New York put its energies into the foundation of the city we know today. From 1873, when Central Park opened, until 1911, when the main branch of the New York Public Library at Forty-second Street and Fifth Avenue opened its doors, the Sixth and Third Avenue elevated railroads were built, the Metropolitan Museum of Art got its permanent home, the Brooklyn Bridge crossed the East River, the Statue of Liberty came from France, the city's first skyscraper rose, its first underground subway line began operation, and Penn Station opened. For all the building being done it was also the "Old New York" of Edith Wharton's great novels.

In 1898 the boroughs of Manhattan, Brooklyn, Queens, Staten Island, and the Bronx united their 320 square miles and 3,393,252 people, and the map of the city was drawn as it remains today. In 1907, 1,285,349 immigrants entered this city. New York had done its work and thrown itself open to the world. If there is little great writing during this period there are at least the American realist novels of William Dean Howells, Stephen Crane, and Theodore Dreiser. New York, expanding, institution-building New York, with its hideous and foul new slums, fresh opportunities, and, by now, old money, was crucial to all three.

By the beginning of World War I, Boston had almost completed its transformation into a university town. The great New England writers of the nineteenth century were long dead, and after them came generations of curators. Boston's last great writer of the nineteenth century, Henry Adams, proclaimed that he had seen the end of his world. New York's time was about to come, and another war would be decisive in bringing it about.

Before World War I, New York was still a horse-drawn city. Because the subway and elevated trains had replaced the omnibus the rhythm in the streets was more sedate, but visitors like Henry James and Ezra Pound were impressed with the size and surge of the crowds who jammed the sidewalks. In 1913 the city's population exceeded 5,600,000. Pound, James, and others were also impressed by that New

World invention, the skyscraper, which created the Manhattan skyline and turned many of the city's streets into caverns. Skyscraper! What optimism—not to say arrogance—in the word.

As New York thrust itself up into the sky its streets began to form the patterns of neighborhoods we know today. Downtown was Wall Street, the citadel of business. Then the slums of Mulberry Street where Little Italy and Chinatown converged. Farther up on the East Side stood the tenements of the Lower East Side jammed with immigrants, largely Jewish, from Eastern Europe. Greenwich Village, which had been laid out before the grid system, had become the home of political radicals, writers, and artists. Its narrow streets were prized for their Old World intimacy, and a way of life that seemed in opposition to the striving and grasping that took place on Wall Street and Uptown, which for Villagers meant above Fourteenth Street. There was Chelsea above the Village and to the east a sort of no-man's-land that still runs up to the posh Turtle Bay and Beekman Place before going on to the Upper East Side. Midtown had become the city's tourist and shopping district. Broadway, made brilliant by electricity and later neon, had become the Great White Way. North of Central Park, Harlem, still a German and Jewish community, had begun to be transformed by blacks migrating from the South. It is the differences, the changes from neighborhood to neighborhood, from the garment district midtown on the West Side to the flower market into Chelsea and then the Village, that were irresistible to walkers. New York, then as now, is a city that reveals itself to whoever takes its measure on foot.

What the First World War did was draw a generation of American writers from their homes across the country to New York because it was now what Paris was to France, the city where men and women of talent and ambition came to make their fortunes. They came, too, with no thought of fortune in mind, but to find themselves in the throng of their own kind. Many expatriated themselves to Europe, but only for a few years, and like Malcolm Cowley, Djuna Barnes, Hart Crane, e. e. cummings, and John Dos Passos, most returned to New York. Others came to stay because the life of the imagination they envisioned for themselves could take place nowhere else. Marianne Moore and Edmund Wilson came to the Village as did the reclusive Edwin Arlington Robinson. Edna St. Vincent Millay came and so did William Carlos Williams. After the war the heart of American modernist writing was in New York City, and then in the twenties everything got turned up a notch. The city became the Big Apple.

The *New Yorker* began in the twenties and so did Henry Luce's *Time*. New publishers led by Horace Liveright, Alfred A. Knopf, and Bennett Cerf's Random House began to publish the new writers. As the city's literary life expanded the many lives within it, the simultaneity of the city's several literary lives became evident. Malcolm Cowley wrote *Exile's Return* about his generation, and nowhere in it does he mention the Harlem Renaissance taking place a few miles away from Greenwich Village. Ignorance? Racism? A combination of both? Cowley knew that Zora Neale Hurston, Langston Hughes, and Wallace Thurman were there, but his generation was Gertrude Stein's lost generation. They had known Europe, and they were simply in another world from the Renaissance, even though they were in the same city.

On Broadway in the 1927–28 season 264 shows opened. The movies had not yet come into their own, and New York was the center of American theater—and of American book publishing, magazine publishing, and radio. The important writing being done in Europe by T. S. Eliot, Ezra Pound, Ernest Hemingway, and F. Scott Fitzgerald soon entered America through New York, and so did the art of Pablo Picasso, Henri Matisse, the dadaists, and the surrealists. So much was happening in the city at once that no one could be a part of it all. In the twenties New York's literary life became many, not as in a collection of fragments but as in more or less independent entities holding to different aesthetic, ethnic, or political standards.

On the eve of the 1929 stock market crash Cowley, Moore, cummings, Hurston, Countee Cullen, Thomas Wolfe, Carl Van Vechten, Edmund Wilson, Dorothy Parker, Dawn Powell, Max Eastman, and Eugene O'Neill were at work in New York. The list of writers active in the city could fill several pages. New York would not see this range and variety again until after World War II.

Within months of the crash the spirit of New York's literary life changed to a fractious, tetchy, political one, and the great experiment of the twenties was replaced by an earnestness and solemnity in keeping with streets filled with men out of work. The writers who had created the Harlem Renaissance split apart to follow their imaginations elsewhere, and so did Cowley's exiles. In their place a group gathered around the *Partisan Review* and a number of the sons and daughters of immigrants, who, having been educated in New York public schools and colleges, becan to write of the world of their fathers and mothers.

By middecade turmoil in Europe had begun to bring intellectual refugees like Hannah Arendt, Erwin Piscator, and Claude Lévi-Strauss to the city. From across America the painters Philip Guston, Jackson Pollock, Robert Motherwell, Mark Rothko, and the others who would invent abstract expressionism, the first absolutely American style of painting, came to the city to work on the mural projects of the WPA. These men and women helped give shape to a new, more cosmopolitan literary life than that of the twenties. In the late thirties the groundwork was laid for the New York that would become the first city in the war following the Allied victory in 1945.

The novelist Gore Vidal has calculated the American century as lasting from the end of World War II to roughly the mid-1950s. These are the years, coincidentally, when Vidal was in New York, a member of that generation of novelists who produced important books before they reached thirty: Truman Capote, James Baldwin, William Styron, and the brightest star, Norman Mailer.

The success of Mailer's World War II novel, *The Naked and the Dead* (1948), combined with his talent, energy, and ambition to place him in the forefront of New York writers. Over the next several years all of literary New York heated up. Ralph Ellison's novel *Invisible Man,* a work often cited as *the* American novel of its time, appeared as did the first work of the Beat Generation, Tennessee Williams's plays, the early work of the New York School of Poets, J. D. Salinger's *Catcher in the Rye,* John Cheever's short stories . . . but Mailer alone cut across the literary circles then in full swing. He knew the Beats and the *Partisan Review* crowd; he went up to Harlem and began a touchy friendship with James Baldwin; he wrote for *Esquire* and was a founder of the *Village Voice,* and he was as fearless in giving offense as he was in pursuing the many impulses of his imagination. In the sixties he even ran for mayor of the city!

The fifties, a decade that actually stretched to the assassination of John F. Kennedy, saw a great surge of energy in New York, the pent-up explosion of energy held in or otherwise channeled by the war and the new energy of those who resisted post-war conformity, who wanted to write and live black lives, gay lives, Beat lives, feminist lives, lives that crossed the boundaries of their smug and complacent country. Somehow all these forces came together to create an even bigger literary Apple.

Then came yet another war to change the New York literary landscape. Before the Vietnam War writers could come to New York more or less confident that they might, with luck, talent, and industry, be able to make a living by their art. To be a freelance intellectual, a writer dependent on the marketplace and not teaching for a living to support a writing habit, was still a possibility. And the city was still cheap enough for young people to live in while they made their way. The war changed all this.

At the war's conclusion in 1975, America's colleges and universities had absorbed much of the nation's intellectual life, and fiction writers and poets had increasingly been taken into creative writing programs. The real estate boom of the late sixties and early seventies caused New York rents to rise. They soared into the Yuppie eighties and remain dauntingly high today. Writers who wanted to live in, say, the Lower East Side in 1975 found rents three to five times what they had been a decade before. Artists and writers opened up new areas like SoHo and TriBeCa, but commercial interests flowed quickly in after them and soon streets of cheap lofts housed trendy shoe and clothing stores. Brooklyn beckoned, but to rent or buy in New York had become a major expense. It is very hard nowadays to spend a bohemian youth writing in New York—hard enough that a musical set in the new bohemia is titled *Rent*.

Still, New York's literary life hums along on several levels. The machines, the publishers, agents, editors, magazines, communications industries that make American writing go are still concentrated in the city. There is hardly a major American, English, Irish, French, or Spanish writer who does not do business in New York, even if he or she visits only by phone or fax. Intellectual life may have gone into the nation's universities, and while this fragmentation has been accompanied by a decentralization in publishing—there are scores of small, independent publishers publishing literary titles across America—New York is where all the big book deals are made.

But those deals are not, in a strictly literary sense, as big as they once were—big as in significant to the culture as a whole. Several forces came together to produce this outcome. In the sixties, rock 'n' roll, that fusion of white with black energy, captured the imagination of the nation's young. New York was only part of the scene where this took place. The Fillmore was the name of a San Francisco concert hall before the rock impresario Bill Graham brought it to New York and put it on a Lower East Side theater. Whether in San Francisco, Atlanta, or Chicago, the guitar heroes and heroines of rock 'n' roll supplanted, to a degree, the literary heroes of past generations. Allen Ginsberg might be welcome on almost any stage, but there was room for few other poets.

Then, specifically in New York, in the late seventies the art world, painting in the lead, held center stage. The great eminence of Andy Warhol, and the sudden ascent of David Salle, Jean-Michel Basquiat, Elizabeth Murray, and Julian Schnabel attracted the big money that is synonymous with both fame and ink, meaning publicity and interest on a large scale, in New York. Where writers were once the artists most likely to be known, now musicians and painters rose above them. This may have little to do with what sort of books actually get written and read, but writing and money, ideas and fame have been inextricably linked in New York since the beginning of this century.

Whatever arts are riding high an astonishing percentage of the nation's readers are in New York—readers, that is, who keep current and live in a literary culture; readers who seek out one of the city's bookstores to buy new books at least a couple of times a month; readers who attend the city's many book launchings and readings. An astonishing array of writers remain at work in the city: Norman Mailer, Louis Auchincloss, Albert Murray, John Ashbery, Susan Sontag, Stanley Crouch, Paul Auster, Oscar Hijuelos, Eileen Myles, Jeffrey Eugenidies, Ann Lauterbach, Jessica Hagedorn, Phillip Lopate, John Yau, the poets of the Nuyorican Café, and those who read at the Ear Inn or the Dia Center for the Arts, and, as always, any number of writers who have yet to make their mark.

In the past few years an enormous number of books about New York, topped by the first *Encyclopedia of New York City,* have appeared. This might be read two ways. Either they are a summing up, perhaps even a kind of elegy to a New York that people have begun to see as vanishing, or all of these books, histories, novels, and memoirs, represent a pause, a deep breath and close look at the city as it is poised to defy all expectations, as it has so often, and change in a new way.

Chronology

1524   The Florentine explorer Giovanni da Verrazano discovers the bay where New York City now stands.

1609   Searching for a route to the Indies, Captain Henry Hudson, an Englishman in the employ of the Dutch East India Company, sails up the river later named after him. He reaches the site of the present-day Albany before turning back.

1610   Captain Adraien Block leads Dutch exploration of Long Island Sound and claims it as New Netherlands.

1626   Director-general Peter Minuit's first act is the purchase of the isle of Manhattan from local Indians for twenty-four dollars in goods. He names the trading outpost of two hundred Dutch and Walloon settlers New Amsterdam.

1647   The one-legged Peter Stuyvesant becomes director-general of New Amsterdam. Eighteen languages are spoken in the town.

1653   Population reaches eight hundred. First prison is built and first poorhouse opened. The City Tavern becomes the City Hall, and a night watch begins. There is now a municipal government.

1664   During the English-Dutch war a British fleet sent by the Duke of York captures New Amsterdam and the city is renamed New York.

1693   William Bradford of Philadelphia brings the first printing press to the city.

1698   Trinity Church at Wall Street is completed. Today Trinity occupies its third building

1703   A battery of cannons is set up at the southern tip of Manhattan, the area known today as "The Battery."

1725   William Bradford publishes the city's first newspaper, the *New York Gazette*.

1735   Trial and acquittal of publisher John Peter Zenger on charges of libel and sedition.

1754   The city's first college, King's College—now Columbia University—opens.

1762   Samuel Fraunces, an immigrant from the Caribbean, buys the building at the corner of Pearl and Broad Street and opens Fraunces Tavern. The tavern, rebuilt and restored, is a museum today.

1763   City population stands at 12,000.

1776   Revolutionary War begins. British capture New York.

1783   War ends and British evacuate the city. General George Washington hosts a victory dinner at Fraunces Tavern.

1785   New York is the nation's temporary capital.

1787   Royall Tyler's *The Contrast,* the first comedy written by an American, is produced in New York City.

1789   The Congress convenes at Federal Hall, formerly City Hall, and George Washington is sworn in as the first president of the United States.

1807   Robert Fulton sails the world's first steamship, the *Clermont,* on the Hudson River.

1811   The Commissioner's Plan lays out streets and avenues north of Houston on a grid.

1816   The village of Brooklyn is incorporated. Its name derives from the Dutch Breuckelen.

1819   31 May, Walt Whitman is born West Hills, Huntington Township, on Long Island

    1 August, Herman Melville is born on Pearl Street, Manhattan.

1820   New York's population exceeds 120,000, making it the nation's most populated city.

1825   Erie Canal linking Albany and Buffalo opens, which means New York City now has a direct connection with the west.

1832   Four thousand New Yorkers die of cholera.

1835   A fire that starts in a Pearl Street warehouse burns down 693 buildings. Not a single life is lost, but property damage amounts to $20 million.

1837   City population reaches 300,000.

1846   Rules for "the New York game," a forerunner of baseball, are agreed upon by a committee under the direction of Alexander J. Cartwright. The New York Knickerbocker Club fields a team.

    Herman Melville's *Typee* becomes a best-seller. Melville, Edgar Allan Poe, William Cullen Bryant, Washington Irving, and Walter Whitman are all active in the city.

1847   City College of New York is founded.

1851   The *New York Times* begins publication on 18 September.

1855   Walt Whitman's *Leaves of Grass,* printed in Brooklyn, goes on sale.

1862   Edith Wharton is born Edith Newbold Jones at 14 West 23rd Street.

1863   Draft riots, half-spontaneous and half-planned by Confederate sympathizers in the city, leave more than 2,000 dead. The diarist George Templeton Strong says of his city, "This is a nice town to call itself a centre of civilization!"

1873   Central Park, designed by Frederick Law Olmsted and Calvert Vaux, opens. It is the first of its kind in the United States.

1878   Sixth Avenue and Third Avenue Els (elevated railroads) are open for business.

1880   Population of Manhattan passes 1,000,000. The Metropolitan Museum of Art moves into its permanent home.

1883   The Brooklyn Bridge, at the time the longest such span in the world, opens. It is the first bridge to cross the East River.

1886   Statue of Liberty is dedicated. A gift of the French, it commemorates the centenary of the Declaration of Independence.

1892   As the tide of immigrants rises Ellis Island takes over from Castle Garden as the processing center. Today the island's Great Hall, where so many entered this country, is a museum.

1898   The boroughs of Manhattan, Brooklyn, Queens, Staten Island, and the Bronx are united to form New York City. Total area, 320 square miles; population, 3,393,252. This came about because of city comptroller Andrew Green, the Robert Moses of the nineteenth century, had a dream of an "imperial city." He was given a medal acknowledging him as "the father of Greater New York."

1902   The city's first skyscraper, the Flatiron Building at 23rd Street and Fifth Avenue, is completed.

1904   The city's first subway line begins operation from City Hall to 145th Street.

1907   1,285,349 immigrants are admitted to the United States through the port of New York.

1910   Pennsylvania Railroad Station begins service.

1911   The main branch of the New York Public Library opens at 42nd Street and 5th Avenue.

1913   The census calculates New York's population at 5,620,048. Grand Central Station opens and so does the Woolworth Building, at 792 feet the world's tallest. Sixteen hundred works of art, including Marcel Duchamp's *Nude Descending a Staircase,* are in the Armory Show from February 17 to March 15 at 69th Regiment Armory on Lexington Avenue at 25th Street.

1924   James Baldwin is born in Harlem.

1925   Harold Ross founds the *New Yorker.*

1927   The Holland Tunnel, running under the Hudson River to link New York and New Jersey, opens.

1928   In the 1927–28 season 264 shows opened in 76 Broadway theaters, the most in Broadway history.

1929   24 October, Black Thursday, the stock market crashes, signaling a worldwide economic crises. The Museum of Modern Art opens.

1930   Population reaches 6,930,446.

1931   Both the Empire State Building and the George Washington Bridge are completed. At 102 stories, the Empire State was the world's tallest skyscraper into the 1970s and remains the world's most famous one.

1939   The World's Fair begins in Flushing Meadows, Queens. No other world's fair will be so celebrated or memorable as this one.

1943   Rodgers and Hammerstein's *Oklahoma!* opens

1946   The United Nations is located in the city. In 1952 the permanent home of the Security Council and General Assembly opens on the East River between 42nd and 48th Streets.

1947   Tennessee Williams's *A Streetcar Named Desire*, starring Marlon Brando, opens on Broadway.

1948   Norman Mailer's *The Naked and the Dead* becomes a bestseller. Idlewild International Airport opens in Queens.

1952   Ralph Ellison's *Invisible Man* is published.

1953   Merce Cunningham founds his dance company with John Cage as its musical director.

1956   Allen Ginsberg's *Howl and Other Poems* appears.

1957   The New York Giants and Brooklyn Dodgers baseball teams move to the West Coast, San Francisco and Los Angeles, respectively, leaving the New York Yankees as the city's only major league baseball team.

1959   Frank Lloyd Wright's Guggenheim Museum opens.

1960   Fidel Castro of Cuba and Nikita Khrushchev come to the United Nations. At one point an outraged Khrushchev pounds on his desk with his shoe.

1965   On 9 November a blackout occurs throughout the Northeast, darkening all of New York City save for Staten Island and a part of Brooklyn. 800,000 persons are trapped in the city's subways. It takes 13 hours to restore electricity, but there is remarkably little civil disturbance. Nine months later the city's birthrate takes a big leap.

The Beatles appear in Shea Stadium before a crowd of 53,275.

1966   The poet Frank O'Hara dies in a car accident on Fire Island.

1969   Police raid the Stonewall Inn, a gay bar on Christopher Street. Gays refuse to go quietly, and their two nights of resistance launch the gay rights movement. The block where the bar stood is now Stonewall Place.

1973   The 110-story twin towers of the World Trade Center are completed.

1974   Duke Ellington dies.

1975   City teeters on brink of insolvency. The "Big Mac" (Municipal Assistance Corporation) under the direction of Felix Rohatyn is appointed to bring the city out of fiscal crisis. Rohatyn serves until 1993 by which time the "Big Mac" has done its job.

1978   New Yorker Isaac Bashevis Singer becomes the first author writing in Yiddish to win the Nobel Prize for Literature.

1980   Population is at 7,071,639, some 1,200,000 of whom are Jewish, making New York City the largest Jewish city in the world. It is estimated that upward of 500,000 illegal aliens live in the city.

John Lennon is shot to death by a deranged fan outside his home in the Dakota.

1984   Bernhard Goetz shoots four black youths on the No. 2 subway at Chambers Street with an unlicensed handgun. Civil suits that result are not settled until a dozen years later.

1987   Death of Andy Warhol and publication of Tom Wolfe's satirical novel *Bonfire of the Vanities.*

1990   David Dinkins is elected New York's first African American mayor. Leonard Bernstein dies.

1991   Miles Davis dies.

1992   John Gotti, "The Teflon Don," is convicted on numerous charges and sentenced to life in a federal prison.

1993   Novelist Toni Morrison becomes the first African American writer to win the Nobel Prize. A car bomb placed by terrorists explodes in the garage of the World Trade Center, killing five.

1996   Farrar, Straus & Giroux celebrates fifty years of publishing and New Directions, sixty.

Academy of American Poets
584 Broadway, Suite 1208

In 1996 the academy declared April National Poetry Month. The hope is that publishers, booksellers, libraries, teachers, and poets across the nation will participate in readings, festivals, and workshops, thus celebrating poetry and its significance in American life. This is exactly the sort of activity Marie Bullock had in mind when she founded the academy in 1934. The story goes that Bullock, an American raised in Europe, returned to the United States to discover poetry treated with far less respect than she had known it to be in the Europe of her childhood. She determined to do something to honor American poetry and sustain the poets who write it. This led to the creation of the academy as a nonprofit organization open to anyone who sent in a contribution. (Today the world is more complicated, and although the academy will accept any contribution, it is best to send in at least twenty-five dollars, because for smaller sums the academy loses money in processing the membership.) In 1963 the academy put on its first public reading, Robert Lowell and John Berryman at the Guggenheim Museum. Today it annually supports more than fifty readings across the country, and residences for poets in the Southwest and Pacific Northwest. The academy also administers a number of prizes from the $100,000 Dorothea Tanning Prize to the Walt Whitman Award, the Lenore Marshall Poetry Prize, the James Laughlin Award, and the Harold Morton Landon Translation Award. Members of the academy receive *American Poet,* a quarterly edited by Bruno Navasky. Plans are currently in the works to make this magazine available on newsstands. William Wadsworth is the academy's executive director.

Ace Books

A sequence of events that began in 1949 at the Columbia Psychiatric Institute caused this mass-market publisher of pulp fiction to bring out William Burroughs's first novel, *Junkie.* It was at the institute that Carl Solomon introduced himself to his newly arrived fellow patient, Allen Ginsberg, by saying, "I am Myshkin." Knowing his Dostoyevsky, Ginsberg replied, "I am Kirilov," and the two men became friends. In 1952, both men now attempting to live "normal" lives in New York, Solomon took a job under his uncle at the publisher A. A. Wyn, Ace's parent company. Meanwhile, Ginsberg had taken on the role of agent for the novels of his friends Burroughs and Jack Kerouac. He tried *Junkie* on two Columbia classmates in publishing, the poet Louis Simpson and Jason Epstein, but got nowhere. He then took the book to Solomon, who bought it for $1,000 and published it back-to-back with *Narcotic Agent,* the memoir of a former agent of the Federal Bureau of Narcotics. The legend under Burroughs's title read "Confessions of an Unredeemed Drug Addict," and the cover showed a man holding a desperate woman in a hammerlock to keep her from the heroin she craved. The twin novels sold for thirty-five cents a copy and, although unreviewed, racked up sales of 113,170 copies in their first year. It would be a decade before Burroughs's next book appeared. Solomon offered Kerouac such a puny advance that they were never able to cut a deal. In 1956 Ginsberg's "Howl," dedicated to Carl Solomon, appeared.

Adams, Franklin Pierce (F. P. A.) (1881–1960)

From after World War I until the early 1950s, the initials F. P. A. were famous because of the literary column "The Conning Tower," which Adams published in several newspapers, the *New York Herald-Tribune* and *New York World* chief among them. There is almost certainly no column like it, one devoted to books, literary gossip, and original work, being published in any major American newspaper today. Young writers from around the country sent Adams their work hoping to break into print in the column. In it, F. P. A. published early writing by, among others, Edna St. Vincent Millay, Ring Lardner, and Dorothy Parker. Although he translated Horace and Propertius from the Latin, Adams published mostly light verse. That he titled a book *Tobogganing on Parnassus* says something about his sense of humor. Along with the drama critic Alexander Woollcott and the sportswriter Heywood Broun, Adams began the weekly luncheon habit at the Algonquin Hotel that developed into the Algonquin Round Table.

Adelman, Stanley (1923–1995)

The *New York Times* printed Adelman's obituary under the headline "Repairer of Literary World's Typewriters." Only in a city of so many writers could there have been a store like Adelman's. A Holocaust survivor, he learned to repair typewriters after gaining his freedom and came to America in 1949. It took him a while to find a job, but eventually he landed one at a shop on the Upper West Side, where he worked his way up from employee to owner. Adelman repaired the old-fashioned manual machines favored by Isaac Bashevis Singer, David Mamet, Alfred Kazin, the novelist Erich Maria Remarque, the sportswriter Roger Khan, Philip Roth, and the playwright Murray Schisgal. One of his longtime customers, the novelist Howard Fast, remembered Adelman convincing him to replace his 1937 Underwood, for which parts had become unavailable, with an Olympia. "I felt as a Jew I could not write on a German typewriter," recalled Fast. Adelman responded, "I was in a concentration camp. If I can sell that typewriter, you can write on it."

Agee, James (1909–1955)

A Tennessean, Agee graduated from Harvard and came to New York in 1932 to work for *Fortune* and live in Greenwich Village. He had a basement apartment at 38 Perry Street and went uptown to his office in the Chrysler Building. The Village and Luce Publications remained constant in his life. His book of poems, *Permit Me Voyage,* won the Yale Series of Younger Poets Award in 1934, but the work that Agee is known for today began in 1936 when *Fortune* commissioned him and the photographer Walker Evans to do a series of articles on Southern tenant farmers. In 1941 this became *Let Us Now Praise Famous Men,* but not before *Fortune* dropped the project after Agee turned in a manuscript many times the expected length. As he struggled to give shape to what was more prose poem than reportage, Agee's life fell apart and the heavy drinking that would lead to his early death by heart attack got the better of him. *Time* hired him as its film critic in 1941, and he took an apartment at 172 Bleecker Street, where he lived for the next decade. Agee wrote the best film criticism of his time, passionate, totally committed to the movies as art, but without pretense—the sort of criticism that makes you want to go out and see the movie right away. It is in print and still readable today. He also wrote screenplays: *The African Queen* for his idol, John Huston, and *The Night of the Hunter,* for the only movie the actor Charles Laughton directed. Agee kept a writing studio at 33 Cornelia Street and spent his last year at 17 King Street. After Agee's death his novel *A Death in the Family* appeared and won a Pulitzer Prize in 1958. His son, Joel, raised in East Germany, also became a writer. There are several photographs of Agee senior in which his handsome, unshaven, gimlet-eyed face is *the* hungover writer.

Agents, Literary

Over the past decade, newspapers have paid increased attention to literary agents, some of whom have become prominent in their own right. The amazing Irving "Swifty" Lazar was a celebrity—he was also much more than just a literary agent—and today Andrew Wylie is nearly as famous as his clients, among whom are Norman Mailer and Salman Rushdie. But literary agents remain absent from the encyclopedias and reference works that cover American literature. For these books literature is a thing removed from the marketplace where agents' toil and authors' income, if not their reputations, are determined. New York City is the capital of American literature because it is where the majority of literary agents, editors, and publishers are located. Agenting begins with James Lawson, a Scotsman active in literary circles between 1820 and 1840. Lawson acted as more go-between than bona fide agent and took no fee for matchmaking between Bryant, Poe, Whittier, and magazines of the day. This was a period when magazines and newspapers flourished in New York, creating competition among themselves and thus giving Lawson room to maneuver on behalf of his clients. Some sources give the 1880s as the dawn of agentry in New York. This, too, was a time when magazines thrived. In 1891 the International Copyright Act went into effect, which gave the books of British authors published in the United States copyright protection and the same for American writers in Great Britain. Because contracts now had to be negotiated at a distance, this opened up a new field for agents. One of the first agents to represent British publishers in New York was Paul Reynolds, who also took on Stephen Crane and Frank Norris in addition to H. G. Wells and Joseph Conrad. Reynolds worked without a contract, which is not unusual even today, and his writers paid him 10 percent of their royalties. Ten or 15 percent remains a standard fee, but today agents receive it from the advance they negotiate for their clients and the royalties the book produces. I asked the agent for this book, Anne Dubuisson, who has now left the business to raise a family in Alaska, how she defined the agent's role today and she responded: "In these days of the mega-merged publishing house, where editors stay probably an average of two years and an author's career is threatened if he doesn't sell as many copies as expected, an agent is basically the author's only steady advocate. She often advises an author on what to write, pre-edits an author's work (jobs the longtime editors performed in the past), finds the best publisher and editor for it, negotiates often complicated contracts for domestic and foreign book rights and film/dramatic rights, collects the author's monies, and basically watches over the publisher/editor to make sure they are doing right by the author." Where Hemingway once spoke his mind directly to his editor, Maxwell Perkins, or Charles Scribner, who headed the publishing house, today's authors rely on their agents to say what needs saying.

Several recent books give a glimpse into the author–agent relationship. Flannery O'Connor's letters to her agent, Elizabeth McKee, are in O'Connor's collected letters, *The Habit of Being*. The first volume of Lyle Leverich's biography of Tennessee Williams goes into detail about the playwright's dealings with and through his agent, Audrey Wood. Diarmuid Russell, Eudora Welty's agent for many years, described their business relationship in his book, *On Being an Agent*.

Important agents past and present include Harold Ober, who worked with F. Scott Fitzgerald, Harold Matson, Sterling Lord, Candida Donadio, Ellen Levine, Scott Meredith, Deborah Karl, Amanda Urban, Brandt and Brandt, McIntosh and Otis, Sanford Greenburger, Mort Janklow, Lynn Nesbit, Elizabeth Nowell, who had a role in shaping Thomas Wolfe's unwieldy manuscripts, Ann Watkins, Carol Mann, Maxine Groffsky, Melanie Jackson, the Curtis Brown Agency, Robert Dattila, Georges Borchardt, and the aforementioned Lazar and Wylie.

Lazar was a bald gnome of a man who wore huge eyeglasses. He earned the nickname "Swifty" by doing deals with a speed that floored his clients and sometimes the parties he was negotiating with. Wylie, dubbed "The Jackal" by the British press after his negotiations on behalf of the novelist Martin Amis, is clever, tough, does not mind his manners, and often comes away with fat contracts for his writers and big money for himself. Just as often he seems to leave behind bruised publishers. He appears to relish a fight, but he has a sense of humor. His agency once represented a travel book it knew to be a hoax. After the book was published and the hoax revealed, Wylie took pleasure in having put one over on the publishing world. That his father was a publisher with Boston's Houghton Mifflin may explain some of his behavior, but he is a man devoted to his writers.

Albee, Edward (b. 1928)

The adopted son of Reed and Frances Albee, part-owners of the Keith-Albee Theater Circuit, Albee came to Greenwich Village as a twenty-year-old with no particular literary ambitions. He lived on the income of a trust fund and, to keep the wolf from the door, took small jobs working as an office boy and record salesman. In the late fifties he and his friend, the composer William Flanagan, worked weekends delivering telegrams for Western Union. Flanagan credited this job with inspiring Albee's first hit play, *The Zoo Story*. But the play did not get written until 1958, when, in Flanagan's words, "it came out of thin air." Albee finished it in three weeks while living at 238 West Fourth Street. He followed this with a number of short plays, each of which was greeted with enthusiasm, and then went on to Broadway with *Who's Afraid of Virginia Woolf?* (1962). He had first seen the play's title in 1954, scrawled as graffiti on a mirror in a now-gone Tenth Street bar. In 1963 *Virginia Woolf* was covered with awards, including a Tony. Albee plowed some of the profits from the play into a group called Theater 64, which produced plays by Samuel Beckett and Harold Pinter at the Cherry Lane Theater and founded the New Playwrights' Unit Workshop, which helped foster the work of LeRoi Jones (Amiri Baraka). Albee's moment as a golden boy of the theater was brief. For a decade and a half he presented plays on Broadway to an audience that greeted them with increasing indifference. Except for *A Delicate Balance*, which would be revived to acclaim in 1996, the critics who had loved early Albee were now hostile. In the eighties the only way he seemed to get into a Broadway theater was to buy a ticket. He left town to teach playwriting in Houston and see his work staged in Europe, where his reputation remained strong.

Algonquin Round Table
Hotel Algonquin
West Forty-fourth Street between Fifth and Sixth Avenues

The wits of the Round Table have been so often sung that they have entered into literary folklore, where they are an ideal of sophistication and humor. Were they as witty as we make them out to be, as we *want* them to be? Perhaps, but as we get further away from their moment their radiance dims. This isn't surprising: Like some wines, most humor fails to travel. "The Round Table," Dorothy Parker remembered, "was just a lot of people telling jokes and telling each other how good they were." Just? Parker clearly meant to deflate romanticized notions about the group. As she said, "These were no giants." But the jokes were once fresh, lively, and immediately repeated, and those who gathered at the Round Table enjoyed each other's company enough to keep the ball rolling. They were smart, literate, absolutely with-it New Yorkers with tongues in their heads and few inhibitions about using them. They became celebrated because they were good copy and because among their

number sat press agents and newspaper columnists eager to report
what they said.

The group probably originated when the press agent John Peter
Toohey introduced *New York Times* drama critic Alexander Woollcott
to the angel food cake in the Algonquin's Pergola Room (now the Oak
Room). Soon Woollcott, Franklin P. Adams, who as F. P. A. wrote the
famous "Conning Tower" column for the *New York Herald Tribune,*
and the sportswriter Heywood Broun began the habit of lunching there
weekly. Word of the fun they were having got around and others joined
them. The famous story is that the playwright Robert Sherwood and
the writers Robert Benchley and Dorothy Parker came to the group
from their offices at *Vanity Fair* because the very tall Sherwood hated to
be mocked by midgets. When Sherwood left the office alone to take
lunch, the midgets from the Hippodrome across the street gave him a
good going-over. He enlisted Benchley and Parker as bodyguards and
led them to the Round Table, where they were joined by the novelist
Edna Ferber, playwrights George S. Kaufman and Marc Connelly, satirical novelist and screenwriter Donald Ogden Stewart, the founder of
the *New Yorker,* Harold Ross and his wife, Jane Grant, and the illustrator Neysa McMein. Guests as celebrated as Harpo Marx, Douglas Fairbanks, Tallulah Bankhead, and the Lunts dropped in to enjoy the
festivities. This was at a time when theater people were as glamorous as
today's movie stars. F. P. A. led the group, but Woollcott, the model for
Sheridan Whiteside in *The Man Who Came to Dinner,* was said to
dominate it. Throughout the twenties the group roared at what some
memoirists, Edna Ferber among them, remembered as a dizzyingly fast
pace. They were sharp and had thick hides and went after the usual cast
of characters, bores, hypocrites, charlatans, the pompous and the socially pretentious, and, inevitably, they put down one another. Theirs
was not good clean fun, and this added immensely to their appeal. By
the end of the twenties the Round Table had begun to disband, one of
the casualties of the Depression. In 1938 the Algonquin's owner, Frank
Case, gave an account of the group in his book, *Tales of a Wayward
Inn.* His daughter Margaret Case Harriman expanded on this in 1951
with *The Vicious Circle,* and the song has been sung again and again as
many of the Round Table members have had their biographies done. In
1995 the actress Jennifer Jason Leigh gave a creepy impersonation of
Dorothy Parker in the movie *Miss Parker and the Vicious Circle.* There
seems no end to our appetite for these people.

Beyond the Round Table, the Algonquin has had a varied literary history. H. L. Mencken stayed in the hotel, and on their first visit to America after twenty-five years in Paris so did Gertrude Stein and Alice B. Toklas. On his visits to New York to confer with his editors at Random House, William Faulkner stayed at the Algonquin. He worked on parts of several novels while in the hotel and wrote his 1949 Nobel Prize acceptance speech on a piece of the hotel's stationery. Tennessee Williams, John Updike (the Algonquin is practically around the corner from the *New Yorker*), Gore Vidal, Thornton Wilder, the novelist Peter De Vries, and a host of other writers have also stayed there.

Allen, Woody (b. 1935)

Born Allen Stewart Konigsberg in Brooklyn and raised in the Flatbush section. By the time Allen entered Midwood High School he had begun to supply New York newspaper columnists like Earl Wilson with gags. He briefly attended New York University and the City College of New York, but the education he needed came in showbiz. He served on the team of writers—Neil Simon and Mel Brooks were among his colleagues—who created Sid Caeser's *Your Show of Shows* and appeared as a stand-up comedian in New York nightclubs and on *The Ed Sullivan Show* and *The Tonight Show*. In 1966 his play *Don't Drink the Water* began an eighteen-month run on Broadway. Allen directed his first feature film in 1969, and although he has published books of short prose pieces, *Getting Even* and *Without Feathers* among them, the movies have been his main form of expression. In his stand-up act Allen created a character—an intelligent, neurotic New York Jew who puts himself down before the world gets a chance to—that he has refined in film after film. He is not as adventurous as Philip Roth's Alexander Portnoy, but they share many of the same worries. Allen has concentrated on New York City, Manhattan for the most part, with an attitude that seems literary. He tells as much as he shows about the city he clearly loves. The prime example of this is the architectural tour of Manhattan in *Hannah and Her Sisters*. Allen's films are the work of a highly literate artist whose eye is at the service of his words. He lives on Central Park West and every Monday night can be found playing clarinet at Michael's Pub.

American Academy of Arts and Letters
632 West 156th Street

Around the middle of May each year, members of the academy convene to award several writers, among other artists, prizes. They hand out not medallions but nice fat checks, and they do it in grand style: drinks before lunch and a public reception afterward, at which drinks are served. The academy was organized in 1904 by Mark Twain, William Dean Howells, the painter John La Farge, the composer Edward MacDowell, and the sculptor Augustus Saint-Gaudens, among others. When the novelist William Burroughs was made a member, he accepted the academy's rosette gladly, saying that honors were always welcome when you had to cross borders and go through Customs to get them.

Arendt, Hannah (1906-1975)

Arendt and her husband Heinrich Blücher, a teacher of political science, got out of France one step ahead of the Nazis and Pétain's collaborators and came to the Upper West Side, where so many intellectual refugees from Europe landed. They lived first on Ninety-fifth Street and then at 130 Morningside Drive, sometimes taking in boarders to make ends meet. Trained in philosophy by Martin Heidegger, Arendt became a political theorist in response to the rise of Hitler, the war that followed, and the Holocaust. Her great work, *Origins of Totalitarianism* (1951), explores why the awful fact of totalitarianism came to be and its consequences for us all. She was sent to Jerusalem by the *New Yorker* to report on the trial of Adolf Eichmann, and her *Eichmann in Jerusalem* (1963) caused a sensation in New York intellectual circles. In this book Arendt used the phrase "banality of evil," which, much debated at the time, has since entered the language. She taught at the New School for Social Research, and seems to have been a teacher outside the schoolroom, too. Some, including Saul Bellow, could not stand being lectured by her. But perhaps her major contribution to the New York literary life of her time was what she passed on to her friends. In his memoir, *New York Jew,* Alfred Kazin, who was Arendt's friend, put it this way: "She gave her friends—writers so various as Robert Lowell, Randall Jarrell, Mary McCarthy, the Jewish historian Salo Baron—intellectual courage before the mortal terror the war had willed us."

Ashbery, John (b. 1927)

Ashbery differs from his colleagues in the first generation of the New York School of Poets in at least four ways: He spent most of the decade 1955–65 in Paris; he has been an active translator from the French; he has employed a wide range of formal patterns: sestina, pantoum, villanelle, haiku, and haibun; and he has been given by far the greatest number of prizes and awards. Like Kenneth Koch, Kenward Elmslie,

Frank O'Hara, and Harry Mathews, Ashbery graduated from Harvard and then came to Columbia for graduate work for which he completed a thesis on the English novelist Henry Green. In 1952 W. H. Auden chose Ashbery's *Some Trees* as the Yale Series of Younger Poets Award winner. The story goes that Auden could not find a worthy manuscript among those submitted and turned to both Ashbery and Frank O'Hara. Ashbery had a manuscript in hand that Auden accepted, trusting his instinct even though he claimed not to understand Ashbery's poems. Kenward Elmslie, on the other hand, came away from hearing Ashbery read for the first time thinking of Cole Porter's patter songs. Between 1951 and 1955, Ashbery worked in publishing, looking out of the window while at McGraw-Hill to write "The Instruction Manual":

> I wish I did not have to write the instruction manual on
>   the uses of the new metal.
> I look down into the street and see people, each walking
>   with an inner peace,
> And envy them—they are so far away from me!

While in Paris Ashbery kept in close touch with New York through letters and frequent visits. He also wrote art criticism for the *Paris Herald-Tribune* and the poems that appeared in perhaps his most radical book, *The Tennis Court Oath.* Poets who would never produce a line remotely resembling one of Ashbery's were turned on by this book's refusal to follow any of the current conventions. When Ashbery returned to New York to become the executive editor of *Art News,* he began to write poetry as if this were the nineteenth and not the twentieth century. A fifth way that he differs from his colleagues is in having written the greatest number of lines. Kenneth Koch is second. In 1975 Ashbery's *Self-Portrait in a Convex Mirror* swept the board, winning a National Book Award and a Pulitzer Prize. The years since have seen him step up his output. He has published a big book of art criticism, *Reported Sightings,* a selected poems, almost a dozen individual books of poems, the long poem *Flow Chart,* and his muse shows no sign of drying up. Over these years he has been given a MacArthur Award, the Lilly Prize, and delivered Harvard's Norton Lectures, following in the footsteps of Leonard Bernstein, T. S. Eliot, and Czeslaw Milosz. For all the demands on his time and energy he has been generous in his attentions to any number of younger artists and poets. What is remarkable about all this is that Ashbery's work has for years eluded a host of critics and been put down, at times, in harsh terms. Obviously he has connected with others. Indeed, there was a time in the late seventies when Ashbery-like poems were a glut. Poets imitated him as poets once had Eliot because his way looked like the only way to write. Ashbery has survived it all—he even handled the transition to the classroom, first at Brooklyn College and now at Bard, with aplomb. After Allen Ginsberg, he is the most prominent poet in New York and a regular at readings, parties, openings, and all manner of literary and art events. Nearly forty years ago his close friend Frank O'Hara sang, "John and the nuptial quality / of his verses (he is always marrying the whole world)." A great river of words has flowed after Ashbery's poems without improving O'Hara's insight. For more than twenty years Ashbery has made his home in the Chelsea neighborhood.

Auchincloss, Louis (b. 1917)

A lawyer-writer with the emphasis on writer, and familiar with the city's aristocracy from birth, Auchincloss has chronicled New York's upper crust since he began writing novels in the late 1940s. In this century no writer has done this as long or as well as he has. Auchincloss was admitted to the New York bar in 1941 and joined the law firm of Sullivan and Cromwell. His first novel, *The Indifferent Children* (1941), appeared under the pseudonym Andrew Lee. He did this for the unusual reason that a man he knew recognized himself as the central character and thought he had been unfavorably described. Auchincloss said he felt like a heel and used the pseudonym to protect the man. In this and in the many novels and stories that followed, Auchincloss explored the themes of family and money. He is one of the only New York writers of his time to have a practical understanding of the world of business and Wall Street, and he has gone again and again into that world for his fiction. When he branched out it was to write one of his most popular novels, *The Rector of Justin* (1964). Many thought of this as a fictional portrait of Endicott Peabody, the founding headmaster of Groton, where Auchincloss had gone to prep school, but this was not the case. He actually read a great many biographies of prep school headmasters and made a composite portrait. Throughout his career Auchincloss has served New York both as president of the Museum of the City of New York and with his pen. He combined excerpts from the diaries of Philip Hone and George Templeton Strong, himself a lawyer, to form a portrait of the city from 1830 to 1875; he wrote an excellent short book on Edith Wharton for the *Viking Vista* series (this book is worth getting out of the library or tracking down in secondhand shops as much for its pithy text as for its photographs and illustrations), and a book on Henry James and a group portrait of figures from the Gilded Age in *The Vanderbilt Era*. Wharton has been Auchincloss's chief inspiration. To say that he lacks her authority and the steel of her genius is not to denigrate his work. He embodies some of her fine qualities of observation and has given himself, as she did, to a world he knows inside and out, a world he has had the imagination to bring alive in his pages. There are always several literary New Yorks overlapping in the city. Imagine Auchincloss, the young lawyer, launching his career as the Beat Generation hangs out in Times Square bars. He has his eye on the Upper East Side while the painters and poets mix at the Cedar Bar in the Village, James Baldwin writes of his native Harlem, Truman Capote throws his masked ball, and, well, New York literary life is lived on many layers far from the boardrooms, offices, and brownstones encountered in Auchincloss's fiction. Auchincloss has produced so many books while lawyering that he must be one of those writers who, like the doctor-poet William Carlos Williams and the insurance executive-poet Wallace Stevens, thrives on two careers. At times he did step away from the law, but from 1954 until he retired in 1987 he practiced at Hawkins, Delafield, and Wood, where he headed the firm's trust and estates department. Auchincloss has lived most of his life on the Upper East Side, at 66 East Seventy-ninth Street from 1935 to 1945, at 24 East Eighty-fourth Street in the early 1950s, and for some years on upper Park Avenue.

Auden, W. H. (1907–1973)

On 16 January 1939, Auden and his close friend, the novelist Christopher Isherwood, sailed through heavy snow into New York harbor, where they had their first sight of what Isherwood described as "the Red Indian island with its appalling towers." Both men were already well known to American readers, and they immediately took part in the city's literary life by being interviewed and giving readings. That 6 April, the eighteen-year-old Chester Kallman (1921–1975) gave Auden the eye at a poetry reading, and soon after they began the tempestuous relationship that would last the rest of their lives. On the day Germany invaded Poland, Auden wrote his famous "September 1, 1939," which begins:

> I sit in one of the dives
> on Fifty-Second Street

Uncertain and afraid
As the clever hopes expire
Of a low dishonest decade . . .

New York was to be Auden's base until he became disenchanted with the city in 1972 and returned to Oxford in England. In New York Auden had three main residences. During the early 1940s he lived in the famed Middagh Street house, which has its own entry in this book, in Brooklyn Heights. From 1945 until 1953 he and Kallman lived at 7 Cornelia Street in the Village, and from 1953 until Auden's departure they lived at 77 St. Mark's Place in the East Village. This last apartment was in the same building where Leon Trotsky had *Novy Mir* published during the time he spent in New York. Although Auden lived downtown and was for a time a regular at the San Remo, the literary and intellectual circles within which he moved were uptown until they evolved into his own circle. The Trillings were his friends as was Hannah Arendt, but Auden had wide interests and was close to Igor and Vera Stravinsky and Robert Craft, the translator James Stern and his wife, Tania, the Russian doctor and novelist V. S. Yanovsky, and the psychologist Oliver Sacks. There are some hilarious descriptions in Craft's Stravinsky chronicles of Auden and Kallman's generous hospitality and slovenly housekeeping. At one dinner Vera Stravinsky went to use the bathroom only to discover that the wash basin was filled with black gunk. She washed it down the drain, thus depriving everyone of the pudding Kallman had made for dessert. It was at this same St. Mark's apartment that the poet James Schuyler, who was Auden's secretary for a time in Italy, went to parties where he just missed meeting T. S. Eliot and Bertolt Brecht. Those who arrived earlier were more fortunate. Auden's birthday parties were famous for their guest lists and for the invitations that read "Carriages at one a.m." Throughout his New York years Auden, who rarely taught, produced a great deal of poetry and the literary journalism and editing that earned him his daily bread. He adhered to a strict schedule that had him working all morning in a curtained study, and he used speed—"the chemical life," he called it—to enhance his concentration and energy. (There is an essay to be written about the use of speed by New York artists as diverse as Auden, Ted Berrigan, and Larry Rivers.) Although Auden was not personally close with the poets of the New York School (James Schuyler is the exception) his work had a great effect upon theirs. Auden's humor, his great verbal dexterity and sense of play, and his use of the city left their mark. Frank O'Hara revered him, and it was Auden who launched John Ashbery's career by choosing Ashbery's first book, *Some Trees,* for the Yale Series of Younger Poets Prize. Perhaps the poet to whom Auden meant the most was Joseph Brodsky, whom Auden welcomed to America and helped in many ways. As Auden aged he liked to lay down the law like a Victorian schoolmaster, but he was modest about his own reputation. "A minor American Goethe," he called himself. Shortly before he left New York he published an article in the *Times* in which he thanked "Abe and his coworkers in the liquor store; On Lok my laundryman; Joseph, Bernard and Maurice in the grocery store at Ninth and Second Avenue . . . ," and others in his neighborhood who had served him over the years. Auden was, as Schuyler remembered him in his elegy, a "kind man and great poet."

Chester Kallman deserves a few words. He published two books of well-made, conventional poems, and he collaborated with Auden on several opera librettos, doing the lion's share of the work on Hans Werner Henze's *Elegy for Young Lovers.* It was Kallman who introduced Auden to opera, and it became an abiding passion for both men. Auden and Kallman were so different temperamentally—Auden was content to be monogamous while Kallman took pleasure in cruising and rough trade—that they eventually had great difficulties in their relationship. Kallman took to spending long periods away from the city.

Auster, Paul (b. 1947)

A graduate of Columbia, Auster spent most of 1971 to 1974 in Paris before returning to the United States, where he worked as a poet, translator (his *Random House Anthology of Twentieth Century French Poetry* is the best of its kind), and essayist while developing what we now know are his considerable abilities as a novelist. These began to form in his memoir *The Invention of Solitude* (1982). The first volume of his *New York Trilogy, City of Glass* (1985), did not appear until he was nearly forty, but once under way Auster published seven novels in quick succession. Fascinated by chance and coincidence, he has adapted popular forms, most important the detective story, to his ends. What distinguishes Auster's work is the lucidity of his prose. You feel you are reading through it to the story. He has the gift of writing sentences that pull the reader along and never pause to admire themselves. No other novelist of his generation has paid so much attention to New York City. It appears as a character, not just a setting, in *The New York Trilogy,* and as a dystopia in *In The Country of Last Things* (1988), and it has a large role in *Moon Palace* and a smaller one in *Leviathan*. This last is, by the way, in this reporter's opinion the best American novel about the generation that came of age in the sixties, twenty years down the road. During his years in Manhattan Auster lived at 456 Riverside Drive and 6 Varick Street. Since he is the sort of writer who takes freely from his life, these addresses appear in several of his novels. He now lives with his wife, the novelist Siri Hustvedt, in Brooklyn's Park Slope neighborhood, and his attachment to Brooklyn is so strong that it came into play when chance led him deeper into filmmaking than most novelists ever go. In 1990 Auster, who is Jewish, accepted a commission to write a Christmas story for the op-ed page of the *New York Times*. The director Wayne Wang read "Augie Wren's Christmas Story" in San Francisco and knew at once that he wanted to film it. He contacted Auster and this led to the collaboration that yielded the film *Smoke*, for which Auster wrote the script, and the improvised comedy *Blue in the Face*, which Auster codirected. Central to both films is a vision of Brooklyn, not as a melting pot in which ethnic identity is diluted, but as a salad where races and cultures retain their flavor. Work on these projects took Auster away from his desk for nearly two years, and when he returned he wrote *Hand To Mouth* (1997), a memoir that deals in part with the variety of literary work he did, and some of the people he worked with and for, before he became a successful writer.

Auster's fiction and films have had wide appeal in Europe, especially in Germany and France. The French critic Gérard de Cortanze became so absorbed by Auster's New York references that he came to the city with a photographer and produced the coffee-table book *Le New York de Paul Auster*.

B

Baldwin, James (1924–1987)

Baldwin is the first major American writer to be born in Harlem, and he happened to come into the world in the middle of the Harlem Renaissance, whose invigorating air must have been among his first breaths. He spent his early years on upper Park Avenue before moving to 2171 Fifth Avenue, now built over by a housing project. Baldwin attended Frederick Douglass Junior High School—the poet Countee Cullen was one of his teachers—and then went to DeWitt Clinton High

School, where he befriended the photographer Richard Avedon, with whom he would one day collaborate, and the critic Emile Capouya. The friendship with Capouya proved decisive, for it was he who put Baldwin in touch with the painter Beauford Delaney. Delaney lived in the Village at 181 Greene Street, and there Baldwin found the man who would be his mentor and lifelong friend. But this gets a little ahead of the story. In junior high and high school, Baldwin caught the eye of several teachers who recognized his intelligence and precocious literary abilities. He remains one of the few significant writers of his generation (Truman Capote is another) not to go to college. Instead, Baldwin got his education in Greenwich Village, where he went to live in 1942–43 following the death of his stern (to the point of being sadistic) stepfather. By this time Baldwin had already got religion, been a storefront preacher, and abandoned religion. The cadences of the Bible stayed in his head, providing the sinew and rhetorical energy for his prose. During his Village years, Baldwin got his start as a writer, and he later remembered that Saul Levitas, the editor of the *New Leader,* gave him his first book to review. This was a time when young writers could earn a little money while sharpening their styles reviewing books for any number of New York-based literary and political magazines. Alfred Kazin and others had broken into print in this way in the thirties, and it was still possible through the mid-fifties. Other editors took an interest in Baldwin, including Randall Jarrell at the *Nation,* Elliott Cohen and Robert Warshow at *Commentary,* and Philip Rahv at *Partisan Review.* Soon Baldwin began to turn out the essays that would make his place in American literature, but before these were published as a book, he spent several years in Paris, where he began the novel that became *Go Tell It on the Mountain* (1953). It is autobiographical and deals with Baldwin's years as a preacher. The novel brought Baldwin a great deal of attention, always a mixed blessing for a black American writer because that writer is then expected to interpret and explain the black world to the white. Baldwin did this with a vengeance, and in his first book of essays, *Notes of a Native Son* (1955), he published work that educated those whites who could hear what he had to say and infuriated some of those who couldn't. He followed this up with a second book of essays, *Nobody Knows My Name* (1961), that continued his exploration not only of what race meant in America but the shared consequences for all Americans of the nation's racial history. Powerful and praised as these essays were, Baldwin wanted to be a novelist, but it must be said that apart from *Another Country* (1962), Baldwin's

novels fall short of being first-rate. By the mid-fifties Baldwin was famous, sought after, and had begun the sometimes frantically peripatetic
life that would take him throughout the American South as a journalist, back and forth to Paris, to Turkey, where he wrote chunks of his
later books, and finally to a house in the south of France, probably the
closest thing to home for him. During at least some of the years from
the early sixties until the end of his life, he kept an apartment at 470
West End Avenue. But whether he was in New York or not, Baldwin's
work had a significant presence in the city and reached beyond its literary life, especially through his many appearances on television in the
sixties and seventies. When "The Fire Next Time," his 1963 report/ser-
mon on the Black Muslims and white America's blind indifference to
black America appeared in the *New Yorker* Baldwin became a national
figure and remained one until his death, two years before which his collected nonfiction, *The Price of the Ticket,* came out. Anyone wishing to
take Baldwin's measure as man and writer while, incidentally, getting a
vivid picture of Harlem during World War II, must begin with this
book. After his death a memorial service was held at the Cathedral
Church of St. John the Divine. Some who had scorned Baldwin, such as
the poet and playwright Amiri Baraka, came to praise him. Baldwin
was a vivid creature who loved to drink and gossip, who drew people
to him as he moved slowly—he was never on time—through the city,
who had a magnificent smile and the face of a Benin bronze, and who,
all his life, loved the late-night heart-to-heart during which all the
truths are told. There have been several biographies of Baldwin, and he
figures prominently in the lives that have been published of his friendly
enemy Norman Mailer and will figure just as prominently in those of
William Styron among many other writers of his generation.

Baraka, Amiri (*See* Jones, LeRoi)

Barnes, Djuna (1892–1982)
Barnes first came to New York as a student at the Art Students League.
From 1913 to 1931 she worked as a journalist and illustrator in the city,
first at the *Brooklyn Eagle* and then for other newspapers. Sun and
Moon Press of Los Angeles has published a good deal of her journalism
under the title *New York*. She covered in her original style a wide vari-
ety of offbeat stories from the tango craze to the closing of the Jacob A.
Stapler floating hotel for girls moored at Twenty-third Street to Coney
Island. "Chinatown," she wrote, "is a period over which the alphabet

of our city has to step." In 1919 she became involved with the Provincetown Players as both actress and playwright. The theater was then at
133 MacDougal Street and under the direction of James Light, from
whom Barnes rented a room at 86 Greenwich Avenue. In the early thirties Barnes left for Paris, where she wrote *Nightwood,* the novel that
was first published and championed by T. S. Eliot and remains one of
the cornerstones of modernism today. Returning to New York at the
end of the decade, she moved into an apartment at 5 Patchin Place,
where she lived the life of a recluse. Her neighbor at number 4, e. e.
cummings, took pleasure in yelling out of his window to her to make
sure she was still alive. She was all but forgotten until the late seventies,
when journalists began to seek her out as a Greenwich Village recluse.
Barnes was imperious and would have none of their sentimental interest, nor would she credit anyone for the success she had enjoyed, not
even Eliot. As a publisher he was in her words simply a "printer." Bill
Zavatsky, the poet and editor of Sun Books in New York, came in contact with her because she was the literary executor of the artist, poet,
and Village character, Baroness Elsa von Freytag-Loringhoven. The
baroness had once offered to infect the poet William Carlos Williams,
on whom she had a crush, with syphilis so that he might more fully realize his genius. Zavatsky called Barnes because he wished to publish a
book of the baroness's poems. Barnes asked to see the sort of books Sun
published, and Zavatsky sent a book of his own poems that the press
had just published. In the author's photo he had very long hair. Barnes
called to say that while he looked like a nice little girl, she would not let
him publish the baroness. Barnes died shortly thereafter. She has been
the subject of several biographies, and Sun and Moon keeps her books
in print; New Directions continues to sell several thousand copies of
Nightwood each year.

Barnes & Noble

"Booksellers Since 1873," say Barnes & Noble's advertisements. This is
true, but only since the mid-1980s has Barnes & Noble become a major
force in Manhattan. (Barnes & Noble is moving into Brooklyn, but
there are as of 1997 no stores in Queens, Staten Island, or the Bronx,
which for some reason is nearly empty of bookstores.) Barnes & Noble
invented the superstore in New York, and East Side, West Side, Astor
Place, Union Square, Rockefeller Center, and elsewhere, they are all
around the town. Each month Barnes & Noble schedules so many read-

ings that it publishes a full-page ad in the *New York Times* listing them all. Across North America there are now 454 superstores and 559 mall shops. The book business has never seen anything like it, and, of course, feelings about Barnes & Noble run high, as small bookstore owners struggle to compete with superstores.

Authors and publishers are divided on the issue, but Barnes & Noble has been seen as a factor in the book industry's current slump. As of October 1997 net sales of hardcover books were down nearly 10 percent from last year. Worse, on average 45 percent of books shipped by publishers were being returned unsold. No one knows for certain why book sales are down. The figures may reflect a trend across the culture away from reading. Barnes & Noble certainly wants to sell as many books as it can so that any drop in the market works to its disadvantage. But returns are another matter. In essence, Barnes & Noble's supermarket approach whereby prominent shelf and display space is at a premium and many titles are not in the store but rather are listed on the store's computer has redefined what *commercial* means in the book business. Publishers, especially small independents and those who publish literary titles, argue that their books are not being given a chance, that Barnes & Noble gives its attention to books that are hot at the moment. Barnes & Noble has countered that New York publishers are elitist and out of touch with the reading public. The company's attitude is that publishers ought to pay attention to what sells and not blame Barnes & Noble for what does not. As independent stores close, a literary culture disappears, and many hate to see this happen.

Barr, Alfred H., Jr. (1902–1981)

As the Museum of Modern Art's first director, Barr brought a great deal of the art being made in Europe in the early twentieth century to New York, thus inspiring countless painters and writers. He also wrote beautifully about it, especially about the art of Picasso and Matisse. The fastidious, scholarly Barr made many trips, "campaigns" he called them, throughout Europe in the years before World War II, accompanied by his wife, Margaret Scolari Barr, who acted as his interpreter to Picasso among others. It was from these trips that Barr brought back the work that made up the museum's first van Gogh, dada, and surrealism shows. In the fifties he was a famous presence on the burgeoning New York gallery scene, wearing his oversized Russian overcoat, looking intently and buying for the museum as well. The work he did at MOMA helped make New York an Imperial City. For years he lived at 49 East Ninety-sixth Street and often walked back and forth to the museum on East Fifth-third.

Beard, James (1903–1985)

When the American food revolution began in California in the 1970s James Beard, who since the late thirties had been living in Manhattan writing about food and teaching cooking, was acknowledged as its grandfather. Beard, who wrote two dozen books and was food editor for the *New York Times,* began holding Beard's Cooking Classes in his Greenwich Village apartment in 1955. For a time the poet John Ashbery was one of his students. Such was Beard's stature in the food world that there have been two biographies of the man. One of these, *Epicurean Delight: The Life and Times of James Beard,* was the work of Evan Jones (1916–1996), a New Yorker by way of Minnesota and Paris, who wrote a number of books about food and who, with his wife, Judith, set a very good table at their East Sixty-sixth Street apartment. Because Beard was one of Judith's authors at Alfred A. Knopf, where she is an editor today, he ate at the Joneses. Julia Child, also a Jones author, has eaten there as well. When not editing Child, the grandmother of the American food revolution, Judith Jones is at work on the books of John Updike, Albert Camus, and Shelby Hearron.

Beat Generation

"So I guess you might say we're a beat generation," said Jack Kerouac in November 1948 to his friend the novelist John Clellon Holmes. The word *beat* was used in carnival, drug, and African American slang to mean exhausted, depleted of energy and prospects, sunk to the very bottom. In a 1952 article for the *New York Times Magazine,* "This Is the Beat Generation," Holmes defined *beat* as "a feeling of being reduced to the bedrock of consciousness." Later, Kerouac and Allen Ginsberg emphasized the beat in *beatific.* The generation came together in New York in 1944 when Lucien Carr, William Burroughs, Allen Ginsberg, Herbert Huncke, and Jack Kerouac met each other. The older Burroughs might be thought of as the group's father figure. Huncke had come from the world of drugs and petty crime: Carr, Ginsberg, and Kerouac were at different times Columbia University students. Neal Cassady came from Denver in December 1946 to become the model for Dean Moriarity in Kerouac's *On the Road.* Burroughs, Kerouac, and

Ginsberg were all passionate writers who through all their travels and the recklessness and mess of their lives kept producing novels and poems. There are enough sensational episodes in each of these men's lives to fill a book twice this size. This is one reason why all three of them have already had multiple biographies.

The Beats' New York was the underside, the other side of post-World War II prosperity and conformism. They loved the carny world of Forty-second Street bars, and the characters who inhabited them. They were men eager to take part in a bad boy's world of drugs, sex, and experience with a capital E. (Very few women played key roles, and one who did, Joyce Johnson, titled the memoir of her relationship with Kerouac *Minor Characters*.) While New York was their base, they moved restlessly back and forth across the country, to Burroughs's Texas marijuana farm, to Mexico City, to Cassady's Denver, and to San Francisco. Today, we can fly to all the places the Beats went and arrive without having had an adventure other than our baggage being lost. They drove across a country considerably less franchised and homogenized than the one we live in today. In Kerouac's books you feel the surge of freedom as his characters move through what were to them still wide-open spaces and the joy as they descend upon New York, roaring across the George Washington Bridge to get their kicks in the city's streets, bars, and pads. For the Beats, life could be improvised like a Charlie Parker solo, and for many this had enormous appeal. When Kerouac's *On the Road* appeared in 1957, America began to notice these Beat writers because they were a New York phenomenon and New York had the communications machinery to make anything famous. The generation became a creature of Luce Publications, and *Life* ran long feature articles on Beat culture. Suddenly, the Village was packed with men wearing goatees and sandals and "chicks" in black leotards. This attention turned the Beats' rebelliousness into a cliché, but their work withstood the onslaught and time has brought greater interest in their lives and writing. You will not find the city they "dug" with such a frenzy, but their books are everywhere. The year 1997 saw not only the fortieth anniversary of Jack Kerouac's *On the Road,* but the deaths of both Allen Ginsberg and William Burroughs. While Burroughs rusticated in Lawrence, Kansas, where he spent the final sixteen years of his life, Ginsberg had been active until near the end. He seemed never to tire of spreading the Beat gospel: First thought best thought.

Bellow, Saul (b. 1915)

While it is taken for granted that Nobel Prize winner Saul Bellow is Chicago's most prominent novelist, more of his books have been set in New York than in the Second City. Bellow did not get to New York until the forties, but he set his first novel, *The Victim* (1944), there. *Set* is perhaps too strong a word since after the opening, "On some nights New York is as hot as Bangkok," the city is in the reader's imagination, but the novel's characters hardly experience the place. In 1950 Bellow returned from Paris, where he had been living, to New York and a teaching job at New York University. For the next two years he lived in the Village, at least part of the time at 17 Minetta Lane, and worked on his Chicago epic, *The Adventures of Augie March*. Bellow next lived at 333 Riverside Drive, an apartment in which only his bathroom gave him a view of the Hudson. The Upper West Side is the setting for two of Bellow's novels. His short novel *Seize the Day* (1956) takes place in the fictional Hotel Gloriana near that great Beaux-Arts pile, the Ansonia Hotel, "like a Baroque palace from Prague or Munich," in Bellow's words, between Seventy-third and Seventy-fourth Streets on Broadway. Polish, intellectual, and a survivor of the Holocaust, the hero of *Mr. Sammler's Planet* (1970) lives on the Upper West Side. Sammler's New York seems on the verge of a moral and civil nervous breakdown. The novel is dark and sardonic, and Bellow, or at least his character Sammler, strikes out at, among others, Hannah Arendt. For the reader who wants an unconventional—and at the time unpopular—view of the effect on New York of the revolutions of the sixties, this book provides quite a workout. At times it reads more like a fire-and-brimstone sermon than a novel. Bellow's Oblomov, Morris Herzog, lives in West Seventeenth Street in the novel *Herzog* (1964), but when he breaks away from the letters he writes but never sends, he goes to the Upper West Side to visit the women in his life. Shortly after the end of World War II Bellow met the writer Delmore Schwartz. They had a tumultuous friendship even for Schwartz, who had many, that ended in estrangement. At the end of his life in 1966, the mad Schwartz came to live in the Hotel Dixie, one step up from a flophouse, in Times Square. On one occasion Bellow passed his old friend but could not bear to speak with him, so deranged and spooky did Schwartz look with his "East River gray" pallor. The wretched Schwartz died of a heart attack soon after. Meditating on Schwartz, their friendship, the dreams of their generation, and the fate of the artist in America led Bellow to write *Humboldt's Gift* (1979), in which Schwartz is Von Humboldt Fleischer and

Bellow, or at least aspects of him, is Charles Citrine. In this book there is something of the New York Schwartz and Bellow knew in the forties and fifties, but it is a large trunk of a book into which Bellow crammed a great deal. Since then Bellow's fiction has not revisited the city in any meaningful way. It is ironic that Schwartz's biographer, the novelist, literary journalist, and Chicago native James Atlas is currently at work on Bellow's biography.

Berkson, Bill (b. 1939)
Born in New York and raised on the Upper East Side, Berkson was in college at Brown when he first read the work of the New York School of Poets, Frank O'Hara's in particular. In 1959 Berkson took Kenneth Koch's poetry writing class at the New School for Social Research and through it met O'Hara, whose close friend he became. Tibor de Nagy Editions published his first book, *Saturday Night: Poems 1960–61;* Berkson also wrote art criticism and was in the thick of the early sixties' downtown poetry/painting ferment. After O'Hara's death Berkson edited the memorial volume, *In Memory of My Feelings,* published by the Museum of Modern Art in 1967. In 1970 Berkson went west to San Francisco, where he has stayed. For many years he lived north of the city in Bolinas, which became a sort of Lower East Side West for Berkson's New York confreres, Joe Brainard, Lewis Warsh, Anne Waldman, Ted Berrigan, and Alice Notley. While in Bolinas Berkson edited the magazine *Big Sky* and in its pages served both coasts. He no longer publishes much poetry but has returned to writing art criticism, which appears in *Art in America* and elsewhere.

Berlin, Irving (1888–1989)
The great migration of Jews from Eastern Europe carried Berlin from his native Russia to New York's Lower East Side, where he began his career in music as a street singer. "Everybody ought to have," he once said, "a Lower East Side in their life." Before he became a well-known songwriter, he learned the ropes as a Tin Pan Alley song plugger, on the vaudeville stage, and in Broadway revues. "Alexander's Ragtime Band" (1911) was his first hit. A self-taught pianist, Berlin composed the music for his words but could play the piano in only one key. He overcame this lack by having a special device fitted to the keyboard that allowed him to shift keys. Not only did Berlin write the best-selling record ever, "White Christmas," but he wrote "God Bless America" and a catalog's worth of songs with New York backgrounds, including "Puttin' on the

Ritz," "Harlem on My Mind," and "Easter Parade." While Berlin was not so successful on the Broadway stage as his contemporaries Cole Porter and Rodgers and Hart, he had two hit shows, both starring that quintessential New Yawk voice of the former Queens secretary, Ethel Merman: *Annie Get Your Gun* (1946) and *Call Me Madam* (1950). For most of his life Berlin lived on the Upper East Side and passed his last years on Beekman Place as a recluse. In his list of things that are "the top" Cole Porter included a "Berlin ballad."

Bernays, Edward (1891–1995)

Bernays has been called the father of public relations, the high-toned name given to press agentry or publicity. It is the art of putting a person or product's name before the public in a good light and keeping it there—or of restoring that person or product's good name after it has fallen from grace. Some have read a good deal into the fact that Bernays was the nephew of Sigmund Freud and assumed that he adapted many of Freud's insights for his own use. While his connection to literature is slight, Bernays did write a great deal of words and cause a great many more to be written. Since New York is the public relations capital of the world, it has to be, in part, his doing. Bernays wrote several books on the subject, and in 1923 New York University hired him to teach the first course in public relations ever offered anywhere. His daughter Anne, a Barnard graduate, has had a successful career as a novelist. *Poor Little Rich Girl* is her best-known title.

Berrigan, Ted (1936–1983)

> New York's lovely weather hurts my forehead
> here where clean snow is sitting, wetly
> round my ears, as hand-in-glove and
> head-to-head with Joe, I go reeling
> up First Avenue to Klein's

And reel around New York, the Lower East Side in particular, Berrigan did, from 1960, when he arrived in the city, until his too-early death in 1983. "Joe," the artist and writer Joe Brainard, was sometimes his partner, but Berrigan had a gift for friendship and he walked the city with Ron Padgett, Anne Waldman, Bernadette Mayer, Lewis Warsh, Jim Brodey—the second generation of the New York School of Poets—and with the third generation as well. A "son" of Frank O'Hara, Berrigan introduced himself into the world of poets and painters to which he became central as the editor of the mimeographed magazine *C.* He published his first book, the collage poem *Sonnets,* in mimeo form. It was this book, later reprinted by Grove Press and still later by United Artists, that made Berrigan's name. At times he wondered if he could ever surpass it. He certainly did as a teacher and inspiration to others at Iowa and then in Chicago. Many of the poets to whom Berrigan brought the news followed him to New York, and for these, as for many others, he was a generous audience, careful enough of their art to tell them exactly how he felt about it. By the mid-seventies Berrigan, who lived for many years on St. Mark's Place with his wife, the poet Alice Notley, and their two sons, had become a legend. Everyone who knew him had a night's worth of stories about him. When he was awarded a National Endowment for the Arts grant, he took the check, having no bank account, to a check cashing store and walked home with some $9,700 cash in his pocket. A visitor to the Berrigan-Notley apartment looked into their cupboard to find it bare save for several bottles of Pernod. Berrigan sold the mail he received in the morning to Robert Wilson of the Phoenix Bookshop in the afternoon and thus supported his family and kept himself in pills. Speed was his drug, and it undermined his health and distorted his personality over the last years of his life, but as difficult as he could be, Berrigan was well loved. After his memorial service at St. Mark's Church, a crowd of some two hundred carried George Schneeman's large portrait of the naked Berrigan down Second Avenue past the Gem Spa, a landmark in his poems. Tom Clark and Ron Padgett, who met Berrigan, then a graduate student, while in high school in Tulsa, Oklahoma, have written memoirs of him, and Anne Waldman edited a book of memoirs and homages, *Nice to See You.*

Best-Seller Lists

The first best-seller list appeared in 1895 in the *Bookman,* a magazine edited by Professor Harry Thurston Peck of Columbia. Anthony Hope's *The Prisoner of Zenda* is the one title on it that is in print today. In 1912 *Publishers Weekly,* which has been called the book industry's Bible, began to publish its own lists and sometime later the *New York Times Book Review* began to publish the list that is most often consulted today by the lay reader. Until fairly recently, best-seller meant a best-selling book and had to do only with numbers sold. Some enterprising graduate student may one day determine more or less exactly the time at which the term began to mean a book that is more a commodity than a work of literature, a book written especially to achieve bestsellerdom. Literary books—Frank McCourt's *Angela's Ashes* and Margaret Atwood's novel *Alias Grace* are on the current *Times* list—can still qualify, but no literary writer expects his book will make the list as did those of Willa Cather, Ernest Hemingway, Norman Mailer, James Jones, and John Steinbeck. For years the list documented books in two categories, "Fiction" and "Nonfiction," and counted only the top ten books in each. Today the list stretches to fifteen and there is a third category, "Advice, How-To and Miscellaneous." Recently independent bookstores have refused to supply the *New York Times Book Review* with sales figures. Their rationale is that the newspaper's web site is linked to Barnes & Noble's online bookstore.

Bishop, Elizabeth (1911–1979)

Shortly before her graduation from Vassar in 1934, Bishop met Marianne Moore, and she first came to New York to see Moore and to learn from her all that she could. After graduation, she worked briefly for the U.S.A. School of Writing in "an old tumble-down building near Columbus Circle." It was one of those places that advertise on matchbook covers to which writers send their work and receive criticism from "famous writers" in return. Bishop did not last long in the job but got a good piece out of the experience. It is in her *Collected Prose*. Throughout her life Bishop visited New York, at times for months, staying mostly in hotels and the Greenwich Village apartments of friends. She has a few poems set in the city, one of which beseeches Marianne Moore to "please come flying" over the Brooklyn Bridge to a Manhattan that Bishop describes as, "all awash with morals this fine morning." There is a love poem, "Varick Street," set in the industrial stretch of Varick north of Canal, and there is also a "Letter to New York," which opens:

> In your next letter I wish you'd say
> where you are going and what you are doing;
> how are the plays, and after the plays
> what other pleasures you're pursuing

One can only wish that Bishop herself had answered this letter and that her keen and original eye had been more often engaged by the New York she knew.

Blackburn, Paul (1926–1971)

Blackburn's mother, the poet Frances Frost, brought him to live in the Village when he was fourteen, and he went on to study at New York University before going to graduate school at the University of Wisconsin, where his encounter with Provençal poetry proved decisive. Under the influence of William Carlos Williams he wrote lightly swinging poems that move with a walker's gait. The city Blackburn encountered was often his subject as was the south of France and the Mediterranean, where he sometimes traveled. In the late 1950s he wrote a number of poems set on the subway ride into Manhattan from Brooklyn, where he then lived. He worked at office jobs, wrote the Cliff Notes for *El Cid,* and did not teach until the last year of his life. In the sixties he organized two important reading series on the Lower East Side, at the Deux Magots Coffeehouse and later at Le Métro Café. These were forerunners of the Poetry Project at St. Mark's Church. Blackburn believed in the community of poets and was a fixture at these readings, manning the portable tape recorder he faithfully lugged from event to event. The bulk of his work, poetry and journals, was published after his death. Among other New York addresses Blackburn lived in Chelsea at 322 West Twenty-fifth Street.

Blackwood, Lady Caroline (1931-1996)

A member of the Anglo-Irish aristocracy, a descendant of the playwright Richard Brinsley Sheridan and, on her mother's side, a Guinness, Lady Caroline, novelist and journalist, died of cancer in Manhattan's Mayfair Hotel at 610 Park Avenue. Her work had a life in England, but it did not travel well. Her connection to New York is through marriage and death. The painter Lucian Freud was her first husband. In the sixties she moved to the city, where she married the composer and pianist Israel Citkowitz. They divorced in 1972, and she married the poet Robert Lowell in England. This marriage was failing when, in September 1978, Lowell flew to New York to see his ex-wife, Elizabeth Hardwick. The taxi stopped at Hardwick's West Sixty-seventh Street address, and the driver turned to see Lowell dead of a heart attack, slumped in the backseat. On his lap he held *Girl in Bed,* a portrait of Lady Caroline painted more than thirty years earlier in Paris by Lucian Freud.

Bodenheim, Maxwell (1893–1954)

Poet, playwright, and novelist (one of his novels was titled *Naked on Roller Skates*), Bodenheim was a bohemian who began as an avant-garde writer in the Village in the twenties and lived the bohemian life until booze and poverty brought him down. Today he is remembered more for having been murdered than for any of his writings. The novelist Dawn Powell entered this in her diary: "Max killed with *The Sea Around Us* on his chest—a sea that engulfed him. I think his wife in drunken fit stabbed him and he was mad enough to stab back and the pal was so outraged he got gun and killed Max." The murders took place in a Third Avenue rooming house. The murderer, Harold Weinberg, was declared insane.

Book-of-the-Month Club

Harry Scherman founded the first of America's book clubs in 1926 to act as a middleman between readers and publishers. Experts such as Dorothy Canfield Fisher, Heywood Broun, and Christopher Morley chose books that were then advertised by the club. Readers who joined selected four books for two dollars and agreed to buy a specific number of future club selections. Book-of-the-Month Club began with 4,700 subscribers and in twenty years reached one million. To attract and hold such an audience, the club's selections had to be middlebrow. William Faulkner, for one, never had a novel chosen until the undistinguished *Reivers* was published after his death. His prose, it is said, made one of the judges giggle. Throughout the club's life, even as it contributed greatly to the success of such writers as George Orwell, Truman Capote, and E. Annie Proulx, it has been a punching bag for many. The critic Dwight Macdonald stated a commonly held view when he said, "The best that could be said is that it could be worse." As club sales and membership began to plunge in the early eighties, partly because of competition from discount stores, the judges, among them the novelists Brad Leithauser and Wilfred Sheed and the journalist J. Anthony Lukas, began to resent the organization's high-handed ways. Although the judges were paid $75,000 a year for their efforts, they were sometimes told that novels by such blockbuster writers as Stephen King were to be on the list even though the judges had not read them, much less voted on them. In the summer of 1994, the judges were eliminated and today a marketing executive will seek to continue the club's revival. No surprise there. The point of the club has always been dollars, and if it did some good for literature along the way that was a bonus.

Books: A Short Bibliography of Books by New York Writers
   or on New York

The major New York writers published in the Library of America's plump, black-jacketed volumes are James Fenimore Cooper, Stephen Crane, Theodore Dreiser, W. E. B. Du Bois, William Dean Howells, Zora Neale Hurston, Washington Irving, Henry James, Herman Melville, Eugene O'Neill, Thomas Paine, Edgar Allan Poe, Edith Wharton, Walt Whitman, as well as John Dos Passos's *U.S.A.* and James Thurber's *Writings and Drawings*. The Library has also published John Hollander's anthology *American Poetry: The Nineteenth Century* in two volumes. These excellent books are where to go for a look at the work of Philip Freneau, Fitz-Greene Halleck, William Cullen Bryant, Emma Lazarus, and others. The biographical notes in every one of the Library's volumes are excellent.

The Encyclopedia of New York City, edited by Kenneth T. Jackson and published by Yale University Press, appeared in the fall of 1995, thank God. This book could have been written without it, but it might have taken twice the time. Jackson and company have put New York at your elbow. While there are errors and omissions inevitable in the first printing of any book of this kind, the encyclopedia is invaluable. Anyone interested in the city will want to own it.

Edward Robb Ellis's *The Epic of New York City* stops at Mayor Robert Wagner's administration in the mid-1960s and is out of print, but no general history of New York City surpasses it. Ellis is both readable and reliable.

In the early 1980s Pantheon republished in paperback *The WPA Guide to New York City* and the Federal Writers' Project's *New York Panorama.* The city has changed several times since these were originally published in the late 1930s, but their maps remain useful, and New York's past is well presented through lively prose and good photographs. Both of these books can be found in secondhand stores. The farther away you are from the city the easier they are to come by. I purchased my copies in San Francisco's Mission District.

New York is the most written about of America's cities. Even its public library has a coffee-table book, *Treasures of the New York Public Library.* To go with all these words there is a wonderful picture book, John A. Kouwenhoven's *The Columbia Historical Portrait of New York: An Essay in Graphic History.* It is in both hardcover and paperback and can be found in secondhand stores.

Books & Co.
939 Madison Avenue

This narrow store devoted to literature, philosophy, and art displayed all of its new books face up, making it a pleasure to browse. Readings were held on the second floor. It was a good idea to get there early for these as the store had readers—Jim Harrison, Ann Lauterbach, Howard Norman—who drew crowds. Recently, Books & Co. began to publish under its own imprint, thus becoming a throwback to those nineteenth-century booksellers, Wiley's and D. Appleton's, in which New York book publishing had its start. Like the Gotham Book Mart, Books & Co. covered some of its wall space with photographs of writers who were friends of the store.

Alas, Books & Co. closed at the end of May 1997. The owner, Jeannette Watson, gave as the reason a hike in the rent by their landlord, the Whitney Museum. This must have been the final straw. The novelist Cynthia Ozick asked the questions that went to the heart of the matter, "What does this tell us? That New York can't support an independent bookstore?" Perhaps. At least the Upper East Side, with its commercial rents as high as $400,000, cannot. The *Times* thought the closing significant enough for an "Epilogue" on its arts page. The story quoted some lines from a poem James Merrill had written for the store's tenth anniversary in 1987:

> Ten years of browsing, and the
>   shelves
> Mysteriously grow more packed
> Full of reflection, silver-packed . . .
> Looking for books, we find
>   ourselves.

Bookstores

Today the superstores are at war with independent bookstores everywhere. Because Manhattan is the nation's book publishing capital, the city is the front line of this war. When the uptown SHAKESPEARE & COMPANY closed soon after the Upper West Side BARNES & NOBLE moved in nearby, the *New York Times* gave the event lengthy coverage.

The issue is simple: superstores offer discounts and a range of stock that independents cannot match. As the superstores separate the casual book buyers from the book lovers, independent stores that do not specialize are finding it difficult, if not impossible, to survive. The demise of the independents is much lamented by the book lovers. As the big guy clobbers the little guy, readers, especially those interested in poetry, experimental fiction, and the sort of books that are reviewed neither widely nor immediately, fear the worst. Superstores answer these charges by saying that they are expanding the market for books and that they do feature a breadth of inventory that goes beyond best-sellers.

At present there are fewer than a half-dozen first-rate literary bookstores in Manhattan: GOTHAM BOOK MART (41 West Forth-seventh Street), THREE LIVES (154 West Tenth Street) and ST. MARK'S BOOKSHOP (31 Third Avenue) are chief among these. If you are in the West Village touring literary haunts Three Lives is worth a visit. There is no warmer and more appealing bookstore in the city.

Although some specialty stores have closed (Samuel Weiser's occult store and Lewis H. Michaux's NATIONAL MEMORIAL AFRICAN BOOKSTORE have yet to be replaced), it is still possible to find most of what you are looking for in New York. The best used store in the city is THE STRAND at Broadway and Twelfth Street. Its aisles are narrow and crowded, but there are upward of two million books in the place and the staff is literate and helpful. The Strand has stacks of remainders in almost every field, and review copies show up in the store so quickly that new books are often here before they arrive elsewhere. If you enter through the lobby next door and go to the third floor you will find the Strand's rare book room, where bargains can be found. ARGOSY (116 East Fifty-ninth Street between Park and Lexington) is also worth a visit if you are looking for out-of-print and out-of-the-way titles.

For cookbooks there is only one store to visit, KITCHEN ARTS AND LETTERS (1435 Lexington Avenue at Ninety-third Street), run by Nach Waxman. Actually, *cookbooks* is too narrow a description; Waxman stocks all manner of books that have to do with food and nutrition. He is proud to say that in his store one can find a copy of books such as Peter Garnsey's *Famine and Food in the Graeco-Roman World*.

Several stores deal in mysteries, the most famous being the MYSTERIOUS BOOKSHOP at 129 West Fifty-sixth Street. Children's books can be found at BOOKS OF WONDER (132 Seventh Avenue at Eighteenth Street), and the BANK STREET COLLEGE BOOKSTORE (Broadway and 112th Street) boasts more than 20,000 titles.

As of September 1997 NEW YORK BOUND became yet another

bookstore in New York City to close. The cause was not competition from the superstores but a makeover of the lobby of Rockefeller Plaza that left no room for retailers. It is hard to believe that Manhattan will go long without a bookstore devoted to New York City, but for now many, including the writer of this book, agree with the *New Yorker*'s Philip Hamburger, who said of the closing, "This is a terrible loss. It's another way of discombobulating New York's soul."

In the past decade the city's art museums have beefed up their bookstores. The widest selection of books across all periods of art can be found at the Metropolitan Museum. The Museum of Modern Art's store, which remains open even on Wednesday, when the museum is closed, has a good stock of books on modern art, films, and photography. The shops at the Whitney, Guggenheim, and Brooklyn museums have smaller selections, but catalogs of recent shows are usually available. Unfortunately, no store in the city has filled the gap caused by the closing of Japp Reitman and Wittenborn, but HACKER (45 West Fifty-seventh Street) does the best that it can and that is very good, especially for out-of-print art books.

In the past fifteen years tabletop booksellers have sprouted in Manhattan, usually on the Upper West Side in the Eighties, on Fifth Avenue near the Plaza Hotel, on the Avenue of the Americas near Eighth Street, and, with less regularity, on Spring Street in SoHo. Of course, they can display only a few titles, but they pay no rent and best-sellers are often on sale cheap. One of the reasons the city lacks the kind of secondhand bookstores that can be found in abundance in Maine, Denver, or San Francisco/Berkeley is that rent on large convenient spaces is too steep. "Booksellers' Row," which once ran up Fourth Avenue between Astor Place and Fourteenth Street, is now represented only by the Strand.

In the early nineteenth century, New York bookstores were important for the book publishing they did. Charles Wiley's shop, at several downtown addresses, including 3 Wall Street, had a backroom that became "The Den" where Cooper, Bryant, and Halleck congregated. At first Wiley published under the John Wiley and Sons imprint only Europeans such as Chateaubriand, Goethe, and Lord Byron, but in 1819 he published Fitz-Greene Halleck's poem *Fanny* and followed this with *The Spy* and other novels by James Fenimore Cooper. George Putnam began his career at Wiley's and went on to run a shop of his own and become a publisher. Daniel Appleton, the founder of one of New York's most prestigious nineteenth-century houses, began as a bookseller. Until recently Charles Scribner's had a bookstore in midtown, and Doubleday operates stores throughout Manhattan today.

Of the bookstores recently gone, Robert Wilson's PHOENIX BOOKSHOP at 18 Cornelia Street left perhaps the biggest hole, at least as far as poets were concerned, when its owner decided to close shop. Wilson had been steadfast in his love of poetry, and his catalogs of out-of-print and hard-to-find books, pamphlets, and broadsides were a great resource in the 1960s. He was among the first to buy the letters and manuscripts of living poets. Many a day Ted Berrigan earned his bread by taking his morning's mail to Wilson, who paid cash for it. These days poets' papers are one of their few assets, and agents negotiate with libraries on behalf of those poets who have been pack rats. There is one great New York poem that spends some time in a bookstore, Frank O'Hara's "The Day Lady Died":

> and in the Golden Griffin I get a little Verlaine
> for Patsy with drawings by Bonnard although I do
> think of Hesiod, trans. Richmond Lattimore or
> Brendan Behan's new play of *Le Balcon* or *Les Nègres*
> of Genet, but I don't, I stick with Verlaine
> after practically going to sleep with quandariness

For more bookstores, see page 316.

Bowles, Jane (1917–1973)

A New York native, Jane Auer married Paul Bowles in 1938 when he was a composer and she had not yet begun to write her highly original fiction. Together they shared the famed 7 Middagh Street house on Brooklyn Heights with W. H. Auden, Carson McCullers, and others in the early forties. After this they left New York, eventually settling in Tangier, Morocco, and only returning to the city for brief visits. Jane Bowles wrote one novel, *Two Serious Ladies* (1943); one play, *In the Summer House* (1953); and one book of stories, *Plain Pleasures* (1966). These were collected and augmented with other published and unpublished work to make up *My Sister's Hand in Mine* (1978). The poet James Merrill once called Elizabeth Bishop "a poet's poet's poet." Jane Bowles is a writer's writer's writer. There is nothing like the eccentric humor and tang of her sentences. You cannot be indifferent to her work, and those who like it—Tennessee Williams, Truman Capote, and John Ashbery so numbered themselves—love it. She has been the subject of a biography, and in Bernardo Bertolucci's film of Paul Bowles's novel, *The Sheltering Sky*, Debra Winger portrayed her.

Bowles, Paul (b. 1910)

Before he turned to writing fiction, Bowles, a native New Yorker, studied with the composers Virgil Thomson and Aaron Copland and pursued a career as a composer best known for his theater music accompanying plays by Tennessee Williams, among others. During Bowles's New York years he moved in the circle of poets, composers, songwriters, and performers that included John Latouche, the singer Libby Hollman, who was a fiend of longstanding to both Bowles and his wife, Jane, Marc Blitzstein, and Edwin Denby. While Bowles's music has been more referred to than heard, a recent CD devoted to his piano pieces shows its charm. The young James Schuyler wrote the text for Bowles's "Picnic Cantata." After living in Brooklyn at the Middagh Street house Paul and Jane Bowles traveled for a time before returning to New York for two years. They spent these on West Tenth Street. Here Jean-Paul Sartre came to lunch because Bowles had translated his *No Exit* for Broadway, taking the play's English title from a street sign. When the Bowleses left New York again they began their years abroad that led to permanent residence in Tangier. After an earlier encounter with that city and the Moroccan desert, Bowles wrote his first and best novel, *The Sheltering Sky*, the inspiration for which came as he rode downtown on a Fifth Avenue double-decker bus. Norman Mailer thought that in the novel Bowles "opened the world of Hip. He let in murder, the drugs, the incest, the death of the Square (Port Moresby), the call of the orgy, the end of civilization . . ." If he did do all this it certainly had an effect on Mailer in, for instance, *The Deer Park*, and also on other New York writers. Bowles has now spent nearly fifty years in Tangier, but he has been a presence on the New York scene in two ways. During the late fifties and early sixties, when William Burroughs lived in Tangier for the easily available drugs and boys, Bowles became friendly with Allen Ginsberg and Jack Kerouac through Burroughs. In the seventies, the young poet Daniel Halpern looked up Bowles, and when he returned to New York and began Ecco Press he honored his mentor by making him founding editor of the magazine *Antaeus* and republishing titles by both Bowles and his wife. Beneath the polished prose of Bowles's 1972 autobiography, *Without Stopping*, little is revealed. His biographer, Christopher Sawyer-Lauçanno, worked closely with Bowles only to have him turn on the book and its author after publication. The elegant Bowles appears as narrator at the beginning and end of Bertolucci's movie version of *The Sheltering Sky*.

Bradford, William (1663–1752)

A Quaker, Bradford became the first and official printer of Pennsylvania and remained in that office until he published a book in Philadelphia that brought the authorities down on him. Tried and acquitted, but reviled, he was about to return to England when New York's British governor Fletcher brought him to the city in 1691 to become its first printer. Thus, sixty-seven years into its life begins New York's literary history. Bradford printed the first American Book of Common Prayer in 1710, the first Bible to be printed in the city, and the first American play, *Androboros,* in 1714. Of greater significance is New York's first newspaper, the Royalist *New York Gazette,* which Bradford began publishing at 81 Pearl Street in 1725 and continued until 1744. In the paper's early years Bradford's apprentice was John Peter Zenger, whose trial for libel in 1735 would fire the first shot in the war for freedom of the press in America. Bradford also printed some of the currency used in the city. He is buried in the Trinity Church graveyard at Broadway and Fulton Street.

Brainard, Joe (1942–1994)

Brainard, to whom this book is dedicated, is one of those "born" New Yorkers who knows he belongs in the city before he has ever set foot in it. He came from Tulsa, Oklahoma, by way of art schools in Dayton, Ohio, and Boston and followed his Tulsa friends, the poets Ron Padgett and Ted Berrigan, to the city in the mid-sixties. Brainard moved at once into the center of the poetry and art world that surrounded Frank O'Hara, with whom he collaborated, as he was to with John Ashbery, James Schuyler, and nearly every other poet in the first and second generations of the New York School, working most often with Berrigan, Padgett, and Kenward Elmslie. Through the seventies he produced not only a torrent of book covers and flyers announcing readings, but his own collages, drawings, and paintings. Brainard's work was everywhere, and then abruptly, in the late seventies, he stopped making art. He returned briefly in the early nineties, collaborating with Elmslie on the book *Sung Sex,* but the old impulse to work was not there. What happened to Joe became a much discussed topic, and the answers offered were as various as his giving up speed, which he had used during the height of his art making, to his simply having realized he had said all he had to say. Brainard would deserve a place in this book on the strength of his art alone, and the way he fused the elegant with the ordinary to play off of the poems of his time, but he was also a writer who

produced an unforgettable book, *I Remember*. At some point in the late
sixties, bored in his studio, Brainard began to amuse himself, writing, "I
remember . . . ," and letting his memory fill in the blanks. Soon he had
pages of "I remember," and after he had shown these to friends and
read from them at readings, poet-publishers such as Anne Waldman
and Lewis Warsh eagerly published them. In 1975 all the small books of
"I remember" were gathered into a complete *I Remember*, which, after
a few years, went out of print. Because dozens of creative writing teachers used Brainard's "form" as an assignment to stimulate their writing
classes, the book achieved an underground reputation. Paul Auster,
who regards the book as a masterpiece, urged Penguin to publish the recent reissue. Brainard, alas, died of AIDS before it reappeared. During
the last twenty years of his life he lived in a loft at 8 Greene Street in
SoHo. The place became more and more spartan as Brainard gave up
his art and periodically gave away the many books he read. He maintained his love for elegant clothes, but in the last years of his life he
could have packed his things into a few suitcases. At his memorial service in St. Mark's Church more than a dozen people spoke and two
dozen more would have gladly taken their place.

Breton, André (1896–1966)

Breton, the pope of surrealism, spent World War II in New York unhappily. Although he had many of his fellow surrealists for company,
Yves Tanguy, Matta, Kurt Seligman, André Masson among them, and
such French intellectuals as Claude Lévi-Strauss, Breton had little
money and he never learned English. His biographer, Mark Polizzotti,
sees this as "a stubborn refusal" on Breton's part, an act born out of
both arrogance and fear of ridicule. Breton announced that he preferred
not to "tarnish" his French by learning English. In any case, while he
enjoyed the city's restaurants and street life, he lost fifty pounds during
his New York years. The painter Willem de Kooning claims to have
seen him swatting away a butterfly on a New York street corner. If Breton had little direct impact on New York literary life, the surrealists as a
whole, poets and artists, had a powerful influence on poets as various
as Charles Simic and John Ashbery. During his New York years Breton
lived at 265 West Eleventh Street.

Broadway

Broadway the street begins at the Battery and follows an old Indian trail
north though Manhattan for seventeen miles; it then runs another four

miles through the Bronx until it leaves New York City, continuing on to Albany and beyond. For the Indians it was one of their main trade routes. From the founding of New Amsterdam it has been one of Manhattan's most vital thoroughfares, but it did not become important to literary New York until the early twentieth century. It was then that the theater district moved up from the Bowery to take over Broadway and Times Square. Because of the intense concentration of electric signs, that stretch of Broadway was named "the Great White Way." At its height in the 1920s this became the center of theater in America and all sorts of plays were produced: from Shakespeare, Ibsen, Chekhov, and Shaw through Eugene O'Neill, Maxwell Anderson, George S. Kaufman, to comedies, farces, and, of course, America's foremost contribution to the world stage, the musical. It was on Broadway that *Of Thee I Sing, Show Boat, Porgy and Bess, Oklahoma, Annie Get Your Gun,* and *West Side Story* premiered. During the 1927–28 season 264 shows opened in seventy-six Broadway theaters. Broadway theater was at its height and literary New York went to the theater as it would later go to the movies. Novelists of every stripe including Fitzgerald and Hemingway wrote plays, and writers across the country dreamed of writing a Broadway hit as today they dream of writing a hit screenplay. Broadway did not escape the effects of the Depression, but the economic catastrophe also brought new life to the theater as leftist political radicals saw it as a way to get their message across and playwrights like Clifford Odets and Lillian Hellman flourished. Then came the Federal Theater Project, which, led by the company put together by Orson Welles and John Houseman, pumped more life into Broadway. The decade and a half after World War II were great years for American playwrights as Tennessee Williams, Arthur Miller, and William Inge came to the fore, but Broadway itself had begun to decline. This happened slowly at first, but by the late sixties one heard Broadway referred to as "the fabulous invalid" and production costs rose as audiences dwindled. First the movies and then television made theater an acquired taste, a luxury that gradually became a very expensive one. Musicals flourished into the early sixties, but there were few new playwrights after Edward Albee and David Mamet, and there seemed room for only one new writer of musicals, Stephen Sondheim. By the early eighties Broadway became a tourist attraction mounting fewer shows each year, some years not even ten, and these ten were often star vehicles or extravaganzas that depended on sensational stage effects. The same holds true today. It is difficult to imagine when Broadway will again play a significant role in New York's literary life.

Brodkey, Harold (1930–1996)

There are careers to which New York is a necessary accomplice. Brodkey's is one. Had he lived in his native St. Louis or in San Francisco, it is doubtful that he would have become famous for a novel he could not seem to complete. Those cities—in fact every other city in America—are too far from the means of publicity, and Brodkey's career thrived on publicity. The novel began life as *Party of Animals,* appeared as such in several Farrar, Straus & Giroux catalogs, but resisted becoming a book. "Publishing," Brodkey told a reporter, "would interfere with working on it." He also said, "It is a dangerous to be as good a writer as I am." Dangerous, almost certainly, to the five publishers who gave him advances on what became *The Runaway Soul,* published in 1991 after thirty-two years in the writing. He also published two books of short stories and a second novel, all the while working at the *New Yorker,* where he was, several memoirs attest, a character—his own most compelling creation. He died of AIDS and wrote about his dying in the *New Yorker* in essays that met with the same mixed reactions that greeted his fiction. Within days of his death, the poet Joseph Brodsky died in Brooklyn. Brodkey's death was all the more remarked upon for being so quickly followed by that of his near namesake Brodsky. It is the sort of celebrity that, courted or not, was his lot in life.

Brodsky, Joseph (1938–1996)

When the exiled Brodsky came from Russia to New York in the early seventies he took an apartment at 44 Morton Street in the Village. Here he lived for many years while he taught in Michigan, Massachusetts, and in New York at Columbia and New York University. A PBS documentary photographed him in this apartment in conversation with fellow Nobel Prize-winning poet Derek Walcott. In the early nineties the now married Brodsky moved to Pierrepont Street in Brooklyn Heights where he was living when he died in his sleep in January 1996. While in that neighborhood he was responsible for persuading the Auden Society to erect a plaque commemorating Auden's years on Middagh Street. Brodsky revered Auden above all other contemporary poets writing in English and wrote an eloquent essay about his poem "September 1, 1939," the first major poem Auden wrote after taking up residence in New York. When asked what he had written about New York, Brodsky replied, "I don't think I've written anything about New York. You can't do much about New York." What he did write while in the city were many of the essays on which his reputation as a writer in English may one day come to rest. Throughout Brodsky's years in the city, Russians, recent émigrés as well as visitors, beat a path to his door. To them he represented the greatness of Russian poetry, no matter how long he had lived in this country, and he was known for being generous with his time and, if it was asked of him, his money. Brodsky is remarkable above all because he refused to leave his career in Russia or in the Russian language. He demanded a great deal of his muse and by main force made himself into an American poet writing in his adopted tongue. At his funeral in a Brooklyn Heights church not far from his home he requested that a recording of a favorite song, "When Johnny Comes Marching Home," be played.

The Bronx

> The Bronx
> No, Thonx
> OGDEN NASH

The Bronx is the only borough of New York City connected to the North American mainland. The other four boroughs are either islands (Manhattan and Staten Island) or part of Long Island (Brooklyn and Queens). Today the Bronx has a population of 1.2 million but very little of literary interest. There is, however, the Edgar Allan Poe cottage at Poe Park on the Grand Concourse and East Kingsbridge Road. Poe lived in it between 1846 and 1849, and while it was then out in the country, he could get into Manhattan by the Harlem River railroad. During the years he lived there, Poe worked on the poems "Annabel Lee," "Ulalume," and "The Bells." The cottage is open to the public, but it is a long trip for very little worth looking at. The other object of literary pilgrimage in the borough is Woodlawn Cemetery, where Herman Melville, George M. Cohan, Joseph Pulitzer, Damon Runyon, and the journalist Nellie Bly are buried. It has an entry of its own here.

For a few years in the first decade of this century Mark Twain lived in the borough's Riverdale section. Paddy Chayefsky, the screenwriter who wrote *Marty* and *Network,* was born in the Bronx, as were Herman Wouk, the critic Harold Bloom, the novelist and critic Cynthia Ozick, and the novelist Don DeLillo. Clifford Odets grew up in the Bronx, the poet Howard Nemerov (brother of the photographer Diane Arbus) graduated from the Fieldstone School there, and the poet John Hollander graduated from the Bronx High School of Science.

The Bronx is as varied as Brooklyn or Manhattan. South Bronx has neighborhoods as rough and dangerous as any of those in the city, whereas Riverdale is posh and suburban. If you enter Manhattan from the north on any of the parkways, you drive through the Bronx. Many who visit the borough do so to attend baseball games at Yankee Stadium, the house that Babe Ruth built.

Brooklyn

Although Brooklyn did not become a borough of New York City until 1898, it enters New York literary life with Walt Whitman in the early 1840s. Whitman's father came from Long Island to take part in the Brooklyn building boom that saw small, scattered settlements and large farms grow from a population of four thousand in 1810 to two hundred thousand in 1850 and into the nation's fourth largest city. Whitman's father built houses on speculation, overextended himself, lost his shirt, and returned to Long Island. His son stayed to edit a number of Brooklyn's newspapers, among them the *Brooklyn Daily Eagle.*

In Whitman's Brooklyn years reaching Manhattan meant taking the ferry across the East River or, in the rare years the river froze, walking across. The numerous trips back and forth Whitman took inspired some of his most beautiful poems. It was to Brooklyn that Ralph Waldo Emerson and, in a visit notable for its discomfort, Henry David Thoreau came to see Whitman. Although he kept a Brooklyn address until after the Civil War, it was really the home of Whitman's youth and the place where he both learned his craft and began work on the poem of his life, *Leaves of Grass.*

Following the Civil War, Whitman's Brooklyn was all but obliterated by the city's rapid growth. As with Manhattan, the people's time and energy went into public works. The designers of Manhattan's Central Park, Frederick Law Olmsted and Calvert Vaux, created Brooklyn's Prospect Park, a design they preferred. In 1883 Washington Roebling finished the work his father, John, had begun, and the Brooklyn Bridge became a reality. Lewis Mumford was to write of it, "In this structure the architecture of the past, massive and protective, meets the architecture of the future, light, aerial and open to sunlight." It would inspire Hart Crane's great poem "The Bridge," and to walk across the bridge today is to be able to imagine the thrill of those who first did so. (One writer worked on the Brooklyn Bridge, the pornographer Frank Harris, who labored for a time in a caisson under one of the bridge towers. He is best known for his autobiography, *My Life and Loves,* which catalogs at great length his sexual life, and for Oscar Wilde's line regarding Harris's years in London: "Frank Harris has been received in all the great houses—*once.*")

At the beginning of the twentieth century Brooklyn's population reached one million as the city attracted Eastern and Southern European immigrants, as well as blacks from the American South. By the thirties Brooklyn's 2.5 million people made it the city's most populated borough, a distinction it holds today.

Until the early 1940s, when writers began to discover the charms of Brooklyn Heights, its low rents and spectacular views of Lower Manhattan, Brooklyn's writers crossed the East River to make their fortunes and live. Alfred Kazin, who grew up in an East New York Jewish neighborhood, was one of these. The poets Charles Reznikoff and David Ignatow were born in Brooklyn, and so were Norman Mailer, J. P. Donleavy, Gilbert Sorrentino, Hubert Selby, Norman Podhoretz, Lillian Smith, the novelist and essayist Michael Stephens, and the poet Edward Barrett. Thomas Wolfe lived in Brooklyn in the thirties. The Nobel Prize-winning Joseph Brodsky died there. Marianne Moore wrote poems to the Brooklyn Dodgers in her Brooklyn apartment. Arthur Miller wrote *A View from the Bridge* on Brooklyn Heights where stood the famous Middagh Street house, home of W. H. Auden and Gypsy Rose Lee, among others. The playwright Neil Simon grew up in Brighton Beach, Joseph Heller in Coney Island, and Terry McMillan in East New York. The playwright William Alfred grew up in the city and set his play *Hogan's Goat* there. Native son Henry Miller wrote of Brooklyn in several of his books. Today Brooklyn is the only borough to have a poet laureate, Dennis Nurkse.

The generation that discovered Brooklyn Heights was followed by one that discovered Park Slope, where a number of writers and literary people have lived or live today. Among them are Paul Auster, Siri Hustvedt, Ian Frazier, Luc Sante, whose *Low Life* is an excellent book on New York's nineteenth-century slums and underworld, the poet Lewis Warsh, the novelists Russell Banks, Mary Morris, Kathryn Fields, and Jennie Fields, the literary agents Gail Hochman and Ann Rittenberg . . . and, well, as you walk the streets of this neighborhood that has Manhattan-sized crowds but a different feel, you are probably passing any number of writers and literary types. The neighborhood supports two bookstores, both of which have reading series: Nkiru Books at 76 St. Mark's Avenue and the Community Bookstore at 143 Seventh Avenue.

Who knows what writers are growing up in the now predominantly Russian Brighton Beach section or in those areas where tens of thousands of Haitians and Caribbean people have moved over the past decade or so or in the largely Hispanic Sunset section down from Park

Slope. To cross Brooklyn by subway is to encounter the city's astonishing racial mix, and to remember that New York City has always been an immigrant city. This has been truer in the past twenty years than at any time since the beginning of this century. Sometime in the first or second decade of the twenty-first century, the children of these immigrants will be American men and women whose writing will, one hopes, invigorate the national literature as has happened so many times before.

In 1994 *The Brooklyn Reader,* edited by Andrea Wyatt Sexton and Alice Leccese Powers, appeared. It collects thirty different writers on Brooklyn and is worth looking up even if it only begins to cover the many and various writers in this city. Pete Hamill, a Brooklyn boy and author of the memoir *A Drinking Life,* contributed an introduction to the book.

Brooklyn College
In response to overcrowding at the City College, Brooklyn College opened in 1937. When John Ashbery came there to teach in the late seventies, the school appeared on New York's literary map. Among Ashbery's students were the poets John Yau and Edward Barrett. Allen Ginsberg replaced Ashbery in the early nineties. The poets Louis Asekoff and Julie Agoos also teach at Brooklyn, as does the novelist Susan Fromberg Schaeffer. The novelist Sapphire is a recent graduate.

Brown, Charles Brockden (1771–1810)
A Philadelphia native trained as a lawyer, Brown lived on and off in New York between 1794 and 1800. He worked as a journalist and wrote novels, and has been recognized as "the first American to adopt literature as a sole profession." His base of operations was a Dr. Smith's house in Pine Street, now in the Wall Street district. Here he wrote the Gothic novels *Wieland* (1789), *Ormond* (1799), and *Arthur Mervyn* (1799–1800). The last takes place in a yellow fever epidemic similar to that which laid low both Brown and Smith. (Smith did not survive.) Brown's novels were widely read in their time and are thought to have influenced both Shelley and Poe. Despite his prodigious output, Brown found himself unable to make a living by his pen and returned to Philadelphia, where he worked as an importer until his death.

Brown, Claude (b. 1937)
Born in Harlem and raised on 145th Street between Seventh and Eighth Avenues, Brown grew up in the street life of pimps, prostitutes, guns,

and drugs. His autobiography, *Manchild in the Promised Land,* appeared in 1965 and helped show white America how short, wretched, and cruel life in Harlem can be. Brown was one of the first African American writers to bring this news to a wide public and the book became a best-seller. He went on to cover some of the same ground, with a sharper focus on the scourge of heroin, in his 1975 novel, *The Children of Ham.*

Broyard, Anatole (1920–1990)

After World War II Broyard came to Greenwich Village from Brooklyn, where he had been raised, and lived the Village life. He wanted to be a writer and took courses at the New School, opened a bookstore while—because of his extraordinary good looks—pursuing and being pursued by women. A thin memoir of this period, *When Kafka Was the Rage,* one of Broyard's four books, appeared after his death. Not enough on the face of it, even if his eighteen years as a book reviewer and columnist for the *Times* are thrown in, to earn him a place in this book. But in the 17 June 1996, *New Yorker* Harvard professor Henry Louis Gates Jr. "outed" Broyard in an essay titled "White like Me." *Outed* is in quotation marks because it seems, as Gates did not deny, that a good many people knew Broyard was passing as white. On this slender thread . . . but there is more. Broyard was the model for the character Henry Porter in his friend Chandler Brossard's Village novel, *Who Walk in Darkness.* "People said that Henry Porter was a Negro," wrote Brossard. James Laughlin of New Directions, who was about to publish the novel, not only knew Broyard but also knew that he was Porter and would object. He sent Broyard galleys, and as Laughlin had foreseen, Broyard demanded a change. In the published version of the novel Porter is illegitimate. Many years later Broyard opened his *Times* review of Brossard's latest novel, "Here's a book so transcendentally bad it makes us fear not only for the condition of the novel in this country, but for the fate of the country." Perhaps there will be more in the future about Broyard's passing and his literary life in New York, but for now it can only be lamented that he never got down on paper what might have been an original and complex view of the postwar Village.

Bryant, William Cullen (1794–1878)

A prodigy, Bryant wrote his two most famous poems, "To a Waterfowl" and "Thanatopsis," before reaching twenty. He is another in the line of New York writers who were also lawyers, but he gave up the law before moving to the city in 1825. Already known as a poet, Bryant became a newspaper editor and edited the New York *Evening Post*, which he owned, for fifty-two years. During that time Bryant rose to prominence not as a writer, but as a citizen. No poet—indeed, no literary man or woman—has approached Bryant's influence over the affairs of New York City. In 1844 his editorials began the campaign that resulted in the construction of Central Park. When the Hungarian patriot Lajos Kossuth visited New York, Bryant presided over the dinner in his honor, as he had when Charles Dickens first visited the city. In February 1860 Bryant introduced Abraham Lincoln, then a candidate for the presidency, to a crowd at Cooper Union whose polite applause Lincoln turned into wild cheers. That April Bryant eulogized the recently dead Washington Irving. By this time Bryant's life was one of banquets, committees, addresses, and influence that goes beyond rank and social position. He founded the Century Club, advised Lincoln on cabinet appointments, served as president of New York Medical College and of the American Free-Trade League. On his seventieth birthday, the Century Club hosted a "Bryant Festival" at which Oliver Wendell Holmes, Bayard Taylor, and Julia Ward Howe spoke. Bryant was one of the founders of the Metropolitan Museum of Art and first chairman of the committee to raise money for the museum. All of this activity did not distract him from his writing. Between 1870 and 1872 he published translations of both the *Iliad* and the *Odyssey*. Through his final years Bryant kept to a busy schedule and his death came, as only seems appropriate for such a public man, when, following his address at the unveiling of the Manzi statue in Central Park, he fell and never recovered from his injuries. He died at 43 West Sixteenth Street, his home after 1867, and is buried in Roslyn, Long Island, where he had a house from the late 1840s. In 1884 Reservoir Square at Sixth Avenue and Forty-second Street, site of the Croton Reservoir, was renamed Byant Park. A statue of Bryant stands today in the park, which is now directly behind the main branch of the New York Public Library. The park has had its ups and downs over the years, becoming such a bastion of the homeless during the 1970s that a Park Restoration Corporation had to be convened to create the grassy space surrounded by a wide gravel walk that is there today.

Bryant makes a number of appearances in Philip Hone's diary, one of which is worth recounting. Hone lived downtown on Broadway and while shaving one morning he looked out his window to see Bryant tussling with another newspaper editor, William C. Stone. Hone saw

Bryant start things by "striking Stone over the head with a cowskin." The cause of their imbroglio had to do with a toast given at a private dinner. Hone found the entire business "disgraceful." Woe to the man of note who lives and works in a small city where a diarist is at work.

Buckley, William F., Jr. (b. 1925)

Two writers ran for mayor of New York in the 1960s. Buckley was the first, and in 1965 on the Conservative Party ticket he racked up 341,226 votes to the 41,000 of Norman Mailer, who ran in 1969. Scion of a wealthy family, Buckley founded the politically conservative *National Review* in 1955 and became its editor. He had already gotten some attention with his book *God and Man at Yale* in which he scolded his generation for its lack of religious fervor. At one time or another former leftists such as Max Eastman and John Dos Passos wrote for Buckley's magazine, as did Clare Booth Luce, Garry Wills, and the newspaper columnist George F. Will. For years Buckley had a television talk show called *Firing Line* on which he skillfully debated or grilled a wide range of guests, including, on one occasion, a very drunk Jack Kerouac. No one who saw the show will forget the way Buckley pursed his mouth, gripped a pen between his fingers, and opened his eyes wide when going in for the kill. Off camera he was said to be friendly with many of his adversaries. He did almost come to blows with Gore Vidal, and for a number of years after they engaged in a nasty legal battle, which both of them claim to have won. In 1990 Buckley gave up the editorship of the *Review* and concentrated on the spy novels and journals of ocean voyages that he has been writing for years. Long before Norman Podhoretz at *Commentary* and the generation of conservatives who came of age during the Reagan-Bush years—not to mention Rush Limbaugh—Buckley and his magazine carried the banner for conservatism. It was lonely work, but he did it with relish.

Buntline, Ned (1823–1886)

This is a case of the man, whose real name was Edward Zane Carroll Judson, being more interesting than the writer. Before Judson landed in New York, he had been a midshipman in the navy, soldier, fur trapper, duelist, and who knows what else. In 1849 he was one of the ringleaders of the Astor Place riot. This occurred over May 10 and 11 and involved a feud between supporters of the English actor William C. Macready and his American rival, Edwin Forrest. Partisans of Forrest, Judson among them, broke into a performance by Macready in the

Astor Place Opera House, and the fight carried outside, growing in ferocity until the militia had to be called in. Twenty-two were killed at the scene and nine died later. Judson went on to name the rabidly anti-Catholic Know-Nothing faction and used it to advance his campaign against immigrants. At least part of the time he was occupied writing what became known as dime novels. He turned out more than four hundred of these, the most famous being *Buffalo Bill, the King of the Border Men* (1869) in which Judson/Buntline gave frontier scout William F. Cody the name Buffalo Bill. This novel and others set in the West caused screenwriters to put a character based on Buntline into several horse operas. The director John Ford had him in mind when he had the editor of the *Shinbone Star* in *The Man Who Shot Liberty Valance* order, "Print the legend."

Burroughs, William (1914–1997)

After graduating from Harvard, Burroughs came to New York in the late 1930s. It is worth noting that the three dominant figures of the Beat Generation—Burroughs, Kerouac, and Ginsberg, the latter of whom went to Columbia—attended Ivy League colleges. If you are going to rebel against the establishment it pays to have seen its face early in your life. Burroughs is often spoken of as the heir to the Burroughs Adding Machine fortune. This is technically true, but by the time his namesake grandfather's fortune got down to him there was little of it left. Yet from 1939 to 1961 Burroughs's parents supplied him with two hundred dollars a month. Given the nature of Burroughs's activities during these years, this stands as an act of parental devotion nearly unparalleled in the annals of literature. Through the early forties Burroughs drifted from job to job and out to Chicago, where he met Herbert Huncke, one of the original Beats, and back to New York where an old St. Louis friend, David Kammerer, introduced Burroughs to the teenage Lucien Carr. Carr was about to enter Columbia and meet Ginsberg and Kerouac, after which one thing led to another and the core of the Beat Generation was formed. By 1944 Burroughs had begun using heroin. He wrote about this in his first book, *Junkie,* which would not be published until 1953. At the outset the older Burroughs was mentor to the younger Ginsberg and Kerouac. He not only had a wide variety of intellectual interests but a boyish appetite for all sorts of criminal adventures. He had cut off the first joint of his left pinkie, liked to run with petty criminals, had a passion for firearms, and was homosexual but was also drawn to Joan Vollmer, whose apartment at 419 West 115th Street became the meeting place for him and his friends. It was at this combination crash pad and commune that the Beat Generation was born. In 1947 Burroughs married the pregnant Vollmer and left New York, not to return permanently until 1974, when he was a celebrated writer and cult hero. During the years away from the city Burroughs did things that would make him a legend. First, he and Joan ran a marijuana farm in eastern Texas (it appears in Kerouac's *On the Road,* in which Burroughs is Bill Lee). Then he took his family to Mexico City, where drugs were easier to come by. It was there that he accidentally shot and killed Vollmer while playing a game of William Tell. Or perhaps he meant to murder her. He later wrote that "demons" made him do it. In any case, he hired a smart lawyer and, with the aid of bribes and his own perjured testimony, spent only thirteen days in jail before being released on bail. He next went into the South American jungle in search of the hallucinogenic drug yage, which he found, took, and carried back to New York, where he stayed for a time before eventually moving to Tangier, Morocco. There he not only descended deeper into drugs but wrote the pages that he then dropped on the floor later to be assembled into the novel Kerouac titled *Naked Lunch.* (Burroughs had given it the title *Naked Lust,* which Kerouac misread, to Burroughs's delight.) Maurice Girodias published this book in Paris in his Olympia Press *Traveler's Companion* series in 1957, and five years later, after an obscenity trial, Grove Press published it in the United States. By the time Burroughs returned to New York he had published several other books, experimented with cut-ups (a collaging of bits and pieces of various texts), and been picked up as an avatar by many rock musicians, including those who would launch punk rock. Back in the city and living on the Bowery in a basement that had once held the locker room and toilets of a YMCA and was now called the Bunker, Burroughs began to write more conventional novels beginning with *Cities of the Red Night* (1981). These years have been chronicled by the pop journalist Victor Bockris in *A Report from the Bunker.* As Burroughs's celebrity grew he began not only to give public readings, snarling out the words in his wonderfully comic, nasal, and nasty voice, but also to appear in the pages of fashion magazines. No writer can come inside in America like one who has been outside. But Burroughs kept his sense of humor about all this success. He accepted election to the American Academy of Arts and Letters because, as he said, he knew the value of medals when it came to going through Customs. In the late eighties, the St. Louis native returned to the Midwest, to Lawrence, Kansas, to write, as well as to paint, his technique being to fire a shotgun at painted-filled balloons tied to boards. For a while these works sold like hotcakes. There have been several Burroughs biographies, and as is true for all the major writers of the Beat Generation so much is known about his life that it seems impossible he was ever really "underground."

In 1997 the last of the men who began the Beat Generation died. First, Herbert Huncke, then Allen Ginsberg, and finally, in August, William Burroughs. "The Beat Writer Who Distilled His Raw Nightmare Life" ran the *New York Times* headline over his half-page obituary, a length that indicated that the publication considered Burroughs an important writer. A few weeks later the *New Yorker,* whose former incarnations never would have come within a mile of Burroughs, published under the title "Last Words" entries from his journal. He had taken this up some years past after he had given up writing for publication. Burroughs recorded his last conversation wtih Allen Ginsberg: "Allen made holes in the Big Lie not only with his presence, his self-evident spiritual truth. Last words 'Two to five months the doctors said,' Allen said, 'but I think much less.' Then he said to me, 'I thought I would be terrified, but I am *exhilarated*!' His last words to me." Burroughs's own last words, at least those he left in his diary, were dated 1 August, two days before his death: "Love? What is it? Most natural painkiller. What there is. LOVE."

Cage, John (1912–1992)

Cage first knew New York City as a student. In 1933 he came to study with his teacher Arnold Schoenberg's former pupil Adolf Weiss. For a year and a half Cage lived in furnished rooms and cold-water flats and took odd jobs. Eventually, he enrolled at the New School for Social Research in the composer Henry Cowell's class. When the now married Cage returned in 1942, he had twenty-five cents in his pocket and the painter Max Ernst's phone number. Ernst and Cage had met in Chicago, and Ernst had told the Cages they could stay with him when they came to New York. In one of the Zen-like stories scattered throughout his first and most important book, *Silence,* Cage tells of phoning Ernst. Clearly, Ernst did not recognize Cage's voice, but after a time he asked, "Are you thirsty?" To Cage's yes, Ernst said, "Well, come over tomorrow for cocktails." When Cage relayed to his wife the outcome of the call she said, "Call him back. We have everything to gain and nothing to lose." This time Ernst recognized him, "Oh, it's you. We've been waiting for you for weeks. Your room's ready, come right over." From then on Cage headquartered himself in New York. In 1945 he and his wife divorced, and he moved into an apartment on Monroe Street on the Lower East Side. Soon he and the dancer Merce Cunningham began their lifelong collaboration, and Cage joined in the whirl of one of the most extraordinary periods of New York cultural life. Already acquainted with the surrealists through Ernst, Cage developed an interest in Zen and introduced several of his friends, the painter Philip Guston among them, to Dr. D. T. Suzuki's classes at Columbia. Cage's apartment became a meeting place for the young composers Christian Wolff, Earle Brown, and Morton Feldman. This was a time when the arts, at least downtown, cut across boundaries. Cage and Cunningham collaborated with the painters Jasper Johns and Robert Rauschenberg, and performances of Cage's music had a significant impact on a new generation of poets, dancers, and artists. The poets John Ashbery and Frank O'Hara attended the 1952 concert at which David Tudor played for the first time Cage's 4'33", four minutes and thirty-three seconds of silence. Ashbery and O'Hara remembered leaving the concert realizing that in art anything could be done, that there really were no rules. Cage had a similar effect on a later generation of American poets, Clark Coolidge prominent among them. This came, in part, through Cage's writing, collected in *Silence* and in several books that followed, including *A Year from Monday* and *Empty Words*. In 1990 he gave the Norton Poetry Lectures at Harvard, creating his text through the use of chance methods that had formed the core of his aesthetic since he encountered the I Ching forty years before. "Everything we do," he famously said, "is music." It is this openness to experience and the blurring of the line between art and life that so many learned from Cage. When he and Cunningham were not on the road with Cunningham's dance company they lived, in their last years, in Westbeth's artists' housing, where they entertained all manner of artists. They set a very good table often enlivened by the mushrooms Cage picked himself. He had become a mycologist out of necessity while living poor for a time in Rockland County, New York. It is typical of Cage and of his aesthetic that he turned a lack of means to his advantage. Schoenberg said of him that he was "not a composer, but an inventor—of genius."

Cahan, Abraham (1860–1951)

Cahan came to the Lower East Side in 1882. He had been born and raised in a shtetl near Vilnius in Lithuania. Arriving in New York already a committed socialist radical, Cahan attended political meetings where a simple suggestion on his part had decisive consequences. The meetings were conducted in Russian, and Cahan argued that they should be held in Yiddish as Yiddish was the true language of the mass of Jewish immigrants. He carried the day and became a sought-after public speaker. During these years he lived in various rooming houses in the East Broadway area but did have "the best years of my life in America" at 213 Clinton Street. In 1893 he joined the staff of a Yiddish labor weekly paper. Here he met William Dean Howells, who had come in search of information about labor unions. Howells encouraged Cahan to write, and when Cahan completed his firsy novel, *Yekl* (1896), Howells used his influence to have the book published by D. Appleton. In 1897 Cahan was one of the founders of the *Jewish Daily Forward.* He soon left the paper after a policy dispute but returned in 1902 to become its editor, a position he held until his death. As a writer he is best known for his novel *The Rise of David Levinsky* (1917), but it was as an editor that he had his most significant impact. The *Forward* became the largest Yiddish paper in the world, and throughout Cahan's years it argued forcefully for trade unions. There are many vivid pages on Cahan in Irving Howe's great book on Lower East Side Jewish life, *World of Our Fathers.* For many years Cahan lived at 224 East Eleventh Street. His seventy years in New York saw American Jewish writing rise out of the ghetto to a place of prominence in the nation's literature. Before Cahan there had been little or no American Jewish writing, but at his death Saul Bellow, Allen Ginsberg, Delmore Schwartz, Isaac Bashevis Singer, and a host of other Jewish writers were at work all over the city.

Calisher, Hortense (b. 1911)

Has there ever been a New York writer with a more euphonious name? Born in Manhattan, educated at Barnard, Hortense Calisher did not start to publish until age thirty-seven, when a short story of hers appeared in the *New Yorker.* Her first novel, *False Entry,* came out in 1962, by which time she had returned to the city from the suburbs and was living with her husband, the writer Curtis Harnack, at 24 West Sixteenth Street, a very literary address. William Cullen Bryant had owned the house; Margaret Anderson and Jane Heap of the *Little Review* had lived in it, and so had, for a short time, Hart Crane. In 1969 Calisher published *The New Yorkers,* a novel that drew on her experience as an investigator for the Department of Public Welfare. But it is not disguised autobiography that distinguishes Calisher's novels, novellas, and short stories. It is her range. She has written a science fiction novel, *Journey from Ellipsia* (1965); a comic novel, *Queenie* (1971), which she has described as "about a girl who was brought up in the world of kept women, but wanted to be a college girl with all the normal repressions"; and an unconventional autobiogrpahy, *Herself* (1972). When the *Paris Review* asked her to account for the origins of this diversity, Calisher responded, "In my genes, certainly. Combined with the family history, all the places we came from. The generation gaps. The enormous diversity of my home town—New York. I come from the admixture we set ourselves up to be."

Capote, Truman (1924–1984)

Time will tell if Capote's career belongs more to the history of ambition or literature. He had an insatiable drive for celebrity and knew how to get what he wanted. He worked the New York publicity machine for all it was worth so that by the end of his life the nation knew him not as a writer but as the television talk show guest with the funny, campy voice and the sharp tongue. Like others of his precocious generation (Styron, Mailer, Vidal, Baldwin), Capote published a novel, *Other Voices, Other Rooms* (1948), in his mid-twenties. The author's photograph on its back cover got him nearly as much attention as the Southern Gothic prose inside. The blond Capote reclines on a sofa and looks soulfully at the viewer with a come-hither stare that says, "I can be counted on to go too far." Capote had actually debuted in New York literary life much earlier. At seventeen he worked as a copyboy at the *New Yorker,* keeping track of cartoons. Harold Ross, the magazine's editor, fired him after Robert Frost complained abut Capote's walking out, "a representative of *The New Yorker,*" on one of his readings. If Capote had a gift for getting noticed, he had an equal one for friendship. Long before he appeared in the cover of *Life* magazine, he moved in the world of the rich and famous, largely through his friendship with the head of CBS, William Paley, and his beautiful wife, Babe. Capote's second novel, *Breakfast at Tiffany's* (1958), was a success and many young women in New York saw themselves in its heroine, Holly Golightly. Fame arrived with *In Cold Blood* (1965), a "non-fiction novel," as Capote described it, about the murder of a Kansas family and the subsequent apprehension, trial, and execution of their killers. The book appeared in four installments in the *New Yorker* and went on to become a best-seller and a movie. Suddenly, Capote was interviewed everywhere about his research methods (he claimed the ability to remember 90 percent of every interview he conducted and so had no need for a tape recorder), the "new" form he had invented, and his stand on the death penalty. On 28 November 1966, Capote hosted a masked ball for five hundred guests at the Plaza Hotel in honor of Katherine Graham, the publisher of the *Washington Post*. No writer has ever thrown a party that even approached this one. It cost Capote sixteen thousand dollars. Jacqueline Kennedy's mother-in-law, Rose, came, and so did Frank Sinatra and his new bride, Mia Farrow. Among the writers in attendance were Glenway Westcott, Katherine Anne Porter, Thornton Wilder, Anita Loos, and Janet Flanner. The Paleys were there, as were Maria Agnelli, C. Z. Guest, Slim Hayward, Lauren Bacall, D. D. Ryan—in short, everybody who was anybody. For Capote it was mostly downhill from there. He signed a big contract with Random House to write the novel *Answered Prayers*, sections of which appeared in magazines, stunning his society friends. "Capote Bites Hand That Fed Him," read one magazine headline, and certainly this is what he had done in dishing the dirt about the rich whose company he had so eagerly sought and long cultivated. When the book appeared after Capote's death, it seemed thin stuff, little more than lightly fictionalized gossip and decidedly not the book Capote had so often bragged about in his television appearances. By the mid-seventies Capote had become one of talk show host Johnny Carson's favorite guests, and his literary gifts had shrunk to one-liners. The novelist Jacqueline Susann was "a truck driver in drag," and Jack Kerouac's books were "not writing but typing." Drink and drugs caused Capote's death just before his sixtieth birthday. (The joke went around that it was a good career move.) In New York Capote lived on the Upper West Side, in a Brooklyn Heights house at 70 Willow Street as the tenant of Broadway lighting director Oliver Smith, and after he hit it big, at the United Nations Plaza apartments at First Avenue and Forthninth Street. He traveled a good deal, wrote much of *In Cold Blood* in Europe, kept a house in Sagaponack on Long Island, but always, as he said, returned to New York as home. He shared much of his life with the novelist Jack Dunphy. Harper Lee, author of but one novel, *To Kill a Mockingbird*, helped him with the research for *In Cold Blood*. Capote wrote the scripts for the movies *Beat the Devil* and, based on Henry James's *The Turn of the Screw*, *The Innocents*. He was born in

New Orleans and died in Los Angeles, but it is impossible to imagine his career taking place anywhere but in New York.

Caro, Robert A. (b. 1935)

A New York native and former reporter for *Newsday,* Caro wrote the great muckraking biography of Robert Moses, *The Power Broker: Robert Moses and the Fall of New York* (1974). Moses may have faded from contemporary memory, but his effect on the city and its environs has not. As an appointed, but never elected official, he was for more than forty years the most powerful force in the shaping of New York City. He hated slums and so he tore down much of the Lower East Side and created the high-rise apartment buildings, the projects, surrounded by lawn that are there today. He built more of these in Harlem and other sections of the city. Moses believed slums to be absolutely evil and assumed, as he did about everything he undertook, that all New Yorkers agreed with him. He met protests, particularly from the poor blacks and Puerto Ricans uprooted by his grand designs, but he swept these aside. His base was the Triborough Bridge and Tunnel Authority, which controlled all the bridges and tunnels leading into and out of the city, the tolls from which he used to finance many of his large-scale construction projects. Because of Moses there is Jones Beach, the Northern and Southern State Parkways on Long Island, the Cross Bronx Expressway, the Brooklyn-Queens Expressway—altogether more than 416 miles of superhighways making up thirteen different roadways. In essence, Moses girded and bisected the city with highways so that those who lived in the suburbs could have access by car and city folk could escape to beaches and parks. To accomplish his dreams he rode roughshod over almost anyone fool enough to get in his way. Today, the car still rules New York and this is the legacy of Robert Moses, a man who never learned to drive.

Carr, Caleb (b. 1959)

The Ur-Beats had few children. Neither Herbert Huncke nor Allen Ginsberg was a father. Of the four children fathered by William Burroughs, Jack Kerouac, and Lucien Carr, three have written novels. Billy Burroughs, the author of two novels, died tragically in his thirties, and Jan Kerouac also died young after a hard life. Caleb Carr is not only alive but very successful. His novel *The Alienist* was a best-seller, and its sequel, *The Angel of Darkness* (1997), has been hailed as a worthy successor. In Dr. Laszlo Kreizler, the alienist or psychiatrist who is expert in minds that are alienated from themselves, Carr has invented a sort of Sherlock Holmes of the mind and surrounded him with a number of lively characters. These are joined in the sequel by historical figures, including Albert Pinkham Ryder, Elizabeth Cady Stanton, and Clarence Darrow. *The Angel of Darkness* is more than six hundred pages long, but as *New York Times* reviewer Christopher Lehmann-Haupt reported, "the reader keeps on turning" them. Carr was born on Manhattan's Lower East Side and lives there today.

Carr, Lucien (b. 1924)

Carr is the most important nonwriting member of the Beat Generation. As a Columbia freshman, he met Allen Ginsberg when Ginsberg wandered into his dorm room. Carr already knew William Burroughs and Jack Kerouac, and early in 1944 he brought everyone together. On 14 August of that year Carr stabbed to death a man named David Kammerer. Two days later, after conversations with both Kerouac and Burroughs, Carr turned himself in to the police. Both Kerouac and Burroughs were arrested and charged as material witnesses. Ultimately Carr was charged with second-degree manslaughter, found guilty, and served four years in the Elmira Reformatory. Kammerer, a friend of Burroughs from St. Louis, had met Carr there when the latter was in grade school. Kammerer developed an obsession with the young, blond, and very handsome Carr—"angelic" was Ginsberg's description of him—and followed him first to Chicago and then to New York. Carr seemed to both like Kammerer's adoration and resent it. Finally, on that August day on the banks of the Hudson, Kammerer, according to Carr, made sexual advances and threatened to harm Carr's girlfriend. Carr plunged the Boy Scout knife he carried into Kammerer's heart twice, and then in a panic attempted to weight the corpse with rocks before pushing it into the water. Kammerer's body did not sink but was found downstream. Carr made the front page of the *Daily News* in what the paper called an "honor slaying." After his release Carr eventually went to work for United Press International and fathered two sons, one of whom, Caleb, wrote the best-selling novel set in nineteenth-century New York, *The Alienist*.

Caterpillar

The poet Clayton Eshelman began this magazine in New York in the mid-1960s before taking it to Los Angeles. With considerable energy, Eshelman brought together the work of the Black Mountain poets, New York poets such as Robert Kelly—the magazine's one contributing editor—Jerome Rothenberg, and Paul Blackburn, and a passionate commitment to poetry in translation. Although not affiliated with the New York School, Eshelman paid attention to the arts, and painters Leon Golub and Nancy Spero did covers for issues. The cover photograph for issue two showed a couple fucking. If this was meant to bring down the wrath of the establishment on the head of *Caterpillar*, it did not do so. The magazine reached twenty issues, among them a still valuable one featuring the work of poets Jack Spicer and Robin Blaser. After a hiatus, Eshelman, with his wife, Caryl, as managing editor, the position she held on *Caterpillar*, began the journal *Sulfur*, which is published today out of Ypsilanti, Michigan.

Cathedral Church of St. John the Divine
1047 Amsterdam Avenue at 112th Street

St. John, the world's largest cathedral, had sponsored poetry readings for several years when in 1976 it created the Muriel Rukeyser Poetry Wall on which anyone can post a poem. In dedicating the wall Rukeyser said, "This is a place where poems will always be accepted. They can be signed or unsigned and in all languages." A New York native, Rukeyser published a great deal of socially conscious poetry and translated the work of the Nobel Prize winner Octavio Paz. Recently, the critic and anthologist Eliot Weinberger has championed her work. In 1984 St. John gave New York and America the Poets' Corner. The television anchorman Walter Cronkite acted as master of ceremonies at the dedication that installed Walt Whitman, Washington Irving, and Emily Dickinson as the first three honorees. Modeled after the Poets' Corner in London's Westminster Abbey, St. John's Poets' Corner has brought new poets into the fold every year. Melville and Stephen Crane are now there, as are Edith Wharton, Langston Hughes, Robert Frost, William Carlos Williams, and Elizabeth Bishop. Poetry readings accompany the installations, which take place in late October at a vespers service. After W. H. Auden's death in 1973 a memorial service was held for him at St. John, and the life and work of James Baldwin was also celebrated in such a service. The memorial service for Nobel Prize winner Joseph Brodsky, who died in January 1996 in his Brooklyn Heights apartment, took place in March of that year. Following readings by Seamus Heaney, Jonathan Aaron, Rosanna Warren, Mark Strand, Derek Walcott, Mikhail Baryshnikov, and others of Brodsky's friends, the crowd stood in silence as Brodsky's distinctive, high-pitched, twittering voice sang out over the public address system.

Cather, Willa (1873–1947)

In 1906 S. S. McClure, publisher of *McClure's Magazine*, brought Cather from Pittsburgh, where she had been teaching school, to New York as an editor of his magazine. She took a studio apartment at 60 Washington Square, and there she met Edith Lewis, who became her friend and companion for life. (Upon Cather's death Lewis became her executor. She is buried beside Cather in Jaffrey, New Hampshire, where their stones look toward Mount Monadnock.) In 1913 Cather and Lewis moved to 5 Bank Street (now demolished). Here Cather's child-hood years in Nebraska came back to her with a force that sustained her writing for the rest of her life. Beginning with *O Pioneers* she wrote six novels, including *My Ántonia,* at this address. We commonly think of the Village as New York's bohemian quarter, but it had another side to it. Cather and Lewis's apartment comprised several high-ceilinged rooms where they hosted Friday afternoon "at homes." D. H. Law-rence was one of their visitors. From Bank Street, Cather and Lewis moved uptown, first to the Grosvenor Hotel at 35 Fifth Avenue and then to 570 Park Avenue. By 1911 Cather had resigned from *McClure's* to become a writer and write she did, with single-minded determina-tion, for the rest of her life. While her novels and stories had a wide popular audience, she insisted that they live only on the printed page and in her readers' imaginations. During her lifetime she refused to sell her work to the movies. After her death, Lewis stuck to this rule.

The straightforward clarity of Cather's prose is as unabashedly American as any prose ever written in this country. Perhaps she would have found her way to this, and to her Nebraska landscape, had she stayed in Nebraska or Pittsburgh, but she is emblematic of the writer who finds the release of her imagination in New York City. It is a com-monplace that the most New York of New Yorkers have come from out of town. You will encounter many of them in this book. Perhaps Cather's Nebraska came to her so powerfully because the energy and freedom of New York had for her a totality, a presence that compelled her back to her past. Nebraska became not an escape from the city but a parallel to it. Cather's Nebraska is so vivid few readers will imagine her writing in a Park Avenue apartment or in a New Hampshire inn. But this is what she did and with an exhilaration that brightens nearly every one of her pages.

Cedar Street Tavern / Cedar Bar
9th Street and University Place

From the mid-forties until it closed in 1962, the Cedar was *the* bar of the New York School of painters. Willem de Kooning and Franz Kline, wearing his habitual raincoat, could be found there almost every night. Jackson Pollock came in from Long Island to see his shrink, and afterward raised hell at the Cedar (one night he tore the men's room door off its hinges) and routinely got himself eighty-sixed. After Larry Rivers won $32,000 on the television quiz show *The $64,000 Question*, his first stop was the Cedar, where he waved his check and cried out, "Drinks are on me!" Philip Guston drank there and so did Norman Bluhm, Joan Mitchell, Grace Hartigan, Mercedes Matter, and ... it was central to the hard drinking social life of the fifties art world. Since Kline and de Kooning had both taught at Black Mountain ("The trouble with Black Mountain," de Kooning had cracked about the perpetually hard-up experimental college, "is that if you teach there they want to give the place to you"), Black Mountain writers like Fielding Dawson and Robert Creeley came to the Cedar. The New York poets, at least those, as James Schuyler wrote, "affected most by the floods of paint in whose crashing surf we all scramble," also came to the Cedar, Frank O'Hara in their lead. Barbara Guest came, too, and the critic Harold Rosenberg, the composers Morton Feldman and John Cage, and even the critic Clement Greenberg, who came to detest the place. "The thing is," Greenberg says in John Gruen's elegy to the fifties art world, *The Part Is Over*, "when you produce good art you don't age. It's when you make the scene that you age." Yes, any scene takes its toll, but Franz Kline had a rejoinder to this. "Half the world wants to be like Thoreau at Walden," he told Frank O'Hara, "worrying about the noise of the traffic on the way to Boston; the other half use up their lives being part of that noise." The tavern's closing on 30 March 1963, was documented by *Village Voice* photographer Fred W. McDarrah, whose photographs taken in the place appear in the book he assembled and wrote with his wife, Gloria, *Beat Generation: Glory Days in Greenwich Village*.

Cerf, Bennett (1898–1971)

A Columbia graduate, Cerf broke into publishing in Horace Liveright's firm, Boni and Liveright. In 1925 Cerf bought the Modern Library from the financially pressed Liveright (he had dropped a bundle producing Broadway flops) for $200,000 and thus set in place the cornerstone of Random House, which he began with his partner Donald Klopfer. The house, now owned by communications tycoon Rupert Murdoch, thrives today at 73 West Forty-fifth Street. It was Cerf who got James Joyce to let him publish *Ulysses* in 1934 and then brought in the lawyer Morris Ernst to fight and win the court case that overturned the ban against the book. That same year Random House brought out Marcel Proust's *Remembrance of Things Past.* Cerf put fine editors such as Saxe Commins, Robert Linscott, and Albert Erskine together with writers such as Eugene O'Neill, Lillian Hellman, Gertrude Stein, and Random House's crown jewel, William Faulkner. Random House also published Whittaker Chambers and Ayn Rand, and had a great success with the playwright Moss Hart's memoir, *Act One,* and even greater success with the documentary novelist James Michener. When Random House acquired Alfred A. Knopf in 1960 the firm became the nation's largest publisher of literary titles. In the sixties the firm had a string of best-sellers: Truman Capote's *In Cold Blood* (1965), William Styron's *The Confessions of Nat Turner* (1967), and Philip Roth's *Portnoy's Complaint* (1969). For his part, Cerf was not the publisher who wore tweed and corduroy, smoked a pipe—although he did smoke a pipe—and ruminated over great books. He was a man about town and celebrity enough in his own right to appear as a panelist on the long-running television quiz show *What's My Line?* At Columbia Cerf had edited the humor magazine, and he edited several compilations of jokes, puns, and humorous sketches for Random House. One of these included the pun he accepted as the longest in English. A Russian husband and wife are walking in Moscow's Red Square. The husband feels a drop of rain. The wife says he is mistaken. He replies, "Rudolph the red knows rain, dear."

Chapman, John Jay (1862–1933)

Before returning to his native New York as a lawyer from Harvard, Chapman punished himself for hitting another man by thrusting his hand into a fire. The offending hand had to be amputated. In New York, Chapman practiced law, joined Teddy Roosevelt's City Reform Club to battle Tammany Hall, and published essays on literary subjects and political writings. At Coatsville, Pennsylvania, in 1912 he did the second most extraordinary thing in his life. He advertised and held a prayer meeting to commemorate the death by lynching of a black man in that town. In the address he gave that day Chapman sounds like both a latter-day abolitionist and a forerunner of the civil rights movement. "This whole matter has been an historic episode," he said, "but it is a part, not only of our national history, but of the history of each one of us." Jacques Barzun edited a *Selected Writings* of Chapman in 1975 for Farrar, Straus and Cudhay, and it is worth looking up to encounter one of the most independent minds of the time.

Cheever, John (1912–1982)

After being thrown out of Thayer Academy at seventeen, and writing about it in a piece that Malcolm Cowley published in the *New Republic,* Cheever came to New York City and served his apprenticeship as a writer over the next seventeen years. His masterwork, *The Stories of John Cheever,* prints none of the stories he wrote before 1946 when he was struggling to learn his craft and earn a living. His work came of age as his generation came out of World War II and moved to the suburbs in the early fifties, as Cheever did himself. Cheever is commonly thought of as the poet of the gin-and-cigarettes middle class, the first generation of American commuters, and the perfect writer of *New Yorker* stories, but his work easily transcends the social class of his characters and the confines of one magazine. For years it has been fashionable to praise good American short story writers by comparing them to Chekov. Cheever is the only short story writer of his generation whose work can stand the comparison. Just as you never see Chekov at work—his stories cannot be dismantled and their parts used to instruct a creative writing class—Cheever's work cannot be reduced to a plan. At their best his stories unfold so that the reader is totally in their grasp and absolutely uncertain of what is to come. In the preface to his collected stories he wrote of their roots in the city: "These stories seem at times to be stories of a long-lost world when the city of New York was still filled with river light, when you heard the Benny Goodman quartets from a radio in the corner stationery store, and when almost everyone wore a hat." These were the years in which Cheever lived in apartment buildings with his young family. In one of these the super let him use a room in the basement for his work. Each morning Cheever left his apartment dressed in a suit like the other men in the building and rode the elevator to the basement, where he took off his trousers so as not to ruin their crease, hung them on a hanger, and typed his pages dressed in his undershorts. In front of an apartment building on Fifty-ninth Street he talked out loud the ending of one of his best stories, "Goodbye, My Brother." Cheever remembered that the doorman politely remarked, "You're talking to yourself, Mr. Cheever." For years the *New Yorker* ran Cheever stories and when he collected them he had thanks for his editors,

Harold Ross, Gus Lobrano, and William Maxwell. Cheever also wrote novels, which were acclaimed, in part, because it was thought then, as it is today, that novels are inherently superior to short stories and readers were eager to see Cheever get out of short pants and into trousers. He wrote four of these, but none of them will live as long as his stories. In the last decade of his life drink pushed Cheever into madness, but he took the cure at Smithers in Manhattan and spent his last years sober. He said of himself, "The constants that I look for are a love of light and a determination to trace some moral chain of being." His friend Saul Bellow said of him in his eulogy, "His intention was, however, not only to find evidence of a moral life in a disorderly society but also to give us the poetry of the bewildering and stupendous dreamlike world in which we find ourselves."

Cheever's daughter Susan, herself a novelist, has written two books about her father, *Home before Dark* and *Life at Treetops*. His son Ben, the author of one novel, edited his father's letters. Cheever's wife, Mary, published two books of poems. The only nonwriting Cheever, at least to date, is son Federico.

Chelsea Hotel
222 West Twenty-third Street

Designed as an apartment building by the then notable firm of Hubert, Pirsson and Company and opened in 1884, the Chelsea had literary associations before it became a hotel in 1905. Upon arriving from Boston in 1888 William Dean Howells took a suite, and his friend Mark Twain stayed there while on a lecture tour. After it became a hotel, the painter and diarist John Sloan had a studio there, and O. Henry was in residence in 1907 and 1910. In the thirties the poet Edgar Lee Masters moved in and took enough interest in the history of the place that he wrote a poem about it:

> Who will remember that Mark Twain used to stroll
> In the gorgeous dining room, that Princesses,
> Poets and celebrated actresses
>
> Lived here and made its soul . . .

In 1937 Thomas Wolfe, stopping at the hotel to inspect the rooms, ran into Masters, who urged him to stay; he did. In May 1938 he extracted the manuscripts of *The Web and the Rock* and *You Can't Go Home Again* from some four thousand pages he had brought from Brooklyn in trunks. In 1940, Virgil Thomson, the composer and writer, whose plainspoken, tart style is one of the wonders of American prose, took rooms in the Chelsea and remained there until his death in 1989. Thomson often entertained in his shipshape quarters. The composer and diarist, Ned Rorem, among other writers, has given accounts of these dinner parties. In the fifties James T. Farrell and Mary McCarthy lived for a time in the hotel, but not together. Its most famous guest during those years was the Welsh poet Dylan Thomas, who stopped there during his reading tours of the States. After drinking something like eighteen straight whiskeys, Thomas was taken from the Chelsea in a coma to St. Vincent's Hospital, where he died. Another hard-drinking writer, the Irish playwright Brendan Behan, checked into the Chelsea in 1961 after having been asked to leave the more sedate Algonquin Hotel, where he had been chasing maids down the halls. In his book *Brendan Behan's New York,* he asked the Chelsea's owner, Stanley Bard, to install a plaque on the hotel's facade commemorating his stay. After Behan's death in 1964 this was done, and there are now plaques to Arthur Miller, who kept a room in the hotel for many years, Thomas Wolfe, and the poet James Schuyler. From the early seventies until his death in 1991, Schuyler lived in room 625 facing Twenty-third Street. Here he wrote many of the poems that are in his Pulitzer Prize-winning *Morning of the Poem* and the last book he published, *A Few Days.* Herbert Huncke spent his last years at the hotel, supported by the donations of admirers and the Grateful Dead's Rex Foundation. As celebrated as it is for the writers and artists who have lived there, the Chelsea is perhaps better known for two recent events that took place in its rooms. Andy Warhol filmed much of *The Chelsea Girls,* and in the 1980s Sid Vicious of the Sex Pistols murdered his girlfriend, Nancy Spungeon.

Today the Chelsea has roughly 250 units. There are single rooms, and there are also five-and-a-half-room suites. At least 75 percent of these are filled by permanent residents. Anyone who spends a night at the Chelsea will quickly learn that the amenities are far from those at an uptown hotel but then the ambience is . . . well, I once rode down in the elevator with the saxophonist and composer Ornette Coleman and that made my stay.

Christopher Street
28 West Twenty-fifth Street
Launched in 1976 by publisher Chuck Ortleb, *Christopher Street*'s focus was gay New York, and it printed the work of older gay writers such as Tennessee Williams, Gore Vidal, Ned Rorem, and Quentin

Crisp, as well as the post-Stonewall generation, including the novelists Andrew Holleran and Edmund White. In tandem with Robert Mapplethorpe, White conducted a series of interviews with Truman Capote and William Burroughs, among others. In January of 1997 the magazine, which had appeared monthly, became a quarterly.

City College of New York
138th Street and Convent Avenue

City College educated generations of New York Jews who were denied admission to Ivy League and other private schools because of discriminatory quota systems. The school was founded in 1847 downtown on Lexington Avenue, and by 1903 three-quarters of its population was Jewish. In 1907 the school moved to its current address, and the student body ballooned until it exceeded 32,000—four-fifths of whom were Jewish—in 1929. The size of the student body led to the creation of what are now Brooklyn College and Queens College. During the thirties City College was a political hotbed, and it was in that decade that most of the writers who graduated from the school were in attendance: Alfred Kazin, Irving Kristol, Gertrude Himmelfarb, Daniel Bell, Irving Howe, who went on to teach there, and Nathan Glazer. Other graduates are the muckraking novelist Upton Sinclair, Lewis Mumford, the songwriter E. Y. "Yip" Harburg, George Gershwin, Bernard Malamud, Irvin Faust, and the creator of the detective Easy Rawlins, Walter Mosley. Among current and recent teachers are the novelist Mark Mirsky, who founded and edited the journal *Fiction,* and Frederick Tuten and poets William Matthews and Ann Lauterbach.

Clampitt, Amy (1920–1994)

Clampitt was the quintessential late bloomer. She came to New York from her native Iowa in the early 1950s and worked first as a reference librarian at the National Audubon Society before becoming a freelance writer, editor, and researcher and an editor at E. P. Dutton, a job she left in 1982 when she finally had a career as a poet. Every poet's apprenticeship is different and takes the time it takes. In Clampitt's case she had been writing poems for some years and sending them to the *New Yorker* only to have them rejected time and again. It was 1978 before Howard Moss, the *New Yorker*'s longtime poetry editor, accepted one of her poems and another five years before Alfred A. Knopf published her first book, *The Kingfishers* (1983). Edmund White, among other critics, went bonkers over her work and a second book quickly followed.

This was met by the sort of praise poets dream about. "She is as 'literary' and allusive as Eliot and Pound," wrote Alfred Corn, "as filled with grubby realia as William Carlos Williams, as ornamented as Wallace Stevens and as descriptive as Marianne Moore." Actually, this is praise so fulsome that no poet could dream of it, but Clampitt's work seems not to have been crushed under its weight. She published three books with Knopf and a complete poems is surely in the offing.

Clurman, Harold (1901–1980)

Born in New York, Clurman fell in love with the theater as a child after seeing the great Yiddish actor Jacob Adler on stage. He graduated from Columbia, studied at the Sorbonne in Paris, and upon returning to New York became first an actor and then in 1931, with Cheryl Crawford and Lee Strasberg, a founder of the Group Theater. In its ten years the Group mounted plays by Clifford Odets and William Saroyan, acted in or directed by John Garfield, Franchot Tone, Morris Carnovsky, and Elia Kazan. Clurman went on to a Broadway career directing Carson McCullers's *Member of the Wedding* and William Inge's *Bus Stop*. As a theater critic he reviewed plays for the *Nation* from 1952 until his death.

Columbia University
Morningside Heights, Manhattan

Columbia began in 1754 as King's College, when eight students met in the vestry room of Trinity Church. It moved to its own building in 1760, and in 1784 it got a new charter and the name Columbia. Alexander Hamilton and John Jay were students in the school's early years. As Manhattan moved uptown, so did Columbia. When the diarist George Templeton Strong, a Columbia graduate, was a trustee the school occupied a building at Forth-ninth Street and Madison Avenue. In 1897 the school, now a university, moved to its present location in Morningside Heights on the Upper West Side at Broadway and 116th Street. In the early decades of the twentieth century the philosopher John Dewey, anthropologist Franz Boas, economist Wesley Clair Mitchell, and historian Charles Beard were all on the Columbia faculty. The art historian Meyer Schapiro and the critic Lionel Trilling, both graduates of the school, were among the first Jews allowed onto the Columbia faculty. They taught at the school for many years, as did Mark Van Doren and his brother Carl, both Columbia graduates, Gilbert Highet, Jacques Barzun, C. Wright Mills, who rode his motorcycle to classes, Daniel Bell, Robert Gorham Davis, Allan Nevins, the historian and editor of George Templeton Strong's diary, F. W. Dupee, and Richard Hofstadter. Over the past thirty years Susan Sontag, Adrienne Rich, Steven Marcus, Michael Wood, Edward Said, and Simon Schama have taught there. Slater Brown, e. e. cummings's pal in cummings's novel *The Enormous Room,* went to Columbia, as did the literary and political radical Randolph Bourne. Bennett Cerf edited the school's humor magazine, *The Jester,* and so did the painter Ad Reinhardt. The poet Louis Zukofsky and Whittaker Chambers were friends while at Columbia. Rodgers and Hammerstein began their collaboration at Columbia. Joseph L. Mankiewicz, who wrote the screenplay for *Citizen Kane,* is a Columbia graduate, as is the screenwriter I. A. L. Diamond, who wrote *Some Like It Hot,* and the mystery novelist Cornell Woolrich. The poets John Berryman, Thomas Merton, later to write the bestseller *The Seven Storey Mountain* about the spiritual quest that led him to a Kentucky monastery, and Robert Lax graduated from Columbia, as did the publisher Robert Giroux and the critic Maxwell Geismar. In the forties Jack Kerouac came to play football for renowned football coach Lou Little, but soon dropped the sport and then the college. Allen Ginsberg, his brother in the Beat Generation, managed to get himself thrown out of Columbia. Clifton Fadiman, whose endorsement for a book was once like the "Good Housekeeping Seal of Approval," graduated from the school, as did the journalist Dan Wakefield, the poet and translator Richard Howard, the poet John Hollander, the novelist Sam Astrachan, Robert Gottlieb, the publisher who followed William Shawn as editor of the *New Yorker,* the poet Ned O'Gorman, the critic and editor Norman Podhoretz, the poet Louis Simpson, and the novelist Ivan Gold. In the sixties and seventies Ron Padgett, Paul Auster, Hilton Obenzinger, David Shapiro, Dick Gallup, Phillip Lopate, Jonathan Cott, Bill Zavatsky, David Lehman, and Luc Sante were at Columbia, and the poet Kenneth Koch taught at least a few of them. Koch remains on the Columbia faculty. The novelist Siri Hustvedt got her graduate degree at the school, and the filmmaker Jim Jarmusch was a poet on the literary magazine during his Columbia years. Perhaps the most famous work written by a Columbia graduate is Clement Clarke Moore's *'Twas the Night Before Christmas.*

In 1889 Columbia formed Barnard College for women. Barnard maintains its affiliation with the university, but has its own administration, governing board, and faculty. Among the writers who attended Barnard are Patricia Highsmith, Zora Neale Hurston, who studied with the anthropologist Franz Boas, the novelist Hortense Calisher, Rosellen Brown, Lynne Sharon Schwartz, Joyce Johnson, Judith Sherwin, Mary Gordon, Francine du Plessix Gray, Tama Janowitz, Ntozake Shange, Laurie Anderson, and Alice Notley. In 1996 the novelist and poet Erica Jong, who graduated from Barnard in 1963, led a fund-raising effort in support of the school's writing program. While on the Barnard faculty Kate Millett, who earned her Ph.D. at Columbia, published *Sexual Politics* (1970), a key work in the reemergence of the feminist movement.

For more than two decades the Writing Program at Columbia has employed so many writers to teach its students that a call to the program office left the person who answered feeling that it was impossible to list them all and so he did not even try. For many years the novelist Robert Towers ran the program.

Commentary

The monthly journal of the American Jewish Committee, *Commentary* has essentially been two magazines in its fifty-one years. Until 1959 under the editorship of Elliot E. Cohen and with art critic Clement Greenberg as associate editor, the magazine was liberal in outlook. Hannah Arendt wrote for it, and so did Harold Rosenberg, George Orwell, John Dewey, Albert Camus, Lionel Trilling, Arthur M. Schlesinger Jr., and Philip Roth. It is doubtful that any of these writers would be at home in today's *Commentary*. In 1960 Norman Podhoretz took over as editor and the magazine drifted rightward until in the early seventies it proudly unfurled its neoconservative banner. Podhoretz published his political memoir, *Breaking Ranks,* in 1979, detailing his own, and the magazine's, shift in attitude. Earlier, Podhoretz had been set, as his memoir of the transition from growing up in Brooklyn to Manhattan's Upper West Side put it, on "making it." That book shows him in the footsteps of Norman Mailer, but Podhoretz did not stay on that path, and his magazine stood as solidly behind Reagan and Bush as any intellectual journal in the nation. If there is any doubt that the majority of writers and intelligentsia in New York are left-to-liberal in their views, measure the heat Podhoretz has taken for his stance.

Comstock, Anthony (1844–1915)

Comstock came to the city after the Civil War and in 1872, outraged by the immorality he encountered, founded a private agency, the New York Society for the Suppression of Vice. At first the police allowed Comstock's society, of which he made himself secretary for life, some powers, but in 1873 he managed to get an antiobscenity statute through Congress. As a special agent of the U.S. Post Office, he used the Comstock Law to hunt out abortionists, pornographers, gambling, and contraceptive devices. Between its inception and 1950, Comstock's society is estimated to have arrested more than 3,500 people and destroyed more than 150 tons of obscene literature and four million pictures. His zeal carried him into art galleries, newspapers, and publishers. In the service of his campaign he wrote novels decrying the dangers of urban life. *Frauds Exposed* and *Traps for the Young* were some of his titles. H. L. Mencken called Comstock a "smut-hound," and George Bernard Shaw coined the word "Comstockery." In thirty years of activity, Comstock came to embody the American obsession with other people's morals. Today his epigones attack the National Endowment for the Arts, and, indeed, they have all but gutted the program. "Comstockery" is a constant of American culture.

Cooper, James Fenimore (1789–1851)

Cooper is the first major nineteenth-century writer associated with New York, but he did not arrive in the city until he was thirty-one and a published author. Cooper was born and raised in Cooperstown, New York, the town founded by his father on Otsego Lake and now famous as the home of major league baseball's Hall of Fame. He went to Yale and lasted until his junior year before being expelled for numerous pranks, one of which involved tying a donkey into a professor's chair. He embarked on a naval career until his father's death left him, for a very short time, a rich man, and he married Susan De Lancey, who came from an old New York family. She is supposed to have dared him to write a novel; he responded with *Precaution* (1820) and began to move in New York literary circles. The sociable Cooper became a regular at Charles Wiley's New Street bookstore, where in 1832 he founded the Bread and Cheese, a lunch club that had as members Fitz-Greene Halleck, William Cullen Bryant, and the inventor of the telegraph and author, Samuel F. B. Morse. By this time Cooper had published *The Spy* and moved his family into the city. They lived on Broadway above Prince Street in what is now SoHo but was then the suburbs. Later they lived at 3 Beach Street and 345 Greenwich Street. Debt resulting from problems with his father's estate hounded Cooper, but he had great success with his 1823 novel *The Pioneers,* which sold more than 3,500 copies the day it appeared. In 1826, the year he left New York for

Europe, Cooper published *The Last of the Mohicans,* the novel that made his name and by which most would identify him today. He spent several years in Europe, where his fortunes improved, and then returned to New York, where he lived on Bleecker Street, near the present La Guardia Place, and on St. Mark's Place. In 1836 he returned to Cooperstown and began to buy up the property once owned by his family. At the end of his life he worked on a history of greater New York City, but he died before finishing *The Towns of Manhattan.*

While Cooper deserves the credit he has been given for establishing the novel in America, his books are little read today. The fault is in their convoluted style. It takes a major act of will to get through pages of sentences like: "His [Deerslayer's] account was both clear and short, nor was it embellished by any incidents that did not directly consider the history of his departure from the village of his people, and his arrival in the valley of the Susquehannah." Gasp! But Melville, Balzac, Joseph Conrad, and D. H. Lawrence sang his praises. These have been largely forgotten while Mark Twain's sharp and funny demolition of Cooper's work is often recalled. Cooper's novels did give America the mythic figures of Uncas and Chingachgook, noble red men, and Hawkeye, the great hunter and woodsman. They made their way into comic books and movies and remain vivid today.

Corso, Gregory (b. 1930)

"Born by young Italian parents, father 17 mother 16, born in New York City Greenwich Village 190 Bleecker . . ." So wrote Corso in his biographical note for *The New American Poetry.* His birthplace, 190 Bleecker, is across the street from the San Remo, where Corso would one day drink with the other writers who frequented the place. But this came only after a wild youth that eventually landed him in prison, where he began to read seriously and to write. In his note Corso described what happened next: "One night 1950 in a dark empty bar sitting with my prison poems I was graced with a deep-eyed apparition: Allen Ginsberg." That was in a lesbian bar, the Pony Stable, on West Fourth Street, and out of this came Corso's affiliation with the Beat Generation. His books have been published by City Lights and New Directions, and his novel, *The American Express,* by the notorious Olympia Press. He is perhaps best known for his poem "Marriage," dedicated to the painter Mike Goldberg and his then wife, the writer Patsy Southgate, who are the Mike and Patsy in Frank O'Hara's "The

Day Lady Died." Corso's poem exclaims "Penguin dust" and "Pie Glue!" and imagines the sort of father he'd be:

> Surely I'd give it for a nipple a rubber Tacitus
> For a rattle a bag of broken Bach records
> Tack Delle Francesca all over its crib
> Sew the Greek alphabet on its bib
> And build for its playpen a roofless Parthenon—

Corso is the only prominent beatnik writer to have been born in Greenwich Village.

Cowley, Malcolm (1898–1989)

Cowley's *Exile's Return: The Literary Odyssey of the 1920s* (1934, revised edition 1951) remains the best firsthand account of the "lost generation" that expatriated itself to Europe after World War I and came home to create Greenwich Village's heyday. What you get from Cowley is the exhilaration of a generation, come to New York from all over America, discovering itself. No matter the unconventional character of their sexual or literary interests, their desire to be free of where they came from and their passion for one another has, in Cowley's prose, a beguiling innocence. As it must for all generations, the glow wore off. Black Friday and the onset of the Depression broke up the gang that gave the Village the bohemian flavor we still think of it as having today. Cowley became editor of the *New Republic,* a literary journalist, and eventually the editor of Jack Kerouac's *On the Road* at Viking. And like many of his fellows he moved out of the city, to Sherman, Connecticut, in his case, where he lived a long life and wrote many books of literary reminiscence. In his Village days Cowley's circle included his old high school friend the critic Kenneth Burke, Hart Crane, Allen Tate, who lived at 27 Bank Street while he wrote his biography of Stonewall Jackson, the writer and editor Matthew Josephson, who wrote a memoir of those years (*Life among the Surrealists*), and Cowley's first wife, Peggy, who became engaged to Hart Crane just before his death. They often ate dinner at John Squarcialupi's speakeasy at 30 Perry Street, which later moved to Waverly Place. Cowley's *Exile's Return* ends on a nostalgic note, not for youth alone but for America before the Depression. Many of Cowley's friends went on to distinguished literary careers, but the generation's coherence evaporated with the new decade. The Harlem Renaissance, which took place coincidentally with the literary world Cowley describes, suffered a similar fate.

Craft, Robert (b. 1924)

A conductor, Craft served as Igor Stravinsky's musical assistant and constant companion from 1948 until Stravinsky's death in 1971. Craft recorded these years in *Stravinsky: Chronicle of a Friendship* (1972). For pure literary interest, there are many pages in the book on W. H. Auden, who wrote the libretto for Stravinsky's opera *The Rake's Progress* and who was a friend of the composer. There is also the hilarious account of a New York dinner with British novelist Evelyn Waugh at which Waugh, who was once described as having "a tigerish charm," declared, "All music is positively painful to me!" Craft has a keen eye and is a good writer. Stravinsky knew everyone, and his musical life and opinions retain their interest. Craft has been a long-time contributor to the *New York Review of Books*.

Crane, Hart (1899–1932)

After Walt Whitman, Crane is the great American prophetic poet. He saw in the Brooklyn Bridge the image of transcendent human imagination and purpose, and he believed the bridge symbolized unity and faith in the future. From April 1924 to June 1925 Crane lived at 110 Columbia Heights in Brooklyn, in the very home from which Washington Roebling had overseen the construction of the bridge designed by his father, John Augustus Roebling. Housebound because of a nervous disorder brought on by the bends suffered while working in the caissons on which the bridge is anchored, Roebling and his wife looked out on the construction of the bridge whose every detail they saw to. Crane may have looked out from the same window. In any event his desk had a view of the bridge ("O harp and altar, of the fury fused," he wrote in his poem "The Bridge"), the East River, and Lower Manhattan. During this time Crane lived with, as his first biographer, Philip Horton, delicately put it, "a person with whom he had fallen deeply in love during the preceding weeks." This "person" was a young sailor who, during their romance, was often at sea. While living in Columbia Heights, Crane worked for Sweets Catalogs in Manhattan, visited his friends Malcolm Cowley, Slater Brown, and Waldo Frank in the Village, and wrote, among other poems, "Voyages II–IV." These poems appear in *White Buildings* (1926). When *The Bridge* appeared in 1930 Walker Evans's magnificent photograph of the Brooklyn Bridge was on its cover. You can hear echoes of the poem in Allen Ginsberg's "Howl" and the poems of Frank O'Hara. The house at 110 Columbia Heights has long been torn down.

Crane came to New York from Cleveland in 1916 and immediately became a vivid presence on the scene. He was in the crowd that gathered around Alfred Kreymborg and his magazine *Others* and published in the *Dial* when Marianne Moore edited the magazine. In his Village years Crane lived mostly in what where then rooming houses at 139 East Fifteenth Street, 54 West Tenth Street, and 25 East Eleventh Street. For a time he lived at 24 West Sixteenth Street, the same house in which Margaret Anderson and Jane Heap of the *Little Review* lived. The house had once been owned by William Cullen Bryant. Crane had a yen for sailors and liked to cruise the waterfront, which was, in his time, a working seaport.

Crane, Stephen (1871–1900)

Crane had nine years of writing life and he made the most of them. Since he crammed so much work into so little time, it is difficult to determine when he wrote what. He seems to have written a draft of *Maggie: A Girl of the Streets,* imagining New York before experiencing the real thing, the Bowery, "the most interesting place in New York." Upon finishing the novel, Crane despaired that a commercial publisher would bring out a story of slum life and prostitution and so published the novel himself under the pen name Johnston Smith. At this point Crane lived with friends at 143 East Twenty-third Street. He sent a copy of the book to the novelist Hamlin Garland, then living uptown, whom he had met during his brief time as a Syracuse University student. Garland read and admired the book and passed it on to William Dean Howells, who responded favorably to Crane's realistic detail and invited the younger writer to tea. Howells went on to champion the novel in interviews and his *Harper's* magazine column. He did not, however, care for *The Red Badge of Courage,* which Crane, who had never seen war, had researched while living with art student friends on East Twenty-third Street. While the *des, dat, dose,* and *dem* dialect of "Maggie" did not deter Howells, he could not abide the soldier's dialect in Crane's masterpiece. Crane's painter roommates gave him the background for his other novel set in New York, *The Third Violet,* which *McClure's* serialized. *McClure's* also employed Crane as a journalist, and it was on their payroll that he sailed from Florida on the steamship Commodore with a cargo of arms to aid Cuba's rebellion against Spain. That ship sank, but Crane made it into a small boat with four others and out of their ordeal came his most vivid short work, "The Open Boat." He returned to Cuba and reported on the Spanish-American War for Joseph Pulitzer's

New York World, seeing action at San Juan Hill and earning the praise of fellow correspondent Richard Harding Davis. In Cuba Crane experienced renewed attacks of the tuberculosis that soon killed him. He returned to New York and sailed for England, where he became the friend of Joseph Conrad and H. G. Wells. His lungs gave out in Germany, where he had journeyed in hopes of a cure.

Crosby, Harry (1896–1929)
Boston born, raised, and schooled, the rich and bohemian Crosby rebelled against his native city throughout his life. Today he is known not for his own poems or for the poets he published at his Black Sun Press, but for his suicide. In *Exile's Return* Malcolm Cowley presented Crosby's death as emblematic of his generation's despair, its sense that the twenties had used up the world's possibilities. The facts are that on 10 December 1929, shortly after Crosby and his wife, Caresse, arrived in New York for a visit, Crosby borrowed the key to a friend's studio in the Hotel Des Artistes at 1 West Sixty-seventh Street. When the friend returned that evening he found the door locked. After Crosby failed to answer the phone, the friend had the door broken down and discovered Crosby's body and that of a young woman, Mrs. Josephine Bigelow, the wife of a Harvard graduate student. Crosby had shot Bigelow and then turned the gun on himself. He left no note, and to all outward appearances the death of two rich, healthy, and attractive young people seemed inexplicable. To the authorities, that is, and to the newspapers, who did not take the time, as Cowley did, to read Crosby's diary and to consider the "books he read and ideas he seized upon for guidance." In "Echoes of a Suicide," the final chapter of his book, Cowley sees Crosby as a "symbol of change." "The religion of art" that had inspired a generation had ended and "a financially bankrupt world had entered the age of putsches and purges, revolutions and counterrevolutions." Crosby's particular religion of art had centered on his own work and that of his press, which published Hart Crane and D. H. Lawrence. Although the novelist Geoffrey Wolff published a well-received biography of Crosby, he seldom appears in the literary histories or encyclopedias that cover the city in which he was front-page news for a day.

Cruz, Victor Hernández (b. 1949)
Born in Puerto Rico, Cruz came to the Lower East Side at the age of six with his parents. He wrote his first book of poetry, *Papo Got His Gun*

(1966), at the age of seventeen and like a number of other poets in that neighborhood, got hold of a mimeograph machine and published it himself under the Calle Once (Eleventh Street) imprint. Cruz dropped out of high school and went uptown to East Harlem, where he co-founded the East Harlem Gut Theater. In 1967 he became the editor of *Umbra,* the magazine of a black and Hispanic writers' group in his old neighborhood, and in 1968 he moved to Berkeley, California, where he still spends some of each year when he is not in Puerto Rico or New York. *Red Beans* (1990), published by Coffee House Press, is his most recent book of poems. Some of Cruz's early work reads like today's rap songs. He is interested in the speaking and singing voice, and you can imagine what he writes coming to his in the voices he hears as he walks down Second Avenue. In "Essay on Williams Carlos Williams" Cruz wrote:

> I love the quality of the
> spoken thought
> As it happens immediately
> uttered into the air

A sentiment to which the slam and performance poets who gather today at the Nuyorican Café might answer Amen.

Cullen, Countee (1903–1946)

It is often written that Countee Cullen was the only writer of the Harlem Renaissance to be born in New York. Cullen himself gave New York as his birthplace, but then he also said he was born in Baltimore and Louisville, Kentucky; no less an authority than David Levering Lewis gives his birthplace as Lexington, Kentucky. In any case, he eventually became the "son"—there was never a legal adoption—of the Reverend Frederick Cullen. He went to live with Cullen and his wife, Carolyn, at 234 West 131st Street and took their name. The family later moved to the parsonage of the Salem Methodist Episcopal Church at 2190 Seventh Avenue. Cullen attended De Witt Clinton High School, where his schoolmates were Nathanael West and Lionel Trilling. At New York University he graduated Phi Beta Kappa the same year, 1925, that Harper's published his first book of poems, *Color.* Cullen then went to Harvard for an M.A., won several prizes and fellowships, among them a prestigious award from *Opportunity* magazine, and was hailed as a genius by Alain Locke. In 1927 his marriage to Yolande Du Bois, the only daughter of W. E. B. Du Bois, was the social event of the

Harlem season, but the marriage soon foundered and was most likely never consummated. Cullen, the recipient of one of the first Guggenheims given to a black American, was soon on his way to Paris with his high school classmate Harold Jackman. Of the major Renaissance poets Cullen was both the most traditional and the one who insisted that he was "going to be a POET and not a NEGRO POET." The novelist Wallace Thurman described him as working with "eyes on a page of Keats, fingers on typewriter, mind frantically conjuring up African scenes. And there would of course be a Bible nearby." When Cullen returned to New York from Europe in 1930 he was at twenty-seven the wonder of the Renaissance, but for all intents and purposes his career was over. He did publish the Harlem novel *One Way to Heaven* in 1932, but it went unreviewed in the NAACP magazine, *Crisis,* and his former champion Alain Locke gave it brief notice among a dozen other books. In 1934 Cullen returned to De Witt Clinton to teach French. One of his students was James Baldwin, who interviewed Cullen for the school paper. He died at forty-two and was buried out of his father's church, where he had been married. Carl Van Vechten and the singer Paul Robeson were among the pallbearers. Du Bois, his ex-father-in-law, saw Cullen's career as unfinished: "It did not culminate. It laid [a] fine, beautiful foundation," he wrote, "but the shape of the building never emerged."

cummings, e [dward] e [stlin] (1894–1962)

Cummings came to New York by way of Harvard and service with the Norton-Harjes Ambulance Corps in France during World War I. While in France he landed in a French prison with his friend the writer Slater Brown, and this experience inspired his first book, the autobiographical novel titled *The Enormous Room.* After the war cummings came to Greenwich Village, where, in 1923, he took a studio at 4 Patchin Place, which would be his address for the rest of his life. "If asked 'why' I live here. I'd answer," he wrote, "'because' here's friendly. unscientific. private. human." Ezra Pound came to visit cummings at this house in 1939, having returned to America for the first time in twenty-five years. Allen Tate brought T. S. Eliot to call, and one night the drunken Dylan Thomas prevailed upon his friend and American agent, John Malcolm Brinin, to bring him to visit cummings. After 1940 the novelist Djuna Barnes lived on Patchin Place; cummings liked to open his window and shout out ribald greetings to her. Although cummings's reputation rests on his poetry, he also painted throughout his life.

Dahlberg, Edward (1900–1977)

Dahlberg, the illegitimate son of a woman barber, came to New York to attend Columbia from which he graduated with a degree in philosophy. He then lived abroad, where he wrote the novel *From Flushing to Calvary* (1932) about New York slum dwellers. Dahlberg lived in on the Lower East Side in the 1960s, but he seems to have had very little contact with the city's literary life. He was, in any case, a curmudgeon and a maverick possessed of a highly erudite and individual prose style. His publisher and friend Jonathan Williams once described Dahlberg as the sort of man who would place an entire cake before you and condemn you as ungrateful if you failed to eat every morsel.

Daniel, Minna Ledeman (1896–1995)

A New York native and Barnard graduate, Daniel edited the influential journal *Modern Music* from 1924 until it ceased publication in 1946. Although it numbered among its contributors Alban Berg, Béla Bartók, and Arnold Schoenberg, its importance stems from its coverage of American music. Virgil Thomson, Aaron Copland, John Cage, Elliott Carter, Roger Sessions, and Marc Blitzstein all wrote for the magazine, as did the young Leonard Bernstein and the poet and dance critic Edwin Denby.

Dawson, Fielding (b. 1930)

Born in New York City but raised in Missouri, Dawson attended Black Mountain College and after serving in the army returned to New York "for keeps" in 1956. At Black Mountain he studied with both Charles Olson and Franz Kline and has had a career as a writer and an artist. His drawings and photocollages have appeared on a number of book jackets, including his own. Dawson wrote a book about his time at Black Mountain and *An Emotional Memoir of Franz Kline* (1967), much of which takes place over drinks at the Cedar Bar. New York is a character in a number of Dawson's stories but most powerfully in his three "Penny Lane" novels. In these his prose writer/narrator meets a poet friend and others for drinks in bars on the Lower East Side. The hour is invariably after lunch, and the dim, cool, quiet of the bars is so accurately rendered you feel you are eavesdropping. Dawson has lived in downtown apartments and lofts throughout his New York years and now teaches writing to prison inmates.

Deep-Image Poets

This loosely formed, and short-lived, group gathered around the poets ROBERT KELLY (b. 1935) and JEROME ROTHENBERG (b. 1931). Both men are native New Yorkers and graduates of the City College of New York. They were active in the city during the years after graduation, but both of them went on to greater things after they left New York. For many years Kelly has taught at Bard College while turning out an enormous volume of poetry. He is said to have consulted Virgil, his finger falling on the line "write everything." Rothenberg founded ethnopoetics and has produced influential anthologies of both oral poetry from around the world and modernist poems. He is one of the few American poets to have written a book of poems about Hitler's death camps. These can be found in the 1989 *Khurbn and Other Poems*.

Delaney, Samuel R. (b. 1942)

A native of Harlem, Delaney got an education at the Dalton School and Bronx High School of Science before dropping out of the City College of New York and heading downtown, where he began to write science fiction novels and get another sort of education. He describes all this and his marriage to the poet Marilyn Hacker in his totally absorbing autobiography, *The Motion of Light in Water*. No other writer of his generation has written so well about what it was like to live as a young writer in New York before and during the hippie sixties. That the writer is beginning to understand what it means to be gay is part of the book's interest, but Delaney is really exploring what it means to become sexually aware at a time when all the rules are changing. And, inevitably, he writes a good deal about what inspired him to write science fiction. The short answer is his experience of New York City. He describes himself as "a quintessentially New York writer" and can trace the genesis of several of his novels to New York locations. Kolhari in the *Nerveryon* series is a scaled-down New York, and some of the books are set in what is clearly the Port Authority Bus Terminal. His million-selling novel *Dahlgren* (1974) is set in the Harlem he knew as a youth, and *The Mad Man* (1994) was partly inspired by New York's homeless people. Today Delaney lives on the Upper West Side, teaches at the University of Massachusetts at Amherst, has won four Nebulas—the sci-fi Oscar—and watched as what he calls "a five-and-a-half inch bookshelf" of books about him have appeared. He is a famous writer, but that fame is circumscribed by his being a genre writer. Hunt down his autobiography and you will see for yourself just how much more than that he really is.

DeLillo, Don (b. 1936)

Born in the Bronx and raised in the South Bronx near Arthur Avenue, DeLillo graduated from Fordham University before working for the Manhattan advertising agency Ogilvy & Mather. He worked as a copy-writer long enough to get a feel for the way American advertising ma-nipulates the American language and to gain an understanding of how American business works. Few American writers know that world as well as DeLillo. When he creates a character who is a businessman, such as Nick Shay in *Underworld,* the nature of his work and what he feels about it are convincingly presented. He published his first novel, *Americana,* in 1971 and followed it up with five more novels in the seventies. *Great Jones Street* (1973), titled after the downtown street where the West Village meets the East, is the story of Bucky Wunderlick, who wants to be a rock star. With that name, what else? Parts of *Libra* (1986) are also set in New York. It is a book whose sentences have the jitters, and is the only novel of consequence to deal with Lee Harvey Oswald and the Kennedy assassination. As research DeLillo read all twenty-six volumes of *The Warren Commission Report,* making him one of the few American novelists to read that monumental work. *Mao II* (1991) opens with a chapter that describes an actual mass Moonie wedding at Yankee Stadium, a wedding uniting thousands of couples who had never met be-fore. No novelist of his generation works so well from the facts. DeLillo knows the wisdom of Wallace Stevens's dictum, "Reality is only the base, but it is the base." When his long story "Pafko at the Wall," which deals with Frank Sinatra, Jackie Gleason, and J. Edgar Hoover in their Polo Grounds box seats during the 1951 Brooklyn Dodgers/New York Giants playoff game, appeared in *Harper's* in 1994 it was so powerful that readers wondered what sort of novel, if any, it might lead to. They had their answer in the fall of 1997 when *Underworld* was published with "Pafko at the Wall" as its opening chapter. Melvillian in its sweep, it is a work of great ambition and imagination, and perhaps the most im-portant novel by a writer of his generation. *Underworld* has had the ef-fect of turning after-dinner conversation among writers away from the movies and back to fiction. The book's hero, Nick Shay, grew up in the Bronx, and in those passages DeLillo's finely tuned ear is beautifully in evidence. Perhaps because of his experience in advertising, DeLillo has shunned the limelight throughout his career. *Underworld* smoked him out, at least for a short time, and he gave interviews, rare for their intelligent clarity, and contributed an essay, "The Power of History," to the Sunday *New York Times Magazine*. This is a work that sheds light not only on DeLillo's novel but also on those of E. L. Doctorow and other American novelists who have built their fictions on a base of fact. When the stir caused by *Underworld* ends, DeLillo presumably will return to his reclusive ways and begin work, seven mornings a week as is his habit, on another of his superb fictions.

Denby, Edwin (1903–1983)

Born in Tientsin, China, where his father was the American consul, Denby was schooled at Hotchkiss and, briefly, at Harvard. He continued his education in Europe, where he received a degree in gymnastics with a specialty in "eccentric dancing" in Vienna. In 1926 he published his first poems in *Poetry*. Until 1934 he traveled in Germany, France, and Switzerland. In that year in Basel, he met his lifelong friend, the photographer Rudolph Burckhardt, when he went into Burckhardt's studio for a passport photograph. Together they moved to New York in 1935 and found a cold-water loft at 145 West Twenty-first Street, where Denby lived for the rest of his life. One day a cat wandered into his loft. The man who came in search of it was Willem de Kooning, who became a friend of both Denby's and Burckhardt's and painted portraits of both of them. Many of Denby's New York sonnets are about de Kooning, Franz Kline, Alex Katz, and other painters of the New York School. In the late thirties Denby collaborated with Orson Welles on *Horse Eats Hat*, a French farce by Michel Labiche, and wrote several opera librettos and occasional dance criticism. From 1942 to 1945, he wrote dance criticism for the arts page Virgil Thomson edited at the *New York Herald-Tribune*. Today Denby is recognized as America's premier dance critic. All of this activity did not make Denby well known outside dance circles, but in the early fifties the poets who would make up the New York School met Denby and he became a valued elder to them, especially to Frank O'Hara. But it was the second generation of the New York School, Ted Berrigan and Ron Padgett in particular, who actively encouraged wider interest in Denby's poetry. Padgett has edited Denby's *Complete Poems*, for which he wrote an introduction that is the best biography we have of Denby until the real thing comes along. Denby was one of those New Yorkers who walks everywhere, and his poems are replete with glimpses of the city in all its moods. He titled one of his books of criticism *Dancers, Buildings and People in the*

Streets, a title that could stand for his collected works. He had a keen sense of New York's wholesome vulgarity and art's place in it. These lines are from his elegy for Franz Kline:

> Who are we sorry for, he's dead
> Between death and us his painting
> Stood, we relied on it
> To keep our hearts on the main thing
> Grandeur in a happy world of shit

Dewey, John (1859–1952)

On Dewey's ninetieth birthday, fifteen hundred dignitaries, colleagues, and friends came to Manhattan's Commodore Hotel to hail him as the nation's chief liberal thinker. For forty years his opinions had been sought on a wide variety of subjects and quoted everywhere. There is no one even remotely like him on the American scene today. He came to teach at Columbia in 1904, stayed there until 1930, and lived in New York until his death. A follower of the pragmatist William James, Dewey believed in the practical consequences of ideas as the measure of their worth and that philosophy must serve as a guide to action. He put his beliefs into practice by helping to found three organizations that continue to this day: the New York Teachers Union, the New School for Social Research, and the American Civil Liberties Union. Perhaps it is inevitable that a thinker as omnipresent as Dewey was in his time must be all but forgotten soon after his death. Today his work is fodder for academicians, and it is doubtful that his reputation will ever return to the heights that led him to be feted that night at the Commodore Hotel.

Dia Center for the Arts
548 West Twenty-second Street

In the fall of 1987 Dia began its Readings in Contemporary Poets series in which more than seventy poets have now read. It has been an all-star lineup—Seamus Heaney, Michael Palmer, Adrienne Rich, Louis Glück, Richard Wilbur, Charles Simic, Denise Levertov—with some pairings that have brought together poets from opposite ends of the American poetry spectrum: Clark Coolidge read with George Starbuck and Barbara Guest and Galway Kinnell appeared together. By far the most famous Dia reading was James Schuyler's in November 1988. The sixty-five-year-old Schuyler had never before given a public reading. His fans turned out en masse and gave him a standing ovation at the reading's conclusion. For a number of readings the Dia produced small books of the poet's work, a short version of a selected poems. Nowadays this has been replaced by a handsomely printed broadside. Tapes of all the readings are available from the Center. Dia, by the way, is Greek for "through," a name that, in the words of the center, "suggests the Center's role in enabling extraordinary artistic projects to be realized." Among these projects are museum-scale exhibitions of painting and sculpture.

The Dial

The first *Dial* appeared in Concord, Massachusetts, in 1840 as an organ of the transcendentalists. Margaret Fuller edited it for the first two years of its life and Ralph Waldo Emerson for the last two. A second *Dial* was published in Cincinnati in 1860 and a third began in Chicago in 1880. This last incarnation moved to New York in 1917, where it was bought by Scofield Thayer and Dr. J. Sibley Watson Jr. in 1920. Their intention was to publish "the best European and American art, experimental and unconventional." They approached this by giving three-quarters of the magazine to criticism and the remainder to fiction, poetry, and reproductions of art. William Butler Yeats, Anatole France, George Santayana, Gertrude Stein, Hart Crane, Edna St. Vincent Millay, Sherwood Anderson, e. e. cummings, T. S. Eliot, Ezra Pound, and William Carlos Williams appeared in its pages. "The Waste Land" was first published in the *Dial* and so were sections of Hart Crane's "The Bridge." No other literary magazine of its time outshone the *Dial*. In 1925 the poet Marianne Moore became the magazine's editor and remained in that position until the magazine ceased publication in 1929. The *Dial* had its offices in a three-story brick building at 152 West Thirteenth Street.

di Prima, Diane (b. 1934)

Di Prima was one of those who was bowled over by Allen Ginsberg's "Howl." She remembers serving beef stew at a communal dinner when someone handed her the small black-and-white *Howl and Other Poems*. "I knew that this Allen Ginsberg," she later wrote, "whoever he was, had broken ground for all of us." Born in Brooklyn and educated at Swarthmore, di Prima was not new to poetry when she read Ginsberg. As a teenager she had corresponded with Ezra Pound and Kenneth Rexroth. In 1958 Totem Press, one of the many small New York presses publishing the new poetry, brought out her first book, *This Kind of Bird*

Flies Backwards, and in 1960 her prose book *Dinners and Nightmares* appeared. By this time she was living on the Lower East Side and editing, with LeRoi Jones, *The Floating Bear,* a forerunner of the mimeo magazines that proliferated in that neighborhood a decade later. She and Jones became lovers, their union resulting in a daughter. One of the few woman Beat writers, di Prima wrote about her adventures as a beatnik in a way that she could not have anticipated. In 1965 Maurice Girodias, publisher of Nabokov's *Lolita,* J. P. Donleavy's *The Ginger Man,* Terry Southern's *Candy,* and a list of "DBs" (Dirty Books) in his Olympia Traveler's Companion series, moved to New York and set up shop in the Chelsea Hotel, opening an Olympia office in Gramercy Park. Now that Grove Press had cleared the way by publishing Henry Miller and William Burroughs's *Naked Lunch* Girodias expected America to be fertile ground. He signed di Prima to do what she called a "potboiler," *Memoirs of a Beatnik.* She wrote the book while living in upstate New York. "Gobs of words would go off to New York whenever the rent was due," she remembered, "and come back with 'MORE SEX' scrawled across the top page in Maurice's inimitable hand, and I would dream up odd angles of bodies or weird combinations of humans and cram them in and send it off again." In one of these combinations she described being in bed with Ginsberg and Jack Kerouac and two others at the same time as "warm and friendly and very unsexy—like being in a bathtub with four other people." Toward the end of the sixties di Prima headed west to San Francisco. Random House has announced a second book of memoirs, and their editorial demands will probably not be for more sex.

Doctorow, E. L. (b. 1931)

Born in the Bronx, Doctorow grew up near the Grand Concourse and graduated from the Bronx High School of Science. After college at Kenyon, he studied drama at Columbia and then went to work in publishing as an editor at New American Library and later as editor in chief at Dial Press. He has published several novels set in New York, all historical in nature. No novelist of his generation has used the city as both backdrop and character more often. Doctorow's very popular *Ragtime* (1975) is set at the turn of the century and mixes historical figures with fictional characters as John Dos Passos did in *U.S.A.* Norman Mailer and his wife Norris Church had roles in the movie made from the book. Doctorow returned to the city in *World's Fair* and *Billy Bathgate* and most recently in *The Waterworks* (1994), which is set in 1871. It takes its title from the Croton Reservoir that stood for many years where the Forty-second Street branch of the New York Public Library and Bryant Park stand today. For many years Doctorow has taught at New York University.

Dodge, Mabel (1879–1962)

Beginning in 1913 at 23 Fifth Avenue, the wealthy Dodge held a salon, in her words, "a meeting place which will be in the nature of a club where both men and women can meet to eat and drink and talk together." Among those who gathered there were John Reed, who had an affair with Dodge, the Wobblies' Big Bill Haywood, the anarchist Carlo Tresca, Elizabeth Curley Flynn, Hutchins Hapgood, Walter Lippmann, Lincoln Steffens, Emma Goldman, and Carl Van Vechten. Each evening was centered on a theme. Emma Goldman talked on anarchism one evening, and on another Dodge's guests heard, many of them for the first time, of psychoanalysis and the theories of Freud and Jung. As Dodge's affair with Reed came to a conclusion at the end of 1913, so did the salon. The art critic Robert Hughes, who did not know her personally, has called Dodge "the manic impressive heiress."

Dodge, Mary Mapes (1831–1905)

Dodge's first book, the worldwide favorite *Hans Brinker; or, The Silver Skates,* remains her best-known work. The native New Yorker wrote other children's books, but more important she edited the children's magazine *St. Nicholas* from its founding in 1873 by Roswell Smith until her death in 1905. Dodge recruited such illustrators as Arthur Rackham and Thomas Nast and published work by Rudyard Kipling and Louisa May Alcott; she also serialized Mark Twain's *Tom Sawyer Abroad.* The magazine continued until 1943. Large, buckram-covered volumes into which a year or more's issues were bound can still be found in summer houses, secondhand bookstores, and church book sales. There is no current magazine for juvenile readers that approaches *St. Nicholas,* and unless television and other eye-candy disappears altogether, there probably never will be.

Dos Passos, John (1896–1970)

The restless, peripatetic Dos Passos never lived for very long periods in New York City, but his experiences there are like bookends to his career. Beginning in 1917, when he lived briefly on East Thirty-third Street, Dos Passos moved in the world of Village writers with an interest in radical politics. Living off Stuyvesant Square on East Fifteenth Street in 1920, he joined his friend e. e. cummings for long walks throughout the city. He published essays, poems, and reviews in the *Dial* and the *Nation* and took art classes (Dos Passos's paintings illustrated his own translations from the French poet Blaise Cendrars) and was on the scene when he wasn't in France, Baghdad, or Damascus. He had a show of his paintings at the Whitney Studio Club on West Eighth Street in 1923 and during the winter of 1924 lived in Columbia Heights within sight of the Brooklyn Bridge, where he worked on his "utterly fantastic and New Yorkish" (his words) novel, *Manhattan Transfer.* This appeared in 1925 to mixed reviews, but Sinclair Lewis gave it a rave. In the novel, Manhattan is a fearsome city. Over the ensuing thirteen years Dos Passos traveled widely while working on his masterpiece, *U.S.A.,* which in 1938 united the three volumes: *The 42nd Parallel, 1919,* and *The Big Money.* New York City figures in this book, but then so does much of the country. Even as *U.S.A.* was hailed by reviewers on the left, Dos Passos had begun to separate himself from the leftist ideals he had once espoused. This drift to the right took years, but Dos Passos came to support Senator Joseph McCarthy's anti-Communist witch-hunt. In 1962 Dos Passos, who had once been thrilled to find himself sitting in a restaurant next to Emma Goldman, stood on the stage at Madison Square Garden and in company with the actor John Wayne and Senator Strom Thurmond accepted an award from the conservative Young Americans for Freedom.

Dreiser, Theodore (1871–1945)

A poor, Midwestern country boy, Dreiser worked his way to New York as a newspaperman, arriving in 1895 to live in the Village. His brother, the songwriter Paul Dresser, already lived in the city, as did their sister Emma whose relationship with a man named Hopkins Dreiser made use of in his first novel, *Sister Carrie.* Hopkins had stolen money from the Chicago bar where he had worked, and left his wife and children to follow Emma to New York. He became the model for Hurstwood in the novel. When Dreiser finished the book he sent it to Doubleday, Page, where the novelist Frank Norris, working as an editor, accepted it and signed him to a contract. The hitch came when Doubleday returned from Europe, read the novel, and, horrified by its contents, tried to get out of the contract. He ultimately published the book in 1900 but barely lived up to his part of the bargain. Doubleday dumped *Sister Carrie,* publishing only a thousand copies on cheap paper and doing no advertising and minimal distribution. The failure of the book crushed Dreiser, and it took him years to come out of the depression that followed and more than a decade to publish another novel. John Dos Passos once praised Dreiser for being "the battering ram" that opened the way for his generation of novelists. Certainly, Dreiser's prose is crude enough to merit that epithet, but Dos Passos meant that Dreiser had made possible the kind of realism about American city life that had not existed before. Crude as Dreiser is, there is no denying the power of his best books. In *Sister Carrie* there may be no middle ground between triumph and tragedy, but it is precisely this lack of subtlety that is true to American city life. During the years he spent recovering from *Sister Carrie,* Dreiser thrived as the editor of a number of women's magazines for Butterick Publications. After *Jennie Gerhardt* appeared in 1911, he gave himself to fiction, publishing his most autobiographical novel, *The "Genius,"* in 1915. Dreiser went west in the early twenties but returned to New York to live at 118 West Eleventh Street, where he wrote his most popular book, *An American Tragedy* (1925). He based this on the Chester Gillette-Grace Brown murder case of 1906. The success of the book made Dreiser a rich man, and he moved uptown to West Fifty-seventh Street. In the early thirties his last New York address was the Ansonia Hotel between Seventy-third and Seventy-fourth Streets on Broadway. By this time he was a Communist devoting himself to a wide variety of social causes.

Dreiser's vision of the city as a force more powerful that human character or will remains with us today. There is a version of it in T. S. Eliot's "The Waste Land" and in hundreds of novels, poems, plays, and films. It helped feed the hippie romance with nature, and sustains those in Idaho and other western states who have gone "off the grid." One value of Dreiser's novels, *Sister Carrie* in particular, is that in them we encounter the sort of innocent wonder that led to his view. As the city overwhelms Dreiser's characters, we can imagine how it overwhelmed him and countless others who came to it as greenhorns from Europe or the American hinterland. Anyone who spends even a few days in New York City today and keeps his or her eyes open will see the same dramatic contrasts that terrified and inspired Dreiser's imagination.

Duberman, Martin (b. 1930)

A New York City native, Duberman is Distinguished Professor of History at the City University of New York's Lehman College and Graduate School, where he founded the Center for Lesbian and Gay Studies.

He has written biographies of Charles Francis Adams, James Russell Lowell, and Paul Robeson, as well as the history of Black Mountain College. He is also a playwright. His most notable contribution to literary New York has been several books on gay themes, *Stonewall* outstanding among them. This tells the story of the Stonewall riots of June 1969 from which the gay liberation movement arose. It was in the streets around Sheridan Square where the Stonewall Inn, a gay bar, stood that gay men faced off the police and the sin that could not speak its name began to shout it out. For some years Duberman lived at 70 Charles Street in that same West Village neighborhood. His most recent book is *Midlife Queer: Autobiography of a Decade, 1971–1981*.

Du Bois, W. E. B. (1868–1963)

Du Bois came to New York in 1910 as the NAACP's director of publicity and research. He was also, and more important in terms of the Harlem Renaissance, the founding editor of the organization's monthly magazine, *Crisis*. In 1919 he brought his protégée Jessie Fauset onto the magazine as literary editor, a role in which she helped, to use Langston Hughes's term, "mid-wife" the Harlem Renaissance into being. Du Bois himself sounded the clarion call in 1920: "A renaissance of American Negro literature is due; the material about us in the strange, heart-rending race tangle is rich beyond dream and only we can tell the tale and sing the song from the heart." He was a revered elder, but his insistence that black writing help in race building sometimes led to friction with the younger Renaissance writers. In 1934 he left the NAACP over the organization's refusal to accept his policy of "voluntary segregation." He saw this as the best way to promote black economic development during the Depression. Du Bois then returned to Atlanta before once again joining the NAACP in the mid-forties, only to resign from the organization for good in 1948. Two years later he ran for the U.S. Senate in New York on the American Labor Party ticket. Du Bois had a number of addresses in the city. Before 1920 he lived at 650 Greene Avenue and then until 1934 at the Paul Lawrence Dunbar Apartments at 2594 Seventh Avenue. Between 1944 and 1951 he lived at 409 Edgecomb Avenue. In 1951 he bought the playwright Arthur Miller's house at 31 Grace Court in Brooklyn Heights. Today Du Bois is represented in the Library of America. While we think of him as an essayist and polemicist, he also wrote novels. *The Dark Princess* (1928) deals, in part, with the early, idealistic years of the Harlem Renaissance.

Dugan, Alan (b. 1923)

Born in Brooklyn, Dugan published his first book, *Poems,* in 1961 to great success. Not only was it in the Yale Younger Poets series, but it also won both a National Book Award and a Pulitzer Prize. *Poems 2, Poems 3,* and so on, have followed. Dugan's *New and Collected Poems* came out in 1983. There is a wiseguy inside the Brooks Brothers formality of Dugan's verse. He has a bracing acerbity, and when he reads aloud his heavily nasal Brooklyn accent gives his words a flavor they don't have on the page. Before he took up teaching he had many jobs, including molding plastic vaginas for life-size medical models in a downtown New York loft.

Duyckinck, Evert (1816–1878)

A lifelong New Yorker, Duyckinck graduated from Columbia and took a degree in law but never practiced. As a writer and editor he was in the thick of New York literary life from 1836, when he founded the Tetractys Club with the poet Cornelius Mathews among others, until his death. Although his own writing is of interest today only to the specialist, Duyckinck was of crucial importance to Herman Melville's career, and he is remembered for this above all. His involvement with Melville began when he published *Typee.* Duyckinck did not think the book much more than a potboiler, but it had already been published in England and so he released it in this country. Melville, whom he did not meet until a few months after publication, became an intimate of Duyckinck's and in the late 1840s he frequented Duyckinck's house at 20 Clinton Street off Washington Square. The house has long been demolished, but in its library a salon gathered and there Melville met Washington Irving and William Cullen Bryant and may have met Poe, to whom Duyckinck was a patron, but of this there is no record. Having the run of the library, Melville made up for lost time at sea by doing a good deal of reading. Of the few letters of Melville's that have come down to us, a number, and they are mostly affectionate, are to Duyckinck. He went on to edit magazines and publish books by Dickens, Carlyle, and Goethe, and, in collaboration with his brother George, produced a two-volume *Cyclopedia of American Literature* (1866). Duyckinck died suddenly, and Melville was the last man to see him alive. His heyday is exhaustively chronicled in Perry Miller's invaluable study of New York writing and literary life in the 1840s and 1850s, *The Raven and the Whale.*

Dylan, Bob (b. 1941)

Born Robert Zimmerman, Dylan took his name from the poet Dylan
Thomas, but his literary influences were the Beats. When he came to
the Village in 1961 the folk music boom had begun, rock 'n' roll had yet
to cross over to white kids, and a Village writer wrote novels or poems,
not songs. Dylan hung around the Kettle of Fish bar on MacDougal
Street, visited Woody Guthrie at Creedmore State Hospital in Queens,
where he lay dying of Huntington's chorea, played at coffeehouses, bars
(he opened for John Lee Hooker at Gerde's Folk City), and apartments
until the producer John Hammond "discovered" him and he recorded
the anthems of a generation: "Blowin' in the Wind," "Like a Rolling
Stone," and "Visions of Johanna." All this happened within so short a
time that Dylan must have served the apprenticeship during which he
fused the blues and country music with his own genius before he
reached New York. After Dylan and the British Invasion—the Beatles
and the Rolling Stones—brought America's black music home to white
audiences young men and women who might have picked up a pen
chose guitars instead. When Dylan hit New York writers were still
heroes, major cultural figures. In the sixties this began to be not the
case, and thirty-five years later there is not an American writer of any
generation whose death will be given the attention the Grateful Dead's
Jerry Garcia's received. Possible exceptions to this are Norman Mailer
and Allen Ginsberg, whose example, Ginsberg's in particular, helped
draw Dylan to the Village. In the decade or so Dylan spent in New York
he lived for a while at 161 West Fourth Street and with his young family at 94 MacDougal. It was here that a "garbologist" named A. J.
Weberman had his fifteen minutes of fame going through Dylan's trash
for . . . well, for whatever he could find. Dylan also lived at the Chelsea
Hotel. During his early years there was some argument among poets
about whether Dylan could be considered a poet. Those who said no
pointed to Dylan's words on paper as not holding up without the music.
Those who thought differently knew that anyone who spoke so intimately to a generation, who put the feelings of so many into words, was
doing a poet's work no matter how he went about it.

E

Eastman, Max (1883–1969)

In 1912, while on vacation from his teaching job at Columbia, Eastman received a telegram, "You are elected editor of *The Masses,* No pay." He accepted the summons and in company with the artists John Sloan and Art Young, who had recruited him, made the magazine a significant voice for leftist causes and one amenable to the arts and literature. Eastman published work by Carl Sandburg, Randolph Bourne, and William Rose Bénet, Floyd Dell, who became the magazine's managing editor, gave the magazine's motto as "Fun, Truth, Beauty, Realism, Peace, Feminism and Revolution." The good times lasted until the *Masses* grew increasingly outspoken against America's involvement in World War I. In 1917 the government killed the magazine by taking away its mailing privileges. Shortly after its demise, the Department of Justice charged Eastman, Dell, and John Reed, a frequent contributor, with "conspiracy" and "interfering with enlistments." Two trials ended in hung juries. John Reed returned from Russia to appear at his trial, and while living with Louise Bryant in Patchin Place he wrote *Ten Days That Shook the World.* Eager to publish Reed's work, Eastman started a new magazine, the *Liberator.* Into its pages he brought William Carlos Williams, Edna St. Vincent Millay, Elinor Wylie, e. e. cummings, John Dos Passos, and Ernest Hemingway. Eastman resigned from the magazine in 1922, passing his position on to Mike Gold, but remained active on the left albeit in bad odor after his support of the exiled Leon Trotsky. Over the years Eastman put more and more distance between himself and the Soviet Union, until following World War II, the Village radical began writing for *Reader's Digest* and then for William F. Buckley Jr.'s *National Review.* Although Eastman's politics moved uptown he remained a Villager, living at 8 West Thirteenth Street for the last twenty-five years of his life.

The story of Eastman's encounter with Hemingway in Maxwell Perkins's office at Scribner's has become legend and is worth retelling. When Hemingway's *Death in the Afternoon* appeared in 1932 Eastman panned it under the headline "Bull in the Afternoon." Sentences such as "Hemingway is a full-sized man, but he lacks the confidence that he is a full-sized man" enraged Hemingway, and he attacked Eastman to Perkins, who was both men's editor. Nothing more came of this until August 1937, when Hemingway dropped in at Perkins's office to find Eastman there. Hemingway wasn't having any of Perkins's lame attempts to defuse the situation. He tore open his shirt to reveal a manly pelt and then tore open Eastman's, revealing a chest as hairless as a baby's bottom. Hemingway next grabbed a book from Perkins's hands and smacked Eastman with it, who then wrestled Hemingway to the floor, where things calmed down but not before a crowd of office workers had arrived on the scene. Perkins thought Hemingway would have killed Eastman, but he admitted to several others, including F. Scott Fitzgerald, that when the dust cleared Eastman had Hemingway pinned to the floor.

Ecco Press

Ecco, now of Hopewell, New Jersey, began publishing in New York in the seventies under the editorship of poet Daniel Halpern with Drue Heinz as publisher. In addition to the books of Nobel Prize winner Czeslaw Milosz, Tomas Tranströmer, Robert Hass, and a series of reprints featuring neglected titles by Elizabeth Bishop and Ford Madox Ford, among many others, Ecco published the magazine *Antaeus*. During its run *Antaeus* was not only one of the top little magazines in the country but had an international outlook. Halpern, who has taught in the Columbia University writing program, now runs Ecco, and Heinz is the publisher of the *Paris Review*.

Editors

In the sixteenth edition of *Bartlett's Familiar Quotations*, edited by Justin Kaplan, who was once an editor for Simon & Schuster in New York, there are three entries under *editor*. One of these is T. S. Eliot's famous line, "Most editors are failed writers—but so are most writers." Eliot was, of course, himself an editor for many years at Faber & Faber in England. Three entries seems awfully few for a profession that deals in words. It is a mystery why there are not more, as surely much wisdom about writing and editing must have flowed between writers and their editors. Perhaps it is because editors naturally stand in the wings, a step or more removed from the finished product. Another mystery is when editing, as we know it today, began. Melville, Whitman, James, and Wharton did not have editors: they had publishers. William Dean Howells was the first major American writer to have a career as an editor, but he worked mainly in magazines, the *Atlantic Monthly* and *Harper's Weekly*. A standard reference on American publishing, John Tebbel's *Between Covers*, does not address the issue. Theodore Dreiser, who arrived in the city before the turn of the century, was an editor, and he certainly had editors, the novelist Frank Norris among them. By the 1920s book editing, by which is meant going over a manuscript with a fine-tooth comb and not just acquiring books, was an established profession in New York. Perhaps to determine the origins of editing the time to investigate is the 1880s, when literacy was on the rise across America. As more Americans became literate more of them became writers, regardless of how much education they had received. Hemingway, for instance, did not attend college, but then neither did Melville or Whitman. As literacy grew, so did the number of newspapers, magazines, and books. Editors must have been required to see all of this into print. In any case, although the history of editing in New York is murky, by the 1920s there were editors at work in New York, Scribner's Maxwell Perkins most notable among them, who had a significant, if unsung impact, on American writing. What follows is a partial list that will be added to tenfold by many writers, editors, agents, and readers who read this entry. Given the number of worthy editors at work in the city, now and in the past, this list can do no more than scratch the surface.

Sonny Mehta of Alfred A. Knopf is probably the city's best-known book editor today. He has become famous for his marathon phone calls—as long as fourteen hours—to writers and for putting some of his authors under near house arrest until they produce the text he wants. Judith Jones, who edits Julia Child and John Updike, has been at Knopf for many years. Drenka Willen of Harcourt Brace is another veteran New York editor who has spent most of her career at one house. Robert Giroux worked at several houses, most famously at Farrar, Straus & Giroux. Pascal Covici edited John Steinbeck and the early Saul Bellow for Viking. Albert Erskine, who spent many years at Random House, edited both Malcolm Lowry and Cormac McCarthy. Nan Talese now has an imprint of her own, as does Elizabeth Sifton. Richard Seaver and Donald Allen were significant editors at Grove Press. James Laughlin did almost all of the editing at New Directions through the early years, but in the 1950s Robert McGregor took on a good many editorial chores, to be followed by Griselda Ohannessian, Peggy Fox, and Barbara Epler. Michael Korda of Simon & Schuster, long on the New York scene, has published a few memoirs about his life and contacts in the *New Yorker*. Robert Gottlieb began at Simon & Schuster, moved to Alfred A. Knopf, and then followed William Shawn as editor of the *New Yorker*, a position he resigned in 1992. Morgan Entriken was a whiz kid in the early 1980s and is now at Grove. Ted Solotaroff was at

Harper and Row, now HarperCollins, for many years. The novelists Toni Morrison, Gilbert Sorrentino, and E. L. Doctorow have all worked as editors in New York, as have Nan Graham (now at Scribner's), Carol Baron, Michael Bessie, Starling Lawrence of Norton, Tom McCormack at St. Martin's, Joseph Fox of Random House, Alice Mayhew, Saxe Commins, and Jonathan Galassi. There are a number of magazine editors already in this book associated with the magazines they worked for. Rust Hills of *Esquire* deserves mention because his long tenure at the magazine made him a force in New York publishing. Another Esquire editor, Gordon Lish, became known as "Captain Fiction" for the aid and encouragement he gave a generation of writers. And then there are the editors of children's books, nonfiction books of all kinds . . . to adequately cover the topic would require a small phone book or large Rolodex.

In January 1997, at a dinner to celebrate Bob Loomis's four decades as an editor at Random House, William Styron, whom Loomis first edited when they were students at Duke University in 1947, had this to say about him as an editor: "What a splendid observer he has been. People have often asked me what it is that has made him such a great editor. With Bob, you can't get by with moments of laziness or failure of clarity or self-flattering turgidity. He pounces like a cobra, shakes the wretched phrase or sentence into sensibility and soon all is well."

Eighth Street Bookshop
17 West Eighth Street

In 1947, on the southeast corner of Eighth Street and MacDougal in Greenwich Village, Eli Wilentz and his brother Ted opened the Eighth Street Bookshop. At the start they paid close attention to poetry, the Beat writers, and whatever was hip. Their store drew W. H. Auden, Delmore Schwartz, LeRoi Jones, and countless other writers whom the brothers treated with warmth and kindness. In the store's basement, in wire drugstore display racks young poets could find the little magazines—*Yugen, Neon, Locus Solus*—where the work of the Beats, the Black Mountain poets, and the New York School had begun to appear. New York and visiting writers relied on the Eighth Street Bookshop to keep them current. In 1965 the store moved across the street to its final address at number 17. Before their partnership broke up, the Wilentz brothers became publishers under the Corinth imprint. Eli published the American Experience series that rescued out-of-print books on American history, and Ted aligned with Totem, another small publisher, to put out books of poetry. Fire destroyed their uninsured store in 1976. Writers joined to raise the money necessary to put the place back on its feet, but Eli Wilentz closed it for good in 1979. This did not end his involvement with literature. An expert on the history of New York City, he led walking tours and fought to preserve literary landmarks, especially buildings associated with Walt Whitman. His son Sean, who teaches American history at Princeton, has followed in his father's footsteps and recently helped discover that Walt Whitman's house at 99 Ryerson Street in Brooklyn still stands.

Elaine's
1703 Second Avenue at Eighty-eighth Street

"Elaine *loves The Paris Review,*" proclaims the advertisement restaurateur Elaine Kaufman places in each issue of the magazine. And well she might, for it was two editors of that magazine, Nelson Aldrich, who eventually wrote the book *Old Money,* and the poet Frederick Siedel, who "discovered" the place for writers. In the seventies it became *the* upscale watering hole for the likes of Norman Mailer and his wife Norris Church, the playwright and gambler Jack Richardson, Kurt Vonnegut and his wife Jill Krementz, the photographer of writers, Willie Morris, editor of *Harper's,* the very funny, very good, and literate alto saxophonist Paul Desmond, and visiting firemen like the novelist Jim Harrison. When they were together Woody Allen and Mia Farrow had "their" table next to the kitchen. A ton of anecdotes gets told about the place, including one about the late Random House editor Joe Fox getting thrown out by Kaufman because he came only to play darts and never ordered a meal. It has had a long run as the place where successful writers go to see, be seen, and do a little business with agents, editors, and movie people.

Ellison, Ralph (1914–1994)

Ellison came north to New York in the summer of 1936. He hoped to earn enough money to return to college at Tuskegee in Alabama, where he had finished his junior year, and continue his studies of sculpture and music. Ellison took a room at the 135th Street YMCA, and the next day he had a fateful meeting with the poet Langston Hughes and the editor Alain Locke on the steps of the library across the street. He never made the money to return to Tuskegee, but he did meet Richard Wright, who asked him to write a book review for the magazine he then edited, *New Challenge.* This set Ellison on his course as a writer, a journey that took him through a number of jobs until he landed in the Federal Writers' Project in 1939. From then until 1945 he lived at a number of addresses in Harlem, read incessantly, and worked to master his craft. In 1945 a Rosenwald Fellowship gave him the wherewithal to get out of the city for a time, and he began his novel *Invisible Man* in Vermont. Returning to New York, he wrote the book over the next five years while living at 749 St. Nicholas Avenue. The novel was hailed upon its appearance in 1952, has never been out of print, and several times has been acclaimed the best American novel written after World War II. That *Invisible Man* immediately became part of the canon of American literature is clear, but it is more difficult to assess the novel's impact. In part this is because Ellison never completed another novel and published but two other books, both essays, after *Invisible Man*. His work did not develop but rather took its place, and events and attitudes changed around it. During the sixties Ellison was vilified for his refusal to align himself with the advocates of Black Power. His thinking on race in America, always subtle, was easy to ignore in the sound and fury of the time. Meanwhile, his novel was read on college campuses across the United States, and if louder voices obscured his, Ellison continued to articulate and clarify his position. And he continued to write fiction. Indeed, it is no fault of his that we do not have a second novel. Sections of it began to appear in the early sixties, and Ellison worked painstakingly on it into the eighties, when tragedy struck. Three hundred and some pages of a nearly completed manuscript were destroyed in a fire at the Ellisons' country house in Cummington, Massachusetts. Ellison attempted to resurrect the novel from notes, drafts, and the memories of his close friends, the novelist Albert Murray among them, but the difficulty of doing this was heightened by the depression he fell into. Toward the end of his life he began working on the book again, and there are rumors that he was nearly finished. If whatever survives of this book can be published it will certainly be among the century's most scrutinized works of fiction.

During the last decades of his life, the much honored Ellison lived with his wife on upper Riverside Drive in an apartment that was often described by the many interviewers who came there to discover what Ellison was thinking. He usually sat in a Mies van der Rohe chair and showed off his collection of Hopi and Zuni kachina dolls. The handsome, graceful Ellison always spoke in measured and well-formed sentences, but it paid to remember that James Baldwin had called him the angriest man he had ever seen. Today, Ellison's friend Albert Murray keeps Ellison's memory alive, and so does the essayist and man-about-jazz Stanley Crouch.

Elmslie, Kenward (b. 1929)

After returning to the city of his birth via Colorado, Harvard, and, of all places, Cleveland, Ohio, Elmslie became friendly with the members of the first generation of New York School poets. Although he is a poet—*Motor Disturbances* (1971) was given the Frank O'Hara Book Award—it has been his involvement in the musical theater, opera, and cabaret collaborations with the artists Ken Tisa and Donna Dennis that makes Elmslie's career unique. In 1957 the Juilliard Opera Theater premiered *The Sweet Bye and Bye,* composed by Jack Beeson with Elmslie's libretto. He collaborated with Beeson again on *Lizzie Borden* (1965), which has been revived several times, most recently in the summer of 1996 by the Glimmerglass Opera Company of Cooperstown, New York. Elmslie has also written librettos for operas composed by Ned Rorem (*Miss Julie* [1965]) and Thomas Pasatieri. Their *Washington Square,* based on the Henry James novel, had a production at a New York University theater around the corner from the square itself. In 1971 *The Grass Harp,* the Truman Capote novella for which Elmslie wrote the book and lyrics and Claibe Richardson the music, opened on Broadway and closed very fast. A resounding flop, it has had a life on records and is now available on CD, and in 1994 the New York Theater presented a staged reading. In the midst of all this Elmslie published a novel, *The Orchid Stories,* and continued to publish poetry; *Tropicalism* and *Moving Right Along* are two of his titles. In the late 1970s he founded Z Press, which published John Ashbery's *Three Plays,* a James Schuyler miscellany (*The Home Book*), and Z magazine. He zigzagged again in the 1980s as he evolved from writer to singer-performer. Ken Tisa designed the visuals for Elmslie's *Palais Bimbo Lounge Show* (1981), which had a run below Canal Street, or off-off-off-off Broadway. The sculptor Donna Dennis did the same for *26 Bars* (1987), which Elmslie has performed in several different venues. His musical collaborator in these shows is Steven Taylor, who also did the music for Elmslie's full-length musical play, *Postcards on Parade.* They performed a two-man version of this work on stage at Brown University, the Naropa Institute, and the Milwaukee Postcard Fair. Elmslie has not only been where poetry meets showbiz in New York, he has had a jukebox song hit "Love-wise," recorded by Nat King Cole and the incomparable New York cabaret singer Mabel Mercer. If that is not enough, he and

Joe Brainard sustained a collaboration for thirty years that yielded *The Champ* (1928), *Album* (1969), and a host of other work before ending with *Sung Sex* (1992). It is impossible to imagine Elmslie's career taking place outside New York, where he has both bridged and mixed into new combinations the various worlds of art, music, theater, and poetry. During the 1960s he lived at 28½ Cornelia Street in a three-room, three-floor house, secreted behind a six-story tenement via arched street door and tunnel. Here Elmslie gave parties famous for their mix of people: Andy Warhol, Marisol, Ned Rorem, John Ashbery, Bianca Jagger, D. D. Ryan, Frank O'Hara, Stella Adler, Red Grooms, and Ruth Ford. In the 1970s he moved to the West Village, where he lives today when he is not in Vermont. His Vermont home, where he summered for many years with Joe Brainard, is the setting of Vermont poems written by such visiting poet friends as Anne Waldman, James Schuyler, and Ron Padgett.

Epstein, Jason (b. 1928)

Now a senior editor at Random House, Epstein has been a member of New York's literary establishment for more than thirty years. It was in 1963, at his West Side apartment, that Epstein and his wife, Barbara, and their dinner guests, the poet Robert Lowell and his wife, Elizabeth Hardwick, hit upon the idea for the *New York Review of Books*. But Epstein's claim to fame dates from the fifties, when he was a boy wonder at Doubleday. His future boss, Bennett Cerf of Random House, put it this way: "The man who really launched the *good*-book paperback was Jason Epstein whose Anchor Books achieved fantastic results. Doubleday was practically conned into doing this series. Doubleday bigwigs didn't think much would come of it, but this brilliant boy, Jason Epstein, opened their eyes." Many Anchor titles were distinguished by the artwork and design of Edward Gorey.

Fadiman, Clifton (b. 1904)

Readers older than fifty may remember the name Clifton Fadiman as being omnipresent in literature promoted on radio, television, and in advertisements for the Book-of-the-Month Club from the mid-1930s through the 1950s. Today his name cannot be found in any of the standard readers' encyclopedias or companions to American literature. Why? In her diary the novelist Dawn Powell described Fadiman as "somberly riding geniuses—the clumsy, overweight jockey on the delicate Arabian steeds." Powell meant that Fadiman was one of those people of letters who come to the fore by reminding us how great and nourishing the classics are. They, as Fadiman did, speak for or pitch the noble virtues of literature. When such people are replaced, as they must be, by the next generation, they are replaced in toto. In Fadiman's case he wrote introductions to more than thirty books, most of which have since had one or more new introductions to keep up with the times. Born in Brooklyn and educated at Columbia, Fadiman was a teacher before he became an editor and radio and television personality. As host of the radio program *Information Please,* which ran from 1939 to 1948, and as a longtime judge of the Book-of-the-Month Club, he certainly had clout in New York's literary world. It seems that he used this solely in support of middlebrow values. In his time he kept the wheels turning, and when he stepped away there were any number of professioanl "jockeys" to take his place.

Farrar, Straus & Giroux
19 Union Square West

Roger Straus founded the house in 1946. Wealthy—he is one of the Macy's Strauses and a Guggenheim—and shrewd, Straus rented office space on Union Square when it was a low-rent district and happily paid $2.75 a square foot, ten to twenty times less than his uptown competitors paid. Over the years Straus and his partner Robert Giroux built up a list that has been heavy with Nobel Prize winners since Isaac Bashevis Singer won in 1978. Straus had begun to publish Singer when he was writing short stories in Yiddish for the *Jewish Daily Forward.* Since then Wole Soyinka, Elias Canetti, and Camilo José Cela have been awarded the prize. So many Nobels came to FSG authors that Straus took to reserving two hotel suites in Stockholm in early December when the prizes are given out. Today, it is the poets that distinguish the FSG list: Nobel Prize winners Derek Walcott, Joseph Brodsky, and Seamus Heaney, and Robert Lowell, Elizabeth Bishop, John Ashbery, Frank Bidart, James Schuyler, Thom Gunn, Robert Pinsky, August Kleinzahler—it is a splendid lineup. Through the years their books have been beautifully served by the designer Cynthia Krupat. For all its literary eminence the most popular recent book published by FSG is probably Tom Wolfe's novel of New York in the Reagan years, *The Bonfire of the*

Vanities. Thanks to the sharp-eyed and fashion-conscious Wolfe we know that Roger Straus used to drive his tan Mercedes-Benz convertible from the east Seventies, where he lived, downtown to the office. Come spring Straus wore tan gabardine suits that went with his car. Today, Jonathan Galassi is FSG's editor in chief.

Farrell, James T. (1904–1979)

Like Theodore Dreiser before him and Saul Bellow after him, Farrell came from Chicago to Manhattan, where his literary career took off. Farrell lived mostly in hotels: at the Brevoort on Fifth Avenue and Eighth Street, where he read pages from the manuscript of *Studs Lonigan* to the novelist Nathanael West, who also had a room in the hotel; at the Sutton Club Hotel at 330 East Fifty-sixth Street, where West, the night manager, let Farrell and his wife stay free of charge; and later at the Chelsea Hotel, where he wrote portions of his Bernard Clare cycle of novels. He became friendly with the early *Partisan Review* crowd, and the first issue of the magazine carried an exerpt from *Studs Lonigan.* It was at a party at Farrell's apartment on Lexington Avenue that Mary McCarthy, then fresh from Vassar, remembered getting her first education in communism. A prolific writer, Farrell is little read today, but Norman Mailer and others of his generation have acknowledged the influence of his work.

Feldman, Morton (b. 1926)

> What was great about the fifties is that for one brief moment—maybe, say, six weeks—nobody understood art. That's why it all happened.

If you want to know what the small, by today's standards, cohesive downtown New York art world of the fifties generated, what the fuss caused by musicians, dancers, painters, and poets was all about, Feldman's essays are an excellent place to start. Unfortunately, they are not easy to find. He wrote a half-dozen for *Art in America* in the sixties and seventies, and several as liner notes for record albums. A company in Germany collected these and published them as *Morton Feldman's Essays,* but, infuriatingly, printed some of them in German. There is an excellent short book of Feldman's writings awaiting the interest of some editor and publisher. A New Yorker who talked with a thick New York accent and dressed like a character out of *Guys and Dolls*—no WASP bohemia for Feldman!—he was twenty-four when he met John Cage and moved into "Bosa's Manor," which was named after the landlord.

Feldman described the place this way: "Cage was living on the top floor of an old building on the East River Drive and Grand Street. Two large rooms with a sweeping expanse of the river circling three sides of the apartment. Spectacular. And hardly a piece of furniture in it." Here, inspired by Cage and the artists who were always coming and going, Feldman began to compose music in earnest, music that was as quiet as he was loud, as soft as his manner seemed rough. It was music that insisted on its own terms and refused to compromise. Feldman pushed duration as far as he could, writing a twelve-hour string quartet and other pieces of unusual length. He was an habitué of the Cedar Bar and found in the painters who gathered there, Philip Guston in particular, the freedom he valued. "It was not the freedom of choice," Feldman wrote, "that is the meaning of the fifties, but the freedom of people to be themselves. This type of freedom creates a problem for us, because we are not free to *imitate* it."

Fitzgerald, F. Scott (1896–1940)
In the Depression when Fitzgerald looked back on New York City, he saw it as "glittering and white." And so it had been for him and his wife, Zelda, but not at first. Fitzgerald lived in a one-room apartment at 200 Claremont Avenue in 1919 and worked in an advertising agency while saving money to marry Zelda Sayre. But in 1920 the successful publication of his first novel, *This Side of Paradise,* reversed his fortunes, and he and his bride were married in St. Patrick's Cathedral before honeymooning in Room 2109 of the Biltmore Hotel. Several raucous parties got them thrown out, and they moved on to the Commodore Hotel, where the fun continued as it would, more or less, throughout the Fitzgeralds' years in New York. Scott and Zelda made a handsome couple, and his books spoke to a generation who took him as its hero. The Fitzgeralds were the toast of the town and got the sort of newspaper coverage that today we give to movie and rock stars, and they thrived on it. They rode down Fifth Avenue on the tops of taxi cabs and danced in the Pulitzer fountain in front of the Plaza Hotel. For a time they had an apartment at 38 West Fifty-ninth Street to which the Plaza catered their meals. Fitzgerald did do serious work in the city with his editor, Maxwell Perkins of Scribner's, but essentially New York was to be conquered and enjoyed. He and Zelda did both. He also put the city at the center of one of the most beautiful American novels, *The Great Gatsby.* Much of the book's emotional life, Tom Buchanan's meetings with his mistress and the scene in which Daisy and Gatsby reveal their love for

one another to Tom, take place in the city, the latter in a room at the Plaza. In the novel, Manhattan is the citadel of commerce, the new America that has drawn Midwesterners Gatsby, Tom and Daisy, and Nick Carraway with its green light of money and possibility. When Nick returns to the Midwest's moral order it is New York's fabulous allure that he refuses. In Fitzgerald's case it was New York that forgot him. By the time he came to write nostalgically of New York in the twenties the city was sunk in the Depression and his own career had gone downhill. He died in California much too young, with most of his books out of print. He had written that in America there are no second acts, but in one of his essays about New York he admitted that if there could be second acts they would take place in the city.

5 Spot
Cooper Square

During the late fifties and early sixties the brother Iggie and Joe Termini, who owned this jazz club, occasionally allowed musicians who did not have New York cabaret cards to perform. This is how Billie Holiday came to sing there the night "she whispered a song along the keyboard / to Mal Waldron and everyone and I stopped breathing." These words end Frank O'Hara's poem "The Day Lady Died," the single most famous poem to be written in New York after 1950. The 5 Spot closed in 1963 to reopen at the corner of Third Avenue and St. Mark's Place, where it lived on into the seventies.

Foster, Stephen (1826–1864)

Foster spent four years, the last and most miserable of his life, in New York. He had already composed the songs we remember today: "O Susannah," "De Camptown Races," "My Old Kentucky Home," "Jeanie with the Light Brown Hair," and "Old Black Joe." In New York his output of songs did not diminish, but everything else in his life fell apart. He separated from his wife in 1862, began to drink heavily, and, impoverished, lived in a Bowery hotel. Some have written that he collapsed and died there, but it seems that he was only injured in that fall and died later at Bellevue Hospital. In Foster's day the Bowery comprised New York's theater district, as it had when the young Walt Whitman was an avid theatergoers. After the Civil War the area went downhill as the theater district moved north on Broadway.

Freneau, Philip (1752–1832)

Freneau's French Huguenot forebears came to New York early in the eighteenth century, his grandfather establishing himself as a wine merchant. At some point the family acquired a plantation, Mount Pleasant, in New Jersey, but Freneau was born on New York's Frankfort Street and got at least some of his schooling in the city. He was educated at the College of New Jersey (now Princeton), graduating in a class of twelve that included the future president James Madison and Freneau's roommate, Hugh Henry Brackenridge, with whom Freneau collaborated on *Father Bombo's Pilgrimage to Mecca in Africa.* It has been accepted as the first published work of American fiction. Freneau also wrote satiric patriotic poems, several of which were published before his writing career got interrupted by the Revolutionary War. He served as a militiaman and a privateer. When his ship, the *Aurora,* was captured in Long Island Sound he landed on the British prison ship *Scorpion,* an infamous hellhole moored off the Battery. Freneau reported his experiences in the poem "The British Prison-Ship." The sage of the *Scorpion* and her sister ship the *Hunter* haunted Walt Whitman, who most probably knew Freneau's poem. Following the war Freneau became a journalist in New York and frequented "Newspaper Row," which was then in Hanover Square. He followed the federal government to Philadelphia and served in the State Department and published the *National Gazette,* in which he passionately attacked Alexander Hamilton and just as passionately supported the French Revolution. He returned to New Jersey where he worked as a printer and bookseller all the while producing Anti-Federalist journalism and patriotic poetry before he retired from journalism to Mount Pleasant and then went to sea. During the War of 1812 Freneau wrote rousing patriotic poems. His "On the Conflagration at Washington" begins:

> Now, George the third rules not alone
> For George the vandal shares the throne
> True flesh of flesh and bone of bone.

A fire at Mount Pleasant destroyed many of his manuscripts, and his last years were spent selling off the plantation to appease creditors. John Hollander, whose essential *American Poetry: The Nineteenth Century* Freneau leads off, has written a sentence describing Freneau's death that for poetic compression cannot be improved upon: "Died when caught in a blizzard while walking home."

Freneau and the radical pamphleteer Tom Paine are New York's first significant writers. Before them the city's literary history is in its news-papers. It must be remembered that while New England and Boston were settled by men and women of the book, New York began as a mer-chant outpost. Its citizens had other things on their minds, and it took the ferment of revolutionary ideas to spark the first important writing in the city.

Friedman, Bruce Jay (b. 1930)

The Bronx-born Friedman got his start in the city's literary life through what he later called "the Bronx mothers' Mafia." His mother met someone else's mother whose son owned the Magazine Management Company. From 1953 until 1965 Friedman edited *Swank*, a training-wheels version of *Playboy*, and then was put in charge of *Male*, *Man's World*, *Men*, and *True Action*. He published his first novel, *Stern*, in 1962, a time when there was much talk of the Jewish novel. Friedman's book is comic, and his main character might be taken as an older, less sexually active brother of Philip Roth's Alexander Portnoy. Or as an un-cle of the neurotic character Woody Allen has come to personify. Fried-man went on to write novels, plays, and short stories, but nothing has approached *Stern* in popularity.

Fuchs, Daniel (b. 1909)

The son of Jewish immigrants, Fuchs published three novels in the 1930s that form a loose trilogy: *Summer in Williamsburg* (1934), *Homage to Blenholt* (1936), and *Low Company* (1939). Neglected when they appeared, when republished in 1961 as *Three Novels* they were praised for their portrayal of Jewish life on the Lower East Side. In the excellent pages that Irving Howe devotes to "The American Jewish Novelists" in *World of Our Fathers*, he singles out Fuchs as the most "regional" of American Jewish writers. He sees Fuchs's novels as deter-mined by a sense of place that is both their source of interest today and where they fit in the line of Jewish novelists that begins with Abraham Cahan's *The Rise of David Levinsky* and goes though Henry Roth and on to Saul Bellow, Bernard Malamud, and Philip Roth. While Cahan, Roth, and Fuchs write of Jewish immigrants in the slums, Bellow, Mala-mud, and Philip Roth write of the Jewish American who has been as-similated but is not totally at ease. Fuchs spent most of his career as a screenwriter in Hollywood.

Fuller, Margaret (1810–1850)

In 1844 Horace Greeley, publisher of the *New York Tribune,* the first American newspaper to be distributed nationally, brought Margaret Fuller to New York from Boston to board in his Turtle Bay home and write for his paper. Fuller spent twenty months in New York, writing book reviews of the major American and English writers of the day and a series of exposés of New York hospitals and prisons. She came to think of the city as "the point where American and European interests converge." The *Tribune* also published her "Women in the Nineteenth Century," which became crucial to the rise of American feminism in the 1850s. By that time Fuller was dead, having drowned in a shipwreck off the coast of Fire Island. She was returning from Europe with her Italian husband and young son. Her friend Ralph Waldo Emerson, with whom she had edited the transcendentalist magazine the *Dial,* dispatched Henry David Thoreau to the site in the hopes that he might find her body, some personal effects, or her manuscript of Garibaldi's revolt in Rome. Thoreau patrolled the beach but found nothing.

Gaddis, William (b. 1922)

This New York native is responsible for two of the most demanding novels written in twentieth-century America, *The Recognitions* (1955) and *JR* (1975). The former is packed with a magpie's hoard of religious, historical, and literary lore and information. It is not a book to be read in bed before going to sleep. The latter begins, "Money . . . ? in a voice that rustled" and ends, "listening . . . ?" It consists almost entirely of unattributed dialogue and has been called an "acoustical" novel. Its setting is the eleven-year-old tycoon JR's East Ninety-sixth Street apartment. These books, and Gaddis's other two novels, resist paraphrase, which is exactly as he wants it. He has won numerous awards, including a MacArthur, but he has also endured more than his share of insulting reviews, and by big names like George Steiner and Alfred Kazin at that. Each of his novels has taken at least a decade to write. To earn his bread Gaddis has worked in many capacities as a professional writer furnishing the words needed by business and industry. All of his novels are in print, but you will find very little of what Gore Vidal calls "book chat" about them. Gaddis believes that the work is the point, not what the writer says about it. Indeed, he agreed to a *Paris Review* interview in the hopes that if he went on record once he could direct other potential interviewers to what he had said there. Fortunately for this book he told one "only in New York" story on that occasion. Because several scenes in *The Recognitions* take place in Hungary, Gaddis wanted these to be in Hungarian. Not knowing the language, he went to the Upper East Side, where there is a large Hungarian community, and into a bar, where he approached the bartender with his problem. "He called someone over," Gaddis remembered. "Finally there must have been ten people around me arguing about exactly the correct accent, the nuance of the phrase. When I had written it all down, the bartender said, 'Now the man who was the leading figure in the conversation, whom everyone else bowed to, as it were, is a great Hungarian actor. If he said you got it right, you know you have it right.'"

Gelber, Jack (b. 1932)

When Jack Gelber got to New York in 1955 he paid $11.20 a month to share an apartment with a saxophone player at 435 East Fifth Street. The sax player had friends who came and went at all hours. Gelber then moved south of Delancey to 11 Pine Street, where he wrote his play *The Connection*. It is set in a "shooting gallery," where junkies come to fix, and has a jazz quartet on stage. Clearly, Gelber picked something up from his time with the saxophonist. In 1959 Julian Beck and Judith Malina mounted a successful run of the play at their Living Theater. Then as now the world of junk was a hip subject and Gelber's play delivered the goods. Malina proudly remembered that "almost fifty men fainted during the run of *The Connection* . . . Always around the same point. The Overdose." In 1962 Shirley Clarke filmed the play from a Gelber script. He wrote several other plays and a novel, but nothing approached the success of *The Connection*. The play isn't often revived, but it is possible to find secondhand copies of the Grove Press edition, which includes photographs of the original production.

Ginsberg, Allen (1926–1997)

Strange now to think of you, gone without corsets & eyes, while I walk on
the sunny pavements of Greenwich Village,
downtown Manhattan, clear winter noon, and I've been up all night, talking

talking, reading the Kaddish aloud, listening to Ray Charles blues
shout blind on the photograph
ALLEN GINSBERG, "Kaddish"

Today Allen Ginsberg has had an international reputation for nearly
thirty years and is the best known of the Beat writers. Beginning with
his breakthrough poem "Howl" (1956) he has been the most public of
American poets and one who has never separated his politics from his
poetry. Ginsberg declared his homosexuality in the fifties when that
sort of thing simply was not done, and since then he has indeed put
his "queer shoulder to the wheel." His literary career began in New
York when as a student at Columbia he encountered first Lucien Carr
and then William Burroughs, Jack Kerouac, and Herbert Huncke—the
Beat Generation. It is typical of Ginsberg that he introduced Gregory
Corso to the group, that he urged Burroughs's novel *Junkie* upon his
friend Carl Solomon, that he was the group's agent and publicist, roles
that he filled whether reading in Prague or teaching a class at the Jack
Kerouac School of Disembodied Poetics, of which he was a founder, at
the Naropa University in Boulder, Colorado. He is as famous for his energy as for his generosity. While at Columbia Ginsberg began hanging
around on the Lower East Side, which became his neighborhood in
1951, when he took an apartment at 206 East Seventh Street. It was here
that some of his earliest photographs of Kerouac, Burroughs, and Neal
Cassady were taken. Ginsberg has never been without a camera, and
today there are tens of thousands of negatives in his Columbia University archive, with more to follow. One day, when all of these have been
cataloged and more have been printed, adding to the number that have
already been published in several books, they will provide not only a
record of Beat activities but a complement to Ginsberg's poems. It was
to the Seventh Street apartment that Burroughs came from South America in 1953 to arrange the letters he had written Ginsberg into the books
The Yage Letters and *Queer*. In the mid-fifties Ginsberg lived in San
Francisco, where he wrote "Howl" and spread the Beat gospel to writers
like Gary Snyder, Philip Whalen, and Michael McClure. He returned to
New York at the end of the decade, living first in an apartment at 704
East Fifth Street, where he wrote what many consider his greatest poem,
"Kaddish," and then in 1959 he moved to 170 East Second Street.
These were the years when Ginsberg was very much outside the New
York literary establishment. The critic and editor Norman Podhoretz
dismissed Ginsberg and the rest of the Beats as "know nothings," but

obviously there were those who regarded Podhoretz's attitude as nonsense. Robert Lowell, for one, said that he learned valuable lessons from Ginsberg's handling of autobiography, lessons he put to use in one of the establishment's favorite books of poems, *Life Studies*. During the Vietnam War Ginsberg was at the center of protests nationwide, and the hippies respected him as a father figure. In 1965 he and his lover Peter Orlovsky moved into 408 East Tenth Street, where they lived for a decade on a city block on which Ginsberg was mugged in December 1974, an event that he characteristically describes in the poem "Mugging." Early in the seventies, with Kerouac dead and Burroughs out of the country, Ginsberg became the only Beat writer of note on the scene, and he made news wherever he went. Jane Kramer of the *New Yorker* wrote a book-length profile of him, and a poster of his bearded head topped by an American flag top hat seemed for a time to be everywhere. He constantly published poems, as many of them appearing in small magazines or alternative newspapers as in national periodicals, and his books continued to be published by City Lights with their signature black-and-white covers. In 1975 he took a walk-up apartment at 437 East Twelfth Street in a building where a number of other poets, including Larry Fagin, lived. Here he remained until 1995, when advancing age made the stairs more difficult and he got a windfall from the sale of his papers to Stanford University, which allowed him to afford a loft in a nearby building with an elevator. Over the last years Ginsberg taught at Brooklyn College, but kept up a killer schedule, often reading accompanied by the guitarist Steven Taylor. When he was in the city he was no less ubiquitous than he was thirty years before. There was no lessening of interest in his work nor in his appetite for reading aloud, which he did with as much passion and command as anyone of his generation. Two years ago a four-CD set appeared, documenting Ginsberg's readings over nearly fifty years. This makes clear how crucial performance of his poems has been, both to the poems themselves and for American poetry in general. There have already been several biographies of Ginsberg and more will certainly follow. He is, of course, a key figure in the biographies of Kerouac and Burroughs and in everything written on the Beat generation. He may or may not be the great American poet after World War II, but he is certainly one of New York City's great poets in a line that runs from his dominant influence, Walt Whitman, through Hart Crane and Frank O'Hara. That these poets are all gay man would not be lost on Ginsberg, nor should it be on us.

Allen Ginsberg died suddenly on 5 April 1997, of a heart attack. He had been diagnosed with liver cancer, knew he had at best a few months to live, and spent his last days working on poems and calling old friends to say good-bye. Ginsberg typically asked his friends, "Do you need any money?" To Amiri Baraka he said, "I'm dying, but I'm not worried. That's how it is." His funeral was held at the Shambala Meditation Center on the sixth floor of an office building in Lower Manhattan. Mourners came and went, chanting and praying during the four-hour Buddhist service. The Kaddish was read, and speakers told funny stories about the poet. During several lulls in the service people came forward to ask for donations to various charities or causes. Since then Ginsberg's remains have been cremated and divided between Buddhist centers in Colorado and Ann Arbor, Michigan, and the Ginsberg family plot in Newark, New Jersey's, B'nai Israel Cemetery. A week after his death the *New Yorker,* which once scorned Ginsberg, published one of his last poems. Memorial services were held for him on the Lower East Side and across the United States.

Giroux, Robert (b. 1914)

Over the past twenty-five years Farrar, Straus & Giroux has been one of the city's foremost literary publishers. Giroux attended Columbia in the late thirties, where he met the poets John Berryman and Thomas Merton, both of whom he went on to publish. While at Harcourt Brace, Giroux edited Jack Kerouac's first novel, *The Town and the City,* and the early books of Robert Lowell. When Giroux joined Farrar, Straus, Lowell and Berryman went with him and so did Elizabeth Bishop, who is perhaps the writer closest to Giroux's heart. He edited her book of letters, *One Art.* Giroux is now semiretired, but as the biographies of the many famous writers he published begin to appear he can be seen everywhere in New York literary life from the 1940s through the 1980s.

Gold, Mike (1894–1967)

Born Irving Granich (Gold is a pen name) on the Lower East Side and raised there, Gold was a son of immigrants who, like Henry Roth and others in his generation, mastered English and wrote of the immigrant experience they knew as children. Gold proclaimed himself a Communist and published first in the *Masses* and the *New Masses* and then in the *Liberator,* the editorship of which Max Eastman passed on to him. In the plays, literary essays, and book reviews he wrote for the *Daily*

Worker Gold held to the party line. He is best known for *Jews without Money* (1930), a novel that quickly became a touchstone of proletarian fiction. Gold wrote not just of "the tenement canyon hung with fire escapes, bed-clothing and faces" where he had grown up, but of the whores he remembered "sprawled indolently, their legs taking up half the pavement." His ambition was more documentary than artistic, but this did not keep him from veering into the sentimental.

Goldman, Emma (1869–1940)

A Russian immigrant, Goldman's fate was sealed on her first day in America, when she met in a Lower East Side café the anarchist Alexander Berkman, who soon became her lover and lifelong friend. It was Berkman who went to Pittsburgh during the Homestead Steel strike and wounded Henry Clay Frick, then in charge of Andrew Carnegie's steel mill. Berkman's act did the strikers no good but got him sent to prison, an experience he wrote about in *Memoirs of a Prison Anarchist*. In New York he and Goldman lived from 1903 to 1913 at 210 East Thirteenth Street, where she published *Mother Earth*, a political magazine that paid sufficient attention to the arts that Strindberg and Ibsen were introduced to America in its pages. The teenage Eugene O'Neill read both of them there for the first time. Goldman was, by all accounts, a mensch who enjoyed a great many friendships among political radicals and writers. She is a good enough writer herself that her personality and a passionate commitment to her ideals come across in her prose. She campaigned for birth control, advocated sex outside marriage, and opposed the United States' entry into World War I. This last led to her arrest. In 1919 Goldman visited Russia, but her anarchism could not be dyed Bolshevik red and in 1925 she published *My Disillusionment in Russia*. Her autobiography, *Living My Life* (1931), remains in print today.

Ironically it is not Goldman or Berkman but Frick who has the most significant presence in New York today. The mansion that he built on Fifth Avenue at 1 East Seventieth Street houses the Frick Collection, which includes paintings by Piero della Francesca, Brueghel, and Vermeer. Today Frick is remembered for these masterpieces, not for the blood that flowed during the Homestead strike.

Goodman, Paul (1911–1972)

Born in New York, Goodman grew up, after his father deserted the family, on the city's streets to become an autodidact. Goodman has been labeled a social critic, which is a way of saying that he wrote a great many books about a great many subjects. He was an intuitive thinker, street-smart, learned, a know-it-all, an anarchist, and a bisexual who liked to show off by French-kissing his dog at parties. In the forties he bragged about how he and his family lived in New York on two thousand dollars a year. He rubbed many people the wrong way, but even some of these thought of him as a genius, and in the sixties he became a guru to the young. Goodman's early work was published by small experimental presses in the Village and then New Directions published a book of stories. He wrote one of the first books on Kafka, *Kafka's Prayer,* and with his brother Percival, an architect, a book on cities titled *Communitas* (1947). (In the 1950s the Goodmans put forth a plan to ban cars from Manhattan.) Goodman wrote a book about gestalt therapy, several novels, including one about New York, *The Empire City,* that wears its convictions on its sleeve, and *Growing Up Absurd* (1960), a book that connected the alienation of America's youth to what Goodman saw as the meaninglessness of work in the postwar world. It made him famous, and for a time he seemed to know more than anyone else about why young people were, in the phrase of the times, "delinquent." Throughout his life Goodman wrote simple, direct, and very often eloquent poems, many of which appeared in his book *The Lordly Hudson.* After his death *Collected Poems* appeared. To Goodman's admirers he was one for whom, in the words of William Blake's proverb, "the road of excess leads to the palace of wisdom."

Gorey, Edward (b. 1925)

Gorey is here, not because he was Frank O'Hara's roommate at Harvard, but because his last name is a perfect descriptive fit for the very funny and morbid Victorian romances he writes and draws. These are mostly short, always droll, and beloved by adults and those precocious children who have a taste for "perfectly well-formed gentlemen" and babies left outside in the snow. For many years the Gotham Book Mart has done a bang-up business in new and out-of-print Gorey titles, and his work has been collected into several *Amphigoreys.* He is also here because in the fifties he designed a series of distinctive covers for Anchor Books, the first quality paperback line. Although Gorey has long since decamped from Manhattan for Cape Cod, when he was in the city he did not miss a performance of George Balanchine's New York City Ballet.

Gotham Book Mart
41 West Forty-seventh Street

Francis Steloff opened the Gotham Book Mart at another location in 1920, but since 1923 it has been in the heart of New York's diamond district. The sign above the entrance reads "Wise Men Fish Here," which is also the title of a book about the store (has a book been written about any other New York bookstore?) by W. G. Rogers. From its inception the Gotham has devoted itself to twentieth-century literature. Under its present owner, Andreas Brown, it has one of the best sections on film of any New York bookstore, but for twentieth-century literature, new and out-of-print, it remains one of the best stores in the city. Since the forties the Gotham has hosted book launches and receptions for visiting writers. Photographs of these events hang in the store today. One of the most famous, and now a postcard sold at the store, shows Dame Edith Sitwell and Sir Osbert Sitwell—the party was in their honor—surrounded by W. H. Auden, on a ladder, Elizabeth Bishop, Marianne Moore, Randall Jarrell, Delmore Schwartz, Stephen Spender, Tennessee Williams, Gore Vidal, and the poet José García Villa. For a time in the fifties LeRoi Jones worked in the store. Robert Lowell frequently called to order books; Philip Lyman was a walking *Books in Print* at the front desk; and parties were held upstairs for everyone from Anaïs Nin to Louis Zukofsky. The James Joyce Society met for years in that same upstairs gallery room. Joseph Mitchell was one of their regulars. The poet Michael Palmer grew up across the street in the Hotel Wentworth, which his father managed, and got at least part of his education at the Gotham. The Gotham's creaky floors, stimulating smell of book dust, and a staff that knows books are pure refreshment for any booklover.

Gottlieb, Robert (b. 1931)

"It is not a happy business now," Gottlieb has said of publishing, "and it once was. It was smaller. The stakes were lower. It was a less sophisticated world." The world Gottlieb remembered as happier was the one he entered when, after graduating from Columbia, he went to work at Simon & Schuster in 1955. This was publishing before houses were taken over by conglomerates, before blockbuster best-sellers, million-dollar advances, superstores, and powerful agents. Gottlieb became editor in chief at Simon & Schuster and then moved to Alfred A. Knopf, where his title was president and editor in chief. Among the many authors he edited were Gloria Vanderbilt, Anthony Lukas, John Lennon, Lincoln Kirstein, Salman Rushdie, John Cheever, Lauren Bacall, Edna

O'Brien, Janet Malcolm, Jessica Mitford, and Arlene Croce. In 1987 S. I. Newhouse, the *New Yorker*'s new owner, asked Gottlieb to replace William Shawn as editor in chief of the magazine. Suspecting that Shawn was being forced out, many *New Yorker* writers signed a petition asking Gottlieb to refuse Newhouse's offer. He did not but instead ran the *New Yorker,* and quite well, too, until Tina Brown replaced him in 1992 and turned the magazine on its ear. Gottlieb then returned to Knopf, where he works on special projects gratis thanks to a large settlement given him by Newhouse. In his more than forty years in New York publishing, Gottlieb has seen a small world grow dauntingly bigger and the pressures to succeed—sales are the sole measuring stick—become the industry's driving force. His *Paris Review* interview in issue 132 of the magazine is worth looking up to see what he, and some of the authors and agents he works with, make of all this.

Gould, Joe (1889–1957)

A literary bum, Joe Gould was the quintessential Greenwich Village character of his time. He graduated from Harvard in 1911 and after some adventures out west came to New York. Most of what we know about Gould comes from Joseph Mitchell's *New Yorker* profiles of him. This is how "Joe Gould's Secret" begins: "Joe Gould was an odd and penniless and unemployable little man who came to the city in 1916 and ducked and dodged and held on hard as he could for over thirty-five years." His secret was the book *An Oral History* to whose title Gould sometimes added "of our times." He wrote this book all his life and showed off sections of it in the bars, diners, and cafeterias where he hung out. One of the chapters described a trip he made to North Dakota to measure the heads of the Mandan and Chippewa Indians. Over the years Gould's book took on legendary status. It was Mitchell, who had first met Gould in the thirties and written about him in 1942, who discovered that the history amounted to just four chapters, endlessly rewritten. Gould did complete at least two poems:

> **My Religion**
>
> In winter I'm a Buddhist,
> and in summer I'm a nudist,

and his performance piece "The Sea Gull." For this Gould stood on a chair, flapped his wings, and screamed, "Scree-eek! Scree-eek!" The painter Alice Neel did a portrait of Gould in which she gave him three sets of genitalia.

Granary Books
568 Broadway, Suite 403
Begun in Minneapolis in the early1980s as a small literary bookshop, Granary Books, under the direction of Stephen Clay, moved to SoHo in 1989. It is now a publisher giving special attention to the work of Johanna Drucker, whose field is the book as visual object. Her work available from Granary falls into two categories: scholarly investigations of typography and book design and historical surveys of artists' books. In 1993 Granary published her essay "Luminous Volumes: Granary's New Vision of the Book." Granary also has an exhibition space and produces catalogs known for their attention to the poets and little-magazine culture of New York's Lower East Side. To date catalogs focusing on the work and archives of Lewis Warsh and Bernadette Mayer have appeared, as has Warsh's *Bustin's Island '68*, a book of photos and text that record a month's visit to that Maine island by Warsh, Anne Waldman, and Ted Berrigan and his family. There are fine presses in New York and places where the books they publish are exhibited and sold, but there is no place that combines the two as does Granary. In late January 1998 "A Secret Location on the Lower East Side: Adventures in Writing 1960–1980," an exhibition of poetry magazines curated by Clay and Rodney Phillips of the Berg Collection opened at the Forty-second Street branch of the New York Public Library.

Grand Street
131 Varick Street
Grand Street has had two incarnations. Under its founding editor, Ben Sonnenberg, the magazine focused almost exclusively on literature, printing literary essays and reviews in addition to poetry and fiction. When Jean Stein took over in 1989, the magazine's focus broadened: Art and photographs were incorporated for the first time and a varied mix of genres became standard. Today it is a sumptuously printed journal in which the reader may encounter a feature on the Grand Guignol, documents on the life and work of Terry Southern, the photographs of Dennis Hopper, an art feature edited by Walter Hopps cheek by jowl with poems by Charles Simic, Fanny Howe, and Kevin Young, and fiction, a good deal of it in translation. Deborah Treisman is the magazine's managing editor.

Grant, Ulysses S. (1822–1885)
When Groucho Marx asked the question "Who's buried in Grant's tomb?" few answered, "A writer." But Grant had more success as a

writer than as president of the United States or New York banker. Mark Twain published Grant's *Memoirs,* completed as Grant suffered the agonies of cancer of the mouth, and Gertrude Stein thought it one of the glories of American prose. That the Library of America has republished the book suggests that Stein's judgment is shared by others. Grant retired to New York City in 1884 and in the short time left to him managed to begin Grant and Ward, a banking house that proved, like so many of his ventures, unsuccessful. He had more impact on the city in death than in life. Grant's tomb on Riverside Drive is the largest mausoleum in the United States. In it beside Grant rest the remains of his wife, Julia Dent Grant, for whose last years the impoverished Grant provided by writing his *Memoirs.*

Greeley, Horace (1811–1872)

Two statues of Greeley stand in New York City today. The one outside City Hall calls us to remember his political career, and the one in Herald Square commemorates his years as publisher of the *New York Tribune.* The *Tribune* was the city's first daily Whig paper, and in it Greeley both took the Whig line and supported pet causes such as abolitionism, unusual for a prominent New Yorker of his day, and the Homestead Act. It was the latter that prompted him to say the immortal words, "Go West, Young Man!"

The success of Greeley's paper led to his influence on the national and local level. He lived for a time in Turtle Bay when it was a farming community (East Forty-eighth and Forty-ninth Streets), and between 1850 and 1853 he lived at 35 East Nineteenth Street, a house that still stands.

Green, Jack (b. 1928)

From 1957 to 1965, Green self-published seventeen issues of *newspaper.* In 1979 he brought out issue number 18. The publication was printed on beige legal-size paper with a high acid content, and original copies that have yet to crumble will do so in a few years. *Fire the Bastards!,* published by Dalkey Archive, is the only generally available book that resulted from this enterprise. In essence, it is a long satiric attack on New York, and on the nation's book review media for their treatment of William Gaddis's novel *The Recognitions.* Green demonstrates that the majority of the novel's reviewers were incompetent or worse, and had no business reviewing any sort of innovative fiction, let alone a novel that Green considers a masterpiece. Green became obsessed and in going too far produced a unique book. He read everything written on the novel at the time of its publication in 1955 and for some years afterward, and tirelessly exposed Gaddis's reviewers for the fakes the reader has no doubt that they were. All who read *Fire the Bastards!* must conclude that novel reviewing is a tyranny of conventional taste. The Gaddis scholar Steven Moore provides a long introduction to this edition that gives a great deal of information about the eccentric, elusive, and fascinating Green. *Fire the Bastards!* is, by the way, in the public domain and a publisher could do worse than bring out a cheap paperback edition.

Greenwich Village

The Village is the lower Manhattan neighborhood bounded to the north by Fourteenth Street, to the east by Fourth Avenue and the Bowery, to the south by Houston Street and to the west by the Hudson River. When New York was Nieuw Amsterdam, the Village was marshlands and hills two miles from the city and called by the Indians "Sapokanican." The name Greenwich is first associated with the area in 1713 and then it was spelled "Grin'wich." As the marshes were drained to become farmland Dutch and English settlers created a suburb of rural estates that survived the Revolutionary War, but in the 1780s the city bought what is now Washington Square and turned it into a potter's field and public gallows. In 1797 Newgate Prison rose on Christopher Street, where it stood until 1829. But it was disease and not civic improvement that brought the Village closer to the city. Between 1789 and 1821 there were four significant outbreaks of yellow fever and cholera in the city. People sought refuge from these by moving to the country, to what is now the heart of the West Village. In 1822 yet another epidemic drove people to settle permanently in the Village, and by 1840 houses lined the crooked streets. Although a grid system had been proposed for New York streets as early as 1806, the Village developed before it was implemented. Narrow, sometimes winding streets and the human-scale brick buildings set the Village apart as the city advanced north in its lockstep of crosstown streets and downtown avenues. There is the intimacy of a village about the neighborhood, and it this quality that drew writers and artists to the area. When Henry James was born in Washington Place in 1843, it was an upscale neighborhood, as was Washington Square when he set his novel by that title there. The first of the Village's bohemians centered around Pfaff's Beer Hall at 653 Broadway just north of Bleecker Street. The place opened in the 1850s, and its claim on our attention is that Walt Whitman liked to go there to drink and meet other aspiring journalists, writers, and actors. Throughout the second half of the nineteenth century the Village became home to any number of writers, publishers, and editors, who found the rents cheap and the company of one another congenial, and while there was always a bohemian fringe the Village of legend began to form its character shortly before World War I. A generation of political radicals and writers as famous today as John Reed, Willa Cather, Theodore Dreiser, and Hart Crane, and as little known as Mary Heaton Vorse, Alfred Kreymborg, and Mabel Dodge, created one of the Village's heydays. This one lasted until the stock market crash in 1929, but after that the Village calmed down rather than changed drastically. During the thirties and forties the Village remained the most literary of Manhattan's neighborhoods, and then after World War II another heyday, fueled by the Beats and a burgeoning arts scene, lasted until the early sixties. Indeed, each succeeding Village generation always seemed to have just missed out on when the Village was really the place to be. Today the Village is in truth not what it once was. The change took place in the seventies, when the Village became prime real estate and one of the most attractive neighborhoods for those who could afford a house in the city. The streets are now quiet and the feel is residential, but it is impossible to walk more than a block without encountering the ghosts of Whitman, Crane, Djuna Barnes, Edna St. Vincent Millay, Eugene O'Neill, Edmund Wilson, James Baldwin, Norman Mailer, Frank O'Hara . . . the list could go on for many pages.

Manhattan yields up its pleasures to walkers. Of no neighborhood is this truer than the Village. If you only have a day to walk its streets that will be enough and a great deal can be seen in a morning or an afternoon. There are all sorts of guides to the Village. This book advises first-time literary visitors to enjoy the streets for themselves before looking for every address. Writers and other literary folk were drawn to the Village because of a character that you can still feel on Bank Street or on Bleecker, Christopher, Perry, and in Sheridan Square and MacDougal and Thomson Streets as they run south from Washington Square. The Village remains congenial to the visitor, and there are small cafés, bars, and restaurants to be discovered throughout the neighborhood.

Green-Wood Cemetery
Twenty-fifth Street and Fifth Avenue, Brooklyn

The 478-acre cemetery was commissioned in 1838 by a private group. David Bates, who created the cemetery, had Cambridge's Mount

Auburn Cemetery as a model. Today Green-Wood is worth visiting for the beauty of its grounds, which are the product of the early-nineteenth-century idea that death ought to be contemplated as a return to nature. While no great writers are buried there, a number of those interred have literary associations. ISABELLA STEWART GARDNER (1840–1924), the friend of Henry James, whose Boston palazzo today houses the museum named after her, is buried here, as is the pianist, composer, and diarist LOUIS MOREAU GOTTSCHALK (1829–1869). Among the notorious individuals buried in Green-Wood are WILLIAM M. BOSS TWEED (1823–1878), ALBERT ANASTASIA (?–1957), the head of Murder Incorporated who was murdered in Manhattan's Park Sheraton Hotel while getting a haircut, and JOEY GALLO (1929–1972), who had fifteen minutes of literary fame in which he hung out at Elaine's. (Bob Dylan wrote a ballad about him, and Jimmy Breslin wrote a novel about him and his brothers.) The newspapermen JAMES GORDON BENNETT (1795–1872), who founded the *New York Herald,* and HORACE GREELEY (1811– 1872), founder of the *New York Tribune,* are buried here as are LEONARD BERNSTEIN (1918–1990), SAMUEL F. B. MORSE (1791–1872), inventor, writer, and artist, and, under her original name of Eliza Gilbert, LOLA MONTEZ (1818–1861), about whom Max Ophuls made a film and Kenward Elmslie wrote a musical. The cemetery affords many other pleasures, is easily reached by subway, and is well worth a visit.

Gregory, Horace (1898–1982)

In the famous photograph taken at the Gotham Book Mart during its reception for Dame Edith and Sir Osbert Sitwell, and now on sale at the store as a postcard, Horace Gregory and his wife MARYA ZATUREN-SKA (1900–1982) are behind Sir Stephen Spender on the left. Gregory and the Russian-born Zaturenska were industrious writers of poetry, critical essays, and biographies. He translated Catullus and Ovid, and together they wrote *A History of American Poetry 1900–1940.* Today their many books are hard to find, even in libraries and secondhand bookstores. They have been dead for less than twenty years and already their lives and careers have interest primarily for the specialist. Perhaps by the time another book like this one gets written, some one or two enterprising graduate students will have shone a light on Gregory and Zaturenska rescuing them from neglect. For now let them remind us of how quickly it all fades and how hard it is to hold the world's attention.

The Grolier Club
47 East Sixtieth Street
Founded in 1884 the Grolier Club is, in its own words, "the mainstay of American book collecting" and "values books not only as vessels of knowledge but also as physical objects." To date the Grolier has mounted more than six hundred exhibitions. These are free and open to the public. The club's reference library of some 90,000 volumes is open by appointment to scholars and bibliophiles. As one enters the Grolier there is a display of some of the books published under its own imprint. These are invariably handsome editions whose subjects range from *One Hundred Books Famous in Medicine* to *Four Hundred Years of Dance Notation* to *British Poets of World War II*. They have been printed at the world's great printers, Stinehour in Vermont and Stamperia Valdonega in Verona, Italy, among them. Some of these books are priced for collectors but many sell for under thirty dollars. Can there be a book lover who does not know the Grolier?

Grove Press
In 1951 Barney Rosset was married to the painter Joan Mitchell, living in the Village, and, after making the movie *Strange Victory,* doing not much of anything. Through Mitchell he met John Balcomb and Robert Phelps, who had begun Grove Press, naming it after Grove Street on which they lived. Rosset, who had some family money, paid three thousand dollars for the press, which brought him its entire assets, boxes of unsold copies of the three books Grove had published: Herman Melville's *The Confidence Man, The Verse in English of Richard Crashaw,* and *Selected Writings of the Ingenious Mrs. Aphra Behn.* At first Rosset kept to the plan of reprinting neglected works by printing Matthew G. Lewis's Gothic novel *The Monk* and two Henry James novels. By 1953 Grove moved to Rosset's apartment at 59 West Ninth Street. The translator Wallace Fowlie, then teaching at the New School, put Rosset on to Samuel Beckett, Jean Genet, and Eugène Ionesco, all three of whom would become Grove writers. As he went after new and experimental writing that was not being published in the United States, Rosset also was determined to fight censorship when and wherever he could, and so he became the publisher of Henry Miller's banned book *Tropic of Cancer.* It ultimately cost Grove $250,000 to defend Miller's work, but Rosset's course was set. By the time he sold Grove he had participated in dozens of lawsuits, making him easily the most combat-

ive New York publisher ever. While battling the censors, Grove simultaneously conducted itself, in the words of novelist Gilbert Sorrentino,
a Grove editor from 1965 to 1970, as "a trade publisher with the spirit
of a little magazine or small press." Indeed, from 1957 to 1973 Grove
published one of the essential little magazines, the *Evergreen Review,*
edited principally by Donald Allen, Richard Seaver, and Fred Jordan.
Grove's heyday roughly coincided with the magazine's life. At its height
the house's authors included LeRoi Jones, Frank O'Hara, Charles Olson,
Kenneth Koch, Jack Gelber, Barbara Guest, John Rechy, Hubert Selby,
Malcolm X, Jorge Luis Borges, Robert Pinget, Marguerite Duras, Witold
Gombrowicz, Paul Blackburn, Boris Vian, and Cesar Vallejo. Among
Grove's famous titles are Beckett's *Waiting for Godot, The Autobiog-
raphy of Malcolm X,* and Donald Allen's anthology *The New American
Poetry.* In 1986, Rosset sold Grove to Ann Getty, a deal masterminded by
the British publisher George Weidenfeld. This resulted in Rosset suing
Ann Getty and being countersued by her. Grove-Weidenfield lasted for
several years, but without the participation of Samuel Beckett, who
remained loyal to Rosset and let him publish his last complete work,
Stirrings Still. Today the house is Grove Press again.

Guare, John (b. 1938)

> INTERVIEWER: Do you think of yourself as a regional writer?
> GUARE: Yes. From the region of New York.

Guare grew up in Jackson Heights in Queens and went to high school
in Brooklyn. The first play he saw was *Annie Get Your Gun* starring
Ethel Merman. Guare's career began off-off Broadway at the Caffe
Cino on Cornelia Street and the theater on Van Dam Street where Edward Albee and his producers sponsored new plays from 1963 to 1969.
His first success was the musical *House of Blue Leaves* (1971), which
won both an Obie and a New York Drama Critics Circle award. In
1990 his *Six Degrees of Separation* became a hit on Broadway. Guare
took his plot from a true story. A young man conned several wealthy
families into accepting him as the son of the actor Sidney Poitier. When
apprehended he gave no satisfactory explanation of why he had undertaken such an adventure. Guare worked this event into a satire of human gullibility and American attitudes toward race and class while
suggesting that the "generation gap" that appeared in the sixties is
permanent. He turned the play into a successful screenplay, a form he

excelled at in *Atlantic City*. For many years Guare has lived in Greenwich Village.

Guest, Barbara (b. 1920)

The lineup of the first generation of New York School poets ought to read Ashbery, Guest, Koch, O'Hara, and Schuyler, but Guest has often been left out, most egregiously by Ron Padgett and David Shapiro in their anthology *The New York Poets*. She came to New York from California in the forties and fell in with the downtown painters and poets whose arts cross-pollinated one another. From 1951 to 1954 she worked as an associate editor of *Art News*, the New York art magazine most congenial to poet-critics. Certainly less prolific than her fellows and, like Schuyler, something of a late bloomer, Guest is the only member of the school to publish a biography, *Herself Defined: The Poet H.D. and Her World* (1986). She also published a novel, *Seeking Air*, and in 1966 Sun and Moon brought out her *Selected Poems*. Perhaps Guest had herself in mind when she wrote in "Santa Fe Trail":

> I go separately
> The sweet knees of oxen have pressed a path for me
> ghosts with ingots have burned their bare hands
> it is the dungaree darkness with China stitched
> where the westerly winds
> and the traveler's checks
> the evensong of salesmen
> the glistening paraphernalia of twin suitcases
> where no one speaks English. I go separately

Gunther, John (1901–1970)

From 1936, when he published *Inside Europe*, until television rendered his sort of reporting superfluous, Gunther was one of the nation's most renowned journalists. He traveled the world to get an "inside" look at countries and continents, and the books he produced made him famous. Gunther belonged to the generation of American writers who got their education working on newspapers. While his journalism has faded, as all journalism must, his memoir of his son, *Death Be Not Proud*, continues to be read today. And perhaps his journalism still has an audience. A paperback edition of *Inside the U.S.A.* appeared in 1997. In the 1950s Gunther and his wife, Jane, lived at 216 East Sixty-second Street, where they entertained writers, politicians, entertainers, musicians, and business people—the sort of mixture on which New York social life thrives. Over the last decade of his life Gunther lived at 1 East End Avenue.

Halleck, Fitz-Greene (1790–1867)

Today a statue of Halleck stands in Central Park, the first poet to receive that honor from the city. He came to New York from Guilford, Connecticut, in 1811 and spent the next eighteen years working in a banking house while establishing himself as a wit, scholar, and poet. Together with his close friend the poet Joseph Rodman Drake, Halleck wrote "The Croakers," a satiric poem that appeared in the *Evening Post* and subsequently in book form. Drake's untimely death in 1820 inspired Halleck's popular lyric, "Green Be the Turf above Thee," two lines from which, "None knew him but to love him, / Nor named him but to praise," are on Drake's monument in Drake Park in the Hunt's Point section of the East Bronx. Halleck was an original member of James Fenimore Cooper's lunch club, New York's first literary club. Because a vote of bread said yes to a member and cheese said no, it later became known as the Bread and Cheese. Halleck frequently contributed to William Cullen Bryant's *New York Review* and became popular as a poet through his public recitations. He served John Jacob Astor, at the time the wealthiest man in America, as confidential secretary from 1832 until Astor's death in 1848, after which Halleck retired on an annuity to his native Guilford. Bryant praised Halleck as "the favorite poet of the city of New York, where his name is cherished with a peculiar fondness and enthusiasm."

Hammett, Dashiell (1894–1961)

A Pinkerton detective who became a mystery novelist and Hollywood screenwriter, Hammett came to New York in the mid-twenties and lived mostly in hotels. Often drunk and sometimes broke Hammett moved around a lot. Several times he relied on the comfort of friends, the novelist Nathanael "Pep" West in particular. As the night clerk at the Kenmore Hall Hotel at 145 East Twenty-third Street, West often let writer friends stay in rooms free of charge. It was here that Hammett finished *The Maltese Falcon*. In the early thirties West moved uptown to the

Sutton Club Hotel at 330 East Fifty-sixth Street. Here West let Hammett and Lillian Hellman stay in the Diplomat's Suite, where Hammett worked on *The Thin Man*. Alcoholic and ill, Hammett spent the last years of his life living in Hellman's home at 63 East Eighty-second Street. He certainly drew on the early years of his relationship with Hellman in creating the tough-talking married couple, Nick and Nora Charles. For her part, Hellman presented a number of idealized portraits of him in the several memoirs that now seem to have been equal parts fact and invention. Hammett died at the Lenox Hill Hospital and was buried out of the Frank Campbell Funeral Chapel at 1076 Madison Avenue, from which many sports starts and mobsters have been sent to their rest.

Hansberry, Lorraine (1930–1965)

The Chicago-born Hansberry is the first black woman to have a play produced on Broadway. *A Raisin in the Sun* (1959) takes its title from lines in Langston Hughes's poem "Harlem":

> What happens to a dream deferred?
>
> Does it dry up
> like a raisin in the sun?
> Or fester like a sore—
> and then run?

The play deals with a black Chicago family's attempt to move to the suburbs, and the forces that thwart them. Hansberry's father fought a similar battle all the way to the Supreme Court. Her play won a Drama Critics Circle Award, became a film, and is in print today. On the day her second play, *The Sign in Sidney Brustein's Window,* closed on Broadway Hansberry died of cancer.

Hardwick, Elizabeth (b. 1916)

A Kentucky native, Hardwick first came to Manhattan for graduate study at Columbia which she abandoned short of her Ph.D. to write stories and essays that appeared in the *Partisan Review.* In 1949 Hardwick met Robert Lowell at Yaddo, the writer's retreat in Saratoga Springs, New York, and married him that same year while he was in the throes of one of his periodic breakdowns. Their tumultuous marriage ended in divorce, but a reconciliation seemed possible in 1977. Instead, Hardwick was summoned from the West Sixty-seventh Street apartment they had shared to find Lowell dead inside the cab that had brought him from the airport. In life, Lowell cannibalized the letters Hardwick wrote to him after their separation to create his book of poems *The Dolphin*. Many writers and friends, including W. H. Auden, found this a barbarous and cruel act. In death, there have been two biographies of Lowell that inevitably portray their marriage from his point of view. One waits for the day when either Hardwick herself or another writer will present her version of events. Hardwick has written novels—*Sleepless Nights* is her best known—and published several books of essays, the most recent being *Bartleby in Manhattan*. She is one of the founding editors of the *New York Review of Books* and continues to live in New York City.

Harlem Renaissance

The northernmost area of Manhattan beginning above 125th Street, Harlem was a farming village in the seventeenth century until the mid-nineteenth century when farms gave way to estates owned by prominent old New York families such as the De Lanceys, Beekmans, Bleeckers, and Rikers. These estates could not hold off the city as it relentlessly advanced north up the peninsula. As transportation made its way into the area—between 1881 and 1901 the elevated reached 129th Street and the IRT Lenox Avenue subway line opened—a neighborhood began to take shape. The beginning of the twentieth century saw a construction boom that resulted in both overbuilding and the arrival of many German-Jewish families who could not fill the existing apartment houses. Philip A. Payton, a black real estate agent, effectively sowed the seeds of the Harlem Renaissance when he convinced neighborhood landlords to rent their empty apartments to blacks. Thus he opened a prime real estate area to the blacks who had lived in the San Juan Hill and Tenderloin areas of Manhattan. Harlem soon drew the black elite, what W. E. B. Du Bois was to call "the talented tenth," as well as migrants from the South. By 1920, two hundred thousand blacks lived in the area, making it by far the largest concentration of African Americans in the nation. In the ensuing decade more than one hundred thousand whites moved out of Harlem as nearly an equal number of blacks moved in. The Harlem of the twenties, the decade in which the Renaissance took place, was not what would later be called a ghetto, nor does it bear much resemblance to the Harlem of today. The neighborhood was not thought of as cut off from the rest of the city by race, and it was on the rise. Those who made the Renaissance were energized by the sudden coming together of blacks from across the country—the poet Countee Cullen was the only native New Yorker among the major participants—and the forces this produced. The stock market crash of 1929 knocked Harlem for a loop as it did the rest of New York City, but in the decade that began after World War I Harlem thrived intellectually and socially. Whites were drawn by the neighborhood's glow and some of them played important roles in the Renaissance, but at its core this was a black enterprise the depth and scope of which America has not seen since. In addition to Cullen and Du Bois, writers crucial to the Renaissance were Zora Neale Hurston, Langston Hughes, Claude McKay, Wallace Thurman, Carl Van Vechten, and James Weldon Johnson, all of whom have entries in this book. But the Renaissance was much broader than just these important writers, and luckily it and the Harlem of its time have been well explored in recent years. The books to consult are David Levering Lewis's *Harlem Renaissance Reader,* which has a valuable introduction and biographical notes, as well as selections from a wide range of writers. Lewis also wrote the full-scale portrait of Harlem, *When Harlem Was in Vogue.* Steven Watson's *The Harlem Renaissance,* one of Pantheon's Circles of the Twentieth Century series, is useful for its photographs, maps, and very lively text. It has been designed like a scrapbook, and oddments of information pop out from its pages. Ann Douglas's *Terrible Honesty* has some excellent pages on the Renaissance.

In these books you will discover that the writers and artists of the Renaissance received an unusual amount of institutional support, support that was not available, or at least not forthcoming, to writers and artists in Greenwich Village at the time. This came from individuals such as Mrs. R. Osgood Mason and Amy Spingarn, foundations such as that of William E. Harmon and Julius Rosenwald, and the General Education Board. The Harlem Renaissance enjoyed such support because, in the words of David Levering Lewis, there were those who hoped it would "improve race relations in a time of extreme national backlash." It also is worth mentioning that as active as the Harlem Renaissance's participants were—at the time it was called the New Negro Renaissance—"not everything that happened," again in the words of Lewis, "between 1917 and 1935 was a Renaissance happening." As Langston Hughes wrote:

> It was a period when, at almost every Harlem upper-crust dance or party, one would be introduced to various distinguished white celebrities as guests. It was a period when almost any Harlem Negro of any social importance at all would be likely to say casually: "As I was re-

marking the other day to Heywood—," meaning Heywood Broun. Or: "As I said to George—," meaning George Gershwin. It was a period when local and visiting royalty were not at all uncommon in Harlem. And when the parties of A'Lelia Walker, the Negro heiress, were filled with guests whose names would turn any Nordic social climber green with envy. . . . It was a period when every season there was at least one hit play on Broadway acted by a Negro cast. And when books by Negro authors were being published with much greater frequency and much more publicity than ever before or since in history.

Harris, Mark (b. 1922)

When Mark Harris was born in the suburb of Mount Vernon, New York City had three major league baseball teams, the Yankees, Giants, and Dodgers. Harris added a fourth, the fictional New York Mammoths. Henry "Author" Wiggin pitched for the Mammoths and "wrote" three novels, *The Southpaw* (1953), *Bang the Drum Slowly* (1956), and *A Ticket for a Seamstitch* (1957). By the time Harris completed his trilogy the Giants and Dodgers had betrayed their fans for the Golden State of California. These novels belong in the same ballpark as the best of American baseball fiction: Ring Lardner's stories, W. S. Kinsella's work, and Robert Coover's *The Universal Baseball Association, Inc. J. Henry Waugh, Prop.* Because it has had a life on television and in the movies, *Bang the Drum Slowly* is probably the best known (New Yorker Robert De Niro played the catcher, his first starring role), but *The Southpaw,* with its gripping pennant race, is the best of the three.

Haydn, Hiram (1907–1973)

Haydn began his publishing career at Crown and then moved on to Bobbs-Merrill and Random House. In the late forties he taught a fiction-writing course (he had published three novels) at the New School for Social Research. Among his students were William Styron, whom Haydn signed to a publishing contract after reading twenty pages of his novel *Lie Down in Darkness,* Mario Puzo, and Bel Kaufman. In 1959 he and Alfred A. "Pat" Knopf Jr. and Simon Michael Bessie raised a million and a half dollars and began Athenaeum. The incorrigible Bennett Cerf called the house "Half-Athenaeum," but it prospered for a number of years and was known for its distinguished poetry list edited by Harry Ford. Haydn gives a vivid account of Athenaeum and his life in book publishing in *Words and Faces,* one of the few books about American publishing in the twentieth century written from the inside.

Heller, Joseph (b. 1923)

Born in the Coney Island section of Brooklyn and educated at New York University and then Columbia, Heller served in the air force during World War II. When he returned to New York he worked in advertising while writing the novel that was to be both a popular and literary success, *Catch-22* (1961). The phrase has entered the language and is used today to mean the rule you overlooked that when invoked will keep you from getting what you need or want. There is the story that when the novel was in manuscript it was titled *Catch 57*. For some reason this did not sound right and other numbers were tried before everyone agreed on 22. Heller went on to write several other novels, none of which commanded the same interest as his first. For a time he lived at 290 West End Avenue, and he still maintains an apartment on the Upper West Side.

Hellman, Lillian (1905–1984)

There are two Lillian Hellmans: one appears in the several biographies that have been written to date and the other appears in the very popular memoirs Hellman published in the last fifteen years of her life. The facts are that Hellman was born in New Orleans and at age six began spending half her year in that city and half in New York, where she lived with her parents on West Ninety-fifth Street. After spending two years at New York University, Hellman dropped out, worked for a time for the publisher Horace Liveright, and married the playwright and press agent Arthur Kober. That marriage ended in divorce. In the early thirties Hellman met the mystery novelist Dashiell Hammett in Hollywood, where she had gone to work on movie scripts. They established a liaison that lasted for the rest of his life. In 1934 Hellman's play *The Children's Hour* opened on Broadway. It was followed by what is today her most famous work, *The Little Foxes* (1939), and then her anti-Fascist play, *Watch on the Rhine*. Throughout the thirties she was a Communist who more or less toed the Stalinist line. Her plays were not only popular, they were made into movies, and Hellman made money during these years, enough to buy in 1944 a house at 63 East Eighty-second Street. During the era of Senator Joseph McCarthy, Hellman was called to Washington to testify before the House Un-American Activities Committee and proved to be a hostile witness. This led to her being blacklisted, in effect, and the fifties were a rough decade for her. She had to sell her country house and scramble for money, but she kept her New York home. In 1970 she sold this and moved to a co-op at 630 Park

Avenue, where she lived until her death. From the time she entered New York's literary life in the late twenties, Hellman moved in a wide circle and had a talent for making both friends and enemies. Dorothy Parker was a particularly close friend and Hellman became her executor. The other Hellman, the woman in the memoirs, reached print in 1969 when Hellman published *An Unfinished Woman* and was embellished in 1973 with the publication of *Pentimento*. Both of these books were very successful, especially the "Julia" chapter of *Pentimento,* which went on to become a movie starring Jane Fonda as Hellman. In 1980, on the *Dick Cavett Show,* Mary McCarthy, no admirer of Hellman's plays, described her as "overrated, a bad writer and dishonest writer." Cavatt wanted to know what was dishonest about her, and McCarthy replied, "Everything. I once said in some interview that every word she writes is a lie, including 'and' and 'the.'" Hellman saw the program and seems to have decided to sue McCarthy upon hearing her words. She duly filed a defamation suit against McCarthy for $2,250,000. Among those who urged Hellman not to persist in this was her friend Norman Mailer. She refused to be dissuaded and only her death brought the suit to an end. Hellman's action had an outcome she never could have intended. Challenges to her veracity came from several quarters. Hellman insisted that she had told the truth in her memoirs. Not so, wrote a number of writers, including Ernest Hemingway's ex-wife Martha Gellhorn and, most damaging of all, a woman named Muriel Gardiner Buttinger, who claimed Hellman's "Julia" was really her story. Buttinger presented a compelling case, and today it is clear that Hellman's memoirs are mostly fiction, persuasively written, but fiction. As to what motivated Hellman, several writers have had a field day drawing her psychological portrait and more will follow.

Helprin, Mark (b. 1947)

Helprin's *Winter's Tale* (1983) is the most original novel about New York by a writer of his generation. Set in a nineteen-century Manhattan that is equal parts history and myth, the book is a fairy tale in which large-scale forces of good and evil struggle. At least that is Helprin's intention, and while the novel is extremely long and at times labored and flat, he mostly achieves what one critic called "a visionary epic of New York City trying to free itself from crime and poverty." Helprin published short stories before this, *Ellis Island and Other Stories* (1981), followed by three well-received novels, *Refiner's Fire, A Soldier of the Great War,* and *Memoirs from Antproof Case.* In the spring of 1966

Helprin stepped up to a sort of fame that rarely comes the way of American novelists. For a decade he had been writing politically conservative columns for the *Wall Street Journal*. One of these caught Bob Dole's eye, which led to Helprin writing the speech Dole gave upon retiring from the Senate. This got such good press that Helprin was brought in to write Dole's speech accepting the Republican Party's 1996 presidential nomination. He did so, but things turned out badly. When the speech was turned over to a team for rewriting, Helprin quit in a huff, according to Dole's aides. To date Helprin has kept his side of the story to himself, which is unfortunate because during the months when he put words in Dole's mouth he spoke to the public like a novelist. On one television talk show he compared Dole with "the woman in the Dorothea Lange photograph" and to a rhinoceros.

Hemingway, Ernest (1899–1961)

Hemingway may really have meant it when he described literary New York as "a bottle full of tapeworms trying to feed on each other," but he enjoyed visiting the city if he didn't have to stay too long. Business brought him to Manhattan to meet with his editor, Maxwell Perkins, at Scribner's. In 1940 when he came to work on the galleys of *For Whom the Bell Tolls* he stayed at the Barclay, a hotel on 111 East Forty-eighth Street, a few blocks from Scribner's office. It has been written that Hemingway completed the book in a binge of ninety-six straight hours of work. The truth is much less dramatic as he had worked on the galleys in Cuba and on the train to New York. No doubt one of the reporters drawn to Hemingway, who was always good copy, originated this story. Late in 1949 he arrived in New York with the manuscript of *Across the River and into the Trees*. On this visit he stayed at the Sherry-Netherland at 781 Fifth Avenue and throughout his few days in the city "sat" for a profile written by the *New Yorker*'s ace reporter Lillain Ross. The result was seen by some as a clever and devastating attack on Hemingway, a judgment Ross dismissed in her introduction to the book publication of the piece, *Portrait of Ernest Hemingway* (1961). Yes, Hemingway talked movie Indian talk—"Book too much for him"; yes, Hemingway splurged on champagne and caviar; and yes, he called his friend Marlene Dietrich "the Kraut," but he was, as Ross pointed out, enjoying himself and she had seen no reason to present him otherwise. The profile makes good reading today, especially for Hemingway's tour of the Metropolitan Museum of Art, whose best picture was, in his opinion, El Greco's *View of Toledo*. In 1959, at the urging of his wife, Mary, Hemingway bought an apartment at 1 East Sixty-second Street. He called it "a safe place" but never spent much time there. Although the painter Thomas Hudson, hero of the posthumously published *Islands in the Stream,* visits New York, the city appears rarely in Hemingway's writing.

Henry, O. (1862–1910)

Most Americans know O. Henry only through the movies and television shows based on his stories. He is one of those popular writers that the academy has forbidden entry to its canon and dismissed as a lightweight sentimentalist. Guy Davenport's Penguin edition of *Selected Stories,* which convincingly presents O. Henry in a new light, is a corrective to this view. O. Henry was the pseudonym used by William Sydney Porter, who spent three years in the Ohio State Penitentiary. Davenport finds this the source of Porter's pen name: *OH* from Ohio and *enry* from Penitentiary. While working as a bank clerk in Texas, Porter was charged with embezzlement and fled to Central America to avoid trial. He returned to Texas, was arrested, tried, convicted, and sentenced to five years in prison. There were rumors at the time that Porter went to jail to shield someone else. The novelist Katherine Anne Porter claimed that she was a relative and knew for a fact that Porter had taken the money, $350, to pay doctor's bills. No one has corroborated her account. In prison Porter worked as a pharmacist and, having once worked on a newspaper, returned to writing and sent his stories to editors in New York. By the time he reached the city in 1902, he already had contacts and an audience. Until his death in 1910 his stories were staples in New York's magazines and newspapers. The city quickly laid claim on his imagination, and he invented the phrase "Baghdad-on-the-Subway," not simply to describe its wonders, but to suggest that the tales he spun were a contemporary Arabian Nights. During his New York years O. Henry lived mostly in hotels. He stayed at the Marty at 47 West Twenty-fourth Street when he got to town and later split his time between the Caledonia at 28 West Twenty-sixth Street and the Chelsea Hotel on Twenty-third Street. Only late in his life did he allow himself to be photographed, and he refused all but a few requests to be interviewed. After his death at the Caledonia, nine empty liquor bottles were found under his bed. In all, he published more than three hundred stories.

Herbst, Josephine (1897–1969)

Usually filed under "proletarian novelists," Herbst moved in wider circles than the category implies. It says something that Hilton Kramer is her executor and that one of her closer friends was John Cheever. She left a book of luminous memoirs, really four chapters of a book but no less beautifully written and evocative for that, *The Starched Blue Sky of Spain.* "In the early months of that year, John Herrmann and I were living in a penthouse on Lower Fifth Avenue," so begins her "Year of Disgrace," which presents the New York literary bohemia of the twenties in forty pages of lucidity and grace. When he edited the magazine *Noble Savage* Saul Bellow published two of the book's chapters. Harper and Row brought out the book in paperback and then quickly remaindered it. It is worth tracking down and so is Elinor Langer's 1983 biography of Herbst. You will discover a wonderful writer with a fresh view of the politics and literature of her time.

Highsmith, Patricia (1921–1994)

Highsmith grew up in Greenwich Village and graduated from Barnard, but she expatriated herself to Europe in the early 1950s and did most of her writing there. Her work has been buried in the mystery or suspense category. Anyone who reads *Strangers on a Train, The Talented Mr. Ripley,* or *Edith's Diary* will understand why Highsmith is put in these categories and by how much she outstrips them. But this entry is less about her work than about an aspect of New York City. In the prologue to the movie *The Naked City* and later to the television show by the same name, a voice intoned the words, "There are eight million stories in the naked city." In other words, everyone, even the seemingly insignificant among us, has one waiting to be told. While waiting for *Strangers on a Train,* her first novel, to be published, Highsmith took a Christmas job selling dolls in a department store. She worked less than three weeks in the job and her time there might have been unremarkable had she not waited on a blond woman who bought a doll. This woman encountered only that one time inspired Highsmith to write a novel about two lesbians in New York City, *The Price of Salt.* She published it under the pseudonym Claire Morgan. The novel sold well enough to be reprinted in paperback where it sold more than one million copies and brought Morgan/Highsmith a ton of fan mail. No one witnessing Highsmith's sale of the doll to that blond woman could have imagined the story that resulted from it. New York literary life is full of such incidents.

Hijuelos, Oscar (b. 1951)

Born in New York of Cuban parents, Hijuelos graduated from the City College of New York. His second novel, the Pulitzer Prize-winning *Mambo Kings Play Songs of Love* (1989), narrates the career of two Cuban brothers who become stars in New York during the mambo craze of the 1950s. Today he lives on the Upper East Side.

Himes, Chester (1909–1984)

Like O. Henry, Himes did time in the Ohio State Penitentiary. His crime was not embezzlement but armed robbery. After his release he spent time on the West Coast and then in Harlem before expatriating himself to France in 1953. There he wrote a series of detective novels for the French publisher Marcel Duhamel's *Série Noire*. These record the exploits of two black detectives, Ed "Coffin" Jones and "Grave Digger" Johnson. Because the movie did so well at the box office, *A Rage in Harlem* (1965) is probably the best known. The others, especially *Cotton Comes to Harlem* and *Come Back, Charleston Blue,* are worth tracking down. Harlem lowlife and grifters come alive in Himes's pages, and the attitudes in the novels are decidedly pre-political correctness.

Holmes, John Clellon (1926–1988)

Benét's Reader's Encyclopedia of American Literature describes Holmes's novel *Go* (1952) this way: "Though he obviously knew his characters first hand, he wrote about them objectively." It is this "objective" quality that sets Holmes's Beat novels apart and limits their appeal. He knew Kerouac, Ginsberg, and the Beat crowd, but he tells stories that he has heard. His books are the most conventional to come from the Beat generation, which is not to say they are without merit, but rather to distinguish them from Kerouac's for one. *Go* was originally titled *The Beat Generation* after the phrase had come up in a conversation between Holmes and Kerouac. When Holmes showed Kerouac the manuscript, it inspired Kerouac to tell the story "like it happened, all in a rush, the hell with these phony architectures." That book became *On the Road.* In 1952 it was Holmes's essay "This Is the Beat Generation" in the *New York Times Magazine* that introduced the generation to a wider public. His best book about those years is the collection of essays and memoirs, *Nothing More to Declare* (1967). Some enterprising publisher ought to bring it back into print. Holmes also wrote *The Horn* (1958), a novel that suffers from its "architectures."

Hone, Philip (1780–1851)

The son of a German immigrant, Hone had scant formal education before going into the auction business at sixteen with his brother. He made a fortune that allowed him to take his place in New York society and politics. In 1825 Hone served a one-year term as mayor during which, accompanied by the Marquis de Lafayette, he opened the Erie Canal. The following year Hone began the diary that he kept until his death. It has never been published in its entirety, but all twenty-eight quarto volumes of the manuscript are in the New–York Historical Society Library. The novelist and New Yorker Louis Auchincloss edited excerpts from Hone's diary and in introducing them wrote: "Hone may have been the last man able to know personally everyone of importance in the United States. Presidents, congressmen, governors, mayors, writers, merchants, educators, scientists, actors, doctors and lawyers—all grist for the ever-grinding mill of his insatiable diary." In its pages Hone chronicled the horrendous fire of 1835 that reduced six hundred of New York's stores to ashes and the panic of 1837 in which Hone took such heavy losses that he was forced to return to work. Politics, social life, the visit of Black Hawk, chief of the Sauk and Fox, Charles Dickens's first lecture tour, dinner at John Jacob Astor's, and the Astor Place riot occasioned by the rivalry of the actors, the Englishman William Charles Macready and the American Edwin Forrest, came under Hone's gaze. The other great New York diarist of the nineteenth century, George Templeton Strong, noted Hone's death on 5 May 1851.

Horace Mann School
231 West 246th Street

Mann was a Bostonian, a legislator, and an educator who improved public schools in Massachusetts before becoming the first president of Ohio's Antioch College. The school that bears his name originally prepared students for Columbia University and was located in the university's Teachers College at 120th Street. William Carlos Williams went there as did Morris Ernst, the lawyer who successfully argued the case that lifted this country's ban on James Joyce's *Ulysses*. In the 1920s the school moved to its present address in the Riverdale section of the Bronx. Before Jack Kerouac entered Columbia in 1940, he spent a postgraduate year at Horace Mann, where he played football. The novelist James Salter, then James Horowitz, the songwriter and mathematician Tom Lehrer, and the cofounder of the Living Theater Julian Beck were in school around the same time. The poet Anthony Hecht, columnist

Anthony Lewis, and Ira Levin, author of *Rosemary's Baby,* also attended Horace Mann. Like Williams before him, the poet August Kleinzahler commuted to the school from New Jersey.

House of Genius
61 Washington Square

Katherine Blanchard ran a boardinghouse at this address where the writers Frank Norris, Alan Seeger, Willa Cather, O. Henry, Stephen Crane, Eugene O'Neill, Theodore Dreiser, John Reed, Lincoln Steffens, and John Dos Passos are said to have lived. Alas, though there is evidence that Frank Norris and the poet and New York native Seeger did have rooms at Mme. Blanchard's, it is not known for certain that any of the others did. Willa Cather lived next door at 60 Washington Square, and Crane, O'Neill, Dreiser, Reed, Steffens, and Dos Passos did live around the square but not at number 61. At some point the desire for a good anecdote concentrated all of them at the same address.

Howard, Richard (b. 1929)

This graduate of Columbia and the Sorbonne has translated more than two hundred books from the French. It is said that he is so fluent a translator that he dictates the English while reading the original. If you have read Roland Barthes, Alain Robbe-Grillet, André Gide, or a host of others you have read the work of Richard Howard. He is also a poet of note, having won a Pulitzer Prize in 1966 for *Untitled Subjects.* He brought these gifts to bear in translating Charles Baudelaire's *Flowers of Evil,* which in addition appeared decorated with myriad beautiful calla lilies courtesy of the artist Michael Mazur. Recently, Howard began a translation of Marcel Proust's *Remembrance of Things Past,* only to abandon the enterprise when he realized how much time it would take. He has lived in the Village for many years.

Howe, Irving (1920–1993)

A native New Yorker, Howe grew up in a poor Jewish neighborhood in the east Bronx and attended City College of New York in the thirties, when the campus was alive with political ferment. Howe briefly became a Trotskyite but later abandoned communism for democratic socialism. Throughout his career he wrote about politics as well as literature, and in 1954 he launched *Dissent* magazine, which is still going today. After some years outside the city, he returned in 1963 to teach at Hunter College, where he remained until 1989. Howe's signal contribution to literary New York is his 1976 book, *World of Our Fathers: The Journey of the East European Jews to America and the Life They Found and Made*. It is that rare combination, a scholarly page-turner. It is indispensable and, best of all, a pleasure to read. For many years Howe lived on Riverside Drive, where he wrote the essays and book reviews that were not afraid to take a stand and give offense.

Howells, William Dean (1837–1920)

Two decisions Howells made in the early 1880s have come to be seen as crucial to New York's becoming America's preeminent literary center. In 1881 Howells resigned as the editor of Boston's *Atlantic Monthly* to devote himself to his own work. In 1885 he accepted Harper and Brothers' offer to supply the New York publisher a book a year and write a monthly column, "The Editor's Easy Chair," for which Howells would be paid the unprecedented sum of three thousand dollars a year. In all, the contract guaranteed him ten thousand dollars a year. The decline of Boston and rise of New York are not so simply explained, but after Howells removed himself, Boston was not to have a resident writer of the first rank until Robert Lowell lived there in the 1950s. It cannot be said that the restless Howells settled in New York, for after 1885 he and his wife became, in the words of his biographer, Kenneth S. Lynn, "gipsies for the rest of their lives." Among their New York addresses were the Chelsea Hotel, which Howells found too expensive, and two apartments on East Seventeenth Street near Stuyvesant Square within walking distance of the Harper office on Franklin Square. It was at 330 East Seventeenth Street that Howells wrote his New York novel, *A Hazard of New Fortunes*. Like Basil March, the novel's hero, Howells had come from Boston to New York to edit a magazine, and like March he was ambivalent about the city. He knew he wanted to get "its vast, gay, shapeless life into fiction," as he wrote Henry James, but New York's "frantic panorama" and the ton of work he had to do to satisfy his Harper's contract weighed heavily on Howells. Influenced by Tolstoy, he had begun to speak out against social injustice, as few American writers of his stature did at the time. He was alone in his public plea for executive clemency in the case of the anarchists convicted of murder, Howells thought unjustly, in Chicago's Haymarket riots. Eventually Howells let his Harper's contract expire, but he was again to occupy "The Editor's Easy Chair" at the beginning of the twentieth century. Sadly, this came at a moment when the realistic novelists he had championed, Stephen Crane and Frank Norris first among them, had been silenced by death and disease. In his last years Howells became an establishment figure. The American Academy of Arts and Letters elected him its first president in 1908, and in 1915 the Academy gave its first Howells Medal for fiction to Howells himself. He died in New York at the Hotel St. Hubert, 120 West Fifty-seventh Street, where he had spent the last decade of his life. Unlike his close friends Henry James and Mark Twain and any number of writers he had championed, not only did Howells's reputation decline after his death but an aspect of his work became so overblown that in 1960 the critic Leslie Fiedler could characterize his fiction as "resolutely cheerful, sane and progressive." While his Boston novel, *The Rise of Silas Lapham,* and his New York novel, *A Hazard of New Fortunes,* are not condemnations of the American Dream, they are uneasy about it to a degree no one could guess from Fiedler's words. The journalism in which Howells railed against American imperialism, the Philippines being his case in point, and spoke out for the work of Zola, Tolstoy, and Ibsen is a matter of record. But he produced an enormous amount of writing with such facility that this led to indifference, if not distrust. It is unfortunate if these attitudes discourage readers. Howells's fiction is essential to an understanding of the last three decades of the nineteenth century, years when the mighty engine the United States became got built.

Hughes, Langston (1902–1967)

Harlem

What happens to a dream deferred?

Does it dry up
like a raisin in the sun?
Or fester like a sore—
And then run?
Does it stink like rotten meat?
Or crust and sugar over—
like a syrupy sweet?

Maybe it just sags
like a heavy load.

Or does it explode?

Hughes came to New York in 1921 after attending seven schools in several different cities and graduating from high school in Cleveland. He lived at the 135th Street Y while spending a freshman year at Columbia, but he dropped out and began to travel. In 1925 he was a busboy in Washington, D.C., where Alain Locke published his work in the *New Negro*. Back in New York he met Carl Van Vechten, who brought his work to the attention of Alfred Knopf. *The Weary Blues* appeared in 1926, the same year Hughes returned to college at Lincoln University in Pennsylvania. Frequent visits helped him maintain close ties in Harlem, but during the thirties he traveled widely and visited both Russia and Spain during the Civil War. He became a Marxist and published poems and plays in *New Masses*. When he did return to New York he stayed in rooming houses and did not have a permanent residence there until 1942 when he took a studio apartment at 141st Street. He lived there until 1947, taking his meals with an adopted aunt and uncle, the Harpers, who lived nearby at 634 St. Nicholas Avenue. In 1948 Hughes moved with them to a three-story brownstone at 20 East 127th Street. During the Harlem Renaissance Hughes was close to Countee Cullen, Alain Locke, and Zora Neale Hurston, but his friendship with Cullen ended, in part because of Locke's interference, and his working relationship with Hurston ended acrimoniously, also with Locke playing a role. Of all the writers active in the Renaissance, Hughes was the best known after things cooled down in the early thirties. In 1938 he founded the Harlem Suitcase Theater on 125th Street, and he was justly referred to as Harlem's poet laureate. Arnold Rampersand has given us a big biography of Hughes, and not only is his poetry well known today but many of its readers regard it with genuine affection.

Huncke, Herbert (1915–1996)

Huncke the Junkie! "Huncke is always the same," wrote his friend Jack Kerouac, "but let him start to tell you stories sometime—he is the greatest storyteller I know, an actual genius at it, in my mind." In Kerouac's *On the Road* he is Elmo Hassel. Born in Greenfield, Massachusetts, Huncke grew up in Chicago, where he began using drugs at the age of twelve and broke into the world of crime as a runner for Al Capone's gang. For years he drifted around the country, sometimes supporting himself as a male prostitute. He did admit that his tendency to fall in love kept him from making a great deal of money at it. In 1940 he landed in Times Square and discovered home. Four years later he met Burroughs, whom he originally took for an FBI agent, and through him Allen Ginsberg and Kerouac. Huncke is said to have introduced the word "beat" to his friends, and the rest is an extraordinarily well-documented story. During those years Huncke held court at the Angle

Bar on Forty-second Street and Eighth Avenue. When the sex researcher Dr. Alfred Kinsey of the *Kinsey Report* worked Times Square bars in 1946 in search of subjects to interview he discovered Huncke, who gave him an earful and then introduced him to Ginsberg and others. Whereas the focus for his friends became writing, for Huncke it was "junk, junk, junk." This meant a little petty crime and a life of waiting for his connection and for someone to drop by that he could put the touch on for a few bucks. He was constitutionally incapable of holding a steady job and proud of it. In 1990 he published his autobiography, *Guilty Pleasure.* Those who saw his powder-white, living death mask of a face will never forget it. He truly looked like death warmed over.

Hurston, Zora Neale (1891–1960)

When she died in her hometown of Eatonville, Florida, Hurston was buried in potter's field. Her books were out of print, and her last years had been shadowed by totally untrue accusations of child abuse. Today, Hurston's work has been put back into print by the Library of America, and thanks to the novelist Alice Walker there is a stone over her grave bearing the epitaph "A Genius of the South." Of all the writers active in the Harlem Renaissance, Hurston is as extraordinary as her work is original. She left Eatonville, the first black incorporated town in America, in her teens and found her way to Howard University, where she encountered Alain Locke, who glimpsed talent in her. He passed her name along to Charles S. Johnson, editor of the magazine *Opportunity,* and Johnson suggested she come to New York. *Opportunity* held award dinners that had become important social occasions. Hurston shone at these and met the popular novelist Fannie Hurst, whose chauffeur and secretary she became, and in whose East Sixty-seventh Street house she lived while attending Barnard on scholarship. She was the school's only black student, "a sacred black cow," as she described herself. When Hurston took courses with the anthropologist Franz Boas, she glimpsed her future work. For his part, Boas saw that Hurston's Eatonville background and natural interest in anthropology equipped her to collect black folklore. In 1927, supported by Mrs. Charlotte Osgood Mason, the "godmother" of the Renaissance, Hurston went south for two years to begin the work that began to bear fruit in the thirties. Returning to Harlem, she was one of the scene's luminaries, a charming, sometimes crude, funny, naive life of the party admired by Carl Van Vechten, Langston Hughes, and others for the stories she told and her inventive tongue. It was Hurston who coined the word *bodacious* and the terms

Niggerati and *Negrotarian*. But Hurston never had an easy time of it. She broke with Langston Hughes over who wrote what in their collaboration, the dramatic comedy *Mule-Bone*. Mason's patronage seemed to stifle her, and it was only after it ended in 1932 that Hurston began to publish books, five in all during the mid-thirties, including her masterpiece, *Their Eyes Were Watching God* (1937), and her collection of folktales, *Mules and Men* (1935). In the forties she published two more books, the second coinciding with the accusation that she had had sexual relations with a ten-year-old boy. Hurston's innocence did not prevent her from sinking into a depression that precipitated a steady decline. Beginning in the early 1970s her work began to be rediscovered. It is now clear that in telling the tale of her people Hurston rescued a world that might otherwise have been lost to us.

I

Irving, Washington (1783–1859)

America's first man of letters and the most highly paid writer of his generation, Irving was born at 131 William Street. His mother named him after George Washington, who, upon encountering the young Irving and his nanny in the street, was induced by the nanny to give Irving his blessing. At the end of his life Irving repaid the kindness by writing a biography of Washington. Instead of attending Columbia, as two of his brothers did, Irving learned the law at a lawyer's office. He is the first in a long line of New York writer-lawyers. Irving began to publish under the pseudonym Jonathan Oldstyle, Gent. (he went on to use many others) in 1802 and that year traveled to Europe for the first time. Returning, he hung out a shingle at 3 Wall Street, but it is unclear that he had any clients. As a lawyer he was more a power broker than a practicing attorney. With his brother William and the writer James Kirke Paulding, Irving wrote the humorous journal entries that appeared serially throughout 1807 and were collected as *Salmagundi; or, The Whim-Whams and Opinions of Launcelot Wangstaff, Esq. and Others*. In its pages is the first use of the word *Gotham* to describe New York City, a nickname still in use today. Irving, who had a sense of humor, must have known that there was a Gotham in England, a village whose inhabitants, according to legend, feigned stupidity so as to make the place unattractive to King John, who wanted to live there. In 1809 Irving published his most popular work, *A History of New York,* under the pseudonym Diedrich Knickerbocker. The name has a tale attached to it. Wanting to create a "real" Knickerbocker, Irving and his friends Paulding and Henry Brevoort pulled off a hoax. The *New York Post* published an item saying that an elderly gentleman named Knickerbocker had left his lodgings some time since and had not returned. Ten days later the landlord published a notice to the effect that "a very curious kind of written book" had been found in one Diedrich Knickerbocker's room and would be auctioned off to pay his outstanding bill. The finale came in a newspaper advertisement announcing the disappearance of *A History of New York,* "found in the chamber of Dr. Diedrich Knickerbocker, the old gentleman whose sudden and mysterious disappearance has been noticed." This book made Irving a celebrity and earned him two thousand dollars, an unheard-of sum at the time. Following the War of 1812 Irving, a lifelong bachelor, went to Europe, where he spent the next seventeen years traveling in England, Germany, and Spain. Irving's *Sketchbook of Geoffrey Crayon, Gent.,* appeared in America in 1819. It contains the stories "Rip Van Winkle" and "The Legend of Sleepy Hollow" by which Irving is best known today. Actually, these stories are more than mere literature. They long ago entered American folklore, and many who know them will have no idea that they are the invention of one author. Irving finished his European sojourn in Spain, where he wrote a biography of Christopher Columbus. Back in the States, he continued his restless travels, used his influence in Washington on several matters, got handsomely paid by John Jacob Astor for a history of Astor's fur trading empire, fell in and out with the New York politician later to be president of the United States, Martin Van Buren, hailed the appearance of Poe's story "William Wilson," and, in 1842, was appointed minister to Spain, a post he held for the next four years. Over the last decade of his life Irving remained in America working on his biography of George Washington as his health deteriorated. He spent most of his time at Sunnyside in the New York suburb of Tarrytown. When he came to the city he often stayed with his nephew John Treat Irving Jr. at his home in Gramercy Park, 46 East Twenty-first Street.

Irving was the most celebrated American writer of his day, rivaled only by James Fenimore Cooper and Ralph Waldo Emerson. The range of his associations—he knew Sir Walter Scott, Thackeray, and Dickens, as well as most of the American presidents of his time; he wrote to Hawthorne praising his work, and Melville read *Typee* to him—is breathtaking and a reminder of how small a country the United States was then and how intimate the worlds of literature and politics were. Today, Irving is one of those writers who is, with the two exceptions cited above, embalmed in his time, and yet when Spike Lee takes his seat at New York Knickerbocker basketball games he cheers for a team named after an Irving creation.

J

Jacobs, Jane (b. 1916)

On the cover of the Modern Library's new edition of Jacobs's *Life and Death of Great American Cities* (1961) is a photograph of Jacobs in the White Horse Tavern. The White Horse plays a small role in the book that remains as visionary today as when it was first published. Essentially, Jacobs argues for mixed use, meaning that cities ought not to organize themselves into industrial, residential, business, and entertainment districts. They should be anarchic and, like her own West Village neighborhood, mix light industry, residences, bars and clubs, and small businesses so that there is always life on the streets. In her New York years—she has lived in Toronto, Canada, for some time—Jacobs fought the good fight against Robert Moses and the almighty automobile. It is thanks in part to her that a major highway does not run from the West Village to the East River. In 1969 her love affair with New York ended abruptly, and she decamped for Toronto, a city she had described as "the most hopeful and healthy city in North America." Jacobs lives there today.

James, Henry (1843–1916)

Of all the great New York writers of the nineteenth century, James spent the least amount of time in the city. He was born at 21 Washington Place, now the site of New York University's main building, and he could have had no memories of the house, for in that year his wealthy father took the family to Europe, not to return to the city until 1847. For the next eight years the Jameses lived at 58 West Fourteenth Street, a house that was visited by Horace Greeley, William Cullen Bryant, Bronson Alcott, and Ralph Waldo Emerson. But the house more closely associated with Henry was that of his grandmother Walsh at 19 Washington Square North. It is standing today. James must have been remem-

bering this house when he set his New York novel, *Washington Square,*
there in "the ideal of quiet and genteel retirement in 1835." The seed
from which came was not from James's New York years, but from an
anecdote told to him by his great friend the English actress Fanny Kemble. He published *Washington Square* in 1881, by which time he had
been out of the city for twenty-six years, or since he was twelve. It is an
upside-down fairy tale in which Prince Charming is a fortune hunter,
the fairy godmother is a "goose," the evil stepmother is the heroine
Catherine Sloper's father, and the heroine lives unhappily ever after. It is
a cruel comedy of manners with money at its heart. Between 1855 and
his death in 1916, James came infrequently to the city. In 1875 he
stayed six months at 111 East Twenty-fifth Street, experimenting to see
if he wanted to return to New York permanently, but he determined
that the city might turn him into a hack and returned to England. On
most of his visits to the city he stopped at the home of Edith Wharton's
sister Mary Cadwalader Jones at 21 East Eleventh Street. Minnie Jones
had something of a salon where she entertained Brooks and Henry
Adams, Theodore Roosevelt, the sculptor Augustus Saint-Gaudens,
and the painter John Singer Sargent. It was to this house that James
came in 1904 after an absence from New York of twenty-four years. On
that trip he explored a good deal of the city, including the Jewish ghetto
of the Lower East Side. He left his impressions in his book *The American Scene* (1907). James remembered his native city late in his life and
wanted to be remembered as its son when he collected his work into
"The New York Edition." It is the definitive version of everything he
wanted preserved. *Washington Square* remains one of the essential
novels of New York.

Johnson, James Weldon (1871–1938)

By the time the Harlem Renaissance began in the 1920s Johnson had
been successful in a variety of careers: newspaperman, lawyer (the first
black man to be accepted by the Florida bar), writer of popular songs,
American consul to Venezuela (he wrote Theodore Roosevelt's campaign song, "You're All Right, Teddy," and Teddy appointed him), and
author of the anonymously published *Autobiography of an Ex-Colored
Man* (1912). In 1920 he became the executive secretary of the National
Association for the Advancement of Colored People (NAACP), a position he held until 1930. Johnson had arrived in New York at the turn of
the century and worked as a songwriter with his brother John Rosa-
mond and the composer Bob Cole, turning out more than two hundred

songs including "Under the Bamboo Tree." He lived at the Marshall Club at 260 West Fifty-third Street, a hangout for black writers, artists, and musicians. Latin America took him out of the city between 1906 and 1913. When he returned he edited the newspaper *New York Age,* wrote poems, and began working for the NAACP. By the time the Harlem Renaissance was in full swing, Johnson, who lived at several Harlem addresses, had become something of an establishment figure and a connection between the uptown Renaissance and downtown whites. During the twenties he edited two important anthologies, *The Book of American Negro Poetry* and the best-selling *Book of American Negro Spirituals.* In 1930, as the Depression began to erode the Renaissance, Johnson published *Black Manhattan.* Although he did not intend it as such, the book became a valediction to the black energy, fueled by migrations from the South, that had made Harlem black and created the New Negro and the Renaissance itself.

Johnson, Joyce (b. 1935)

For a few years around the time *On the Road* (1957) appeared, Jack Kerouac and Johnson, then Joyce Glassman, were lovers. They met in a Howard Johnson's on Eighth Street, Kerouac having called Glassman after he got her number from Allen Ginsberg, whom she knew slightly. She had attended Barnard and now worked for a publisher while writing her first novel. Kerouac had just come back from Mexico and was about to set out again. He was also about to become famous, which made him even more restless. Johnson tells their story and much else about the Beats she knew in her memoir, *Minor Characters.* The book also deals most affectingly with her struggles to find her place as a woman and writer in what was decidedly a man's world. It is one of the few books by a woman associated with the Beats and has been in print since it appeared in 1983. Johnson went on to publish novels and *What Lisa Knew* (1990), an account of the grisly Steinberg murder case.

Jones, Hettie (b. 1934)

Hettie Cohen met LeRoi Jones (now IMAMU AMIRI BARAKA) when they worked together on the *Record Changer,* a small jazz magazine, on Morton Street in the Village. They fell in love, married, and for a decade starting in the mid-fifties had a series of apartments that became meeting places for their poet friends. The first was in Chelsea at 402 West Twentieth Street and has six large rooms Here the Joneses began the poetry magazine *Yugen* and Totem Press. Their tastes cut across the various schools, Black Mountain and New York, and ranged over much of the poetry that appeared in Donald Allen's *New American Poetry* anthology. At their parties one could find Gilbert Sorrentino and Hubert Selby from Brooklyn, Frank O'Hara, Allen Ginsberg, Jack Kerouac, Joel Oppenheimer, and visiting firemen like Ed Dorn and Robert Creeley. Their next place was at 324 East Fourteenth Street. Again it was large and cheap, fifty dollars a month, and became headquarters for the various poets then turning American poetry on its ear. As their marriage began to deteriorate the Joneses moved to 27 Cooper Square. They had nearly split apart when on February 21, 1965, while they were drinking champagne at a party to celebrate the reopened Eighth Street Bookshop, word came that Malcolm X had been gunned down in Harlem. Almost immediately Jones moved uptown, leaving Hettie behind. She tells the story of their marriage in detail in her memoir, *How I Became Hettie Jones*. Along with her friend Joyce Johnson's memoir, *Minor Characters,* it is what we have to date of the woman's side of New York's downtown literary bohemia in the fifties. Jones is especially good on the complications surrounding and impinging upon her having married a black man.

Jones, LeRoi (b. 1934)

Although he has been AMIRI BARAKA since 1965, it was as LeRoi Jones that he was one of the most animating presences on the downtown literary, theater, and jazz scenes. When he came to the Village after growing up in Newark, New Jersey, attending Howard University in Washington, D.C., and completing a tour in the air force, Jones later remembered that "suddenly I *was* free"—free to be a poet, and to move in the art world in which he wanted to make his place. The addresses he lived at are the same as those for his wife at that time, Hettie Jones, whose entry precedes this one. Beginning with the launching of their little magazine *Yugen* and Totem Press, the Joneses drew poets to their apartments, which became gathering places where many famous parties were held. Jones himself was as active and respected as a poet as he was in any of his other roles. Grove Press became his publisher, and he began to write plays, *Dutchman* being the most prominent. Of course, Jones knew that he was one of the few black men on the scene and the only black poet to appear in Donald Allen's anthology *The New American Poetry*. As Baraka he dealt with this in *The Autobiography of LeRoi Jones*. When he and his wife moved to 27 Cooper Square, their last address together, Jones plunged even deeper into the world of music, both by going to clubs and in his writing. He frequented the Half Note on Hudson and Spring Streets and the 5 Spot across from his apartment. One night outside the latter he and the bass player Charles Mingus scuffled. In 1963 Jones wrote *Blues People* and taught from the book at the New School. Malcolm X's murder in 1965 galvanized Jones into leaving the Village for Harlem, cutting himself off from white poet-friends like Frank O'Hara, John Wieners, and Ed Dorn and becoming a black nationalist. As Baraka he continued to make things happen. In Harlem at 146 West 130th Street he founded the Black Arts Repertory Theater School, which is now defunct. In the thirty years since he transformed his life Baraka has made his peace with many of the white poets whose world he once turned his back on. His journey from Newark to the Village to Harlem and back to Newark has obviously been an extremely complex one on several levels. In his Village years he distinguished himself by his generosity to fellow poets and enthusiasm for the art. To many he made a great deal of difference. *Transbluesency (1961–1995)* is his selected poems.

Kael, Pauline (b. 1919)

Kael came from the Bay Area to review movies for the *New Yorker* in the sixties. She possessed an instinctive understanding of the rich vulgarity of movies, their *Kiss Kiss Bang Bang,* as she titled one of her books. Her forceful reviews praised those directors and actors who had, in her words, "true movie-making fever." She communicated this fever to a generation of readers who came to feel they had not seen the movie until they read Kael's review. Her review of Bernardo Bertolucci's *Last Tango in Paris* remains the standard of over-the-top criticism. Kael periodically collected these reviews into books, and also wrote a book about *Citizen Kane.* With her accustomed passion she argues that the screenwriter Herman Mankiewicz was the movie's true auteur and not director Orson Welles. Kael retired from the *New Yorker* in 1991, but thumbnail versions of her reviews still appear in the magazine. Her swagger and colloquial directness, and the joy with which she sank her teeth into her subject, influenced a generation of journalists who write about movies, dance, music, and sports in New York.

Kazan, Elia (b. 1909)

A Greek born in Istanbul when it was still called Constantinople, Kazan emigrated to New York with his parents in 1913. He was active in the Group Theater as an actor and director, and it was there that he picked up the nickname "Gadge," from gadget, for his ability to fix things. Kazan got to Broadway in the forties, where he directed Thornton Wilder's *The Skin of Our Teeth,* Arthur Miller's *Death of a Salesman,* and, in his most famous collaboration, Tennessee Williams's *Streetcar Named Desire* (1947), starring Marlon Brando. The first movie Kazan directed was *A Tree Grows in Brooklyn.* He is probably best known for *On the Waterfront,* which starred Brando and had a script by the novelist Budd Schulberg. Kazan also directed the movie made from John Steinbeck's *East of Eden.* In the sixties movies and theater paled for Kazan, and he began to publish novels, beginning with the autobiographical *America, America* and followed by several others. In 1988 he published his autobiography, *A Life.*

Kazin, Alfred (b. 1915)

No other writer of his generation has written about New York so often, so deeply, or so well as Kazin, and it is probably also true that no other reader of his generation has so assiduously read the novels and poetry written in and about New York. Kazin grew up on Sutter Avenue in Brooklyn's Brownsville section, from which Manhattan seemed as far away and exotic as Paris. While living at 91 Pineapple Street in Brooklyn Heights in the late forties, Kazin wrote of his Brownsville youth in his first book of New York memoirs, *A Walker in the City.* All of Kazin's memoirs, essays, journal entries, and reviews that have dealt with New York essentially have a walker's intimacy with his city. In 1935 Kazin graduated from City College and went out to make his way as a writer in the middle of the Depression. He got started by sitting in editors' waiting rooms in the hopes of being given books to review. Malcolm Cowley of the *New Republic* proved to be the most helpful of editors, and in *Starting Out in the Thirties* (1965) Kazin describes those years and his relationship with Cowley. In 1938 Kazin enrolled at Columbia, where he not only earned an M.A. but became inspired by the historian Carl Van Doren to write his first book, *On Native Grounds: An Interpretation of Modern American Prose Literature* (1942). He did most of his reading for this book in the great reading room of the New York Public Library's main branch at Forty-second Street. Throughout much of his career while Kazin has taught at New York University,

Hunter, and City College, among other schools, he has been a freelance intellectual, and, in the words of Edmund Wilson, who was one himself, a "metropolitan critic." This not only means a person who lives and writes in the city, but one who draws energy and ideas, a sense of how the world works, from life in the city. Kazin has held editorial positions at *Fortune* and *American Scholar* and written for nearly every major New York literary journal from *Partisan Review* to the *New Yorker*. In 1978 he published the third chapter of his autobiography, *New York Jew*, covering many of the years in which he had been a working New York intellectual and writer living on West End Avenue. With the photographer David Finn, Kazin published *Our New York* in 1989. It has several long sections on writers, focusing on Truman Capote, Norman Mailer, Isaac Bashevis Singer, and James Baldwin. There are also several insightful pages on New York writers in his *Writer's America: Landscapes in Literature*. In these he decries the city's indifference to its writers. The city leaders have recently begun a campaign to place commemorative plaques on several buildings where important writers have lived, but as with so much else in the city, literature tends to get lost in all the living that takes place. Recently, Kazin has published excerpts from his journals and a short memoir of his early writing life. At this writing he remains active as a writer and as a professor of the City University of New York Graduate School, and one hopes he possesses the desire and stamina to add a final chapter to his autobiography.

This entry errs somewhat in its narrow focus. Kazin's books, and his published journals, reveal just how wide the range of his attention has been. He knew a good many of the New York School of painters, and has not by any means kept his nose in a book throughout his career. Throughout Kazin's work there runs a sensitivity to the city's streets, buildings, and people. *Our New York* begins with a Henry James quote from *The American Scene*. Kazin may well have chosen it because in James's words on New York he sees his own attitude expressed: "The subject was everywhere—that was the beauty, that was the advantage; it was thrilling, really, to find oneself in the presence of a theme to which everything directly contributed, leaving no touch of experience irrelevant."

Keene, Donald (b. 1922)

Several years ago a Japanese television crew traveled to northern Vermont, where Donald Keene was vacationing, to film an interview with him. As the principal translator of Japanese fiction and literature into

English since World War II, Keene is a renowned figure in Japan. Here he suffers the fate of most translators, and his name does not appear in literary reference books or guides. This neglect cannot diminish his stunning achievements. He has given Americans the novels of Osamu Dazai, the anthologies of Japanese literature published by Grove, his selections from Japanese diaries, and other translations too numerous to mention. He also has opened postwar Japan to Americans through his scholarly articles and mainstream essays about Japan life and culture. For many years he taught Japanese language and literature at Columbia, where he received his education.

Kerouac, Jack (1922–1969)

Kerouac came to New York a football hero for a year of postgraduate work at Horace Mann before entering Columbia in 1940 on an athletic scholarship. He had starred at halfback while in high school in the mill town of Lowell, Massachusctts, catching the attention of Columbia's legendary coach, Lou Little. But a broken leg ended Kerouac's first year in football, and when he tried to resume play his heart wasn't in it. He stayed part of three years at Columbia, a time in which he discovered he did not want to follow the conventional path the university presented him but rather would be a writer. In 1944 the Beat Generation came together. Kerouac met Lucien Carr at the West End Bar on West 113th Street, and then he met Allen Ginsberg, like Carr a Columbia student, and William Burroughs. Over the next several years the Beats, with Herbert Huncke and Neal Cassady added to the company, had the adventures in New York and on the road that Kerouac, "The Great Rememberer," as his friend the novelist John Clellon Holmes called him, spent his writing life transforming into fiction as if he were a bohemian Proust. Between 1946 and 1948 Kerouac wrote his first novel, *The Town and the City*, in his mother's Ozone Park, Queens, apartment. This is not only the most conventional of Kerouac's novels and the first to be published, but also the first book by any of his group to see print. Harcourt Brace was the publisher and Robert Giroux the book's editor. When the book appeared in 1950 Kerouac posed for his author photograph dressed in a suit, very uncomfortable at the prospect of having to be in the public eye. This discomfort was to plague him throughout his writing life. Kerouac became the first Beat celebrity, not just because *On the Road* became a hit novel, but because of his dark good looks. He looked the part of a romantic bohemian writer, and while he was eager enough for literary success, he turned out to be much more fragile than Burroughs or Ginsberg, who would also partake of it. Like the painter Jackson Pollock, Kerouac froze in the glare of publicity as if he were a deer caught in the headlights of an oncoming car. Kerouac wrote *On the Road* in three weeks in an apartment at 454 West Twentieth Street. Reliable sources indicate that he wrote it in Lucien Carr's loft at 149 West Twenty-first Street. Carr did provide Kerouac with the scroll of teletype paper on which he wrote, but it was at the former address, where Kerouac lived with his wife, Joan, that he did the actual writing. The cause for the confusion may be Kerouac's desire to subsequently forget that he ever had a wife. In any case, he stoked himself on Benzedrine inhalers and the cups of coffee his wife brought him while he sweated through one T-shirt after another, and in three weeks he had a 120-yard-long novel totaling 186,000 words. Several months later, after hearing alto saxophonist Lee Konitz, Kerouac opened up the novel and added some "spontaneous bop" transitions inspired by listening to Konitz improvise. *On the Road* went the rounds of New York publishers until Viking finally published it, with Malcolm Cowley, a bohemian of another era, as its not always friendly editor. Kerouac's novel *The Subterraneans* also had its genesis in New York. In 1953 at Allen Ginsberg's East Seventh Street apartment Kerouac met the young woman who would become Mardou Fox in the novel. They lived briefly in "Paradise Alley," now a parking lot, at 501 East Eleventh Street. In writing of this adventure, Kerouac transposed the events to San Francisco and placed the apartment on Heavenly Lane. Beginning in the early fifties and lasting until 1963, Kerouac's mother lived at 94-21 134th Street in Queens. He actually wrote *The Subterraneans* at her apartment, and over the years returned to her when he needed the solace that his work demanded. It is not where most expected to find the King of the Beats, but Kerouac was a dedicated writer who needed quiet and respite, home cooking, away from the world into which he had thrown himself in search of both kicks and enlightenment. New York has a wondrous glow in his books, and the charge of a boy's first encounter never really dims no matter the sadness Kerouac encountered in the city. His prose has the exhilaration you can hear in a Charlie Parker solo, and his New York is as beautiful as the "big glazed cakes and creampuffs" Dean Moriarity and his girl, Marylou, eat at Hector's Cafeteria when they first arrive in the city.

Kerouac, Jan (1952–1996)

The only child of Jack Kerouac, Jan saw her father twice, once at age nine and again at fifteen. She was born to Kerouac's second wife, Joan Haverty, and her parents were estranged at the time of her birth. Jack Kerouac denied being her father. Indeed, he battled her mother in court until he took a blood test and when the results came in acknowledged that he was Jan's father. She went on to become a novelist, publishing her first novel, *Baby Driver* (1981), which dealt with her adventures on the Lower East Side during the hippie sixties. Over the last few years of her life, she sought to wrest control of her father's archives from the Sampas family, relatives of her father's last wife, Stella. She died of kidney failure before the case she brought could go to trial.

Jack Kerouac was not the only absentee father among the core of the Beat Generation. William Burroughs's son, Billy, also a novelist, suffered years of neglect. Billy followed in his father's footsteps, not only as a writer but also a drug addict, and he died in his early thirties. Lucien Carr's two sons somehow survived a volatile upbringing and are now active in New York. One of them is a painter, and the other, Caleb, wrote the best-selling novel *The Alienist*. Neither Herbert Huncke nor Allen Ginsberg had children. In a recent *New York Times* profile of several of the children of Beat Generation luminaries, Ginsberg came across as more caring than most of the parents.

Kinnell, Galway (b. 1927)

A poet laureate of Vermont, Pulitzer and MacArthur Award winner, Kinnell has long taught at New York University. This emphasizes the success he most certainly is, but the poems he has written about New York tend to concentrate on the areas of the city where "the great and wondrous sun will be shining / On an old spider wrapping a fly in spittle-strings." It is not exactly the underside that activates Kinnell's imagination, but the out-of-the-way and overlooked and the man in the street. In 1974 his long poem "The Avenue Bearing the Initial of Christ into the New World" focused on all of these and with Whitmanic compassion and plenitude gathered together the life he encountered on the Lower East Side's Avenue C.

Kirkus Reviews
200 Park Avenue

Kirkus provides prepublication reviews to publishers and other interested parties on a subscription basis. A good Kirkus review is prized because their anonymous reviewers are seen as hard graders, harder, that is, than those at *Publishers Weekly, Library Journal,* or *Booklist,* where the other prepublication reviews appear. Publishers often use reviews by either one or both to advertise books before "commercial" reviews come out in newspapers and magazines. Bookstores use the reviews as a guide to ordering.

Kirstein, Lincoln (1907–1996)

Boston-born and a Filene's department-store heir, Kirstein came to New York after Harvard, where he had founded and edited the magazine *Hound and Horn,* whose title came from an Ezra Pound poem. Begun in 1927, the magazine lasted until 1934. Pound liked to call it *Bitch and Bugle.* While in college Kirstein also helped form the Harvard Society of Contemporary Art, a forerunner of the Museum of Modern Art, an institution Kirstein came to condemn as "one of the worst influences in cultural history." In 1933 he met the Russian dancer George Balanchine in Paris. Kirstein invited Balanchine to New York, and when the dancer accepted, the course of both men's life was set. They formed the School of American Ballet, which became the New York City Ballet, and for more than forty years their partnership guided and sustained this foremost of New York's cultural institutions. But the ballet, about which Kirstein wrote, was only one of many interests. He wrote poems (New Directions published his *Rhymes of a PFC,* which chronicled his service as a private in World War II), essays on photography, painting (he thought Matisse a "clumsy decorator" and adored the work of Paul Cadmus), film, and theater, and an elegant autobiography, *Mosaic.* This last appeared a year before his death and takes Kirstein up to the moment he and Balanchine begin their work in New York. A section of the book describes Kirstein's affair, in the early thirties, with Carl Carlsen, a merchant seaman and fledgling writer, who had been one of Hart Crane's lovers. The book has an aristocratic candor and ornate style that never masks real feeling. It will be a pity if Kirstein left behind no more writings about his life. The best introduction to his work is the miscellany of his writing edited by Nicholas Jenkins, *By With To and From: A Lincoln Kirstein Reader,* published by Farrar, Straus & Giroux. Alfred Kazin said of the tall, heavyset, massive-headed, black-suited, imposing Kirstein that he was "the American Diaghilev, the most intelligent, passionate and indomitable of aesthetes." He was also the most individual of men, who went against the grain of his times even as he shaped its taste.

Knopf, Alfred A. (1892–1984)

A New York native, Knopf seems to have had no other career in mind but publishing. He graduated from Columbia and worked briefly for Doubleday and Page and for Mitchell Kennerly. Knopf was asked to leave Kennerly's firm after he approached the novelist Joseph Hergesheimer, then under contract to Kennerly, about one day publishing under the Knopf imprint. In 1915 Knopf set up shop for himself and the following year he married BLANCHE WOLF (1894–1966), who, as he said, "did everything." She became a director of the firm in 1921 and its president in 1957. From the start, Knopf's colophon was a running borzoi and their first advertisements proclaimed: "BORZOI Books are good books and there is one for every taste worthy of the name." The Knopfs may have chosen the borzoi because they liked the breed or wanted to emphasize their interest in Russian literature. In any case, Knopf has been distinguished by its commitment to European, Latin American (Blanche was fluent in Spanish), and Japanese literature. They have published Thomas Mann, Albert Camus, Gabriel García Márquez, and Yasunari Kawabata. Another distinguishing feature is the attention to design and production. Knopf books are always beautifully made, and each of them carries a note on the typeface used. Of all the major New York publishers, Knopf has conducted its business with the most class. Among its prominent writers are Wallace Stevens, John Updike, Julia Child, André Gide, Elizabeth Bowen, and Langston Hughes. Knopf brought out James Baldwin's *Go Tell It on the Mountain,* John Hersey's *Hiroshima,* and the hard-boiled detective fiction of James M. Cain and Dashiell Hammett. In 1960 the firm merged with Random House but maintained itself as "a separate and distinct imprint under the direction and editorial control of ourselves." This control passed to Robert Gottlieb in 1968, and when he left to become editor of the *New Yorker* he appointed Sonny Mehta, who runs the firm today, as his successor. Knopf himself was a colorful character given to blunt talk and sharp clothes. He took pleasure in wine and food, and these interests were well served on Knopf's list. Alfred A. Knopf Jr., the Knopfs' only son, became a publisher himself and one of the founders of Athenaeum.

Koch, Kenneth (b. 1925)

Along among the first generation of the New York School, Koch has had a teaching career. He has been at Columbia since receiving his doctorate there. Not that these years in the academy have rubbed off on his poems and plays: Koch is the least academic of poets. He graduated from Harvard, served in the Pacific in World War II, and spent three years in Europe, principally Italy and France, which had a profound impact on his work. His first book, *Poems,* appeared with prints by the painter Nell Blaine, and he has, in keeping with the other members of his school, collaborated with a good many artists, Larry Rivers among them. Koch has written a mock epic about a Japanese baseball player, two dozen or more plays, some of which have been produced Off-Broadway, a novel, and a stream of poems from which he made a *Selected Poems* in 1994. He won the Bollingen Prize in 1995. Koch has given considerable energy to a series of books beginning with *Wishes, Lies and Dreams* (1970) that are meant to teach children and others how to write poetry. They are original and inspiring books. James Schuyler thought that Koch could "teach a golf ball to write a pantoum." As a young man in the city, Koch had an apartment that looked out on the Third Avenue Elevated subway, which meant that the riders could look in. To amuse his guests Koch sometimes donned a gorilla mask and peered out of his window as the train roared by. No wonder a Frank O'Hara poem names him "the excitement prone Kenneth Koch." He later lived on Perry Street in the Village and has had an apartment on Claremont Avenue near Columbia for many years. Koch's genius is as a comic, and in his work the ridiculous becomes sublime.

Kosinski, Jerzy (1933–1991)

Kosinski's death by suicide was as unexpected, and bewildering, as any of the famous literary suicides since World War II. It is a mystery why the sort of attention that has been paid to the suicides of Ernest Hemingway and Sylvia Plath has not been focused on Kosinski's death and life. Perhaps this is yet to come, and certainly James Park Sloan's excellent 1996 biography is a start, but one wonders if Kosinski is simply not, as least for the moment, taken seriously as a writer. In 1982 the *Village Voice* published the article "Jerzy Kosinski's Tainted Words," whose main contention was that Kosinski's novels had received so much editorial assistance that his authorship of them was now in question. At the time Kosinski was a celebrated writer whose first novel, *The Painted Bird* (1966), not only created a sensation upon publication but had long been accepted as a masterpiece of Holocaust literature. He was also the author of the enormously popular *Being There* (1971), an actor in Warren Beatty's movie *Reds,* and a man who moved easily in the top New York literary, political, and show business circles. Although friends and supporters of Kosinski, the *New York Times* among them, came to his defense, his reputation has yet to rebound from the *Voice*'s attack. But if he is not taken seriously as a writer today, there is still the fascinating life of the man who came to New York in 1957 to study at Columbia, where he began to write in English. In Sloan's biography the egomaniac, mythmaking, highly intelligent, vital Kosinski reinvented himself after his experiences as a child in Poland during World War II with a ferocity equaled only by another amazing rogue and impostor, the psychologist and writer Bruno Bettelheim. Kosinski's is yet another of those American lives in which an immigrant takes full advantage of the freedom to be whoever he wants to be for however long he can sustain it. At the time of his death he had an apartment in the Hemisphere House on Fifty-seventh Street, not far from the old Russian Tea Room.

Krassner, Paul (b. 1932)

During the 1960s Krassner edited the *Realist,* a cheaply produced satirical magazine that nearly always went too far. It managed to offend not just the Catholic church, whose prowling monsignors tried to keep it off Boston newsstands, but almost everyone else. The issue that appeared after William Manchester's book on President Kennedy's assassination printed excerpts from the book that the president's widow purportedly had asked Manchester to cut. In one of these Lyndon Johnson is described as mounting the president's corpse in order to have intercourse with it in a most unorthodox manner. So eager were the *Realist*'s hip readers to believe the worst of Johnson that they fell for the hoax, hook, line, and sinker. When Krassner published his memoirs of the *Realist* years he titled them *How a Satirical Editor Became a Yippie Conspirator in Ten Easy Years,* which gives an idea of what came next for him. He is now a stand-up comic, and his satirical writings have been collected under the title *The Winner of the Slow Bicycle Race.*

Kreymborg, Alfred (1883–1966)

Born in New York, Kreymborg was a poet, critic, and literary historian, but he is remembered today for his role as editor. He began by editing a magazine with the unfortunate name *Glebe,* Old English for soil, for the publisher Boni and Liveright. This lasted a half dozen issues and was followed in 1913 by *Others,* which had a six-year run and gathered around it the poets Wallace Stevens, Marianne Moore, and William Carlos Williams. For a time this crowd met in Kreymborg's Bank Street apartment in the Village. He went on to edit *Broom* with Harold Loeb, who is probably best known as the model for Robert Cohen in Hemingway's *The Sun Also Rises*. From 1927 until 1936 Kreymborg edited the annual *American Caravan* in company with Paul Rosenfeld, Van Wyck Brooks, and Lewis Mumford. His own poems, alas, have not survived into current anthologies and must be tracked down in the library.

Krim, Seymour (1922–1988)

Born, in his words, "in the shadow of the George Washington Bridge" and educated at De Witt Clinton High School in the Bronx, Krim worked on a number of New York magazines, beginning with *Dime Western* and including *Show, Nugget,* and *Evergreen Review.* He was a Beat Generation/New Journalism man of letters whose collection of fiction and essays, *Views of a Nearsighted Cannoneer* (1968), had praise from Norman Mailer, James Baldwin, and William Styron. The book closes with an essay on his friend and fellow Villager Milton Klonsky, who was very much on the Village scene from the mid-forties through the sixties. At the time he encountered Klonsky, Krim lived at 224 Sullivan Street, and his picture of the Village catches the nervous energy of the time. His book appeared only in paperback and so will have to be hunted down in secondhand stores. He did not go on to write the books he dreamed of writing and this became part of his story.

Kunitz, Stanley (b. 1905)

A painstaking craftsman, Kunitz has produced relatively little poetry over a long career. His first book, *Intellectual Things,* appeared in 1930 and his *Selected Poems* won a Pulitzer Prize in 1958. Born in Worcester, Massachusetts, Kunitz came to New York at twenty-three about the same age as his mother when she landed as an immigrant from Russia. For many years Kunitz lived around the corner from e. e. cummings's Patchin Place home at 157 West Twelfth Street. While unaffiliated with the New York School or, for that matter, any group of poets, Kunitz had strong ties to a number of the New York painters including Philip Guston, Mark Rothko, and Franz Kline. He was instrumental in getting Poets House off the ground.

Lauterbach, Ann (b. 1942)

Born and raised in New York City, Lauterbach spent much of the late sixties and seventies abroad, mostly in London. Returning to New York, she lived in SoHo and worked in art galleries while writing the poems that appear in her first book, *Before Recollection* (1987). She now lives in TriBeCa, teaches at the City College of New York and at the City University of New York Graduate School, is a contributing editor of the magazine *Conjunctions,* and has been awarded a MacArthur Fellowship. *On a Stair* is her most recent book. It shows her to be a poet who has absorbed the influence of John Ashbery, which during the seventies was as easy to inhale as the air, and extended herself into a poetry of dislocation and rapture.

Lazarus, Emma (1849–1887)

The New Colossus

Not like the brazen giant of Greek fame,
With conquering limbs astride from land to land;
Here at our sea-washed, sunset gates shall stand
A mighty woman with a torch, whose flame
Is the imprisoned lightning, and her name
Mother of Exiles. From her beacon-hand
Glows world-wide welcome; her mild eyes command
The air-bridged harbor that twin cities frame.

"Keep, ancient lands, your storied pomp!" cried she
With silent lips. "Give me your tired, your poor,
Your huddled masses yearning to breathe free,
The wretched refuse of your teeming shore.
Send these, the homeless, tempest-tost to me,
I lift my lamp beside the golden door."

The last five lines of this, Emma Lazarus's most famous poem, are inscribed on a brass tablet mounted on the pedestal of the Statue of Liberty. Although her poem had been picked for this spot in 1886, the year of the statue's dedication, it did not take its place there until 1903. Lazarus herself was not one of the "huddled masses" she wrote about. Her father, Moses, was a wealthy Sephardic Jewish sugar merchant whose roots in New York City went back to the eighteenth century. He was a founder of the exclusive Knickerbocker Club. Her mother was of

German descent. Educated at home, Lazarus was a prodigy whose first book of poems, published at her father's expense, appeared when she was in her teens. As Walt Whitman had a generation before, she sent her book to Ralph Waldo Emerson, who encouraged her, engaged in a correspondence with her, and responded to her future work with editorial comment. She wrote novels and verse drama, and translated Heinrich Heine's poems. In 1881 she accompanied a rabbi to Ward's Island, where Jewish immigrants landed, a visit that impelled her into a range of Jewish causes. To aid in the fund-raising effort to build the pedestal beneath the Statue of Liberty, Lazarus wrote her sonnet "The New Colossus," which she read at the statue's dedication. Within a year she was dead of cancer of the mouth, having been nursed during her fatal illness by Nathaniel Hawthorne's daughter, Rose.

Harvard University paleontologist and writer Stephen Jay Gould, New York born and raised, has recently called attention to a scandal involving Lazarus's most famous lines. Entering the International Arrivals Building at John F. Kennedy Airport he looked up to see these Lazarus lines in gold:

> Give me your tired, your poor
> Your huddled masses yearning to
>   breathe free . . .
> Send these, the homeless, tempest-
>   tost to me.
> I lift my lamp beside the golden
>   door.

Having been made to memorize this poem in grade school, Gould knew at once what phrase had been eliminated. In an editorial on the op-ed page of the *New York Times* he saw the "language police" at work. "We may call people 'homeless' and 'tempest-tost,'" he wrote, "but they may not be, even with poetic license, 'wretched refuse.'" Which is, of course, exactly how the immigrants of any time may have been considered in the lands they left, were often forced to leave, to come to America. Lazarus knew this, but the powers at JFK have taken pains to assure that today's immigrants arriving by plane will not be insulted by her words. This censorship in the name of good taste and not hurting anyone's feelings is as odious as any other, but there is another issue here. As America's politicians debate the nation's immigration policies, few, it can be certain, will advocate accepting "wretched refuse," especially if Lazarus's words are no longer here to remind us that it was precisely in this condition that many of our forebears came to these shores.

Levertov, Denise (1923–1997)

Born in England, Levertov attended neither school nor college and is self-educated. Her reading of Wallace Stevens and William Carlos Williams while still in Europe were crucial to her formation as a poet. In December 1948 she and her husband, the novelist Mitchell Goodman, took up residence in New York. They lived at several Village addresses, 52 Barrow Street and 727 Greenwich Street among them. Through Goodman she met Robert Creeley and thus got to know a number of the poets involved with Black Mountain College. Levertov has often been lumped together with these poets, but she never so much as visited the school, and it was the San Francisco poet Kenneth Rexroth who championed her work and introduced it to James Laughlin of New Directions. There is a *Poetry U.S.A.* film of Levertov made in the early sixties in her New York kitchen and neighborhood. She actively opposed the Vietnam War and took part in many of the mass poetry readings of that time. In the late sixties she moved out of New York and lived in the Pacific Northwest.

Lion's Head
59 Christopher Street

When the Lion's Head closed in October of 1996 Pete Hamill, the newspaperman, novelist, and anthologist who had been one of the bar's regulars through the sixties and early seventies, did not go to the wake. As he wrote in the *Times* a few days later, he "didn't want to spend a night carousing with ghosts." By the time "the Head," as it was known to habitués, closed, its days as a writers' bar were over, but its walls still held the book jackets—they covered them like wallpaper—of the writers who drank there. "Is this the place where writers with drinking problems go?" a woman once asked. Someone assured her that it wasn't but was the place where drinkers with writing problems hung out. Among these writer-drinkers were a hoard of newspapermen, including Jimmy Breslin and Joe Flaherty. The poet Joel Oppenheimer was a fixture until he, like Hamill, went on the wagon and stayed there. Norman Mailer also dropped by, but in the main the writers who came to the Lion's Head were not famous. It was less a scene than a working writers' bar crowded with copy editors, rewrite men, and the like. The Clancy Brothers also frequented the place, and for a while the actress Jessica Lange waited on tables there.

The Little Review

Brought from Chicago to New York in 1917 by its editor, Margaret Anderson, and associate editor, Jane Heap, the *Little Review* had a short but eventful life in the city. In 1918 the magazine's foreign editor, Ezra Pound, sent Anderson chapters of James Joyce's *Ulysses*. Anderson was bowled over by the prose and decided at once that she wanted to publish the book in installments. She did so and the Post Office intervened, confiscating and burning four issues of the magazine. This did not deter Anderson and Heap. They published yet another installment of Joyce's book, which caught the attention of John Sumner, the secretary of the New York Society for the Suppression of Vice. Sumner took Anderson and Heap to court on obscenity charges, where they were defended by the New York lawyer, and friend of Joyce's, John Quinn. Beginning on Valentine's Day 1921 several hundred Greenwich Villagers packed the courtroom to hear Quinn argue the case. For their part Anderson and Heap hoped for a jail term so as to publicize their cause. In Paris, Joyce hoped that whatever battle might be joined, the upshot would be to clear the way for publication of his book in America. Anderson and Heap did not get their wish. The judge found them guilty and fined them fifty dollars apiece. The verdict scared off one publisher who had shown interest, and it was not until 1934 that Random House brought out an American edition of *Ulysses*. In 1924 Anderson and Heap moved their magazine to Paris, where Heap took over most of the editorial duties. They spent their New York years at 24 West Sixteenth Street in a house once owned by William Cullen Bryant. The offices of the magazine were in a basement studio at 31 West Fourteenth Street.

Liveright, Horace (1884–1933)

How is it that Horace Liveright, who began his publishing career with Charles Boni as Boni and Liveright in 1917, got to publish the young Ernest Hemingway and such expatriates as Ezra Pound and T. S. Eliot? Part of the reason is that old-line New York houses were not interested in the avant-garde, and so these writers could fall to a Jewish neophyte just as many of the great European writers like Tolstoy and Thomas Mann could fall to another Jewish publisher, Alfred A. Knopf. Liveright was a publisher for less than twenty years in which he had a helluva time launching the careers of dozens of writers and those of two prominent publishers, Richard Simon of Simon & Schuster and Random House's Bennett Cerf. On Liveright's list were Theodore Dreiser—Liveright kept a bust of Dreiser in his office—Hart Crane, Eugene

O'Neill, Djuna Barnes, e. e. cummings, and Sherwood Anderson. He published Era Pound, who thought him "a pearl," and T. S. Eliot's "The Waste Land." Indeed, it was Liveright who prevailed upon Eliot to append notes to the poem so as to make a more substantial book. Eliot did not return Liveright's interest and left him for the "Christian publisher" he preferred. On the recommendation of Sherwood Anderson, Liveright published the early work of both Hemingway and William Faulkner. He published Nathanael West's *Miss Lonelyhearts* and had best-sellers with Dorothy Parker's *Enough Rope* and *Sunset Gun*. Among his other authors were Anita Loos, S. J. Perelman, and Bertrand Russell, and in 1930 he brought out Mike Gold's *Jews without Money*. During his boom years the core of Liveright's business was the Modern Library. He and Boni had published the first twelve titles of the series in 1917. They sold for sixty cents each. Classic books in a standard format at a cheap price proved a winning formula. So appealing was the Library that it survived a fishy odor that came from the bindings of many of the first books when summer heat released the cod liver oil that had been used in the glue. Had Liveright held on to the Modern Library he might have been able to ride out the Depression, but he sold the series to his former employee Bennett Cerf—it became the rock on which Random House was built—in order to pay debts. Liveright had accumulated these in several noble ways. He gave large advances to writers, kept open house at his 61 West Forty-eighth Street office, and plunged repeatedly into the musical theater, where his hopes for a hit were always dashed. His interest in the theater led to his auditioning shows and their casts in his office. Writers often showed up for an editorial conference to find a party in progress featuring chorus girls and abundant liquor supplied by Liveright's bootlegger. When the end came Liveright went for a time to Hollywood but was not a success there and returned to New York, where he held court in seedier and seedier lodgings, becoming something of a ghost. Among those who worked at Liveright (he flipped a coin with Boni in 1928 and won the house) were the essayist Louis Kroneberger, the playwright Lillian Hellman, who remembered the parties with "lush girls and good liquor," and Edward Weeks, who went on to edit the *Atlantic Monthly* for many years.

Living Theater
Of all the theater companies spawned "Off-Broadway" the Living Theater became the most notorious. Julian Beck and Judith Malina, both native New Yorkers, met as teenagers, married in 1948, and devoted their

lives together (Beck is now dead) to the Theater, which had its first home in their large apartment at 789 West End Avenue. It next moved downtown to the Cherry Lane Theater for one season, then back uptown to the Loft at Broadway and 100th Street, where they put on Jean Cocteau's *Orpheus,* and then moved again to its final "permanent" home at Fourteenth Street and Sixth Avenue. The Theater's most successful productions were William Carlos Williams's *Many Loves,* Jack Gelber's *The Connection* (the play's theme was heroin addiction and the Freddie Redd Quartet with Jackie McLean on alto was onstage throughout), and Kenneth Brown's *The Brig.* The IRS closed the Theater in 1963 for nonpayment of taxes and the now politically radical company went to Europe, returning in 1968 with *Paradise Now,* a play in the spirit of the time that had the naked cast beckoning audience participation. The company was often busted and became a minor cause célèbre before running out of energy. Judith Malina can be seen onscreen as Al Pacino's mother in Sidney Lumet's film *Dog Day Afternoon* and Julian Beck plays a gangster in Francis Ford Coppola's *Cotton Club.*

Lowell, Robert (1917–1977)

Lowell's first significant time in New York came during the early days of World War II, when he was, in his words, "a fire-breathing Catholic C.O." He had responded to his draft notice with a letter to President Roosevelt and a "Declaration of Personal Responsibility" explaining why he refused induction. As the scion of two old New England families with Revolutionary War heroes, famous poets, and Harvard presidents among his ancestors, Lowell made the *New York Times* and newspapers across the nation. After his arrest and trial, but before he was sent to the Federal Correction Center in Danbury, Connecticut, Lowell spent a few days in New York's West Street Jail, where the man in the next cell was Murder Incorporated's Louis "Lepke" Buchalter. Another C.O., Jim Peck, remembered this exchange between Lowell and Lepke. "Lepke says to him: 'I'm in for killing. What are you in for?' 'Oh, I'm in for refusing to kill.' And Lepke burst out laughing." Out of this encounter Lowell got the wonderful poem "Memories of West Street and Lepke" that appears in *Life Studies.* Lowell's next significant time in the city came in September 1960, when he left Boston intending to spend the year in New York on a Ford Foundation grant to work on an opera. He took the theater chronicler, editor, and Brecht expert Eric Bentley's apartment at 194 Riverside Drive and in company with his friend the poet William Meredith began to spend his time "around the Met." "Four Puccinis in a week," he crowed. No opera came of this, but Lowell found himself at home in New York's intellectual life. By now Boston had become a university town, its intellectual life fragmented into the several academic factories on either side of the Charles River. While Lowell continued to teach off and on at Harvard, New York and then England were home for the rest of his life. In January 1961 he and his wife, the novelist Elizabeth Hardwick, took an apartment on West Sixty-seventh Street that Hardwick described as "built in the 1900s for artists." The Lowells' New York intellectual friends can be found in the early issues of the *New York Review of Books,* which they helped found. It was made up of the old *Partisan Review* crowd and its offshoots, an Upper West Side crowd that included Lowell's great friend Hannah Arendt. Lowell did not mix with the poets of the New York School, although he did once read with Frank O'Hara at Wagner College on Staten Island. On the way to the reading O'Hara spontaneously wrote, as was his habit, a poem that he then read. Lowell had to admit that he himself had nothing that new to offer. Nor did Lowell have much to do with Allen Ginsberg and the Beats. In Lowell's New York a half-dozen literary circles revolved at once. These came into contact with one another, but few writers moved in more than one at the same time. In the mid-sixties Lowell's Ford Foundation-financed course in opera resulted in three plays that opened to good notices on Broadway. His own poetry seemed to be treading water except for the great farewell to Boston, "For the Union Dead," which appeared in the 1964 book by the same name. Throughout his years in New York, Lowell was beset by the manic-depression that so often derailed him. Usually the illness struck while he was in Cambridge teaching at Harvard, and he was sent to McLean's Hospital. But the disorder had been with Lowell since his youth and in 1949, a time when relatively little was known about manic-depression, he had been a patient in Manhattan's Payne Whitney Hospital; Lowell's stay was kept quiet out of concern for what people might think. In 1970 Lowell, having grown stale in New York, went to England to teach; there he ended his marriage to Elizabeth Hardwick, causing great pain all around, and married the novelist Lady Caroline Blackwood. Lowell returned to New York regularly, and in 1977 on September 12, his marriage to Blackwood in ruins, he took a cab to Hardwick's door. The cabbie found him slumped in the backseat, dead of a heart attack. On his lap was a portrait of Blackwood by her former husband, the painter Lucian Freud. Lowell's funeral was held in his native Boston.

When Jacqueline Kennedy's possessions were auctioned, among them were a few books signed by Lowell "to my friend across the park."

Luce, Henry (1898–1967)
Luce Publications: *Time, Life, Fortune,* **and** *Sports Illustrated*
Luce, Clare Booth (1903–1987)

> Are you going to let your emotional life be run by Time Magazine?
> I'm obsessed by Time Magazine.
> I read it every week.
> Its cover stares at me every time I slink past the corner candystore.

Allen Ginsberg wrote these lines in his 1956 poem "America," when *Time* mattered as much as its founder Henry Luce thought it did. Today the magazine has been eclipsed by television and "the media," but these agents do not represent the foursquare Americanism *Time* and the other Luce publications stood for, the sort of Americanism that told Ginsberg, "Businessmen are serious / Movie producers are serious. Everyone is serious but me." Luce and a friend, Britton Hadden, began *Time,* the nation's first weekly newsmagazine, in 1923 on money borrowed from the families of their Yale classmates. It quickly became a success, and except for the few years its editorial office spent in Cleveland, of all places, *Time* has been published in New York. Hadden died in 1929, and Luce launched *Fortune,* a monthly devoted to business. It prospered even in the Depression, and a number of writers, James Agee, Dwight Macdonald, and Alfred Kazin among them, were on its staff. In 1936 *Life,* a weekly picture magazine, was added to the stable and soon became Luce's crown jewel. In the fifties it seemed that every American home subscribed. Eventually, television gave us all the images we could handle, and the *Life* that exists today is the shadow of a once great magazine. In 1954 Luce launched *Sports Illustrated.* Today it is perhaps the most widely read of the Luce publications.

Luce married the playwright Clare Booth in 1937. Her best-known play is *The Women,* which had a solid Broadway run before being made into a movie. Active in Republican party politics, she was elected to Congress from the Connecticut district in which the Luces had a second home. President Dwight Eisenhower named her ambassador to

Italy in 1953. The New York novelist Wilfred Sheed has written her biography. From the time he came to New York Luce lived on the East
Side, at 435 East Fifty-second Street and on Fifth Avenue near Seventy-
seventh through the decades when his fame rivaled that of the newspaper barons of the preceding generation, Pulitzer and Hearst

Lynch, Anne Charlotte (1815–1891)

First at 116 Waverly Place and then on Thirty-seventh Street west of
Fifth Avenue, Lynch, a poet and teacher of composition, entertained
many of New York's writers and artists. Or as Theodore F. Wolfe wrote
in his *Literary Haunts and Homes* (1898), her "parlors were during
four decades opened regularly for brilliant receptions to the kindred
guilds of letters and art, at which were welcomed many most illustrious
in Europe and America." Herman Melville attended Lynch's annual
Valentine's Day party in 1848. Among the other guests were Fitz-
Greene Halleck, the painter Asher Durand, William Cullen Bryant, the
novelist Catharine Maria Sedgwick, Bayard Taylor, Grace Greenwood,
Seba Smith, and Nathaniel Parker Willis.

M

Macdonald, Dwight (1906–1982)

Born in New York City and educated at Yale, where he became a friend
of Fred Dupee, who would bring him onto the *Partisan Review,* Macdonald was a lifelong New Yorker, pacifist-anarchist, and literary journalist. Before joining the *Partisan Review* he worked as an editor at
Fortune. He went from the *Partisan Review* into his own journal, *Politics,* which ran from 1944 to 1949 and reflected his respect for Leon
Trotsky. The magazine stood opposed, as does nearly all of Macdonald's own writing, to doctrinaire political attitudes of any stripe. Much
later Macdonald, who called himself a man of the "middle," raised the
hackles of old *PR* friends William Phillips and Clement Greenberg by
arguing that in the ongoing Arab-Israeli conflict the Arabs had a point,
too. In 1925 he became a staff writer for the *New Yorker,* and in 1962
he published a controversial essay on popular culture, "Masscult and
Midcult." This appeared in his first book of essays, *Against the American Grain* (1962). In 1974 he published a second book of essays, *Dis-
criminations,* for which Norman Mailer, who is not treated with kid

gloves in the book, wrote an introduction when it was reissued in paperback. Mailer remembered great parties at Macdonald's apartments on East Tenth Street and later on East Eighty-seventh Street:

> When you went to his house, you never knew if the evening would end in an acrimonious debate between two intellectual figures who might on occasion not speak well of one another for years, or whether you might hear or learn something you never knew before, or whether you might just get drunk, meet a good woman, and have a good time. His were the only literary parties I know where you could count on something flirtatious—a rose hue, so to speak—stealing into the salon.

Of himself Macdonald accepted Paul Goodman's judgment, "Dwight thinks with his typewriter," admitting that he did not know exactly what he was thinking until he discovered it in the process of writing.

Mailer, Norman (b. 1923)

Mailer is the most famous and notorious writer of his generation. He has led his remarkable life in public, and for fifty years has held New York's and the nation's interest. At one time or another every serious American reader has had an opinion about some aspect of his life and work. Born in New Jersey, Mailer grew up at 555 Crown Street in Brooklyn. He went to Harvard imagining himself as an engineer and came out with dreams of becoming a writer. After "modest" service in the South Pacific, he returned to Brooklyn, married for the first time, and settled down to write his novel in an apartment at 102 Pierrepont Street in Brooklyn Heights. Mailer's neighbor in that building was the playwright Arthur Miller, with whom he exchanged small talk when getting the mail. "I can remember thinking," Mailer said in an interview, "this guy's never going anywhere. I'm sure he thought the same of me." If Miller indeed thought as Mailer imagined, he knew better by 1948 when *The Naked and the Dead* appeared to such great acclaim that Mailer became immediately famous and soon wealthy. Few writers have achieved Mailer's initial success, and fewer still have done so at twenty-five. "Did you dig your sudden fame?" the *Playboy* interviewer asked him. "Of course I dug it. I had to dig it. I mean," Mailer answered, "to be brutally frank for all our swell *Playboy* readers out there: it enabled me to get girls I would not otherwise have gotten." His celebrity also left him with a tough act to follow. His second novel, *Barbary Shore* (1951), did not go down so well with the critics but it was by no means a disaster. The book's characters, FBI agents and old Bolsheviks, get together in a Brooklyn Heights rooming house. Some years later life was to mirror art for Mailer when he took a studio in Fulton Street, not realizing that on the floor below him lived Colonel Rudolph Abel, the most important Russian spy in America during the fifties. "I am sure," Mailer remembered, "that we used to be in the elevator together many times." In the early fifties Mailer lived on the Lower East Side, first on Pitt Street in "a grim apartment, renovated in battle-ship gray" and then in a large loft on Monroe Street in the shadow of the Manhattan Bridge. Here he gave large, wild parties that brought together Beat writers like Allen Ginsberg, movie stars, including Montgomery Clift, all sorts of other writers and artists, and, inevitably, trouble. A neighborhood gang crashed one party and gave Mailer a few hammer blows to his head. In 1955 his third novel, *The Deer Park,* appeared, and it was savaged. At this point Mailer might have gone off to lick his wounds, but he had become a fixture downtown and because he had, he claims, long ago determined "to move from activity to activity" he soon found himself launching the *Village Voice.* He did this with Dan Wolf and Edwin Fancher, who had lived in the building next to his when Mailer lived on 39 First Avenue. Mailer put up five thousand dollars in start-up money, and for a time he contributed a long-winded and arrogant column. He seemed to take pleasure not only in stirring things up but in calling attention to himself. His next and most New York of books in its audacious bid for notoriety, *Advertisements for Myself* (1959), did a lot of both. Mailer not only revealed his dreams and ambitions in it (more flaunted than revealed) but in essence he also began to blur the line between fiction and nonfiction. He put himself forward as if he were as important as his work, and when he wrote, "I am imprisoned with a perception which will settle for nothing less than making a revolution in the consciousness of our time," it was up for grabs whether or not this perception would find its home in a novel. He had, without knowing it, begun to invent what came to be called New Journalism. During this period Mailer lived with his second wife, Adele, on Perry Street, where he had one of psychologist Wilhelm Reich's orgone boxes. In 1960 they were living uptown on West Ninety-fourth Street when, after a drunken party at their home, Mailer stabbed Adele. This landed him on the front page of the *Daily News* and in Bellevue. The incident also ended his marriage and many thought, and some must have hoped, that it would be the end of Norman Mailer, but it wasn't. He went on to marry three other women before settling down in the marriage of his life with number six, the painter Norris Church. In 1965 Mailer took on the challenge of writing a serial novel for *Esquire,* promising a chapter a month. This became the lurid *American Dream,* in which the hero, Stephen Rojack, murders his ex-wife. As the Vietnam War heated up Mailer became active in his opposition to it. This led first to a bizarre, but powerful, novel *Why Are We in Vietnam?* set in Texas and Alaska and then to *The Armies of the Night* (1968). This account of Mailer's role in the march on the Pentagon won him a Pulitzer Prize. He was now more of a journalist than a novelist and covered political conventions and major prize fights. He had also become a fixture on television talk shows, and he had begun to make movies. In 1969 he decided that, as he said, he "wanted to make actions rather than effect sentiments," and so he ran for mayor of New York. The newspaperman Jimmy Breslin was his running mate, and they received more than 40,000 votes in a campaign both serious and doomed. Mailer's next book chronicled NASA's attempt to land a man on the moon, and the book that followed, *The Prisoner of Sex* (1971), attacked the ideology of the women's liberation movement. This caused Mailer to become a punching bag for the feminist movement and led to a raucous public debate at New York's Town Hall, the sort of event he thrives on, between him and Germaine Greer, among others. Before returning to the novel in 1983 with *Ancient Evenings,* Mailer published his second Pulitzer Prize-winning book, *The Executioner's Song* (1979). While researching the life of Gary Gilmore, the executed murderer whose story the book tells, Mailer began receiving letters about prison life from one Jack Abbott. Impressed by both Abbott's prose style and his experiences in prison, Mailer helped him get a book of letters published, *In the Belly of the Beast,* and, with other literary figures, to win his release from prison in 1981. Abbott came directly to New York, where within a matter of weeks he murdered a waiter during an altercation at the Bini-Bon Café on the Lower East Side. The spotlight naturally fell on Mailer, and in his usually combative manner he stood up both for Abbott and his having helped him. As Mailer moved into his sixties and then his seventies, his energy showed no signs of diminishing. He has published novels, journalism, and over the past half-dozen years written two huge books, the novel *Harlot's Ghost* and a nonfiction book on Lee Harvey Oswald that *required* several months' research in Russia. He has indeed gone from one activity to another in a career that has zigged and zagged all over the map. Part of the reason for this must have been the burden of his alimony and child-support payments (Mailer has had nine children by his six wives). He has been offered big paydays that he could not afford to turn down, and he is clearly not afraid to make a fool of himself. But Mailer is also the sort of writer whose imagination kicks into overdrive when there is a new project set before it. He seems to be able to see a place for himself, whether it is at NASA, in ancient Egypt, or in the life and mind of Marilyn Monroe, Oswald, and Picasso, the subject of a recent book. No New York writer in Mailer's time has cut across so many of New York's literary circles. Lillian Hellman, Diana Trilling, José Torres, George Plimpton, James Baldwin, Allen Ginsberg, and a phonebook's worth of other writers, agents, and publishers have at one time or another been his associate, colleague, partner, friend, and/or friendly enemy. Since the sixties he has lived in Brooklyn Heights.

Malamud, Bernard (1914–1986)

Born in Brooklyn the son of Russian Jewish immigrants, Malamud went to Erasmus Hall High School, where he later taught, then on to City College before doing graduate work at Columbia. Although he is grouped with Saul Bellow and Philip Roth in the first rank of American Jewish novelists, Malamud's first novel, *The Natural,* has not a single Jewish character. It takes baseball as a central American myth and draws all sorts of allegorical implications from the adventures of its hero, Roy Hobbs. The novel bears only superficial resemblance to the movie based on it that starred Robert Redford. Malamud's second novel, *The Assistant* (1957), is one of the great New York novels. Working from his experience of growing up in just the sort of barely-making-it, mom-and-pop grocery store that he describes in the book, Malamud creates not only a parable of Jewish suffering but a powerfully stark tale of the immigrant's struggles in the New World. The novel's action could take place in any of New York's immigrant neighborhoods. Malamud's prose is like a grainy black-and-white photograph, and the grimness of the book's landscape is relentless. New York City is barely mentioned, so that when it is the reader almost recoils. Can these events involving the grocer, Morris Bober, and his assistant, Frank Alpine, really be happening in the city of Times Square, Central Park, and Wall Street? Bober and his grocery store seem to be in another and impossibly distant world. Malamud wrote this novel, as he did most of his work, while teaching outside New York, first in Oregon and then for many years at Bennington College. He set another novel, *The Tenants* (1971), on the Lower East Side. In this allegory two writers, the white Harry Lesser and the black Willie Spearmint, work out their shared destiny in the abandoned tenement where they are both squatters. Several of Malamud's very fine short stories are also set in the city.

Malcolm X (1925–1965)

Malcolm X had two New York periods, before and after prison. He arrived in the city from Boston in 1941 and spent most of the next five years as a petty crook, pimp, and drug dealer. He sold dope to Billie Holiday, among others, using the name "Detroit Red." He also worked as a waiter at Small's Paradise at 136th Street and Seventh Avenue and lived for a time, as so many other black writers had, at the 135th Street Y. In 1946 he was arrested in Boston for burglary and sent to prison from which he emerged in 1952 a Muslim and man transformed. He returned to New York in 1954 as Malcolm X and established Temple 7 at 116th Street and Lenox Avenue. During the last, tumultuous decade of his life he and his family lived at 23-11 Ninth Street in East Elmhurst, Queens. The week before his death this house was firebombed. On 21 February 1965, Malcolm X rose to give a speech at the Audubon Ballroom on 166th Street between Broadway and St. Nicholas Avenue. He was gunned down by assassins and died at the scene. His autobiography, written with journalist Alex Haley, became a best-seller in the sixties and remains a keystone of black American literature today. James Baldwin turned it into a film script, *One Day When I Was Lost* (1972), that was never made, but in 1992 Spike Lee filmed X's life casting Denzel Washington in the title role.

Marquis, Don (1878–1937)

Best known for his characters archy, a cockroach, and mehitabel, a cat, Marquis wrote about them or, rather, archy wrote about them sans capital letters (he could not hit the key) for the *New York Sun* and the *Tribune*. Marquis devoted several books to these characters and after his death an omnibus, *The Life and Times of archy and mehitabel*, appeared with drawings by the great George Herriman, inventor of the comic strip "Krazy Kat." The books were very popular in their time and are still read today. Here's a sort of limerick from archy:

> coarse
> jocosity
> catches the crowd
> Shakespeare
> and I

are often
low browed

Marquis is one of those writers who is often described as well loved. The affection his public held for him did not keep his end from being hard, however. He died at his home at 51 Wendover Road in the Forest Hills section of Queens, improverished after several years of failing health.

Mathews, Harry (b. 1930)

A New York native, Mathews went to Harvard, the feeder school for the New York poets—Ashbery, O'Hara, Koch, and Elmslie are all Harvard graduates—with whom he is associated. For many years he has lived at least part of the year in Paris, where he is a member of Oulipo, the group of writers and scientists whose interest it is to develop new literary forms. In Mathews's case that has led to inventing systems that produce hilarious results. He has, for example, joined two halves of different proverbs, "A stitch in time is worth two in the bush," and he has written a memorial poem to the poet James Schuyler using only the letters in Schuyler's name. He has published half a dozen novels, the first of which, *The Conversions*, unfolds, in part, in New York.

Max's Kansas City
Park Avenue South off Union Square

Veteran Village bar and club owner Mickey Ruskin opened Max's, nicknamed by the poet Joel Oppenheimer because Union Square was so far from the Village it might as well have been Kansas City, in 1965, and the place became, in the words of Andy Warhol, who hung out there, "the exact place where Pop Art and pop life came together in the sixties—teeny boppers and sculptors, rock stars and poets from St. Mark's Place, Hollywood actors checking out what the underground actors were all about, boutique owners and models, modern dancers and go-go dancers—everybody went to Max's and everything got homogenized." Among the poets Warhol had in mind were Anne Waldman and Lewis Warsh, whose St. Mark's Place apartment was a hangout for poets in the sixties; Michael Brownstein; Gerard Malanga, who was a member of Warhol's entourage; and Jim Carroll, who went on to a career as a rock 'n' roll singer. Lou Reed, who wrote poems as well as songs, played Max's with the Velvet Underground, as did Patti Smith, who once danced on the tables kicking drinks in the laps of record company executives there for the show. For a time Dorothy Dean, a legend in gay New York in the seventies, served as Max's social arbiter. She could usually bounce the unwanted with a look or tart word, but Robert Creeley remembered her in his poem "Dorothy Dean": "I sadly loved / it that you wopped me with your purse." The waitresses at Max's were famous for their good looks and take-no-shit attitude. They often had their hands full as Max's was fueled not only by drink but also by drugs and the money that had begun to flow into the music and art worlds. The painter Julian Schnabel worked as a cook at the place, and put some of his memories into his one published book, *CJV.*

Maxwell, William (b. 1908)

For forty years Maxwell edited fiction at the *New Yorker* and all accounts attest that he was a model of tact, intelligence, generosity, and sympathy. He knew how to tell writers what was good, and how to help them to make what wasn't good better. He edited Frank O'Connor, John Cheever, John O'Hara, Mavis Gallant, and a host of others. At times all of the writers he worked with must have thought they had died and gone to heaven. Now that the letters to and from Maxwell are being published, they will amount to a textbook of the *New Yorker's* painstaking, often nit-picking, word-by-word way of editing. When the Faber & Faber editor T. S. Eliot was told that most editors are failed writers he tartly responded, "So are most writers." Maxwell is an editor whose own fiction rivals that of the best writers he edited. His novels and stories are typically set in the Midwest of his childhood—he was born and raised in Illinois—and have a slow, pre-automobile, pre-World War I pace and a poetry distilled out of place and time that can break your heart. *The Folded Leaf* (1945), *So Long, See You Tomorrow* (1979), and his collected stories are where to begin. He has also written *Ancestors* (1971), an original family history in which historical fact is vivified by the novelist's art. It is a quiet book, as are his others, which may explain why his reputation is not as large as his accomplishment, even though all of his books remain in print today. He has published a single book of essays and book reviews, *The Outermost Dream.*

Mayer, Bernadette (b. 1945)

Born in Brooklyn, a graduate of the New School for Social Research, and possessed of one of the most unconventional imaginations in the New York School, Mayer has been an inspiration through her teaching, readings, and the work itself, to a number of young poets. She did live in Lenox, Massachusetts, in the Berkshires, where she dreamed of opening a stationery store and calling it the Scarlet Letter, but she has spent most of her writing life living on the Lower East Side, where she has raised her three children. She has edited mimeo magazines (*United Artists, 0-9*), been a teacher at, and director of, the Poetry Project, collaborated with her former husband, Lewis Warsh, Alice Notley, Clark Coolidge, and others, and published one original book after another— even a *Utopia*! New Directions has become her publisher, which is appropriate because she is the most "new directional" of writers. They have brought out a *Bernadette Mayer Reader* and in the summer of 1996 published *Proper Name*, a book of stories that redefines the word.

McCarthy, Mary (1912–1989)

McCarthy took her motto from Chaucer: "I am mine own woman well at ease." After graduating from Vassar in 1933, she came to New York and began her literary career as a freelance writer. She lived at 2 Beekman Place near where Kay, the heroine of *The Group* (1963)—perhaps McCarthy's best novel—has an apartment. In 1936 McCarthy married, quickly divorced, and moved to a single room at 18 Gay Street in the West Village. Her Vassar friend Elizabeth Bishop lived around the corner on Charles Street. Bold and beautiful, McCarthy took lovers when she chose to. After her death an account of her affair with Philip Rahv appeared in *Intellectual Memories: New York 1936–1938* (1992). McCarthy had met Rahv, Dwight Macdonald, and others of the *Partisan Review* crowd at one of James T. Farrell's Sunday evening open houses in 1937. She began at once to write theater criticism for the magazine and to get involved in radical politics. From the outset she had a tart tongue and was tenacious in argument. In 1941 she published in *PR* one of the most famous short stories of her generation, "The Man in the Brooks Brothers Shirt." It details the seduction of a young woman by a man named Breen as they travel cross-country by train. The rumor got started that Breen was actually the Wall Street financier and Republican presidential candidate Wendell Willkie. That there was such a rumor at all suggests how notorious the story was in its time. In 1938 McCarthy wed the critic Edmund Wilson. Theirs was a volatile marriage, a picture of which is in her novel *The Oasis* (1949). When they divorced in 1946 they were living at 14 Henderson Place off East Eighty-sixth Street. For a time McCarthy left the city and taught at Bard College, which like her marriage and years at Vassar found its way into a novel, *The Groves of Academe* (1952) in this case. Between 1952 and

1954 she spent many months residing at the Chelsea Hotel after which she left for Europe, to return to New York only as a visitor. *The Group* enjoyed enough of a popular success when it appeared—it is worth reading today for its portrait of literary New York in the thirties—that a movie was based on it. But in the late 1960s and early 1970s McCarthy was best known for her journalism. She traveled to Hanoi during the Vietnam War and filed a report from there, and she covered the Watergate hearings for the *New York Review of Books*. On the whole her work was less well known than it might have been had she been living in America rather than in Paris. In 1979 she returned to the public eye in a remarkable way. In New York to publicize her current novel, *Cannibals and Missionaries*, she appeared on *The Dick Cavett Show*, on which intellectuals and writers were frequent guests. Toward the end of the interview Cavett tried to get a rise out of McCarthy by asking her what writers she thought "overrated." He got more than he bargained for and so did McCarthy, who answered that Lillian Hellman was "tremendously overrated, a bad writer and dishonest writer . . . I said once in some interview that every word she writes is a lie, including 'and' and 'the.'" Hellman was at home alone watching the show and after talking with her lawyer brought suit against McCarthy, Cavett, and Channel 13 for $2.25 million, claiming McCarthy's remarks had caused "mental pain and anguish" and left her "injured in her profession." McCarthy's animosity toward Hellman dated from the political battles of the 1930s, but it was Hellman's memoir of the McCarthy years, *Scoundrel Time*, that was fresh in her mind and had set her off. For Hellman's part, once the suit had been brought she wanted to break McCarthy, to bankrupt her. Much of literary New York took sides, some seeing Hellman as a victim and siding with her while others stood by McCarthy and thought that regardless of the intemperance of what she had said, she was within her rights in saying it. As the suit moved forward and McCarthy's motion for dismissal was denied, Norman Mailer, playing peacemaker, got himself into the middle of the affair, managing to end his long friendship with Hellman while bringing the two camps no closer together. Harold Baer Jr., the judge in the case, saw that the issue embraced whether or not First Amendment right to free speech extended to what might be said on television. It was, he reasoned, one thing for McCarthy to air her opinion in the confines of a magazine but another to say what she did in a medium where millions might hear her. Hellman's death brought the suit to a close before this issue could be argued. This chapter in McCarthy's life, and in the intellectual history of New York City, is treated in depth by her biographer, Carol Brightman, in *Writing Dangerously: Mary McCarthy and Her World*. Since McCarthy's death a volume of the letters she and Hannah Arendt wrote to each other over nearly forty years has been published. This not only sheds light on the life and work of two fascinating women, but adds immeasurably to our picture of those New York writers and intellectuals who began their literary lives in the politically tumultuous 1930s.

McClure, S. S. (1857–1949)

McClure launched *McClure's Magazine,* one of the nation's first mass-circulation magazines, in 1893. After a decade in which it published the work of Robert Louis Stevenson, O. Henry, Arthur Conan Doyle, and Booth Tarkington, the magazine hit its stride when it began to publish the muckrakers. Ida Tarbell's nineteen-part history of Standard Oil appeared in its pages as did Lincoln Steffens's "The Shame of the Cities." Their work and that of Roy Stannard Baker and William Allen White had national impact and is credited with inspiring President Theodore Roosevelt's reformist zeal. McClure tirelessly brought new writers to the enterprise. He discovered Frank Norris in San Francisco, and found Willa Cather writing music and drama criticism in Pittsburgh. She wrote a less-than-flattering profile of Mary Baker Eddy for the magazine. *McClure's* had a whirlwind five years before a policy dispute caused McClure's partner, John Phillips, to team with Tarbell and White in starting a new magazine, the *American.* McClure kept going until 1911, but debt caused him to lose control of the magazine and it eventually wound up, in a much watered down form, a Hearst publication.

McCourt, Frank (b. 1931)

This is a fairy tale: A teacher of writing at Stuyvesant High School on East Fifteenth Street known to writers, but not heretofore known as a writer himself, writes a memoir. His subject is growing up dirt-poor in Limerick, Ireland, in the 1930s and 1940s. He has the aid of two fairy godmothers, R'lene Dahlberg, wife of the novelist Edward Dahlberg, and Nan Graham, editor-in-chief at Scribner's. The book, *Angelas's Ashes,* is published in 1996, the Year of the Memoir, to rave reviews. By the end of 1997 it is still in hardcover and has sold more than one million copies worldwide. McCourt, an excellent reader, who once trod the boards in company with his younger brother, the Third Avenue saloon keeper and actor, Malachy, is in demand everywhere. In Manhattan, writers and others who know the man seem genuinely grateful for his success. Here the fairy tale ends, for in Limerick his reception is mixed. While there to receive an honorary degree McCourt meets many who say they love the way the book is written but disagree with his picture of poverty. They are unable to accept as true the misery they say McCourt overemphasizes. A bookseller named Gerard Hannan has even written and published a retort to McCourt. He calls his book *Ashes*. McCourt is philosophical. "Begrudgers," he says. "What would Ireland be without them?"

McCullers, Carson (1917–1967)

At seventeen McCullers, then Lula Carson Smith, arrived in New York by boat from Savannah, Georgia. Following her high school graduation she had convinced her parents that she ought to come north to school at Juilliard or Columbia. The characters who would appear in her first novel, *The Heart is a Lonely Hunter,* were already, as she told an interviewer, "Walking around in her head." She did attend writing classes at Columbia, but school was not for her. She returned to the South, where she got a good deal of her novel written. In September 1940 she was back in New York and had moved into her friend George Davis's 7 Middagh Street house on Brooklyn Heights. W. H. Auden was already living there, and since McCullers was the only woman in residence, he and Davis assumed she would do the cooking. McCullers quickly corrected that assumption. During the five years she lived at the now legendary Middagh Street house, her friend the novelist Richard Wright and his wife, Ellen, moved into the ground floor, and countless guests, many invited by McCullers, visited the house. "Comparing the Brooklyn that I know," she wrote in her essay "Brooklyn Is My Neighborhood," "with Manhattan is like comparing a comfortable and complacent duenna to her more brilliant and neurotic sister." In 1945 she left that duenna for the house in Nyack, New York, where she lived out a life increasingly compromised by illness. She was one of those who were hurt and angered not to be invited to Truman Capote's 1966 ball at the Plaza Hotel. She soothed her feelings by taking a suite at the hotel and inviting her friends in to celebrate her fiftieth birthday.

At the peak of McCullers's career Broadway was still congenial and attractive to novelists. McCullers adapted her novel *The Member of the Wedding* (1946) in 1950 and had a hit starring Ethel Waters, Julie Harris, and Brandon De Wilde. In 1952 the play became a movie with the same cast. Edward Albee adapted McCullers's short novel *The Ballad of the Sad Café* for Broadway in 1963, by which time the relationship between Broadway theater and novelist had all but ceased to exist.

McElroy, Joseph (b. 1930)

A Brooklyn native and Columbia Ph.D. who has taught at Queens College since 1964, McElroy has published six novels marked by their structural audacity. He began with *A Smuggler's Bible* (1966), reached his widest audience with *Hind's Kidnap* (1969), and published the thousand-page *Women and Men* in 1987.

McInerney, Jay (b. 1955)

McInerney is one of a number of writers—Truman Capote is another— who worked in lowly positions on the *New Yorker* before publishing their first books. A fact checker at the magazine, McInerney drew on this experience to create the Department of Factual Verification in his first, and most popular novel, *Bright Lights, Big City* (1984). Few recent novels have struck the nerve this one did, the same nerve that Hemingway and Fitzgerald struck when they wrote of their generation in *The Sun Also Rises* and *This Side of Paradise*. McInerney is not nearly so original as either of them, but he caught a moment, and any number of Yuppies saw themselves and their youthful torments in his novel. Since then he has published several novels to the sort of reviews that remind him that he has yet to live up to the promise of his first book. Fame in literary New York is always a double-edged sword.

McKay, Claude (1889–1948)

Claude McKay came to the United States from his native island of Jamaica to attend Booker T. Washington's Tuskegee Institute in Alabama. From there he moved to Kansas before arriving in Greenwich Village in 1917. In Jamaica McKay had published two books of dialect poems, and his first American publication was also poetry under, for obscure reasons, the pseudonym Eli Edwards. McKay became an editor of Max Eastman's magazine the *Liberator*. He was the only African American writer of the time to be in such a position on a white magazine, dealing mostly with white writers. In 1922 McKay published *Harlem Shadows,* a book of poems that is generally accepted as the first major book in the Harlem Renaissance. He loved Harlem when he first set foot there in 1917 and had written, "It was like entering a paradise of my own people." But his attitude had changed, and McKay, now a Communist, left America the year the book appeared and did not return until 1934. By then he had published the novel *Home to Harlem* (1928), the story of a black soldier's return from France after World War I. The novel became the first best-seller by an African American writer, but it met with a decidedly mixed reaction in Harlem. After he read the book W. E. B. Du Bois said, "I feel like taking a bath." The younger generation, symbolized by Langston Hughes, thought it "the finest thing 'we've' done yet." When McKay returned to America—he had left before the Renaissance actually began and returned when it was over—he was well known, but because of quarrels with the leaders of the New Negro movement and loss of faith in the Communists, he had few prospects. He wrote two autobiographical volumes and endured being dismissed as the enfant terrible of the Harlem Renaissance. McKay as a writer and man seems to have been one of those who, in the words of David Levering Lewis, the Harlem Renaissance historian, "strives for success only to find it intolerable." It may also be that McKay, like many another successful African American, always felt alien in America and rootless in the world at large. One thinks of both Richard Wright and James Baldwin, who, for all their celebrity, never felt at home in their own country.

McKenney, Ruth (1911–1972)

McKenney's *My Sister Eileen* (1938), partially set on Gay Street in the Village, had many lives. It became a best-seller, then a Broadway play of note (1941), and then a Broadway musical, *Wonderful Town* (1953). The high-spirited froth of her memoir had even longer legs. Both play and musical were made into movies. McKenney's sister Eileen, her book's namesake, married the novelist Nathanael West and died tragically with him in a California automobile accident just three days before the play of the book opened on Broadway. In 1952 McKenney gathered all her writings about her sister into the omnibus *All about Eileen*.

Melville, Herman (1819–1891)

There now is your insular city of the Manhattoes, belted round by wharves as Indian isles by coral reefs—commerce surrounds it with her surf. Right and left, the streets take you waterward. Its extreme downtown is the battery, where that noble mole is washed by waves, which a few hours previous were out of sight of land. Look at the crowds of water-gazers there.

Circumambulate the city of a dreamy Sabbath afternoon. Go from Corlears Hook to Coenties Slip, and from thence, by Whitehall, northward. What do you see? —Posted like silent sentinels all around the

town, stand themselves upon thousands of mortal men fixed on ocean reveries.
Moby-Dick

Melville was born at 6 Pearl Street in the midst of a heat wave that had turned New York into what his father, Allan, described as a "baby-lonish brick kiln." Both of Melville's grandfathers had distinguished themselves in the Revolutionary War. His grandfather Thomas Melvill (the *e* was added in the 1830s) was one of the "Indians" who dumped tea in the harbor at the Boston Tea Party. Peter Gansevoort, his mother's father and a descendant of an old Dutch patroon family, had become a hero in defending Fort Stanwix. (Manhattan's Gansevoort Street is named after him.) Like the other great New York writers of the nineteenth century, Walt Whitman, Henry James, and Edith Wharton, Melville spent considerable time outside the city. He was educated in Albany and often visited relatives in Pittsfield, Massachusetts, where he would later have a home. But it was New York, in particular the sailing ships, piers, and harbor activity, that fired his imagination. After the failure of his father's business and his father's subsequent death, Melville taught school and tried an office job in the city. Nothing on land compelled him as much as thoughts of putting out to sea did, and off he sailed, first to Liverpool and then in 1841 on the whaling ship *Acushnet* to the whaling grounds of the Pacific, an adventurous voyage that would last more than two years and propel him into life as a writer. Upon his return to America, Melville had plenty of tales to tell his relatives, who urged him to write them down, which he did, producing his first novel, *Typee,* in 1846. Instant success! *Typee* sold well enough not only to make Melville's name but to define him for his time as a travel writer, the man who had sojourned among Polynesian cannibals. Over the next dozen years Melville wrote and published eight novels, one of which was *Moby-Dick,* and numerous stories and occasional pieces. He did most of this work in Arrowhead, his farm in the Berkshires, and not one of these books nor all of them together increased his stature as a writer. Indeed, he never got out of debt to his publisher, Harper's, nor was he accepted as the equal of Hawthorne, his close friend in the Berkshires, or the Concord writers. "Dollars damn me," he wrote Hawthorne, and had it not been for the generosity of his wife Lizzie's father, the Boston jurist, Lemuel Shaw, Melville might not have been able to do the work he did. By the time *Pierre* appeared, perhaps as strange a book as Melville was to write, the *New York Day Book* ran the headline

"HERMAN MELVILLE CRAZY." After the failure of *The Confidence-Man* and a solitary trip to England and the Holy Land, Melville gave up writing novels. In 1863 he traded Arrowhead for his brother Allan's house at 104 East Twenty-sixth Street, and lived there until his death in 1891. Roused and appalled by the carnage of the Civil War, Melville wrote the poems that made up *Battle-Pieces and Aspects of the War.* These grim and powerful poems had few readers and in the year the book appeared, 1866, the forty-seven-year-old Melville went to work as a Customs inspector. It was his first nine-to-five job, and he held it until retirement, working six days a week for four dollars a day, twelve hundred dollars a year with national holidays off and two weeks for vacation. (Such was the corruption in New York at the time that 2 percent of all Customs inspectors' salaries went to the Republican State Committee.) In 1867 his son Malcolm died by his own hand in his room on Twenty-sixth Street. This seems to have been Melville and his wife's lowest moment. Recent evidence suggests that he nearly went mad, and the couple came close to divorcing but somehow their marriage survived. Melville did not give up writing, but worked assiduously at his poetry. Although he did see his old friend and early champion Evert Duyckinck, he did not move in literary circles and never met Mark Twain, William Dean Howells, or any of the other writers famous in his last years. Occasionally, readers of his early books sought him out, and they were almost invariably surprised that he was still alive. In 1888 and again in 1891 he privately published books of his poems in editions of twenty-five copies. At his death in 1891 his funeral was held in the house on Twenty-sixth Street with burial in Woodlawn Cemetery next to Malcolm. On Melville's stone, above his dates, there is an empty scroll.

Melville set very little of his work in New York and, except for the years after *Typee,* did not mix in the city's literary life. Yet, he wrote one unforgettable New York story, "Bartleby, the Scrivener," and the city must have played a role in inspiring *Moby-Dick.* The crew of the *Pequod* could have come off New York's streets at almost any time in the city's history. America, in all its diversity, sailed under Ahab, killed whales, and worked in that factory ship. The meanings of a novel, if that name fits it or any other of Melville's long prose books, as rich as *Moby-Dick* constantly reveal themselves. It may be the great poem of the end of Puritan America, but it is also a catalog of wonders as stuffed to the gills as any Walt Whitman wrote. "Bartleby, the Scrivener" has been read by some as Melville's own "I would prefer not to" to the world. Perhaps, but Bartleby seems a distant relative of Kafka's "Hunger Artist," and the story reads like a parable that could have a score of applications. There is something in Bartleby, that pillar of intransigence, that makes him a New Yorker. The one piece of fiction Melville did write entirely in New York, *Billy Budd,* was found, incomplete, after his death. It was not published until 1924 by which time Melville's work had undergone the reevaluation that ultimately led to its place in the pantheon of American letters. Raymond Weaver, a professor at Columbia, was largely responsible for this. Today, Twenty-sixth Street is also called Herman Melville Avenue, a designation Melville would have smiled at. He often said time would tell about his work and it has done so. In spite of Melville's stature today, or perhaps as much because of it, the twelve years of white-hot inspiration through which he wrote and the void into which each of his books fell, the sheer indifference of his world to his work, is sobering. Dollars did damn him, for in his lifetime the 35,000 copies of his books sold in America brought him $5,900, but had he been a best-selling author and grown wealthy would the last four lines of his poem "The Ravaged Villa" ring true?

> The spider in the laurel spins,
> The weed exiles the flower,
> And, flung to kiln, Apollo's bust
> Makes lime for Mammon's tower.

Merrill, James (1926–1995)

Merrill was born in New York, the son of Charles Merrill, a founder of the stock brokerage that exists today as Merrill, Lynch. Thus he began life with a silver spoon, and he was, he said, "as American as chiffon pie." As a youth he lived first in a brownstone on West Eleventh Street and after his parents divorced, in an apartment building on East Seventy-second Street. Upon graduating from college, Merrill settled in New York and became a regular at the San Remo on MacDougal Street in the Village. Shortly after his first book of poems was accepted by the first publisher who read it, he went to Europe. He eventually came back to New York and although he maintained an apartment in the city throughout his life, he lived for the most part in Stonington, Connecticut. In 1955 his play *The Immortal Husband* was produced Off-Broadway and another play, *The Bait,* was done by John Bernard Myers and Herbert Machiz in the Artists Theater. When his father died, Merrill put some of his inheritance into the Ingram Merrill Foundation, which has given grants to numerous writers and artists. His poetry is among the most elegant in diction and form to have been written by an American since World War II.

7 Middagh Street
Brooklyn Heights

Middagh Street has not been a viable address since 1945, when the entire street was condemned and all the houses on it razed. Number 7 remains on the map of literary New York because of the extraordinary collection of writers who lived there from 1940 to the house's demise. George Davis, fiction editor at *Harper's Bazaar,* saw the house in a dream, he claimed, and searched Brooklyn Heights until he found it and rented it. His friend Carson McCullers, separated from her husband, joined him, and W. H. Auden, for whom Davis was a sometime agent, became a third. Auden collected the rent, twenty-five dollars a floor, a landlordly duty he officiously dispatched. Soon the company grew to include Auden's friend Golo Mann, son of the novelist Thomas Mann; the Broadway theatrical designer Oliver Smith, who had a small room on the third floor; Davis's fiancée, Gypsy Rose Lee (they were working on Lee's mystery novel, *The G String Murders*); and, for a year, Paul and Jane Bowles. Bowles remembered the place as "a nice old house with a comfortable atmosphere and rather uncomfortable furnishings" where people minded their own business. In addition there were transient guests, some of whom—Anaïs Nin, Lincoln Kirstein, Salvador Dalí—stayed for a night or two and others—the Irish poet Louis MacNeice, and the Englishmen Benjamin Britten and Peter Pears—who stayed longer. For a time in 1940 the novelist Richard Wright and his wife, Ellen, friends of McCullers's, lived in the house, but they took their meals apart from the others. The inhabitants of 7 Middagh Street did not immortalize the house in poems, novels, or plays. They were there to live and work, not to provide material for one another.

Millay, Edna St. Vincent (1892–1950)

In the Village west of Sixth Avenue at 75½ Bedford Street, there stands a house so narrow it looks no wider than a person's outstretched arms. It is actually seven feet six inches wide, and in it lived Edna St. Vincent Millay in 1923–1924, her last year in the city. A terra-cotta plaque put there by the Historic Landmarks Preservation Center identifies the house as the place where Millay wrote "Ballad of the Harp Weaver." She had come to the Village in 1917, the year in which her first book, *Renascence and Other Poems,* appeared. For a time she acted with the

Provincetown Players at 133 MacDougal Street and directed two of her own plays there. The beautiful, liberated Millay took lovers on her own terms. The critic Edmund Wilson was one, and through him her poems began to appear in *Vanity Fair*. In 1920 *A Few Figs from Thistles* came out. The "First Fig" contains her most-quoted lines:

> My candle burns at both ends:
> It will not last the night;
> But ah, my foes, and oh, my friends—
> It gives a lovely light . . .

The Harp Weaver was given a Pulitzer Prize in 1923 and soon after, Millay and her husband Eugene Boissevain moved to a farm in Austerlitz, New York. She wrote a good deal of poetry after the twenties, but she is associated with that decade for which her "candle burns" lines became first motto and then epitaph.

Miller, Arthur (b. 1915)

Miller was born on West 111th Street when Harlem still had a population of German Jews. His family moved to 45 West 110th Street before moving to Brooklyn in 1929, eventually settling in a small house at 1350 East Third Street, a house that Miller later said was similar to the one in which Willy Loman lived. Miller remembered this neighborhood as being "psychologically divorced" not only from Manhattan but from the rest of Brooklyn as well. "My neighborhood," he wrote, "was bounded by Gravesend Avenue and Ocean Parkway, a matter of six blocks, and from Avenue M over to Avenue J. Once you got out of there you might as well have been taking a voyage to Kansas." Instead of Kansas, Miller went to college at the University of Michigan, where he discovered that he wanted to be a writer. Returning to Brooklyn, he and his first wife lived at 62 Montague Street in the Heights and then a few streets over at 18 Schermerhorn. The restless Miller then moved to a duplex at 102 Pierrepont Street, a building in which Norman Mailer also lived, and here he wrote *All My Sons*. The play opened on Broadway in 1947, won awards, and launched Miller's career. In that same year he bought 31 Grace Court, which he sold in 1951 to W. E. B. Du Bois (Du Bois bought because he felt that he would not be allowed to rent in the neighborhood). Here Miller wrote his masterpiece, *Death of a Salesman* (1949). It met with immediate success, winning a Pulitzer Prize and a Tony Award, and placing Miller in the first rank of American playwrights. From Grace Court, Miller moved to 155 Willow Street, a brick row house. He walked from here to the rough Red Hook neighborhood, where he liked to explore the docks. These walks ultimately led to *A View from the Bridge* (1955). Following this he moved to 444 East Fifty-seventh Street in Manhattan and from 1962 until 1968 he kept a room at the Chelsea Hotel. Miller has set a number of his plays in the city: *A Memory of Two Mondays, The Price, The American Clock,* and *Broken Glass.* In 1987 he published his autobiography, *Timebends.* Since *After the Fall* (1964) Miller has had a difficult, and at times hostile, relationship with the New York theater. That play dealt with his marriage to Marilyn Monroe and was the opening production at the new Lincoln Center. For reasons that are still not quite clear, not only were the critics cool to it but some of the reviews read like personal attacks. While Miller's plays have continued to open in New York, his work has been greeted with more enthusiasm in London and abroad. His New York experience is similar in some regards to that of both Tennessee Williams and Edward Albee. Williams too had his early plays, *Streetcar Named Desire* and *The Glass Menagerie,* hailed, only to have later work practically run out of town on a rail. Early in his career Albee too could do no wrong, but then after *Who's Afraid of Virginia Woolf?* he suddenly could do no right. Like Miller he too found European theaters more congenial to his art than those on Broadway.

Miller, Henry (1891–1980)

"I am a patriot—of the 14th Ward of Brooklyn, where I was raised. The rest of the United States doesn't exist for me, except as idea, or history, or literature." So wrote Miller in *Black Spring,* which appeared in Paris in the thirties but was not published in America until 1963. Born in Manhattan's German American Yorkville section, Miller came to Brooklyn as an infant and liked to describe himself as "just a Brooklyn boy." He spent his first ten years, years that colored indelibly his imagination, at 662 Driggs Avenue in Williamsburg near the bridge. This was Brooklyn's Fourteenth Ward to which Miller returned again and again in his books because he had been so happy there. The family later moved to 1063 Decatur Street, "the street of early sorrows," in the Bushwick neighborhood, and later Miller lived at 91 Remsen Street in Brooklyn Heights. In 1909 Miller entered City College but left after two months. He drifted west for a few years before returning to Brooklyn, where he worked first in his father's tailor shop and then for Western Union, a job that provided him with the material for *Tropic of Capricorn* (1939). Miller left New York for Paris in 1930 and there he became a writer. Beginning in the forties James Laughlin's New Directions published Miller in the United States, but his most famous books remained banned until 1961 when Grove Press released *Tropic of Cancer* and beat back the government's attempt to have it suppressed as obscene. Miller returned to New York in 1940, but stayed only briefly before moving to Big Sur in California, which he made his base for the rest of his long, and increasingly celebrated, life. His work has been condemned by feminists like Kate Millett and championed by Norman Mailer. Miller's work is in the tradition of another Brooklyn boy, Walt Whitman. Like Whitman Miller insists that the reader encounter a man, that the body of the writer lives and breathes in his pages. "In my dreams," Miller wrote in *Black Spring,* "I come back to the 14th Ward as a paranoiac returns to his obsessions."

Miller, Warren (1921–1966)

The author of several novels, Miller hung around Harlem in the early sixties and came away with the material for his novel *The Cool World.* It deals with the initiation of several young men and women into Harlem's criminal street life of drug dealers, pimps, and whores. Few whites had taken the trouble to see what Miller saw, and his novel added to the picture of Harlem then coming into focus. James Baldwin had high praise for the book, and Shirley Clarke made it into a movie. She recruited black kids off the streets for many of the roles and shot it using cinema verité techniques. The documentary filmmaker Frederic Wiseman produced the film. Before his untimely death Miller visited Cuba, then a daring thing to do, and reported on what he encountered in *90 Miles from Home.*

Mitchell, Joseph (1908–1996)

A North Carolina native, Mitchell arrived in New York in 1929 four days before the stock market crash. Over the next eight years he worked for several newspapers, gaining renown for his feature articles. These were collected in the now very difficult to find book, *My Ears Are Bent.* Harold Ross hired Mitchell at the *New Yorker* in 1938, and there he remained for the rest of his writing life. In 1964 the magazine published "Joe Gould's Secret," the last and greatest of Mitchell's stories. He came to work for the next thirty-two years but never published another word. Pantheon collected most of his *New Yorker* work in 1992 under the title *Up in the Old Hotel.* It became a best-seller, and deservedly so. Mitchell mastered a plain, forceful, and vivid prose style.

He roamed the city and looked into corners of it no one else had, and he invented New Journalism before it was given the name. His New York is long gone, but it lives on in his work, where he accomplished, as he put it, "tragedy and comedy all balled up into one thing." Other *New Yorker* writers of nonfiction have approached his standard—A. J. Liebling, Lillian Ross, and John McPhee come to mind—but none have exceeded it.

An "About the Author" note at the end of *Up in the Old Hotel* recounts his frequent trips home to North Carolina and his birding in Ashpole Swamp:

> Once, deep in the swamp, looking through binoculars, he watched for an hour or so as a pileated woodpecker tore the bark off the upper trunk and limbs of a tall old dead blackgum tree, and he says he considers this the most spectacular event he has ever witnessed.

Montague, John (b. 1929)

Montague's breech birth was "the worst," according to his mother, "in the annals of Brooklyn." It occurred at St. Catherine's Hospital on Bushwick Avenue while the Montagues, having fled Ireland to avoid the Troubles, lived at 59 Rodney Street. Montague spent four years in Brooklyn before his family returned to Ireland, where he completed college. He spent his postgraduate years in America at Yale, Iowa, and Berkeley, and then, after several years in Ireland, returned in the seventies to teach at the State University of New York at Albany, a position he holds today. In 1991 White Pine Press collected his Brooklyn work under the title *Born in Brooklyn*. There is nothing quite like it in American letters. The Irish are a powerful presence in New York, and Montague's angle is unique. He writes from both inside out and, by virtue of his years in Ireland, outside in. He remembers

life under

a crumbling brownstone
roof in Brooklyn
to the clatter of
garbage cans

and returns to find "another, wild, raunchier Brooklyn." But the heart of his book is in what Montague calls "the complex fate of being an Irish American." This has its dark moments, but in his case his natal city supplies a light touch: "If the borough of Brooklyn ever decides to recognize me as a lost poetic son they will not have to go to any trouble to honor me, for there is already a Montague Street."

Moore, Clement Clarke (1779–1863)

Had Moore not written *A Visit from St. Nicholas,* sometimes titled by its first line "T'was the night before Christmas," he might be remembered today as author of the foremost Hebrew dictionary of his time and the developer of the farmland that became the neighborhood of Chelsea. Moore wrote the poem for his six children in 1822, but it was a friend who heard him recite it that Christmas Eve who got it published. She submitted it to the editor of the Troy, New York, *Sentinel* where it appeared anonymously the following year. Moore's name became attached to the poem fifteen years later, but he did not acknowledge it as his work until 1844. The poem has not only endured, it has given us the Santa Claus we know today. St. Nicholas was celebrated in New Amsterdam on December 5, the eve of St. Nicholas. Moore gave him the sleigh and reindeer, and had him enter and exit through the chimney. In 1860 the cartoonist Thomas Nast, who made Republicans elephants and Democrats donkeys and whose caricatures of Boss Tweed helped drive that scoundrel from office, illustrated Moore's poem with the jolly, rosy-cheeked, red-suited fellow who now comes to town during Macy's Thanksgiving Day parade. Santa Claus is a New York creation. Moore is buried in Trinity Cemetery at 115th Street. John Jacob Astor and Charles Dickens's son Alfred Tennyson Dickens are in the same graveyard.

Moore, Marianne (1887–1972)

> the savage's romance
> accreted where we need the space of commerce—
> the centre of the wholesale fur trade,
> starred with tepees of ermine and people with foxes . . .

"New York"

Moore came to Greenwich Village with her mother in 1918 and remained in the city for the rest of her life. This most individual and unbohemian of women joined the crowd that included Hart Crane, William Carlos Williams, and Edna St. Vincent Millay around Alfred Kreymborg's magazine *Others.* Kreymborg described Moore as "an astonishing person with Titian hair" and Williams called her "straight up and down like the two-by-fours of a building under construction." At this time she and her mother lived at 14 St. Luke's Place across from the

Hudson Park Branch of the New York Public Library, where Moore worked from 1921 to 1925. Moore seemed to know about everything. Determined to stump her, Kreymborg figured that no woman could know anything about baseball and so took her to the Polo Grounds for a Giants–Cubs game. Christy Mathewson was on the mound for the Giants, and Moore, who many years later wrote poems about her beloved Brooklyn Dodgers, surprised Kreymborg by knowing all about "Matty." Moore was the first of the *Others* crowd to have poems accepted by the *Dial,* which gave her second book, *Observations,* its prestigious Dial Award in 1924. The next year Moore became the magazine's editor, continuing until its demise in 1929. She greatly enjoyed "the compacted pleasantness" of her days at the *Dial's* office at 152 West Thirteenth Street. In 1931 Moore moved with her mother to 260 Cumberland Street in Brooklyn's Fort Greene Park neighborhood. To George Plimpton, who came to interview her in 1964 for the *Paris Review,* she identified her building as having "what look like moth balls on iron stands flanking the entrance." It was to this apartment that the young Elizabeth Bishop, who had met Moore through a teacher at Vassar, came to visit. When Moore crossed the East River to Manhattan, she liked to take the Manhattan Bridge so as to get a good view of the Brooklyn Bridge downriver. From this vantage point there is a moment in which the Statue of Liberty can be glimpsed through the bridge's cables. "Enfranchising cable, silvered by the sea," Moore wrote in "Granite and Steel," her 1965 tribute to the Brooklyn Bridge, "of woven wire, grayed by the mist, / and liberty dominate the Bay." After her mother died Moore returned to the Village, where she lived until her death at 35 West Ninth Street. Over the last twenty-five years of her life, Moore became famous partly because of her correspondence with the Ford Motor Company, which asked her to name their car. *Life* magazine published these letters (although the ill-fated Edsel was named after Ford's son in the end), and Moore appeared in *Life's* pages wearing her trademark unicorn hat. Her love of baseball added to her appeal, and she had the pleasure of throwing out the first ball on Opening Day at Yankee Stadium in 1968. This public face obscured, perhaps to Moore's delight, both the grace and difficulty of her work and her commanding personality. Although she was given a Pulitzer Prize, a National Book Award, and the Bollingen Prize, her poetry has been more praised and admired than imitated. She has an essayistic quality, a way of gathering a great deal of information, often quoting sources, into deliberate, measured cadences, that is entirely her own.

Morley, Christopher (1890–1957)

During the twenties Morley, who wrote poems, novels, and plays, was active in New York as a literary columnist. His confrères were F. P. A., whose "Conning Tower" was the most widely read literary column, and Don Marquis. Nothing like these columns has existed in daily newspapers since the early fifties. They published literary news, gossip, poems submitted by readers, miniature essays, and the columnist's own ruminations and poems. Morley lived at 46 West Forty-seventh Street across from the present Gotham Book Mart at 41 West Forty-seventh Street, a space he helped find. He also helped make the store a hangout for literary types by convening the Three Hours for Lunch Club with the poet William Rose Benét and Buckminster Fuller, who would one day invent the geodesic dome and write poems. Morley had one great popular success, the best-selling novel *Kitty Foyle* (1939), which was made into a movie the following year.

Morrison, Toni (b. 1931)

After several years of teaching Morrison came to New York in the late sixties to work as a textbook editor at Random House. She wrote much of her first novel, *The Bluest Eye* (1970), in the hours just after dawn when her young children were still asleep. Morrison returned to teaching while still working at Random House, now in the trade department, and continuing to write. Since she spent a lot of time in the car between jobs, she tried to write using a tape recorder, but this was a "disaster" and she returned to her favored number 2 pencils. At Random House she edited the books of Angela Davis, Toni Cade Bambara, Gayle Jones, Andrew Young, and Muhammad Ali. *Song of Solomon* (1977), which won a National Book Award, and *Beloved* (1987), winner of a Pulitzer Prize, are her best-known novels. In 1993 she became the first African American to be given a Nobel Prize.

Moss, Howard (1922–1987)

For some twenty years Moss served as the *New Yorker*'s poetry editor and his *Selected Poems* won a National Book Award in 1971, but he is here primarily for the anthology he edited and published in 1980, *New York: Poems*. Whitman aside, Moss focuses on the twentieth century, and he is even-handed enough to have Paul Blackburn follow Elizabeth Bishop. There could be more Allen Ginsberg and there is nothing from the second generation of the New York School or from Cole Porter and other songwriters, but every anthology is open to quibbles. There are pleasures here, in particular the poems by visitors Federico García Lorca, Vladimir Mayakovsky, and Léopold Senghor. In his introduction Moss points out that while there are ample poems about Manhattan and Brooklyn, the other three boroughs, the Bronx, Queens, and Staten Island, are rarely sung. The same is true in prose. In literary New York City those three are the shadow boroughs. Avon published Moss's book as an original paperback. It is now out of print and worth keeping an eye peeled for in secondhand stores.

Mumford, Lewis (1895–1990)

Born in Flushing and educated at City College, Columbia, and the New School, Mumford made cities one of his prime intellectual interests. He wrote a number of books, including *The City in History* (1961), exploring the rise and development of cities throughout the world. For over a decade in the twenties and thirties he lived in the planned community of Sunnyside Gardens in northwestern Queens, but he did much of his thinking and writing about cities in the upstate New York town of Amenia. Mumford was the *New Yorker*'s architecture critic for many years. He possessed a vigorous prose style, and his short book *The Brown Decades* remains one of the best on America, with emphasis on the arts, between the Civil War and the beginning of the twentieth century.

Murray, Albert (b. 1916)

After growing up in Mississippi, graduating from Alabama's Tuskegee Institute, and serving in World War II, Murray came to New York, where he received a graduate degree at New York University and hooked up again with his college friend Ralph Ellison. Over the next few years while Ellison finished *Invisible Man,* Murray and he were very close. Murray was also writing at the time, but he let few people see his work. In 1951 he went back into the air force and served until 1962, when he retired and returned to New York. He resumed his friendship with Ellison and began to publish essays and articles. During the sixties both Murray and Ellison stood in opposition to the rising tide of black nationalism. While this led to Ellison's being vilified by some, it did not obscure his work. Murray, who had published *The Omni Americans* by this time, was all but unknown because no one, black or white, seemed to want to hear what he had to say. The core of his argument is that America is as much a black society as a white one. In Murray's view blacks cannot be separated from nor integrated into American culture, for they have always been indivisible with it. In 1976 he published *Stomping the Blues,* which explored how the blues had shaped the national character and brought him a wider audience before he disappeared again, this time into the person of Count Basie, whose autobiography he spent years writing. Throughout this time Murray lived in Harlem's Lenox Terrace where he lives today, suddenly a writer celebrated by profiles in the *New Yorker* and the *Village Voice.* He has come out from under Ellison's shadow and been hailed as a mentor by young black writers such as Stanley Crouch. Murray did not have to change to achieve his current status. He held to his convictions and the world, black and white, came to him.

New Criterion
850 Seventh Avenue

In 1996 editor and publisher Hilton Kramer celebrated his magazine by declaring that is has been "a voice of embattled dissent . . . from the baleful influence of a Left-liberal ideology in politics and an ugly 'postmodernist' assault on the arts." Kramer sees his magazine as an antidote to much that has dominated New York intellectual and literary life since the thirties, and a bastion of the sort of traditional values espoused by T. S. Eliot, who edited the *Criterion.* Allan Bloom published in Kramer's magazine and so has Roger Kimball, the art critic Jed Perl, Bruce Bawer, John Simon, and Deborah Solomon. While the *New Criterion* publishes poetry and trumpets the "new formalism," the bulk of each issue is given over to essays and reviews. For many years Kramer was the lead art critic for the *New York Times,* and he continues to write an art column for the *New York Observer.*

New Directions
80 Eighth Avenue

While still a Harvard undergraduate James Laughlin began New Directions in 1936. Ezra Pound, whose work Laughlin had been introduced to by his prep school teacher, the poet and translator Dudley Fitts, was his mentor. Pound put Laughlin on to the work of Henry Miller and William Carlos Williams, both of whom published with New Directions throughout their long careers. "One good writer leads to another,"

Laughlin has said. While this is certainly true in his case, how many publishers have listened as closely to their writers? Laughlin's original intention was to publish the avant-garde, "new directional" writers, and he stuck to it, refusing all purely commercial projects into the sixtieth year of the press. New Directions writers include Tennessee Williams, Djuna Barnes, Dylan Thomas, Robert Creeley, Denise Levertov, Bernadette Mayer, Michael Palmer, Jerome Rothenberg, Delmore Schwartz, Thomas Merton, Kenneth Rexroth, Robert Duncan, and the list could go on for pages. More than any other press—Alfred A. Knopf is the only one close—New Directions introduced foreign writers to America: Rimbaud, Apollinaire, Céline, Nabokov, Michaux, Pasternak, García Lorca, Montale, Neruda, Gustafsson, Paz, Borges . . . another list that could fill pages. New Directions is America's premier literary publisher. How did all this come to a Harvard undergraduate? In the thirties Pound, Williams, Miller, and other avant-garde writers were not of interest to the major New York houses. Laughlin had the good taste to commit himself to their work. He also went looking for books in Europe, where other American publishers had not ventured, and there he had the advantage of knowing French and other languages. The offices of New Directions did not move to New York until the forties. For a time Laughlin, always eager to limit his expenses, shared office space with other publishers. One such office gave him a view of the B-52 bomber that crashed into the Empire State building in 1945. In New York Laughlin kept an apartment in the Village and often dined at the Century Club. Tennessee Williams liked to persuade Laughlin to take him there, in part because Laughlin famously did not treat his authors to expensive lunches. Nor did he spend money on large advances or advertising. What he believed in was publishing good books and keeping them in print. When the paperback revolution led to college course adoptions in the fifties, New Directions books, with their distinctive black-and-white covers, were everywhere. They educated that generation, and have continued to do so for subsequent ones. The poet Kenneth Patchen worked for New Directions when it was headquartered in a stable in Norfolk, Connecticut, where Laughlin had a house. In New York the poet May Swenson worked in the office, as did Donald Allen, who would go on to become an important editor at New York's other major avant-garde publisher, Grove Press. While Laughlin was out of town in the forties and fifties developing a ski resort in Utah and working for the Ford Foundation, Robert McGregor, called Bob McHOORSe by Pound in tribute to the hard work he did, held down the fort. Today Griselda Ohannessian, Peggy Fox, and Barbara Epler are in New York. Until his death in November 1977 Laughlin was in semiretirement in Norfolk, Connecticut, where New Directions had its first office.

The New Formalists

It is not only poets of a Beat or bohemian stripe who hatch their movements in Greenwich Village. In 1981 the poets Dick Allen, Frederick Fierstein, and Frederick Turner met at the Minetta Tavern and agreed that it was time for a regeneration of formal poetry. They sought, as their credo, written by Allen and titled "Transcending the Self," suggests, to get beyond the self-absorption they found in so much American free verse. Like most literary groups, their approach to poetry is far from monolithic. Other New York poets who more or less belong to this most low key of movements are Molly Peacock, Rachel Hadas, and Karl Kirchway.

New School for Social Research
66 West Twelfth Street

After resigning from Columbia University during World War I, the historians James Harvey Robinson and Charles A. Beard founded the New School in 1919. Beard's resignation had protested Columbia's expulsion of a colleague for his pacifism. From the start the New School strove to be experimental and to focus on the social sciences. In its early years the economist Wesley Clair Mitchell and the social theorist Thorstein Veblen taught there. In the thirties the school welcomed many European exiles to its faculty, the theologian Jacques Maritain, the linguist Roman Jakobson, and the anthropologist Claude Lévi-Strauss among them. Erwin Piscator came from Berlin to found and run the Dramatic Workshop. Tennessee Williams was one of his students. Meyer Schapiro have a series of standing-room-only art lectures at the school. Hiram Haydn taught the fiction workshop that had William Styron and Mario Puzo as students. Alfred Kazin, Hannah Arendt, and John Cage taught there, as did the poet Kenneth Koch. The poet Bill Berkson took Koch's course and later taught a class at the school himself. One of his students was the poet Bernadette Mayer, who graduated from the school in 1967. Today Robert Polito, poet and biographer, runs a large and active writing program.

New York Public Library

Although the system is less than a hundred years old, which means that great libraries like the British Museum in London had many years' head start in building their collections, the New York Public Library of eighty-one branches can boast of having the seventh largest research library in the world and the fourth largest in the United States. This is, of course, the landmark main branch at Fifth Avenue and Forty-second Street, the library that serves the majority of the more than one million borrowers and visitors who use the system every year. The main branch is worth visiting for three reasons above all. First, it is a beautiful public building, one that by its monumental character proclaims the significance of books and writing to our culture. Second, the great public rooms and main reading room are magnificent. On any day sitting in one of these rooms it is easy to imagine the many men and women, some of them famous writers, but most not, who have found nourishment and inspiration here. Third, the staggering shows put on in the Berg Exhibition Room are not to be missed. Where else can one see the very violets Shelley plucked from Keats's grave in Rome's Protestant Cemetery and Shelley's note identifying them as such? In every one of its shows there are an enormous number of delights whose range extends far beyond books and manuscripts. The recent "Hand of the Poet" exhibit displayed a postcard from Marianne Moore to James Merrill that showed a man in drag under a banner reading, "Warning Idaho is Full of Beautiful Women." Visitors stand and peer into old-fashioned vitrines that snake around the large room. It is almost impossible not to get lost in these shows.

Behind the main branch is the newly refurbished Bryant Park, named after William Cullen Bryant. For years the Park was overrun by prostitutes and junkies, but now all is air, light, grass, gravel pathways, and French folding chairs. It is the perfect place to be at rest in the middle of the city and watched over by busts of Goethe and Gertrude Stein and a full-scale statue of the seated Bryant.

There are two other branches worth a visit: the Schomburg Center for Research in Black Culture housed in the 135th Street branch and the Library and Museum of the Performing Arts at Lincoln Center. The Schomburg began as the collection of Arthur Schomburg, who on modest means accumulated thousands of books, prints, drawings, manuscripts, and pamphlets devoted to the black experience. In 1926 this was purchased by the New York Public Library and housed in the 135th Street branch, where it has grown to be the single most important collection of its kind in the nation. Exhibitions here are just as staggering as those at the main branch.

The 135th Street branch played a significant role in the Harlem Renaissance as a gathering place for writers. In 1936 it was on the library steps that the newly arrived Ralph Ellison met Langston Hughes and Alain Locke. Ellison asked Hughes if he could introduce him to Richard Wright, which Hughes shortly did, and Ellison was soon in the thick of things.

While not as well known as either the main branch or the Schomburg, the Library of Performing Arts has large holdings in dance, theater (the Billy Rose Theater Collection), opera, motion pictures, recorded sound (the Rodgers and Hammerstein Archives) . . . again the range and numbers (24,000 posters!) are staggering and the exhibitions delightful.

Treasures of the New York Public Library, a coffee-table book published by Henry N. Abrams, documents these treasure houses up until 1988. Since then who knows how much has been added to these astounding collections?

New York Review of Books

In the winter of 1963 New York was going through one of a series of newspaper strikes that narrowed down the number of daily papers in the city from seven to the present three. That February in the West Sixty-seventh Street apartment of Random House editor Jason Epstein and his wife, Barbara, the Epsteins and their guests, Robert Lowell and his wife, the novelist Elizabeth Hardwick, dreamed up the *New York Review of Books*. Robert Silvers and Barbara Epstein became the *Review*'s editors and Hardwick, advisory editor, positions they hold to this day. The *Review* flourished, perhaps beyond the wildest dreams of its founders, and today has a national circulation of more than 125,000. (During the 1963 newspaper strike Edmund Wilson noted, "The disappearance of the *Times* . . . book section at the time of the printers' strike only made us aware that it had never existed.") The city was ready for a serious book review, and *NYRB* signed up high-level writers (Edmund Wilson, F. W. Dupee, Hannah Arendt, Gore Vidal, Susan Sontag) to write essay-length reviews of a wide variety of books. Although left-wing in political orientation and focusing on history, politics, and sociology, the *Review* has paid more attention to science—Stephen Jay Gould is often in its pages—than any other mainstream American intellectual publication. Always conservative in aesthetic matters, at least in terms of the fiction and poetry it reviews, in the past fifteen years the paper has covered art exhibitions (John Updike reporting) as it never has before, and gone in heavily for English reviewers. Indeed, Anglophilia is one of the paper's distinguishing features. Among the newer writers are Louis Menand, Joan Acocella on dance, Ian Buruma and the South African novelist J. M. Coetzee. Old hands Garry Wills, Theodore Draper, Joan Didion, Robert Craft, and Michael Wood remain frequent contributors. The historian Richard Hofstadter once joked that the paper's name ought to be the "New York Review of Each Other's Books." Sharp as his wisecrack was in the sixties, it has held little sting since then. When the *Review* began New York could conceive of itself as America's intellectual center, and intellectuals on the Upper West Side could imagine themselves as the center's bulls-eye. Largely because of forces unleashed during the Vietnam War that intellectual center exploded across the country and fragmented into hundreds of colleges and universities. No one at the Epsteins' dinner table could have foreseen this, but somehow the paper they invented has kept pace.

New York School

The New York School of Poets is named after the group of abstract painters such as de Kooning, Kline, Pollock, and Guston, who were given the name "New York School" as a joke. There had once been a School of Paris made up of conventional, establishment painters. De Kooning and his brethren were anything but. At one time or another all the poets in the New York School have taken pains to point out that while they are connected through friendship and the magazines in which they publish, their work is very different. *School* in their case suggests a loose grouping rather than rows of assigned seating and rigorously followed lesson plans. The first generation is made up of John Ashbery, Kenward Elmslie, Barbara Guest, Kenneth Koch, Frank O'Hara, and James Schuyler. Harry Mathews held down the Paris office, and Edwin Denby, a contemporary of de Kooning's, was a Dutch uncle. Except for Koch and Ashbery in his later years, these poets have worked outside of academe. They all write unconventional free verse, and when they do employ received forms they tend to put them to original use. They have all collaborated with painters, with O'Hara leading the way. Cutting across generations and styles, he worked with Larry Rivers, Michael Goldberg, Norman Bluhm, and Joe Brainard. Except for Guest and Mathews all the poets have written for the theater. They also share a significant impact on a second generation of poets and through them a third. In the second generation are Bill Berkson, Lewis Warsh, Charles North, Paul Violi, John Godfrey, Bernadette Mayer, Ted Berrigan, Alice Notley, Ron Padgett, Maureen Owen, Joseph Ceravolo, Joe Brainard, Jim Carroll, Jim Brodey, Larry Fagin, David Shapiro, Michael Brownstein, Anne Waldman, and Frank Lima. It was this generation that administered the Poetry Project at St. Mark's Church and who produced a flood of mimeographed magazines and small-press books during the sixties. They in turn have influenced a third generation that includes Yuki Hartman, the late Michael Scholnick, Eileen Myles, Gillian McCain, Rochelle Kraut, Bob Rosenthal, Ed Friedman, Jo Ann Wasserman, Cliff Fyman, Mitch Highfill, Simon Pettet, and David Abel, among others. Magazines associated with the school range from *Locus Solus,* begun in Paris by Harry Mathews, through the dozen issues of the still valuable *Art and Literature*—John Ashbery was one of the editors—to *Angel Hair,* which mutated into *United Artists,* and *The World,* the ongoing magazine of the Poetry Project. To date only Frank O'Hara, who died in 1966, has been the subject of a biography, but acres of prose have been used to explain and corral Ashbery's work, and he, as well as others of the first generation, will surely draw biographers.

New York University

Founded in Washington Square in 1831 as the University of the City of New York, NYU has had, until recently, the fewest literary lights of any major New York University. As a private university it could not compete with the more prestigious Columbia for students, and during the Depression it was too expensive for the sons and daughters of New York's immigrants. Poets Countee Cullen, Delmore Schwartz, and Ed Sanders graduated from NYU, as did the novelists Joseph Heller and Jerome Weidman. Lillian Hellman, Carson McCullers, and Woody Allen studied at the university, but none of them completed a degree. In the 1970s NYU began a creative writing program in which a host of writers have taught, Russell Banks, Galway Kinnell, Sharon Olds, the Australian novelist Peter Carey, E. L. Doctorow, and Mark Rudman among them. The poet and critic M. L. Rosenthal taught at NYU for many years, as has the Irish critic and memoirist Denis Donoghue.

The New Yorker
20 West Forty-third Street

More books have been written about the *New Yorker* than any other New York literary institution, single writer, or group of writers. Harold Ross, founder of the magazine, has had at least three biographies written about him, including *The Years with Ross* by one of the *New Yorker*'s most famous contributors, James Thurber. Thurber himself has had several biographers, the most recent of whom turned out a book of more than one thousand pages. E. B. White and his wife, Katherine, the magazine's top fiction editor for many years, have had their lives written down and in 1976 Brendan Gill did a group portrait titled *Here at the New Yorker*. The reason for this river of ink is not that the writers associated with the *New Yorker* are major. Most of them— White, Thurber, Robert Benchley, Dorothy Parker, Woolcott Gibbs, Lillian Ross, A. J. Liebling—were among the best journalists and humorists of their time, but their work has dated and will continue to do so. What they, led by Ross, did accomplish was the creation of a magazine that over several generations has been read by the most literate Americans in all walks of life, business, government, literature, science, etc. The *New Yorker* exists today, albeit in a changed and sensational form, because Ross and his writers and artists put together a magazine that they believed in. Pride in the *New Yorker,* often to the point of smugness, marks nearly every memoir about the magazine. Along the way the magazine discovered a formula that appealed to readers and advertisers alike. It somehow connected its readers with its advertisers so that many who subscribed to the magazine could say, with their own touch of pride, that they really didn't read the magazine but the ads were great. Whatever the mix that formed and nurtured this enterprise, few American writers today would refuse to be in the magazine's pages and few, if any, readers do not get pleasure out of at least something in every issue. Harold Ross, an experienced newspaperman, founded the magazine with his wife, Jane Grant, in 1925, the backing coming from members of the Fleischmann yeast family. Initially, the *New Yorker* was a humor magazine that listed the city's amusements and covered the local goings-on in its "Talk of the Town" columns. It did so to distinguish itself from the other humor magazines of the moment, *Judge* and the original *Life*. The *New Yorker* also went in for longer journalistic pieces and developed a biographical feature called the "profile" that was central to it until recently. Ross was adept at putting together, and keeping amused by his antics, a staff that in the case of White, Thurber, and many of the others not only produced for the magazine but wrote books that made them well known, adding to the magazine's luster. Ross gave his writers three things all writers thrive on—time, space, and money. He also gave them editing that is still notorious for its nit-picking fact checking. (The novelists Truman Capote, Chandler Brossard, and Jay McInerney have been among the *New Yorker*'s fact checkers, and McInerney's novel *Bright Lights, Big City* has great fun with this aspect of the magazine.) Ross balanced journalism with fiction, cartoons (for some the art of Thurber, Peter Arno, George Price, William Steig, Saul Steinberg, George Booth, Roz Chast, Edward Koren, and a host of others is the magazine's signature), poetry, and criticism. Then as now the magazine presented the serious and the jokey, and in the case of writers from S. J. Perelman to Ian Frazier, the seriously funny. The magazine has published fiction by John O'Hara—for years a mainstay—Vladimir Nabokov, Mavis Gallant, John Cheever, Ann Beattie, William Maxwell—also one of its top fiction editors—Frank O'Connor, Flannery O'Connor, J. D. Salinger (many of his stories including his last published one), John Updike, whose boyhood dream it was to write for the magazine and who has by now contributed to most of its departments, Donald Barthelme, Alice Munro, Isaac Bashevis Singer . . . the list, as is true of those that follow, could go on for pages. In 1951 William Shawn became editor. While opposite in temperament to the flamboyant Ross, the quiet, meticulous Shawn continued to edit a magazine that was by Ross's dictate not for "the old lady from Dubuque." And where Ross had given an entire issue to John Hersey's *Hiroshima*, Shawn, in the sixties and seventies printed James Baldwin's *The Fire Next Time*, Hannah Arendt's *Eichmann in Jerusalem*, Charles Reich's *The Greening of America*, and Jonathan Schell's *The Village of Ben Suc*. Shawn also published in four installments Truman Capote's *In Cold Blood*. Edmund Wilson reviewed books during Shawn's years as editor; Whitney Balliet reported on jazz, popular singers, and songs, as he does today, developing his own version of the "profile" that reads like an extended monologue or solo; Janet Flanner wrote letters from Paris; Kennedy Fraser commented on clothing styles; Pauline Kael, one of the most influential of the *New Yorker* critics in terms of style, reviewed movies; Andrew Porter covered classical music; and Arlene Croce dance and that is just a dip into the cream of the magazine. To these should be added Philip Hamburger; the great Joseph Mitchell, perhaps the champ of all *New Yorker* writers; Lewis Mumford; poetry editors Louise Bogan, Howard Moss, and Alice Quinn;

Robert M. Coates, Rogers E. W. Whitaker, who wrote on trains; Roger Angell, who has written memorably on baseball; Alexander Woollcott; Ingrid Sischy; Thomas Whitehead; Jamaica Kincaid; Mark Singer; George S. W. Trow; Lucius Beebe; Edith Iglauer; S. N. Berhman, whose *Duveen* is a first-rate example of a *New Yorker* profile; Janet Malcolm; John McPhee, who enjoyed a great vogue in the seventies and eighties; Lois Long; Helen Hokinson; Gus Lobrano; George Steiner; St. Clair McKelway; E. J. Khan Jr.; Andy Logan; Elizabeth Oliver; Mollie Painter-Downes; Robert Caro; Penelope Gilliat; and Rea Irvin, whose drawing of the top-hatted dandy, Eustace Tilley, inspecting a butterfly through a monocle appeared on the magazine's first cover and has appeared on every anniversary cover in some form. In 1985 the magazine was sold by the Fleischmann family to S. I. Newhouse, and William Shawn was soon replaced, to the consternation of many, by Robert Gottlieb, who edited the magazine for seven years. Tina Brown took over as editor in 1992. She came from editing the successful and celebrity gossip / true crime-driven *Vanity Fair,* and she is English. The current *New Yorker* reflects her background. The magazine now prints four-letter words, has given up long discursive essays for shorter, punchier ones, likes to dish the dirt, and is often closer to London's literary world than New York's. While defiantly not a magazine for whatever old lady still lives in Dubuque, the magazine is being talked about again.

Nin, Anaïs (1903–1977)

Born in Paris, Nin came to Manhattan as a teenager, living from 1914 to 1919 in a rooming house at 158 West Seventy-fifth Street with her mother and brother. Here she began the voluminous diary for which she is best known. Her original intention was to keep a record for her father, who had abandoned the family. She returned to Paris and remained there through the twenties and thirties. It was there that she met Henry Miller, who became her lover and then her friend. In January 1940 Nin returned to New York and took an apartment at 215 West Thirteenth Street. Two years later she moved to a studio at 145 Mac-Dougal Street, bought a printing press, and began to publish books. Her novel *Winter of Artifice* appeared in 1942 and two years later she published the collection of short stories, *Under a Glass Bell,* whose good review by Edmund Wilson was the beginning of their friendship. As the seven volumes of Nin's diary began to appear in the late sixties, the surge of the women's movement carried her and her work on its tide. She became famous and was seen as a feminist heroine because she had dictated the terms of her sexual life. A second look at the diaries reveals not only that there were no other women in her life but that Nin clearly desired to be defined by the men she wrote about. Beside Miller and Wilson other writers in the diary are Gore Vidal, Carson McCullers and the denizens of Brooklyn's Middagh Street house, and the young poet Robert Duncan, then named Robert Symmes.

Ninety-second Street Y (M-YWHA)
1395 Lexington Avenue

The initials stand for the Young Men's-Young Women's Hebrew Association, but the Y is a "nonsectarian agency." Since 1940 it has housed the Unterberg Poetry Center. Years ago *Poetry* meant Poetry; today the center offers poetry with a small *p*. In 1966, for example, the Center hosted readings by a large, diverse group: Louise Bogan, Robert Creeley, Carolyn Kizer, John Wieners, and Louis Untermeyer among them and a William Carlos Williams Memorial featuring Denise Levertov and Robert Lowell. A few prose writers were on the program—Isaac Bashevis Singer, the German novelist Uwe Johnson, and Elie Wiesel— but the emphasis was on poetry. That emphasis has now shifted to prose. Not only do novelists have the majority of readings at the Y, but they appear in various symposiums and are interviewed onstage for the *Paris Review*. A partial list of those reading in the spring 1997 program gives an idea of the Y's range: Larry McMurtry, Ruth Prawer Jhabvala, John Montague, August Wilson, James Salter, Gary Soto, Amy Tan, William Trevor, Ann Lauterbach, and A. S. Byatt. Poetry, fiction, and nonfiction workshops are also offered, as are master classes in fiction and poetry as well as literary seminars taught by such luminaries as Helen Vendler. Half-season memberships are available. The center's calendar appears in all the major New York papers and a poster and brochure advertise the series.

Nuyorican Poets Café
236 East Third Street, between Avenues B & C

Miguel Algarin, poet and coeditor of *Aloud: Voices from the Nuyorican Poets Café,* defines Nuyorican as "(New York + Puerto Rican) 1. Originally Puerto Rican epithet for those of Puerto Rican heritage born in New York: their Spanish was different (Spanglish), their way of dress and look were different." Definition 3 is "A denizen of the Nuyorican Poets Café." Readings were first held at the café in 1974 in a space called the Open Room founded by Miguel Pinero, Ntozake Shange, and Piri Thomas. Poets who wanted to read showed up, gave their names to Algarin, who kept each evening's roster, and performed their work. By the early 1980s the café had become a scene, and soon poetry slams were held on Wednesday and Friday nights, as they are to this day. The emphasis at the Nuyorican is on poetry as performance. Bob Holman, formerly of the Poetry Project and coeditor of *Aloud,* exclaims in his introduction to the anthology, "DO NOT READ THIS BOOK! You don't have to: *This book reads to you.*" There are more than 150 individual voices in *Aloud,* and they chant, shout, croon, belt out, and rant their poems. The anthology, which was a 1994 American Book Award winner, bears this epigram from jazzman-astronaut of inner and outer space, Sun Ra:

> If you're not suitable in the future
> you probably won't make it in the present either.

Some of those who have performed at the café and appear in the anthology are Paul Beatty, Maggie Estep, Edwin Torres, Jimmy Santiago Baca, Wanda Coleman, David Henderson, and Sapphire.

Obenzinger, Hilton (b. 1947)

In 1982 Obenzinger, a New York native and graduate of Columbia, contracted to produce a pictorial yearbook devoted to heroic firefighters for the firefighter's union. That book never appeared, but out of the research he did for it Obenzinger wrote the documentary poem *New York on Fire.* Its multitude of voices range from George Templeton Strong to H. Rap Brown. It chronicles all the city's famous fires including that sparked by the 1863 draft riots and the Triangle Shirtwaist Company fire in 1911, but Obenzinger uses his poetic license to treat both the great blackout of 1965 and the mythic firefighter, the seven-foot-tall Old Mose. As Obenzinger says in his note, "I can assure you that as much as the book is fiction, all of it is based on true events." It is a remarkable angle from which to look at the city. Here is an excerpt from the section titled "Triangle Shirtwaist Company March 25, 1911":

Put up the ladders! the people cry out
But the fire horses can't pull up to the building,
The bodies litter the sidewalk, quivering
The horses panic at the pelting bodies.
Oh God, they are falling, so many falling.

Off-Broadway

The longtime theater critic at the *Village Voice* Ross Wetzsteon says that Off-Broadway began in 1956 with the Circle-in-the-Square production of Eugene O'Neill's *The Iceman Cometh* or with Joseph Papp's first Shakespeare in Central Park (it was staged on the back of a truck) in 1957 *or* with the Living Theater's production of Jack Gelber's *The Connection*. Regardless of the year or production, the idea animating Off-Broadway was the creation of an alternative to Broadway's commercial theater. Off-Broadway, located primarily in the Village, did this by mounting avant-garde plays from Europe and America and neglected classics. *Experiment* was the watchword. Theaters were small but actors and audiences eager, and soon Off-Broadway was roaring. It nurtured such American playwrights as Edward Albee, John Guare, Sam Shepard, Lanford Wilson, Marie Irene Fornes, David Mamet, and Christopher Durang. Samuel Beckett's plays opened Off-Broadway, and Jean Genet's *The Blacks* had more than a thousand performances at St. Mark's Playhouse. The scene thrived into the seventies, but is now, as we say, history.

Off-Off Broadway

Off-Off Broadway took the freedom and idealism of Off-Broadway a few steps further. The Living Theater, begun by Judith Malina and Julian Beck in the early fifties, with its anarchist-pacifist political agenda and near total indifference to commercial concerns became the inspiration for many of the theater groups that started up in the early sixties in Village coffeehouses and lofts. These productions were mounted on a shoestring or less. Indeed, the Judson Poets' Theater in the Judson Memorial Church put on a double bill of Joel Oppenheimer's *The Great American Desert* and Guillaume Apollinaire's *The Breasts of Tiresias* in 1961 for $37.50. Joseph Cino's Caffe Cino on Cornelia Street put on several years' worth of productions on next to no money. It was, one of its playwrights said, "a theatrical Garden of Eden." Many of the plays were by gay men or had gay themes, and there was no attempt to have a hit or audition for a move uptown. As with Off-Broadway a number of writers, directors, and actors, both gay and straight, got their start here and at Ellen Stewart's Café La Mama at 82 Second Avenue, 122 Second Avenue, and finally at 74 East Fourth Street. Among those who cut their theatrical teeth in this scene are Sam Shepard, John Guare, Lanford Wilson, the actor Harvey Keitel, Tom Eyen, Bernadette Peters, Jean Claude van Itallie, and Tom O'Horgan. The scene was clubby and while this was perhaps a drawback, it had an openness suggested by Ellen Stewart's description of her club as a "pushcart." Off-Off Broadway did not follow Off-Broadway into history in the eighties. A glance at the listings on the *New York Times* theater pages shows that New York theatrical life still flickers in unlikely places.

O'Hara, Frank (1926–1966)

At O'Hara's funeral on 27 July 1966, in Springs, Long Island, the painter Larry Rivers spoke: "Frank O'Hara was my best friend. There are at least sixty people in New York who thought Frank O'Hara was their best friend." Most who knew O'Hara—and his poems are evidence that he seemed to know everyone in the New York art world of the fifties—have remarked on the man's great charm. He had the gift of intimacy that made those he focused his attention on feel they were special in his affection. O'Hara was the first of his generation of New York poets to die, and while a poet's early death often delivers him or her from obscurity, O'Hara was already famous. After growing up outside Worcester, Massachusetts, service in the navy during World War II, and four years at Harvard, where he met his close friend John Ashbery, O'Hara came to New York in 1951. He began working at the Museum of Modern Art, where he remained, first at the front desk and eventually as a curator, with a hiatus or two, until his death. Had he lived he almost certainly would have risen higher in the museum's administration. O'Hara's first permanent New York apartment was at 326 East Forty-ninth Street, an address that no longer exists. Here he roomed with the poet James Schuyler and then with Joe LeSueur, who lived with O'Hara in three future apartments. While O'Hara published in a great many little magazines, he had few books before his death and was casual about his career as a poet. Not that he was indifferent. To his friend LeSueur, O'Hara "didn't make a big deal out of it, he just sat down and wrote when the spirit moved him. For that reason, I didn't realize right away that if you took poetry as much for granted as breathing it might mean you felt it was as essential to your life." It was essential to O'Hara's life, but so were movies, nights at the Cedar Bar, parties (the fifties New York art world thrived on parties), gallery openings, music

and dance concerts, and the theater, and . . . O'Hara once said he never
wanted to go to sleep! In 1957 O'Hara and LeSueur moved to a loft at
90 University Place and then to 441 East Ninth Street, but neither place
really suited them. During these years O'Hara's life was at full tilt. He
had his work at the museum, his nonstop social life, collaborations with
painters Norman Bluhm, Larry Rivers, and Mike Goldberg, and his numerous friendships with what seems like a cast of thousands but especially with Edwin Denby, Jane Freilicher, Grace Hartigan, Joan Mitchell,
and Patsy Southgate. In 1963 O'Hara and LeSueur moved to their final
apartment at 791 Broadway, across the street from Grace Church,
where the society wedding in Edith Wharton's *Age of Innocence* takes
place. The city of New York has put up a plaque commemorating this
as O'Hara's address. In 1971 O'Hara's *Collected Poems* appeared from
Knopf in what essentially was a plain green wrapper. The original cover,
a nude portrait of the poet by Rivers, had been deemed inappropriate.
This big book revealed that O'Hara had been much more prolific than
most had dreamed. His work, already influential in New York, now
touched countless poets around the country and continues to do so
today. In inventing what he called the "personal poem," O'Hara introduced these poets to the possibilities of poetry coming directly from
their lives and experience. "You just go on your nerve," he wrote, and
such was the charge in his work that many were eager to do likewise.
After his death the Museum of Modern Art published a volume in tribute to him, *In Memory of My Feelings,* in which artists from Willem de
Kooning to Jasper Johns and Philip Guston illustrated his poems. In
1978 Bill Berkson and LeSueur edited *Homage to Frank O'Hara,* which
is worth looking up not only for its many photographs and illustrations
but for the poems to O'Hara and memoirs it contains. Brad Gooch has
published a biography of O'Hara that met with a lukewarm response.
The composer Morton Feldman, who first encountered O'Hara at the
Cedar Street Tavern, wrote in his memoir of the downtown fifties art
world, *Give My Regards to Eighth Street,* that O'Hara deserved "a volume all to himself." In the future there will be many.

O'Hara, John (1905–1970)

A very popular writer in his time, O'Hara focused so intently on the details that communicate class and wealth—brand names, makes of automobile, schools, clubs—and got so many of them right that his work
now seems hopelessly dated. His first novel, *Appointment in Samarra*
(1934), is still considered his most successful. He began it while living
in the Pickwick Arms Hotel, which then stood at 230 East Fifty-first

Street. His other New York addresses were 470 West Twenty-fourth Street, where he lived in 1937, and 55 East Eighty-sixth Street, where he spent the years between 1945 and 1949 and wrote many short stories and the novel *A Rage to Live.* His short stories often appeared in the *New Yorker,* and he had a stage success when he and others adapted his epistolary novel, *Pal Joey,* as a musical.

O'Neill, Eugene (1888–1953)

As befits the only American playwright to be awarded a Nobel Prize, O'Neill was born in a hotel that stood at the corner of Forty-third Street and Broadway. His father, James, was an actor famous in his day for playing the lead in *The Count of Monte Cristo,* a role he undertook nearly two thousand times. O'Neill attended Catholic schools in the city before graduating from prep school in Connecticut and spending one year at Princeton. From 1907 until he began to write plays in 1913 he was in New York, when he was not sailing on the high seas. He often stayed in Jimmy the Priest's rooming house at 252 Fulton Street on the waterfront. O'Neill described the place as "awful" and later claimed, "The house was coming down and the principal housewreckers were vermin." Jimmy the Priest and other men and women O'Neill encountered during these years would later be used as models for characters in his plays. After working as a reporter in New London, Connecticut, where he had spent his childhood summers, O'Neill returned to New York in 1915 with several one-act plays in his suitcase. He lived first in what he called "the garbage flat" at 38 Washington Square. A year later he moved to 48 Washington Square, where he carried on an affair with Louise Bryant, the wife of his friend the journalist John Reed. During this time O'Neill drank—and he drank heavily when he was not drinking ferociously until 1926, when he stopped—at the Golden Swan, popularly known as the Hell Hole, at the corner of Sixth Avenue and Fourth Street. O'Neill's first play to be produced, the one-act *Bound East for Cardiff,* was mounted by the Provincetown Players during their first season in 1916. Over the next three years the Players produced ten of O'Neill's one-act plays at their 133 and 139 MacDougal Street theaters. In 1920 O'Neill had a hit with his first play produced on Broadway, *Beyond the Horizon.* It won the first of his four Pulitzer Prizes and was followed by a number of hits—*The Emperor Jones, Anna Christie, The Great God Brown, Strange Interlude*—and a few total, if ambitious, flops like *Dynamo.* O'Neill had become the most celebrated playwright in the American theater when in 1934 what is taken to be his worst play, *Days without End,* failed miserably. Between then and 1946 no play of his opened on Broadway. At first it was thought that O'Neill fell silent after returning to the Catholicism of his childhood, a possibility hinted at in his last play. But this was far from the case. Instead, he was at work on an extremely ambitious cycle of plays meant to chronicle America from the Revolution to the Depression. He completed only one of these, the posthumously produced *Touch of the Poet,* but during this period, in addition to accepting the Nobel Prize in 1936, he wrote two of the plays that are today judged among his crowning achievements: *Long Day's Journey into Night* and *The Iceman Cometh.* During this period he was largely absent from New York, but while he attended rehearsals in 1946 for *The Iceman Cometh,* which is set in the Hell Hole of O'Neill's youthful drinking days, he and his wife, Carlotta, lived in a penthouse at 35 East Eighty-fourth Street. In 1943 O'Neill's hands had begun to tremble so that he could not hold a pen, an illness that doctors could neither explain nor cure. Since he found it impossible to write other than in longhand, this tremor effectively ended his life as a playwright. His mind remained clear and he had ideas for plays, but he simply could not put anything down on paper. O'Neill died in a Boston hotel room a decade later, and while not exactly forgotten, his work had fallen from its earlier eminence. In 1956 his widow allowed the director José Quintero to stage *The Iceman Cometh* at the Circle-in-the-Square Theater in Sheridan Square in Greenwich Village. Jason Robards starred as the salesman, Hickey, and the play was such a resounding hit that Carlotta permitted Quintero to mount *Long Day's Journey into Night.* Its success restored O'Neill's luster.

Ozick, Cynthia (b. 1928)

Born in the Bronx and educated at New York University, Ozick is a late bloomer whose first novel, *Trust,* did not appear until 1966. Since then several novels and three books of essays have placed her in the first rank of American writers, and she is considered a dominant voice in Jewish-American writing. New York City has not figured prominently in her work, and when it does, as in the long essay about her friend the novelist Alfred Chester, it serves as a backdrop. In her essays, the form that brings out the best in her, Ozick is a public intellectual whose passionate commitment to ideas is neither obscured by academic jargon nor watered down to suit the marketplace. Her most recent collection of these is *Art and Ardor.* She is a writer enlivened by contraries who has taken the line of Abraham Cahan, Saul Bellow, Bernard Malamud, and Philip Roth in a new direction.

At an October 1997 forum on the state of book publishing held at the main branch of the New York Public Library, Ozick was verbally roughed up by Leonard Riggio, Barnes & Noble's chief executive. She questioned the degree to which publishers have created their own problems. "Must you," she asked, "give astronomical advances to O.J.'s girlfriend? Must you give a full-page ad for a celebrity book? Whoopi Goldberg?" At a later point in the evening Riggio answered Ozick's questions in a roundabout way by saying, "Publishing seems to be divided between the stuffed-shirt elites and the more commercial. In the middle, I don't think the average publisher understands the depth to which people are embracing serious literature." Then he added a disclaimer to show that this depth is not very deep, and he used the current sales figures of one of Ozick's books as an example. Some thought Riggio unkind, but Ozick, who can take it as well as dish it out, said, "I think he was making a telling point. He was telling me that I'm pretty damn lucky to be there at all."

Padgett, Ron (b. 1942)

From his native Tulsa Padgett was in touch with Allen Ginsberg and Frank O'Hara while still in high school. In 1959 he edited the *White Dove Review* (Padgett's friend from grade school Joe Brainard was its art editor), and Donald Allen listed the magazine in the bibliography of *The New American Poetry*. The following year Padgett arrived in New York to attend Columbia. Ted Berrigan, a friend since their meeting in Tulsa, where Berrigan was in graduate school, was already in the city. Brainard soon joined them, and the "Tulsa Mafia" was complete when the poet Dick Gallup made a fourth. While in college Padgett edited the first important New York mimeo magazine, *C,* which brought out his first collection of poems, *In Advance of the Broken Arm.* From the start Padgett participated in collaborations with Berrigan and Brainard. He has continued this interest, working with painters George Schneeman, Jim Dine, Trevor Winkfield, and Alex Katz. In 1970 Padgett teamed with poet David Shapiro to edit for Random House the first generally available anthology of the New York School, *An Anthology of New York Poets.* Padgett has been an active translator from the French. Early in his career he translated Pierre Reverdy and he has published translations of *The Complete Blaise Cendrars* and Apollinaire's *The*

Poet Assassinated. For several years he served as the director of the Poetry Project, introducing more than one hundred readers during his tenure. Since the late seventies he has worked at Teachers and Writers. In 1994 he published a memoir of his friend Ted Berrigan that moves from their early joyous comradeship as they discover poetry, art, and New York to the decline of their friendship. The book's candor is magnified by its discretion. In 1996 Padgett's *New and Selected Poems* appeared. The Disney character Goofy (a blown-up detail from a Brainard painting) on the cover reminded Padgett's readers that the author's photo on another of his books showed him half-shaved and half-bearded. In his poetic soul dada lives alongside an old-fashioned American smart aleck. Since the late sixties Padgett and his family have lived on the Lower East Side.

Paine, Thomas (1737–1809)

While Paine is associated with numerous addresses in Lower Manhattan and Greenwich Village, he spent only the last years of his life in New York City. English by birth, Paine worked at a number of occupations before, at the urging of Ben Franklin, emigrating to Philadelphia in 1774. On Franklin's recommendation Paine became editor of the *Pennsylvania Magazine.* He was ahead of his time in speaking out for women's rights, freedom for slaves, national and international copyrights, and, perhaps reflecting his Quaker upbringing, the kind treatment of animals. At the outset of the Revolutionary War Paine joined George Washington's troops. Near Newark, New Jersey, he is supposed to have used a drumhead for a desk on which he wrote the first words of the pamphlet that began the series "The American Crisis." They remain the most famous words to come from Paine's pen:

> These are the times that try men's souls. The summer soldier and the sunshine patriot will, in this crisis, shrink from the service of his country, but he that stands it *now* deserves the love and thanks of man and woman. Tyranny, like hell, is not easily conquered; yet we have this consolation with us, that the harder the conflict, the more glorious the triumph.

Washington had this read to his troops, and perhaps Paine's words played a part in their victory a few days later at the Battle of Trenton. In his pamphlet "Common Sense," Paine set forth a clear case for independence. It became hugely popular and helped form public opinion in support of the patriot cause. In 1787 Paine returned to Europe, to England first, with the intention of perfecting iron bridge construction, but France's revolutionary tumult distracted him from this, and soon he was once again engaged in his life's work, liberty for all. He stayed away from America for sixteen years, during which he wrote the book that offended many and caused Paine to be vilified as an atheist, *The Age of Reason*. His espousal of the French cause had already put him at odds with Thomas Jefferson and John Adams, and in the country where he had once been hailed his name was now, in Adams's words, "the filthy Tom Paine." When he returned to America in 1803 he was poor, in ill health, and—to add insult to injury—roundly attacked from several quarters. He lived first in New Rochelle, but spent more and more time in New York City with congenial freethinkers and Republicans. Paine moved to the city and resided in boarding houses at 16 Gold Street and 36 Cedar Street before living with the portrait painter John Wesley Jarvis and his family at 85 Church Street. In 1808 Paine lived at 309 Bleecker Street in then rural Greenwich Village. His last New York address, 59 Grove Street, was next door to a French friend, Marguerite Bonneville. There Paine died lonely and all but forgotten. Over the next century and a half biographers and political historians restored to him the honor and stature he deserved.

Paley, Grace (b. 1922)

Born and educated in New York City, Paley began writing short stories when "in 1954 or '55," she has written, "I needed to speak in some inventive way about our female and male lives in those years." Speak she did, but no one heard her until the father of friends of her children asked to take a look at her stories. He was Ken McCormick, an editor at Doubleday; he liked what he saw and encouraged Paley to write more. She did and so was born her first book, *The Little Disturbances of Man*. These stories had a spoken directness and an intimate sense of everyday life that touched many readers. Paley tried a novel, but found her talent unsuited to the form. She might have produced more than the 380-some pages of her *Collected Stories*, but she has led an active life as a feminist, beginning in the late fifties, when there were few of her kind, and as an advocate for peace. In 1961 she helped found the Greenwich Village Peace Committee. Those who have heard Paley read will not forget how hand in glove the sound of her voice fits the words on the page. She is married to the poet Robert Nichols.

The Paris Review

Founded in Paris in 1953 by George Plimpton and others, including the novelists H. L. "Doc" Humes and Peter Matthiessen, the *Paris Review* is wherever Plimpton is, and for years that has been on East Seventy-second Street in Manhattan. The magazine has now published more than 140 issues. Thousands of little magazines have been born and flamed out in its lifetime. The masthead has a cast of thousands, which suggests just how social Plimpton is and why the magazine has never been associated with a core of writers as, say, *Partisan Review* has. Fairly early on the point became coverage and not coterie. But the magazine has had from the start a distinct and distinguished feature: its interviews with writers beginning with E. M. Forster. Sadruddin Aga Khan was the magazine's first publisher, and Drue Heinz, who was once the publisher of *Antaeus,* fills that role today. Although he has not published a great deal of late, the genial Plimpton did hit upon a formula that produced two funny and charming books. Walter Mitty-like, he pitched to major league hitters in *Out of My League* and played a quarterback in training camp for the Detroit Lions. He has written a book on fireworks and authored a hoax in *Sports Illustrated* about a fabulous baseball pitcher from Maine. Plimpton's parties are famous, and he seems to go about everything he does with gusto, enjoying himself thoroughly.

Parker, Dorothy (1893–1967)

Born in New Jersey, Parker, then Dorothy Rothschild, grew up in Manhattan at 57 West Sixty-eighth Street. She attended school at Blessed Sacrament Convent on West Seventieth Street, and worked first for *Vogue* magazine, where she invented the advertising slogan "Brevity is the soul of lingerie." She went on to become drama critic at *Vanity Fair* but was fired for her harsh reviews. She found fame as a member of the Algonquin Round Table wits. *The* member might be more appropriate, as more one-liners and wisecracks are attributed to Parker than to anyone else in the group. It was she who, sitting in the middle of a crowded theater, had whispered in her ear, "Calvin Coolidge is dead. Pass it on," and whispered back, "How do they know? Pass it back." It is she whom Clare Booth Luce waved ahead with the insult "Age before beauty," only to say over her shoulder to Luce, "Pearls before swine." It was she whose review of an early Katharine Hepburn performance stated, "She ran the gamut of emotions from A to B," and she who wrote of the play *Man with a Camera,* "Me no Leica." It was she who said at a party, "One more drink and I'll be under the host." If Parker said half the things she is supposed to have . . . well, she probably did. She also wrote short stories, "Big Blond" is the most notable of these, and poems that on the whole have not aged well, although she did manage the couplet "Men seldom make passes / At girls who wear glasses."

Her work is often harmed by the sentimental effect of the wisecrack that is meant to hide a clearly visible broken heart. After the Round Table Parker spent many years in Hollywood working on movie scripts. When she returned to New York in 1963 she was a forlorn and mostly drunk lady whose life seemed to have been foreshadowed by the many stories of failed love she had written. Until her death in 1967 she lived at the Volney, a residence hotel at 23 West Seventy-fourth Street. Her friend and literary executor, Lillian Hellman, found numerous un-cashed checks in Parker's writing desk after her death. Her spirits had sunk so low that money could not lift them. She left her royalties to Martin Luther King's Southern Christian Leadership Conference. Many who knew Parker found her as cruel as she was funny. She had the reputation of never saying a kind word about someone if she had a nastier one on hand. Still, it's hard to believe that she wasn't great company. She once suggested that her epitaph read, "Excuse My Dust."

Parnassus

In 1973 Herbert Leibowitz saw that "new books of poetry were greeted grudgingly like distant cousins, and assigned cramped space or rejected into the cold." What he did to remedy this was publish *Parnassus,* a magazine made up almost entirely of reviews of books of poetry. Lei-bowitz wanted a "Hyde Park Corner where contrary ideas and diverse voices . . . might blend into a harmonious ensemble." He achieved this by giving a wide range of poets, critics, and writers who are simply readers of poetry the space to develop their responses and ideas. The magazine appears twice a year and some issues have been as thick as a Manhattan phonebook. The University of Michigan at Ann Arbor now publishes *Parnassus,* but its editorial offices remain in New York, where they have been from the start. Leibowitz has also published a book on American autobiographies that treats Jane Addams, William Carlos Williams, and Edward Dahlberg, among others.

Partisan Review

Although the magazine is now a pale version of its former self and its address is Boston University, *Partisan Review* was for more than thirty years a journal with powerful literary and political influence. Founded in 1934 as the magazine of the New York City John Reed Club, it merged in 1936 with William Phillips's magazine *Anvil* and then reappeared in 1937 as, in Phillips's words, "an independent Left literary and cultural review." Phillips and Philip Rahv were the magazine's founding editors, and Fred Dupee, Mary McCarthy, Lionel Abel, Eleanor Clark, Clement

Greenberg, Dwight Macdonald, Sidney Hook, Lionel and Diana Trilling, and William Barrett were in at the beginning. Phillips has identified members of the second generation as Daniel Bell, Nathan Glazer, Irving Howe, Alfred Kazin, Norman Mailer, Bernard Malamud, Robert Motherwell, Norman Podhoretz, Philip Roth, and Arthur Schlesinger Jr. These writers represented many shades of the Left political spectrum and worked both inside and out of the academy. The magazine published Saul Bellow's first story, Delmore Schwartz's incredible debut story, "In Dreams Begin Responsibilities," many of Lionel Trilling's important essays, and work by a number of European writers including Ignazio Silone, Nicola Chiaromonte, Simone de Beauvoir, and George Orwell. Indeed, its international outlook was and is a distinguishing feature. The magazine's symposiums, in which a range of writers responded to questions posed by the editors, made for the sort of public forum no longer seen in today's academicized intellectual world. The last major new voice to appear in *Partisan Review*'s pages was that of Susan Sontag, whose essays, looked at thirty years later, seem a swan song to the magazine's glory days. In the late sixties the magazine began to decline, but thirty years is a long run. No other magazine in this century shaped New York intellectual and literary life as *PR* did. The biographies of McCarthy, Macdonald, and Schwartz and the memoirs of Abel, Barrett and Diana Trilling make this abundantly clear. There is also a ton of delicious gossip about this group awaiting the reader with a desire to pursue it through these books and the many others that have been written by and about members of the *PR* crowd. The *PR* office was at 45 Astor Place for many years, and the crowd often gathered at the homes of Macdonald and Rahv on West Tenth Street and of Phillips on West Eleventh. The editors published several anthologies drawn from the magazine, and in 1987 Phillips edited *Partisan Review: The 50th Anniversary Edition*, which includes many of the old contributors and a few new ones.

Payne, John Howard (1791–1852)

> Be it ever so humble, there's *no* place like home.

Payne led one of those nineteenth-century lives so astonishing they seem like a novelist's invention. Along the way he wrote the song "Home, Sweet Home," which contains a line so memorable it found its way into American speech, leaving its author behind. Born in New York but raised elsewhere, Payne returned to the city in his teens to work as a clerk. At fifteen he revealed himself as a prodigy and had his play *Julia;*

or, The Wanderer" in production. Friendship with Washington Irving and other literary figures followed, as did debt, college, and a return to the New York stage. He played up and down the nation, appearing at least once with Edgar Allan Poe's mother, Elizabeth, but his star faded and he went to England, where Charles Lamb, Samuel Taylor Coleridge, and William Hazlitt were his friends. Payne wrote at least sixty pieces for the theater but failed to support himself. Indeed, he landed in London's Fleet Street Prison for debt and upon release went to Paris where "Home, Sweet Home" (Harry Bishop wrote the music) appeared in his play *Clari; or, The Maid of Milan*. While in Paris Payne collaborated with Washington Irving on several plays and romanced Mary Shelley. Back in London to edit a theatrical magazine, he once again came up penniless. In 1832 Payne returned to America, where the actors Edwin Forrest and Charles and Fanny Kemble raised $10,000 for him in a benefit performance. Plans to launch a magazine of the arts sent him south in search of money and contributors. There he became involved with the Cherokee Nation, planned to write a history of that embattled tribe, completed at least one volume (now lost), and journeyed to the tribe's new lands in Oklahoma. Daniel Webster somehow became Payne's champion, persuading President Tyler to appoint him consul in Tunis in 1843. President Polk relieved him of that position in 1845, and after travels in Europe Payne returned to Washington to seek a new post. In December 1850 Payne was in the audience, as was President Millard Fillmore, when Jenny Lind brought down the house with her rendition of "Home, Sweet Home." Fillmore sent Payne back to Tunis, where he died two years later.

Peale, Norman Vincent (1898–1993)

Peale became the pastor of Manhattan's Marble Collegiate Reformed Church, descendant of the first Dutch Reformed Church of New Amsterdam, in 1932. Twenty years later he published the best-selling book *The Power of Positive Thinking*, and his sermons routinely attracted crowds of more than four thousand to the church. His message was Optimism with a capital O. Coming at a time when everything was going America's way, people ate it up like ice cream. Peale's book sold in the millions and he became famous enough to be courted by politicians like Richard Nixon. A syndicated radio program, the magazine *Guideposts*, a newspaper column, more books, and numerous speeches kept Peale in the public eye until the 1970s. Throughout that time he was one of the nation's foremost religious leaders, so well known, in fact, that a striptease dancer named herself Norma Vincent Peel.

PEN—International Association
      of Poets, Playwrights, Editors, Essayists, and Novelists
Pen American Center
47 Fifth Avenue
PEN was founded in London in 1921 by the writer Catherine Ann
Dawson and the novelist John Galsworthy, who was elected its first
president (a smart move on the membership's part, considering that
Galsworthy endowed the organization with the money from his 1932
Nobel Prize). PEN's first outpost was in New York in 1922, and the
novelist Booth Tarkington was its president. Today there are more than
eighty-five chapters active in over fifty-five countries. There are several
in the United States, but the association remains centered in New York,
where it maintains a number of committees. The most important are
Freedom-to-Write, which defends writers worldwide against government interference; Writer's Watch, which keeps an eye out for government censorship and works against it wherever it occurs; and the
Writer's Fund, which provides small sums for writers with emergencies
on their hands. There is also a Translation Committee, which publishes
guidelines for contracts and standard fees for translators and presents
four awards in translation. Norman Mailer once served as PEN president, and the novelist and lawyer Louis Begley and the writer Anne
Hollander have been recent presidents.

Perkins, Maxwell (1884–1947)
In 1909 Perkins went to work in the advertising office of the publisher
Charles Scribner. When he died thirty-eight years later he was the firm's
senior editor, and he had edited Ring Lardner, Edmund Wilson, Erskine
Caldwell, Sherwood Anderson, John P. Marquand, Marjorie Kinnan
Rawlings, S. S. Van Dine, Taylor Caldwell, and James Jones. Sixty-five
of his writers had dedicated books to him. But the title "Editor of Genius" was bestowed on him by his biographer Scott Berg for his work
with F. Scott Fitzgerald, Ernest Hemingway, and Thomas Wolfe. No
other editor of his time worked so long and intimately with three writers of their caliber. For all of them Perkins fulfilled many functions,
from friend to psychologist, that went beyond what was required of
him as an editor. In Wolfe's case, Perkins did everything but write the
books. Wolfe could not stop himself from writing to gargantuan
lengths, and when asked to edit his own work on one occasion he was
able to prune only eight pages from a manuscript of more than one
thousand. He delivered his manuscripts to Perkins's office in a trunk!
To wring from this mass of words the novels that we now have, Perkins

worked so closely with Wolfe, line by line, sentence by sentence, that they were all but collaborating. Wolfe dedicated *Of Time and the River* to Perkins in thanks, but he also left Scribner's for Harper's because he wanted to show that he was the writer, that he could produce a book without Perkins's help. During the thirties Perkins lived at 246 West Forty-ninth Street, where his editorial conferences with Wolfe took place after office hours. Scribner's office was at 597 Fifth Avenue, where for many years the publisher ran its own bookstore. Upon Perkins's death the poet John Hall Wheelock became the firm's senior editor. Since Perkins there has been no New York editor like him, and as publishing now stands there may never be another one. Editors rarely stay in one house for forty years. They move about so often that unless their writers move with them, which because of contracts and other considerations is not so easy, long-term associations are next to impossible. It is more likely that an agent will have the sort of relationship that Perkins had with his writers.

Phelps, Robert (1922–1989)

The French novelist Colette was Robert Phelps's chief subject, and his passion for her life and work produced two original books. *Earthly Paradise* is "Colette's Autobiography drawn from the writings of her lifetime." His *Belles Saisons: A Colette Scrapbook* is in the wonderful, and too seldom used, form of photographs with commentary. Phelps's other major book was his compilation of Jean Cocteau's autobiographical writings, *Professional Secrets*. His accomplishments notwithstanding he would be absent from this book if not for the beautiful passages on him and his work in James Salter's autobiography, *Burning the Days*. Salter came to know Phelps as a result of receiving a fan letter from him, and he visited Phelps often at his apartment on Twelfth Street just around the corner from Fifth Avenue. Phelps was for Salter, as for others, including the painter Philip Guston, the composer and writer Ned Rorem, the poet Louise Bogan, and the poet and translator Richard Howard, a fount of gossip, literary and otherwise, and good talk about books. Two of Phelps's most original books never, alas, got written. The first of these he titled *Following,* and in it he was concerned with people he followed in the street as well as those whose lives or careers he "followed" with close attention. The other was *1922,* a diary of his birth year describing everything that happened in the year that had relevance for his life. Above his writing desk Phelps kept two quotations; Gertrude Stein's "I am coming to believe that nothing except a life-work can be considered" and W. H. Auden's "We were put on earth to make things." As Salter presents him, Phelps is a man you can only regret not having met.

Plath, Sylvia (1932–1963)

The month Plath spent in New York in 1952 as guest editor of *Mademoiselle* (she was a student at Smith College) had such a traumatic effect on her that upon returning to her Massachusetts home she attempted suicide. Plath stayed at the women-only Barbizon Hotel—the Amazon in her novel—at Sixty-third Street and Lexington Avenue. This did not prevent her from having several wounding sexual experiences. During that same month she also suffered a near rape. These events eventually formed the core of her autobiographical novel, *The Bell Jar,* published in England under the pseudonym Victoria Lucas in the year of her suicide. At that point Plath was regarded as a talented writer whose life had been cut short. This began to change after the publication in 1965 of *Ariel,* a book of poems that Robert Lowell, who wrote the book's introduction, celebrated as having been *written* as if she were already dead. Plath became a heroine of the newly revived feminist movement and over the past fifteen years has been an industry in academe.

PM

Although this daily newspaper had only an eight-year run in the 1940s, it is remembered today for its refusal to carry advertising and its crusading on behalf of many consumer issues before consumer issues became buzzwords. *PM* was one of the first to publish the link between cancer and cigarette smoking, and this was when advertisements had "seven out of ten doctors" advising Americans to smoke Camels. Ralph Ingersoll, an editor at Luce Publications, started the paper, which had a magazine format and whose writers included Ben Hecht, Ernest Hemingway, the eagle-eyed journalist I. F. Stone, James Weschler (later of the *New York Post*), and Max Lerner. Margaret Bourke-White and the wondrous Weegee, whose photographs of crime scenes are for many what New York looked like in the forties, were among the paper's photographers. In 1946 Marshall Field, one of the paper's backers, insisted on running advertising to make up the paper's deficit. Ingersoll soon resigned, and the paper went downhill, changing its name to *Star* before disappearing in 1948.

Poe, Edgar Allan (1809–1849)

In thinking about Poe, it is difficult to imagine how he wrote as much and as well as he did while living harassed by poverty, illness, his own and that of his loved ones, debt, drunkenness, and a perpetual motion that would have worn out most men. He first came to New York in 1831 after being thrown out of West Point and, penniless, wrote begging letters to his stepfather while seeing through the press the second edition of his *Poems*, a book of 124 pages dedicated "To the U.S. Corps of Cadets." We know that Poe came again to New York in 1837 and 1838 for as long as fifteen months and that he lived in the Village at Sixth Avenue and Waverly Place and at 133H Carmine Street, among other addresses. During this time he published very little, but he did work on the novel *The Narrative of Arthur Gordon Pym*, which Harper Brothers brought out in July 1838. Poe next shows up in the city looking for work in 1842, but he ran afoul of the "juleps" and drank himself into a blackout. In April 1844 Poe and his wife, Virginia, moved from Philadelphia to New York, where Poe declared, "I intend living for the future." The future lasted two months, and Poe moved five miles outside of town to a farmhouse at what is now Eighty-fourth Street. He enjoyed the solitude, but could "play the hermit" for only a few months before the need for money, and the flourishing magazine and newspaper scene where he could earn it, called him back to the city. But he could not make enough money—in 1845 he netted $425—to live on the farm and work in the city, so in February 1845 he left the Brennan farm and again plunged into the New York literary world. It was the very month that his poem "The Raven" appeared in the *American Review*. A hit from the start, the poem was reprinted at least a dozen times within a few weeks, and readers so loved to read it aloud, loved to croak out "Nevermore," that the poem quickly made its way into a textbook of school recitations. Through the poet James Russell Lowell's good offices Poe became a coeditor of the weekly *Broadway Journal*. "The whole tendency of the age," Poe proclaimed, "is Magazine-ward." In the *Journal* Poe took a strong stand for an international copyright law. At the time American books could be placed under copyright but not English or European books. This meant that American publishers had to pay American writers while English writers were paid nothing. Since they were free to pirate English books, publishers put a glut of them on the market, and American writers were forced to earn their livelihood from magazines. The lack of copyright protection led Americans to starving their own literature while, because of the availability of English books, looking to England for literary standards. Poe caused more of a stir when he started the fracas that became known as "The Longfellow War." He had already accused Longfellow of plagiarism in other New York papers, and he continued his attacks in the *Journal*.

For his part, Longfellow remained aloof, but Poe kept up a barrage of increasingly personal attacks, which had the effect of hurting not Longfellow but Poe. The driven Poe's behavior became more and more erratic, and he took to drinking heavily. These and other personal setbacks occurred at the same time Poe came into control of the *Journal*. Late in 1845 he had the magazine to himself but did not have the money to produce it. After his desperate pleas—and Poe had a gift for pleading letters—did not raise the money needed, he took on a partner, but the magazine died in 1846. Later that year Poe moved to a farm in Turtle Bay, where he rented the top floor and, debt ridden as usual, left behind his bed to pay the rent when he moved out. Poe's last New York address was in the village of Fordham in what is now the Bronx. The house, known as the Poe Cottage, still stands at 2640 Grand Concourse near East Kingsbridge Road. Poe needed this country retreat to soothe his nerves and because he hoped its peace and quiet would improve his wife's health. Neither happened. Poe's own health deteriorated, and Virginia succumbed to tuberculosis in 1847. While in Fordham Poe managed to embroil himself in another literary feud and returned to writing poems. The feud grew out of his series "The Literati of New York." Poe meant to satirize, and his targets resented what he wrote, but when he accused the poet T. D. English of plagiarism, English fought back. He hit Poe below the belt whenever possible, a tactic Poe himself had often used on others. English got to Poe so often that Poe took out a libel suit against the owners of the *New York Mirror,* publishers of English's assaults. Poe eventually won the suit, but his reputation had been badly damaged and his always fragile equilibrium upset. The poems he wrote in Fordham, "Ulalume—A Ballad" and "The Bells," came from a vein of genius Poe was in touch with no matter the distraction caused by his literary battles and the depth of his personal squalor. A restless Poe spent very little time in Fordham after his wife's death, but he did use it as a base until 1849. He was returning to New York from Richmond, Virginia, when he died in Baltimore of an alcohol overdose and exposure. At least that was thought to be the cause of death until recently, when a doctor advanced the notion that Poe had actually died of rabies.

It is often written that Poe composed "The Raven" while living at 85 Amity Street, now West Third Street. We know that he lived on Amity in 1845, which is also the year "The Raven" appeared in print, but he may have written the poem in Philadelphia just before coming to New

York. Whatever the actual place of composition, "The Raven" is one of those poems we want to give an address to, a room where we can imagine the poet receiving his muse and fulfilling his vision.

From our contemporary point of view the literary world of New York in the late 1840s is remarkable because three of the nation's greatest writers, Poe, Whitman, and Melville, were active in the city. Yet they had little to do with one another. Poe and Melville may have met at the home of the publisher and critic Evert Duyckinck, but there is no firm evidence that they did. Whitman published in Poe's *Journal* just before it ceased publication, but we know of no meeting between the two. The three writers were at different stages in their careers. Melville became a best-selling author in 1846 when *Typee* appeared; Poe was famous and infamous by turns; and Whitman had begun to cut his teeth as a journalist. Their New York was a city bursting at its seams as the population nearly doubled in the 1840s to more than 500,000, half of whom were immigrants from Germany and Ireland. It was a rough, volatile city that would not be smoothed out and tamed until the aftermath of the Civil War. Their New York was much like the city of the 1920s, the next period in which distinguished writers could work in absolute independence from one another. Had Poe, Melville, and Whitman been in Boston or Philadelphia a meeting would have inevitably occurred, but their New York was already a city that could swallow up several or seven dozen geniuses.

New York, it must be added, continues to have an ambivalent attitude toward Poe. When a sign was put up to commemorate his West Eighty-fourth Street address it misspelled his middle name as Allen.

Poetry Calendar
611 Broadway, Suite 611

You can't tell the players without a scorecard! There are enough poetry readings given in New York City to support the *Poetry Calendar,* which appears monthly from September to June. Martin J. Paddio is the *Calendar*'s publisher and Molly McQuade is the editor. Not only does the *Calendar* list most of the readings that take place in the city each month, but it publishes poetry and excerpts from books by poets or about poetry. In its pages you will also find advertisements for literary prizes, workshops, and bookstores, as well as for a psychologist who will help you overcome writer's block. Subscriptions to the *Calendar* are available.

Poetry Project
St. Mark's Church
Second Avenue and Tenth Street
The Project, now over thirty, shows no signs of flagging and remains
the one institution devoted to poetry, body and soul, by hosting Monday and Wednesday night readings, workshops, special events, and a
New Year's Day reading/benefit extravaganza, as well as a newsletter
and a magazine (*The World*). There are other reading series in New
York City but none matches the breadth of the Project, nor has any
other developed a community whose devotion to poetry is half so intense. In 1966 the poet Joel Oppenheimer became the Project's first director and began the reading series at the church. This did not plant an
acorn so much as convene a congregation of poets who would over the
next few years make the Project into the city's most active poetry scene.
Anne Waldman, a Village native and the Project's second director, Ted
Berrigan, Ron Padgett, the Project's third director, Larry Fagin, who
edited the mimeo magazine *Adventures in Poetry* from the Project,
Lorenzo Thomas, Lewis Warsh, Tom Clark, the fourth director Bernadette Mayer, Jim Brodey, Jim Carroll, Alice Notley, Tony Towle, John
Godfrey, and Joe Brainard were among this company and they attracted the participation of their elders, Allen Ginsberg, Edwin Denby,
John Ashbery, James Schuyler, Barbara Guest, Kenneth Koch, and Kenward Elmslie. The Project was first the home of the New York School
and the other poets in Donald Allen's anthology *The New American
Poetry*. But over the years hundreds of poets of all stripes, genders, political and sexual persuasions have read at the Project. A partial roll call
shows Clark Coolidge, Fanny Howe, Robert Lowell, Ted Greenwald,
Eileen Myles, the Project's fifth director, Michael Palmer, Robert Creeley, Fielding Dawson, Amiri Baraka, David Henderson, Bill Berkson,
Philip Whalen, Ed Sanders, Jaime Manrique, Rochelle Kraut, John Yau,
Gregory Corso, Diane di Prima, William Burroughs, Jerome Rothenberg, Susan Howe, Wang Ping, David Rattray, Yuki Hartman, Maureen Owen, Bill Zavatsky, Charles North, Paul Violi, Bruce Andrews,
Charles Bernstein, Charlotte Carter, Bob Holman, and not just poets
but novelists, translators, filmmakers, and performance artists. What is
most remarkable about the Project is the sense of community that has
grown through and around it, exemplified by the memorial services held
there for Ted Berrigan, James Schuyler, and Joe Brainard, the launchings of new books and magazines, and the ability of the Project to
always find room for the new and innovative. Thirty years ago the place

was more a social scene than it is now, but the Project survived the end of one counterculture era to open its doors to others. Ed Friedman is the Project's sixth and current director, Jo Ann Wasserman coordinates readings, and Lisa Jarnot edits the newsletter, which covers Project activities while mixing in essays, book reviews, poems, and a little gossip.

Peter Stuyvesant's private chapel stood where St. Mark's now stands. The site has been in use by a Christian congregation longer than any other in the city, but the church itself is the second oldest in the city, after St. Paul's Chapel at Broadway and Fulton Streets. It was completed in 1799; the Greek Revival steeple was added in 1828 and sometime later the interior was given a Georgian finish. Peter Stuyvesant is buried in the church graveyard. W. H. Auden, who lived nearby on St. Mark's Place, was a member of the church's congregation.

Since the church was built the area around St. Mark's has undergone considerable transformation, the most extraordinary of which was the influx of Jewish and other Eastern European immigrants in the late nineteenth century. The Jewish presence can be seen in the few delicatessens still in the neighborhood, but Polish and Ukrainian restaurants, butchers, and social clubs remain. These may well be gone in a generation. One recent development has been an influx of Indian restaurants into the area. West Sixth Street off Second Avenue is almost completely taken up by them. When the Project began the Lower East Side was full of cheap apartments and railroad flats, perfect for young writers who wanted to survive on a shoestring. At 39 St. Mark's Place Lewis Warsh and Anne Waldman had an apartment that served as a sort of salon where people hung out; Ted Berrigan, for one, showed up nearly every day. Today there is no area in Lower Manhattan where young writers can find cheap places to live. The community that formed around the Project did so in part because through the sixties young people just starting out could afford to live in Manhattan.

Poetry Society of America
15 Gramercy Park

"The Poetry Society of America places poetry directly in the paths of millions of people every day—more than any other literary organization in this country." A boast? Absolutely, but one that "Poetry in Motion" has made good. Through this project PSA has placed poems by Seamus Heaney, Laura Riding, Ogden Nash, Sandra Cisneros, Gwendolyn Brooks, and numerous other poets on placards in New York, Chicago, and Boston subway cars and buses. Two new poems are mounted every month, and soon more cities and more poets will join the program. What they do for strap-hangers PSA also does for couch potatoes through their collaboration with New York City's Opportunity Channel. The show *Poetry on Television* features poetry "spots," the same poems that are riding the buses and subways, and occasional hour-long tributes that focus on the work of renowned poets. PSA also presents "Poetry in Public Places," with readings in such venues as Brooklyn's Botanical Garden, Manhattan's Hayden Planetarium, and the Art Institute of Chicago; arranges tributes to poets at the New York Public Library and in other libraries across the country; organizes poetry festivals that have ranged from the Caribbean Poetry Festival to the Festival of the Living World: Voices of the African Diaspora and Native America; and, at its Gramercy Park headquarters, offers a lineup of seminars each fall and spring. In the spring of 1997, Frank Bidart gave a seminar titled "The Long Short Poem," Robert Pinsky followed with "Refrain, Repetition and Recurrence," and Heather McHugh ended with "Ends." Last, and very welcome to the poets who receive them, PSA hosts a veritable Oscar night of awards each year, including the Alice Fay Di Castagnola Award, the Shelley Memorial Award, and, as of 1995, the Robert Frost Medal. All of this activity and much else including poetry, tributes to poets, essays, interviews with the poetry editors of magazines that run the gamut of those that publish poetry, is reported in the *Journal of the Poetry Society of America*. Membership is open to anyone who loves the art as it has been since 1910 when the society was founded by Witter Bynner and George Santayana among others. Elise Paschen is the society's current director.

Poets & Writers
72 Spring Street

Poets & Writers is, in the words of its executive director, Elliot Figman, "a nonprofit organization dedicated to helping poets and writers with the business of writing." Founded in 1970 it has evolved and grown to provide a wide range of publications, programs, and services. Most conspicuous among these is *Poet & Writers Magazine,* which is available in bookstores and by subscription. It appears six times a year and in addition to all kinds of news—grant and award deadlines, lists of prize winners, calls for manuscripts—the magazine publishes interviews with writers and "publishing pros" and essays about writing. The most invaluable of the organization's services is surely its *Dictionary of American Poets and Writers.* This comes out each year in an updated version that for 1997–1998 lists more than seven thousand poets and writers, complete with addresses, phone numbers, E-mail addresses, and so on. The Poets & Writers catalog lists a host of other available books, including Adam Begley's *Literary Agents: A Writer's Guide,* and even features a "General Store," which offers P&W coffee cups, sweatshirts, and mouse pads. Poet Galway Kinnell and novelist E. L. Doctorow are members of the organization's advisory board.

Poets House
72 Spring Street, Second Floor
Elizabeth Kray and the poet Stanley Kunitz began Poets House as "a comfortable, accessible *place for poetry.*" It contains a library of more than 30,000 volumes, all acquired by donation, and an archive of hundreds of audio tapes of readings and other poetry events. The collections do not circulate, but are open to anyone who cares to use them. Each fall there is an exhibit of as many as 1,200 of the books of poems published that year in the United States. There are also at least thirty readings and other programs presented within the library. To top it off, Poets House compiles and distributes the *Directory of American Poetry Books.* Schedules and membership forms are available from Poets House. Visitors should be sure to pick up a copy of their "Manhattan Poetry Map," which identifies fifty-four addresses connected with poetry and poets on the island of Manhattan.

Powell, Dawn (1897–1965)
In 1962 Edmund Wilson asked, "Why is it that the novels of Miss Dawn Powell are so much less well known than they deserve to be?" Three years later when Powell died, nearly all of her fifteen novels were out of print. Susan Edmiston and Linda D. Cirino's *Literary New York* (1976) has no listing for Powell. The author of a dozen novels set in Manhattan had dropped from sight. Then Gore Vidal, who had known Powell, published a long essay on her work in the *New York Review of Books* and this led to a revival, which thanks to Steerforth Press in, of all places, South Royalton, Vermont, is going great guns today. An Ohio native, Powell came to New York in 1918, after graduating from Lake Erie College, and lived in the city for the rest of her life. By 1925, the year she published her first novel, she was married and settled in Greenwich Village. Although she moved house a number of times—40 West Ninth Street, 72 Perry Street, and 106 Perry Street were some of her addresses—she remained a Village resident until her death.

Throughout the 1920s, 1930s, and 1940s Powell published novels and wrote movie scripts and plays. She began to hit her stride in 1940 with the publication of the beautifully titled *Angels on Toast,* set in the New York advertising world. Another novel, *The Wicked Pavilion* (1954), takes place in a café resembling the one in the old Hotel Lafayette on East Ninth Street at University Place. In 1962 she published *The Golden Spur,* in which a young man from Ohio comes to the Village in search of the father he has never known. All three of these novels were reissued in 1990 following Vidal's essay. In 1995 interest in Powell's work rose with the appearance of her diaries, edited by Tim Page. She kept these from 1931 to 1965, and they tell the story of a writer who, although she had much to contend with in life, stayed true to her work. Page enumerates her difficulties as "an unconventional and sometimes deeply unhappy marital life, near-constant money troubles, the demands of a mentally and emotionally impaired son, heavy drinking that was debilitating at times, and what might be described as a 'bipolar' personality." There was so much in Powell's life to weigh her down it is little wonder that she is essentially a comic novelist. Readers of the diary will feel the sadness in her life, but they will be delighted by her sharp tongue—she combined this with a warm heart, which Logan Pearsall thought of as the perfect character for a friend—and they will get an intimate, intelligent view of thirty years of New York literary history and of one writer's commitment to her craft.

Publishers Weekly
249 West Seventeenth Street

This is the bible of the American trade book industry and has been for so long that no one can remember when it was not. It actually began life in 1872 when Frederick Leypoldt launched *Publishers' and Stationers' Weekly Trade Circular.* The following year the publication took on the name it bears today. *PW* has the power to kill the dreams of publishers and writers or to give them the kiss of life. This comes from their anonymous reviews, which are actually previews because the books have not yet been released. Thus the "buzz" that publishers hope to start on important new books may end, or be limited, at the start. A good review does not necessarily mean a book will be a success, but a star from *PW* will lift the spirits of any writer and keep them up until the first reviews come in.

Pulitzer, Joseph (1847–1911)

A Hungarian immigrant who fought for the Union in the Civil War, Pulitzer began his newspaper career as a reporter for a German-language newspaper in St. Louis. Eventually, he bought the *St. Louis Dispatch* and made a success of the paper before coming to New York and buying the *World* from financier Jay Gould. In raising the *World*'s circulation he went up against William Randolph Hearst and his *Journal*. The papers went head-to-head creating "yellow journalism," meaning that they competed to print the most sensational story first. The phrase actually derived from the comic strip "The Yellow Kid," which appeared in both papers. From 1895 the *World* and the *Journal* were in fierce competition until the battleship *Maine* blew up in the harbor at Havana, and they went into a frenzy of warmongering. When President McKinley finally declared war against Spain and sent American troops to Cuba, both papers were credited with influencing his decision. The newspaper war made both Pulitzer and Hearst millionaires. Pulitzer gave freely to Columbia University's School of Journalism and in his will left an endowment of $16,500 to fund eight prizes in journalism and letters. The Pulitzer Prizes were first given in 1917 and continue today with twenty-six prizes, eighteen in journalism and eight in letters. Prizes are given to the year's most deserving novel, book of poems, and play. These rank among America's most prestigious literary awards.

Puzo, Mario (b. 1920)

Born in the West Side Manhattan neighborhood then known as Hell's Kitchen, Puzo attended Hiram Haydn's writing class at the New School for Social Research. He published two novels before he mined the rich vein of New York Mafia history, lore, and gossip to produce *The Godfather* (1969). In setting one of America's favorite tales, a family's rise from rags to riches, in the underworld, Puzo came up with a great pulp novel. The book became a best-seller, and then, in the hands of writer and director Francis Ford Coppola, it became a movie to rival *Citizen Kane*.

Q

Quinn, John (1870–1924)

There is a famous photograph taken in Paris during the twenties of Quinn with James Joyce, Ford Madox Ford, and Ezra Pound. The severe-looking Quinn, dressed in high, stiff collar, cravat, and morning coat, seems to have wandered in from an earlier era, but he was as much a part of twentieth-century literature and art as the other three men. A New York lawyer, Quinn early on became a patron of the arts, especially of things Irish and of modern art. It was he who arranged for the rental of the 69th Regiment Armory at Lexington Avenue between Twenty-fifth and Twenty-sixth Streets for the landmark Armory Show of 1913. Not only did he lend some seventy-seven works from his own collection to the show, but he bought more of the art exhibited than any other single collector. The library in his apartment at 58 Central Park West held more than 18,000 items, by far the largest assemblage of its kind in the city. Quinn was the patron of John Butler Yeats, who lived the last years of his life in the city, James Joyce, Joseph Conrad, Ezra Pound, and, of particular significance for New York, T. S. Eliot. With writers Quinn's patronage took the form of buying manuscripts, help-ing finance publication, and all manner of other kindnesses. It was Pound who put Quinn onto the work of Eliot, and Quinn was immedi-ately helpful. This included working out the agreement between the *Dial* and Horace Liveright over the publication of "The Waste Land." The *Dial* published the poem first and without notes and awarded Eliot its $2,000 poetry prize. Liveright then published the poem as a book with the notes, and the *Dial* agreed to buy 350 copies. In return for this and other favors, Eliot sent the original manuscript of "The Waste Land" as a gift to Quinn. We know that it arrived at his 39 Nassau Street office but from there what happened to it is a mystery. It was not listed in the contents of Quinn's will. His papers went to his sister, who passed them on to her daughter, Mrs. Thomas F. Conroy, and it was not until the late 1950s that Mrs. Conroy discovered the manuscript. In 1958 she sold it privately to the New York Public Library's Berg Collec-tion. Neither Eliot nor Ezra Pound, who had edited the manuscript, were informed of this. Indeed, a single attempt was made to reach Eliot, but when it proved futile no other effort was undertaken. Eliot's widow, Valerie, was informed of the manuscript's existence in 1968, and two years later she edited and introduced a facsimile of the manuscript.

Quotes

A Collection of Quotes about New York City

One need never leave the confines of New York to get all the greenery one wishes—I can't even enjoy a blade of grass unless I know there's a subway handy or a record store or some other sign that people do not totally *regret* life.
Frank O'Hara

Somehow or other, truly or falsely . . . when you see yourself as a New Yorker you talk faster, you walk faster and you think faster.
Honorable Edward I. Koch, Mayor of New York

. . . submit to no models
    but your own O city!
Walt Whitman

I think this is a city full of people wanting inconceivable things.
Ellen Thatcher in John Dos Passos, *Manhattan Transfer*

It is not so much that I am an American: I am a New Yorker.
Willem de Kooning

He [the traveler] may know that New York City is made up of five boroughs, four of which—Brooklyn, Queens, Richmond, The Bronx—compose like crinkled lily pads around the basking trout of Manhattan.
Federal Writers' Project, *New York Panorama*

Fancy a good romance about Wall Street, so written that the public could understand it! There is of course a tremendous romance there; but only a financier can really know the machinery, and his knowledge is technical. But what can the mere literateur do, walled up to heaven in a world of Mathematical Mystery and Machinery.
Lafcadio Hearn

It is only the young man who supposes there is anything new in Wall Street. The merchant who figures . . . is very old business.
Ralph Waldo Emerson

Only the dead know Brooklyn . . . It'd take a guy a lifetime to know Brooklyn t'roo and t'roo. An' even den, yuh wouldn't know it at all.
Thomas Wolfe

New York City isn't a melting pot, it's a boiling pot.
Thomas E. Dewey, Governor of New York

New York is striped with parallel, incommunicable meanings. I walk among the small brick houses, the color of dried blood. They are younger than European houses, but because of their fragility they seem much older . . . It occurs to me that New York is about to acquire a history, that it already has its ruins. This is to adorn with a little softness the harshest city in the world.
Jean-Paul Sartre

In Boston they ask, How much does he know? In New York, How much is he worth?
Mark Twain

Mammon, n. The god of the world's leading religion. His chief temple is the holy city of New York.
Ambrose Bierce, *The Devil's Dictionary*

As they're putting up the Christmas trees on Park Avenue
I shall see my daydreams walking by with dogs in blankets,
put to some use before all those colored lights come on.
Frank O'Hara, "Music"

New York made Modernism: Modernism made New York.
Robert Hughes

The Bronx?
No, Thonx!
Ogden Nash

Skyscrapers are machines for making money.
Le Corbusier

We [New Yorkers] are arch-modernists with no feeling for modernity.
Morton Feldman

I live in Brooklyn, By choice.

    Those ignorant of its allures are entitled to wonder why. For, taken as a whole, it is an uninviting community. A veritable veldt of tawdriness where even the *noms des quartiers* aggravate: Flatbush and Flushing Avenue, Bushwick, Brownsville, Red Hook.
Truman Capote

If you live in New York long enough, what you thought was an age of lead will look like an age of gold.
Murray Kempton

Besides, New York was then a very Russian city, so we had Russia all over the place. It was a case, as Lionel Abel said, of a metropolis that yearned to belong to another country.
Saul Bellow, *Humboldt's Gift*

I want this new novel to be delicate and cutting—nothing will cut New York but a diamond.
Dawn Powell

This metropolis has all the symptoms of a mind gone berserk.
I. B. Singer, "The Cafeteria"

Baghdad-on-the-Subway

It couldn't have happened anywhere but in little old New York.
O. Henry

New York makes some think of the collapse of civilization, about Sodom and Gomorrah, the end of the world. The end wouldn't come as a surprise here. Many people already bank on it.
Saul Bellow

The present in New York is so powerful that the past is lost.
John Jay Chapman

There is a flash packet, flash packet of fame
She hails from New York, and the "Dreadnought's"
    her name
Anon

East Side, West Side, all around the town.
The tots sang "Ring-a-rosie," "London Bridge is
    falling down";
Boys and girls together, me and Mamie O'Rourke
Tripped the light fantastic on the sidewalks of
    New York.
James Blake

It was three years before we saw New York again. As the ship glided up the river, the city burst thunderously upon us in the early dusk—the white glacier of lower New York swooping down like a strand of a bridge to rise up into uptown New York, a miracle of foamy light suspended by the stars. A band started to play on deck, but the majesty of the city made the march trivial and tinkling. From that moment I knew that New York, however often I might leave it, was home.
F. Scott Fitzgerald, "My Lost City"

I would give the greatest sunset in the world for one sight of New York's skyline. Particularly when one can't see the details. Just the shapes. The shapes and the thought that made them. The sky over New York and the will of man made visible. What other religion do we need?
Newspaper magnate Gail Wynand in Ayn Rand's *The Fountainhead*

These stories seem at times to be stories of a long-lost world when the city of New York was still filled with a river light, when you heard the Benny Goodman quartets from a radio in the corner stationery store, and when almost everybody wore a hat.
John Cheever, Preface to *The Stories of John Cheever*

The city is so conveniently situated for trade and the Genius of the people so inclined to merchandise . . . that letters must be a manner forced upon them not only without their seeking, but against their consent.

John Sharpe, Chaplain to His Majesty's garrisons in New York, 1713.

No woman was ever ruined by a book.

Mayor James Walker, 1923

Where does the evil of the year go

>   when September takes New York

and turns it into ozone stalagmites

>   deposits of light

Frank O'Hara, "Poem"

I think New York is not the cultural center of America, but the business and administrative center of American culture.

Saul Bellow

The ultimate modern artist might be defined as someone who likes living in New York City.

Federal Writers' Project, *New York Panorama*

Who knows the Palisades as I do
knows the river breaks east from them
above the city—but they continue south
under the sky—to bear a rest of
little peering houses that brighten
with dawn behind the moody
water-loving giants of Manhattan.

William Carlos Williams, "January Morning"

New York, inhabited by six million strangers, is the metropolis of curiosity and suspicion. It is the city without landmarks, the home of lasting impermanence, of dynamic immobility.

Malcolm Cowley

We'll have Manhattan
The Bronx and Staten
Island too
Lorenz Hart

I've long believed that people from Brooklyn single each other out in later life because Brooklyn is a real place, a real culture, and there is something about growing up there that has a lasting effect.
Norman Podhoretz

When I was a boy, the Battery was way uptown.
Robert Benchley

There now is your insular city of the Manhattoes, belted round by wharves as Indian isles by coral reefs—commerce surrounds it with her surf. Right and left, the streets take you waterward.
Herman Melville, *Moby-Dick*

Speaking of New York as a traveler, I have two faults to find with it. In the first place, there is nothing to see; and in the second place, there is no mode of getting about to see anything.
Anthony Trollope, 1862

We saw the mystic city of the new world appear far away, rising from Manhattan. It passed us at close range: a spectacle of beauty and savagery. In contrast to our hopes the skyscrapers were not made of glass, but of tiara-crowned masses of stone. They carry up a thousand feet in the sky, a completely new and prodigious architectural event; with one stroke Europe is thrust aside.
Le Corbusier upon arriving in New York for the first time aboard the
Normandy

In New York, after one week of living on cocktails in taxicabs, I have to go to a doctor. The doctor always says—get out of New York before it kills you.
Kenneth Rexroth

It was he who had given the taxi driver an address in Greenwich Village and Maigret had discovered, in the heart of New York, a few minutes away from the skyscrapers, a little city within a city. It

was almost a provincial town, with houses no taller than those in Bourdeaux or Dijon, with little shops, quiet streets along which one could stroll leisurely, and inhabitants who appeared to pay no heed to the monster metropolis surrounding them.
Georges Simenon, *New York's Underworld*

How much New York resembles bacon and eggs, especially when you've been away.
Barry Gifford

It is as beautiful a land as one can hope to tread upon.
Henry Hudson

New York is essentially national in interest, position, pursuits. No one thinks of the place as belonging to a particular state, but to the United States.
James Fenimore Cooper

I did everything with that great mad joy you get when you return to New York City.
Jack Kerouac

A gray hush
in which the boxy trucks roll up Second Avenue
into the sky.
James Schuyler, "February"

It's 8:54 a.m. in Brooklyn it's the 8th of July and
it's probably 8:54 in Manhattan but I'm
in Brooklyn I'm eating English muffins and drinking
Pepsi and I'm thinking of how Brooklyn is New
York City too how odd I usually think of it as
something all its own like Bellows Falls like Little
Chute like Uijonghu
Ted Berrigan

    I too walked the streets of
Manhattan island.
Walt Whitman

There is no question there is an unseen world; the question is, how far is it from midtown, and how late is it open.
Woody Allen

New York is my Lourdes, where I go for spiritual refreshment . . . a place where you're least likely to be bitten by a wild goat.
Brendan Behan

City of dreadful height.
James Bone

If you live in New York, even if you're Catholic, you're Jewish.
Lenny Bruce

New York is a sucked orange.
Ralph Waldo Emerson

It wasn't until I got to New York that I became Kansan.
William Inge

Literary New York (is) a bottle full of tapeworms trying to feed on each other.
Ernest Hemingway

I remember fantasies of opening up an art gallery on the Lower East Side in a store front (I'd live in back) with one exposed wall (brick) and everything else white. Lots of potted plants. And paintings by, you guessed it, me.

I remember fantasies of all of a sudden out of the blue announcing "An Evening with Joe Brainard" at Carnegie Hall and surprising everybody that I can sing and dance too, but only for one performance. (Tho I'm a smash hit and people want more) But I say "no": I give up stardom for art. And this one performance becomes a legend. And people who missed it could shoot themselves. But I stick to my guns.
Joe Brainard

One of the longest journeys in the world is the journey from Brooklyn to Manhattan—or at least from certain neighborhoods in Brooklyn to certain parts of Manhattan.
Norman Podhoretz

I like *pavement,* The sound of my shoes on pavement; stuffed windows; all-night restaurants, sirens in the night—sinister but alive; book and record shops that, on impulse, you can visit at midnight. And in that sense, New York is the world's only city *city.*
Truman Capote

New York was, and is, reckless about scholars.
Perry Miller

If the planet grows cold, this city will nevertheless have been mankind's warmest moment.
Paul Morand

Jazz is New York. You can feel it in the air.
Thelonious Monk

My first impression of New York was overwhelming. Everybody appeared to be young. It was not possible to imagine that people so alive could be old.
Dame Edith Sitwell

I expect some new religion
to rise up like tear gas
from the streets of New York
erupting like the rank pavement smell
released by the garbage-trucks'
baptismal drizzle.
Audre Lorde

New York is cocaine, opium, hashish.
Ambrose Bierce

If Paris is the perfect setting for a romance, New York is the perfect city in which to get over one, to get over anything.
Cyril Connolly

New York is something awful, something monstrous. I like to walk the streets, lost, but I recognize that New York is the world's great lie. New York is Senegal with machines.
Federico García Lorca

They say the neon lights are bright
On Broadway
They say there's always a magic in the air
On Broadway
But when you're walking down the street
And you ain't got enough to eat
The glitter all rubs off
And you're nowhere
On Broadway
Barry Mann, Cynthia Weil, Jerry Leiber, and Mike Stoller

Whenever I hear the words "New York," the first thing that comes to mind is looking out the window of my grandparents' sixth-floor apartment building at the corner of Central Park South and Columbus Circle. The window is open, and I'm standing there with a penny in my hand, about to let go of it so I can watch it fall to the street. I couldn't have been more than four or five years old at the time. Just as I started to open my hand, my grandmother looked over at me and shouted, "Don't do that! If that penny hits someone, it will go straight through his head!"
Paul Auster

In Manhattan surrealism is invisible.
Rem Koolhaas

Have you ever noticed that no American writer of any consequence lives in Manhattan? Dreiser tried it . . . but finally fled to California.
H. L. Mencken in 1922

In New York who needs an atom bomb? If you walked away from a place they tore it down.
Bernard Malamud

Rand, Ayn (1905–1982)

Rand's novels have been popular with readers and loathed by the literati. A Russian immigrant, she worked up a philosophy of radical individualism that she called Objectivism. It stands for "upholding capitalism in politics, egoism in ethics and reason in epistemology." To broadcast her views Rand wrote two novels that, to the amazement of many reviewers, struck a chord in readers who have made them bestsellers to this day. *The Fountainhead,* the story of the misunderstood genius architect Howard Roarke, appeared in 1943 and *Atlas Shrugged* in 1957. It is remarkable that Rand's views cut through her turgid prose and cardboard characters. In the thirties and forties Rand had a sort of salon at the Objectivist Book Service on East Thirty-fourth Street. One of its habitués, Alan Greenspan, became the head of the Federal Reserve.

Reader's Digest

In 1922, when Greenwich Village was the city's bohemian literary center, the most un-bohemian, indeed, *the* white-bread, middle-class magazine, *Reader's Digest,* began in a basement on Minetta Lane. DeWitt Wallace and Lila Acheson Wallace, its founders, quickly took it to the New York suburb of Pleasantville, where it remains today. The *Digest* became enormously successful, and today some of the money it earns is given away by the Lila Wallace Reader's Digest Fund to aid writers and magazines who would be more at home in Greenwich Village than Pleasantville.

Reznikoff, Charles (1894–1976)

> Feast, you who cross the bridge
> this cold twilight
> on these honeycombs of light, the buildings of Manhattan

Born in Brooklyn to immigrant Jewish parents, Reznikoff followed high school in that city with college at the University of Missouri School of Journalism. Returning to New York he went to New York City Law School and after graduation hung out his shingle, but soon took up work that left him more time for his writing. He wrote law cases for *Corpus Juris,* a legal encyclopedia published in Brooklyn. In 1931 his poems appeared in the Objectivist issue of *Poetry Magazine,* edited by Louis Zukofsky, and Reznikoff became known as a member of the

Objectivists. He wrote prose as well as poetry, including a book about his family, *Family Chronicle,* and a novel set in Hollywood (where he worked as a lawyer for a few years), *The Manner Music.* Reznikoff's poetry uses simple and clear language in a quiet way. He had a wonderful eye for city detail honed by the many long walks he took up and down Manhattan and all over Brooklyn. "The house-wreckers have left the door and a staircase, / now leading to the empty room of night." New Directions published Reznikoff's selected poems, *By the Waters of Manhattan,* in 1962 to fine reviews, and Black Sparrow Press brought out nearly all of his work in the seventies and eighties. His work is neglected at present, but a poet of his quality cannot disappear for too long. Toward the end of his life a group called Poets in Public Places had him read on the promenade of Brooklyn Heights overlooking the waters of Manhattan. Among his New York addresses were Eighteenth Street and Ninth Avenue and the Lincoln Towers in Lincoln Center. One of his champions, the critic Eliot Weinberger, believes that Reznikoff is this century's great poet of New York and that one day there will be a plaque at his last New York address, 180 West End Avenue.

Riis, Jacob (1849–1914)

Today in Port-au-Prince, Haiti, there are rope hotels. In shacks and concrete cells, rope is strung like clothesline chest high from wall to wall. A man rents a length of rope, flops his body across it, and hopes for a night's sleep. We think of this as typical of conditions in Third World countries, and some of us think that nothing like this ever existed in the United States, much less in Manhattan. During his years as a police reporter and advocate for the poor in New York, Jacob Riis saw, wrote about, and photographed far worse. A Danish immigrant, Riis became a police reporter for the *New York Herald* and in the years that he worked there (1877–1888) he described the "foul core" of New York's slums. These occupied what is now Little Italy, the neighborhood where Mulberry Street meets Houston. He took his camera with him and in the series "Flashes from the Slums" documented the miserable poverty that was the lot of the mass of recent immigrants. The police-run "lodging houses," where the "lodger" slept on the "soft side of a plank," and early flophouses like "Happy Jack's Canvas Palace," where for seven cents a person could spend the night in a strip of canvas hung hammock-like between rough timbers, drew his special attention. When Teddy Roosevelt became New York's police commissioner he was moved by Riis's articles to shut down the police lodgings. After Riis left the

Tribune to go deeper into the problems created by the intense and un-remitting poverty he had seen, he took his camera into the blackest New York holes where "street Arabs," homeless boys of grade school age, slept, as did immigrant shoemakers and their families. These places were without heat, light, or water. Riis recorded the activities of "Growler Gangs" who preyed on the poor, the interiors of the many sweatshops on the Lower East Side, and the nooks and crannies where lawlessness ruled. Beginning with *How the Other Half Lives* (1890), he published a number of muckraking books that were to have an effect not only on writers such as Stephen Crane but also on public policy. Riis saw Mulberry Bend between Bayard and Park Streets, "the worst pigsty of all" with which he had been in a "death-grapple," turned into a park by the Small Parks Act of 1887, and he saw acres of slums he had decried fall to the wrecker's ball. For his own part Riis found that "the deeper I burrow into the slum, the more my thoughts turned, by a sort of defensive instinct, to the country." In 1887 he built a house in Rich-mond Hill, Queens, at 84-41 120th Street. He lived there until 1911, when he moved to 524 North Beech Street. Aperture Inc. published *Jacob A. Riis: Photographer and Citizen* in 1974. Excerpts from Riis's writing supply captions to the book's many powerful photographs. There is also a short biographical essay by Alexander Alland Sr.

Robinson, Edwin Arlington (1869–1935)

There will always be writers in New York who live and write in isola-tion. For many years the poet Edwin Arlington Robinson was one of them. He came to Manhattan from Maine in 1896 and spent the next decade living a solitary, impoverished, bohemian life, working fitfully on his poetry or sunk in drink and depression. He later said these years were "nothing but the bottle." During them he lived mostly at 450 West Twenty-third Street in a room given him by a kindly barkeep. In 1906 a miracle occurred. President Teddy Roosevelt read Robinson's poems in a book brought home from prep school by his son Kermit. Impressed, Roosevelt sought out the poet and offered him a consular position in Mexico or Canada, but Robinson did not want to leave New York. He managed to wangle his way into a sinecure at Customs. And there he stayed for four years, living in the Judson Hotel, until the Taft adminis-tration relieved him of his post. He stayed on in the city a dozen years after this sustained by two patrons: Mrs. Clara Potter Davidge at 121 Washington Place and James Fraser, the sculptor who designed the buf-falo nickel, and his wife, Laura, at 28 West Eighth Street.

Roebling, Washington (1837–1926)

Washington's father, John, designed the Brooklyn Bridge but died before he could build it. The son saw to completion the father's dream even though an attack of the bends, suffered while working in one of the caissons under a bridge tower, left him in great and constant pain. As Washington watched the bridge go up from a room in his house in Brooklyn Heights, he depended on his wife, Emily Warren Roebling, to see that his orders were carried out. This she did with intelligence, fortitude, and dispatch. It is a wonderful story well told by David McCullough in his book on the building of the bridge. Toward the end of his life Roebling wrote a biography of his father and then lost all two hundred pages of it. We know about the book only from letters Roebling wrote.

Rorem, Ned (b. 1923)

For the composer Ned Rorem it has been a life of Monteverdi and rough trade and . . . well, it seems presumptuous to gloss the work of a diarist who has, as Rorem has done so many times, told all or at least given the impression that he has. Beginning in 1966 with the appearance of *The New York Diary*, Rorem's career as a writer paralleled that as a composer. He has since published many books written with wit and authority about music, but his diary has been—how can it be otherwise?—near the center of his life. The reader who is interested in gay New York and Paris from World War II to the present and in Virgil Thomson, Aaron Copland, Frank O'Hara, Kenward Elmslie, with whom Rorem wrote the opera *Miss Julie,* Leonard Bernstein, Marc Blitzstein, John Cheever, Myrna Loy, and a cast, literally, of thousands will want to read Rorem's diaries. As a composer Rorem has set to music the poems of O'Hara, James Schuyler, and John Ashbery, among others. He appears, of course, in O'Hara's poetry: "Ned's glad / not to be up late / for the sake of his music and his ear." But Rorem was up late many other nights and writing books for us to devour like the rich slabs of cake they are. For many years Rorem has lived on West Seventieth Street.

Rosten, Norman (1914–1996)

Poet, novelist, and playwright, Rosten was born in the city and graduated from Brooklyn College and New York University. While in graduate school at the University of Michigan he and Arthur Miller were in the same playwriting class. They kept up their friendship in Brooklyn, and through Miller, Rosten got to know Marilyn Monroe, about whom he wrote the book, *Marilyn: An Untold Story*. Rosten was also friendly with Norman Mailer. His greatest success came in the theater with his adaptation of Joyce Cary's novel *Mister Johnson*. He began his career by winning the Yale Series of Younger Poets award and ended it as Brooklyn's poet laureate, a position he held from 1919 until his death. Brooklyn Borough president Howard Golden named Rosten to that position and was pleased when Rosten responded with the poem "Glad Words for Howard." Rosten's successor is Dennis Nurkse. Brooklyn is the only one of the city's five boroughs to have a poet laureate.

Roth, Henry (1906–1995)

Roth's Yiddish-speaking parents emigrated from Galicia to the Lower East Side in 1909. There Roth grew up in what he described as "a virtual Jewish mini-state. All transactions, work and play were conducted in Yiddish." In 1934 Roth recreated this world in the novel *Call It Sleep*. The book received good reviews and sold some four thousand copies. Roth went on to write seventy-five pages of a second novel, but he abandoned it despite encouragement from Maxwell Perkins. By 1939 he had fallen off the literary map. Sometime in the mid-thirties Roth joined the Communist Party, after which he either gave up writing, set it aside, or suffered writer's block (it is unclear exactly what happened). In any event, he worked at a series of blue-collar jobs that read like those novelists once took for experience: a precision tool grinder in New York, pulpwood cutter, blueberry picker, maple syrup maker in Maine, an attendant in a mental hospital, a farmer of ducks and geese. Then something extraordinary happened. *Call It Sleep* was reissued in paperback in 1964, and following Irving Howe's enthusiastic front page review in the *New York Times Book Review*, the book found a wide audience and has to date sold nearly one million copies. Roth had written the novel in the late twenties and early thirties while living in the Greenwich Village apartment of a New York University writing teacher Eda Lou Walton. Twelve years his senior, Walton met Roth when he was a student at City College, saw great talent in him, and supported him while he worked to complete his novel. Roth later described her as "a mistress and a mother. It was good, and it was bad. It was maybe good for the writer, but it was bad for the person." *Call It Sleep* is dedicated to her. They split up in 1938, and in the following year Roth married the composer Muriel Parker and disappeared into the years of manual labor. It was not the success of *Call It Sleep* that brought him back to writing, but the 1967 Arab-Israeli War. Roth explained to the novelist Leonard Michaels that since the Communist Party supported the Arabs he could no longer give it his allegiance. "I felt," Roth said, "as if I were personally under attack." This led to what he called a "rational reunion" with Judaism and "a slowly awakening desire to write." What began slowly turned into a torrent, and while Roth was living in Albuquerque, New Mexico, he wrote six novels under the overall title *Mercy of a Rude Stream.* The complete series is in the process of being published.

Roth, Philip (b. 1933)

A native of Newark, New Jersey, Roth came from Chicago, where he had been in graduate school, to a basement apartment on the Lower East Side in 1958. While waiting for his first book, *Goodbye Columbus,* to be published, he became entangled with a woman named Josie. He tells the story of what happened between them and how it figured in his writing in his autobiographical *The Facts.* Some of the *mishegas* resulting from Roth's tumultuous life with her made its way into his 1974 novel *My Life as a Man* and helped inspire his masterpiece *Portnoy's Complaint,* a good deal of which takes place in Manhattan. Along with that novel's great success came the charge that it was anti-Semitic. A number of New York writers and intellectuals mounted a campaign against Roth and his book. Roth's alter ego, the novelist Nathan Zuckerman, suffers a similar fate after writing a best-selling book, and he is fearful of fans and foes alike as he walks the streets of New York. During this time Zuckerman lived on the Upper East Side in an apartment from which he could see Frank Campbell's Funeral Home, out of which members of the Mafia and other New York celebrities get buried.

Rudman, Mark (b. 1948)

Somewhere in Lower Manhattan there is the Millenium Hotel, one *n,* whose name inspired Mark Rudman's long poem *The Millenium Hotel.* The poem evolved out of another long poem, *Rider,* and the structure is open enough to allow autobiographical elements, translations from Boris Pasternak and others, and a host of characters who speak in their own voices. At this point it appears to be the poem of a life that will expand to include all that Rudman deems necessary. He has also published a book of essays on poetry, *Diverse Voices,* and, perhaps his most original work, *Realm of Unknowing.* In the book's subtitle these essays are called "meditations," which suggests their quality of going into a subject and then stopping or stepping back to approach it from another angle. On the page they resemble a series of notes divided into discrete sections, a form that Rudman calls "forays." The title essay on his uncle Herbert Leeds is exceptional, as is the essay on his friend William Arrowsmith. In his essay "On Place: City and Country," Rudman describes the peculiar emptiness that one sometimes encounters in Manhattan: "There are times when the avenues are so empty New York reminds me of an abandoned city in the desert." He has lived for years on the Upper West Side and has taught in the writing programs at both Columbia and New York University.

Rukeyser, Muriel (1913–1980)

Soon after her death Muriel Rukeyser's poetry began to disappear into that limbo from which so much is never recovered. Perhaps this happened because she was such a passionate social activist that the content of her poems came to seem like yesterday's newspapers. And once the content no longer engaged readers her rhetorical flourishes may have sounded windy. Yet, limbo has been held off, at least for a time, by a new interest in Rukeyser's work led by the poet Jane Cooper and others. This is good to see not only because Rukeyser wrote socially conscious poetry of a high order but because she had an original career. Born in Manhattan, she went to Vassar, where she teamed up with Elizabeth Bishop, Mary McCarthy, and the novelist Eleanor Clark to found the *Student Review* as an alternative to the authorized student magazine. As the *Review*'s correspondent Rukeyser went to Alabama to cover the trial of the Scottsboro Boys. Thirty years later she would be arrested and jailed in Washington, D.C., while protesting the Vietnam War, and in 1972 as president of PEN she journeyed to South Korea to protest the imprisonment of poet Kim Chi-Ha. In 1937 Rukeyser won the Yale Series of Younger Poets Prize for her first book, *Theory of Flight*. She published eleven more books of poems, ending with *Collected Poems* in 1979. Rukeyser, who remained fascinated by technology throughout her life, also published a biography of the scientist Willard Gibbs, *Willard Gibbs: American Genius* (1942) and, in 1971, a study of the English scientist Thomas Hariot, *The Traces of Thomas Hariot*. Perhaps her most unusual book was her 1957 biography of the Wall Street financier and Republican presidential candidate Wendell Wilkie. In this book she combined prose, documents, and verse somewhat in the manner of William Carlos Williams's *Paterson*. Rukeyser translated the poetry of Octavio Paz and Gunnar Ekelof, and wrote a number of children's books as well as several plays. Those who are busily reviving her work have a great deal from which to choose. Her last New York address was 463 West Street.

Runyon, Damon (1884–1946)

Harry the Horse, Nathan Detroit, Sky Masterson, Nicely Nicely Johnson, Adelaide: the characters of the musical *Guys and Dolls,* whose score Jo Swerling, Abe Burrows, and Frank Loesser wrote, came from the pen of Damon Runyon. He had been a war correspondent before landing in New York, where he covered sports and wrote a column for the Hearst papers. Many of the stories that he wrote about the Broadway characters, the gamblers, and chorus girls—innocent professions by today's standards—were published in the *Saturday Evening Post* before appearing in *Guys and Dolls* (1932) and other books. These books may not be much read today, but the musical is often revived and the adjective *Runyonesque* is still used to describe someone with the attributes of the characters he created. That the poet Tom Clark, once a denizen of the Lower East Side poetry scene, wrote a biography of Runyon suggests his continuing appeal.

Salinger, J [erome] D [avid] (b. 1919)

A New York native raised in and around the city, Salinger spent the greater part of his childhood on the Upper West Side at 390 Riverside Drive. He was sent to Valley Forge Military Academy outside Philadelphia, which became the model for "Pennsy Prep" in his novel *The Catcher in the Rye* (1951). Returning to New York, Salinger studied briefly at Ursinus College and attended Whit Burnett's short story class at Columbia before serving in France during World War II. He began publishing short stories at twenty-one. Those that he collected appeared first in the *New Yorker* and then in *Nine Stories* (1953). Eight years later he published the first book of the Glass family stories, *Franny and Zooey,* and this was followed by *Raise High the Roof Beam, Carpenters* and *Seymour: An Introduction* (1963). In its issue of 19 June 1965, the *New Yorker* published a last Glass family story, "Hapworth, 16, 1924," and since then Salinger has not published a word. He lives as a recluse in New Hampshire and defends his privacy ferociously. He stopped the publication of a pirated edition of his early stories and kept the British biographer Ian Hamilton from using unauthorized material from his letters. Hamilton's book was in galleys and had been sent to reviewers when Salinger brought suit. The book appeared as *In Search of J. D. Salinger,* but without the letters. The only other contemporary American writers of comparable fame to so determinedly avoid the public eye are the novelists Thomas Pynchon and Cormac McCarthy. They have been successful, but perhaps they have not been so hounded as Salinger has been. A few years ago the *Paris Review* published snapshots of an enraged Salinger charging a woman who had just photographed him on the streets of the New Hampshire town in which he lives. Even a magazine of its reputation was prepared to act like a supermarket tabloid where he was concerned. Given Salinger's own problems with fans, it is more than ironic that Mark Chapman, the fan who murdered John Lennon in front of the Dakota on Central Park West, was carrying a copy of *The Catcher in the Rye* at the time. In response to police questions about why he had killed Lennon, Chapman said that the answer could be found in Salinger's book.

Now that *The Catcher in the Rye* has been given the label "minor classic" and we are nearly fifty years from its original fame, it becomes difficult to remember how all this unwarranted attention came to Salinger. Readers who loved the book—and there were many—often identified with its teenage hero, Holden Caulfield, on his weekend wanderings in Manhattan to such a degree that they felt the writer who created them was their buddy, that they ought to be able to just pick up the phone and give him a call. The novel became and remained such a popular success (it was routinely assigned to high school students and, perhaps unwisely, to those entering prep school) that Salinger's fame grew as his desire for privacy increased. The relative dearth of his output further heightened interest in him as did, of course, his refusal to make himself available to the public.

Norman Mailer put down Salinger as "no more than the greatest mind to ever stay in prep school," but Samuel Beckett read and admired *The Catcher in the Rye.* Today the novel seems dated and quaint, especially in its response to an obscenity scrawled on the wall of the Museum of Natural History, an obscenity that is now freely admitted into the pages of even the *New Yorker.* Still, Salinger and Caulfield's New York is a city many readers knew to be real at the time.

Salter, James (b. 1925)

Born in Manhattan as James Horowitz, Salter is that rare phenomenon, a writer educated at West Point. Edgar Allan Poe also went to school there, but he neither stayed long nor had a career in the military. Salter served as a pilot in the air force, flew missions over Korea during the Korean War, and was on his way to having a military career when he decided to become a writer. It was at this time that he changed his name on the premise that a new vocation needed a new name. Of Salter's several novels only *Light Years* is set in New York City, and it is a beauty, spare and luminous. The years are 1958 to the mid-1970s, and Viri, an architect, and his wife, Nedra, have charm, intelligence, beauty, and enough money to move in an upper-middle-class bohemian world. The subject matter—the disintegration of a marriage—is common enough; it is Salter's style, bright sunlight burned at the edges, clear and sad and driven by well-deployed sentence fragments, that sets the novel apart. Salter is a sensualist whose tone is elegiac. The brilliant New York his characters move through fades quickly as they age. The city has rarely felt more glamorous or merciless. Since then Salter has published his memoir, *Burning the Days,* which is at times reticent, a quality that dismayed some reviewers, and at others fulsome. I have never read better descriptions of what it is like to both pilot a plane and pilot one in combat. The sections on his work in the movies, where he earned his bread while serving his apprenticeship as a writer, are entertaining because, in part, Salter does not take himself too seriously. But the book lives, as does all of Salter's best work, because he makes beautiful sentences.

Sanders, Ed (b. 1939)

Sanders took a degree in classical Greek at New York University, and then embarked on his career as poet, member of the rock band the Fugs, editor of *Fuck You / A Magazine of the Arts,* and owner of the Peace Eye Bookstore. The store at Tenth Street near Avenue A in the East Village had once been a kosher chicken market and the words "Strictly Kosher" were visible on its windows throughout the time Sanders sold poetry books and magazines and promoted free speech. Writers such as Allen Ginsberg and Norman Mailer contributed to *Fuck You,* but this was the mid-sixties, when the expression was not the literary commonplace it is today. Sanders endured police harassment and got busted, as was surely his intention. Among his other publications was a pirated edition of W. H. Auden's hitherto unpublished pornographic poem, "The Platonic Blow." At the time Sanders was perhaps better known for his singing with the Fugs, a band of inspired lunacy that included the poet Tuli Kupferberg. William Blake's songs were featured on its playlist as was the nonsense anthem "Nothing": "Nothing, nothing, Franklin Delano Nothing, Monday nothing Tuesday nothing . . ." In *Tales of Beatnik Glory* Sanders remembered those years. He went on to write a book about Charles Manson, record a country album, write and publish several books of poetry, and retire to Woodstock, New York, out of the limelight.

San Remo
Northwest Corner of Bleecker and MacDougal

In the late forties the San Remo was *the* writer's bar in the Village. James Agee drank there, as did the forlorn Maxwell Bodenheim, a bohemian poet and novelist from the twenties. Michael Harrington, who arrived in New York from Chicago in 1949, just in time to catch the San Remo in full swing, described the crowd as "heterosexuals on the make; homosexuals who preferred erotic integration to the exclusively gay bars on Eighth Street; Communists, Socialists and Trotskyists; potheads . . ." And then the Beats came. William Burroughs, Allen Ginsberg, Jack Kerouac and nonwriting Beat legends such as Lucien Carr and Bill Cannastra were habitués. Chandler Brossard, who wrote the novel *Who Walk in Darkness* about this generation of Villagers, drank there as did William Styron, Norman Mailer, Harold Norse, James Baldwin, W. H. Auden, and most of the literary folk who lived downtown. This was not only a hard-drinking generation but one that did not have television to keep them at home. They read books and wanted to make the scene with others who did.

Saroyan, William (1908–1981)

On Saroyan's first visit to Manhattan he had the sort of experience no one ever forgets, especially if he goes on, as Saroyan did, to become the toast of the town. Arriving from his native Fresno, California, the nineteen-year-old Saroyan lost both his luggage and the hundred dollars he had with him. He found his way to the YMCA across from the Chelsea Hotel at 215 West Twenty-third Street and there, using the dollar's worth of change he had in his pocket, rented a room. In the mid-thirties Saroyan returned to the city, a success following the publication of *The Daring Young Man on the Flying Trapeze*. This time he stayed uptown at the Great Northern Hotel at 118 West Fifty-seventh Street, and he loved it so much that he stayed there on a number of visits until, as he wrote, "I had become wealthy, and the world itself had changed, so I moved on and up, as the saying is." Saroyan's wealth came not only from his very popular books, but from his plays, most prominently *The Time of Your Life* (1939), for which Saroyan received a Pulitzer Prize that he refused to accept.

Schapiro, Meyer (1904–1996)

Schapiro's obituary, written by Picasso's biographer John Russell, appeared on the front page of the *New York Times,* attesting to his eminence as teacher, art historian and critic, and political radical in the New York intellectual life of his time. Born in Lithuania, he emigrated to New York as a boy. In grade school he showed an interest in art that led to his taking an evening class taught by the painter John Sloan. Schapiro continued to paint and draw throughout his life, but after he finished high school and entered Columbia he knew he did not have the talent to became a practicing artist, so he plunged into a varied curriculum that eventually led to a Ph.D. in art history. In 1928 he was appointed lecturer in that subject at Columbia, and he married Dr. Lillian Milgrim, a pediatrician. For more than sixty years they lived in the same Greenwich Village townhouse. Schapiro's greatest impact came as a teacher at Columbia, where he taught for nearly half a century, and at New York University and the New School for Social Research. He championed abstract painting and became important to many painters and writers as the New York School of painters came to the fore. But his real attraction was not timeliness, it was breadth. Schapiro saw more than all but a few art historians because he saw the intellectual, historical, and social context in which art is created, be it medieval mosaics, Cézanne's apples, or de Kooning's women. It was Schapiro who advised de Kooning that his *Woman I* was not a failure as de Kooning feared but a success that would generate others. Allen Ginsberg, who took courses with Schapiro at Columbia, remembered that his lectures on Cézanne's landscapes were decisive in forming his aesthetic outlook. For many years Schapiro resisted publishing his lectures and papers in book form. It may be that he discovered so many of his insights in the act of teaching that he did not want to put a stop to that process by the finality of print between hard covers. In any case, he published only a few brief books before 1977, when the publisher George Braziller began a four-volume series of selected essays on Romanesque, Early Christian, Medieval, and Modern Art that display in clear but workmanlike prose Schapiro's vast and humane erudition. As American intellectual life becomes increasingly specialized we may not encounter Schapiro's like again.

Schultz, Dutch [Arthur Flegenheimer] (1902–1935)

One of Prohibition's most notorious gangsters, the hot-headed, violent Schultz controlled beer and numbers in the Bronx and Harlem. He is supposed to have taken his nom de crime because it fit neatly into newspaper headlines. After all, Arthur Flegenheimer not only sounds like the name of a grocer, it is also awfully long. When Thomas E. Dewey became federal prosecutor and vowed to drive the underworld out of the city, Schultz had a simple plan—kill the man. His hoodlum associates, Lucky Luciano and Meyer Lansky, did not like the idea, but Schultz was determined to go it alone. He never had the chance. Gunned down in the men's room of a New York City restaurant, he spent two days dying, throughout which a police stenographer sat by his bedside taking down every word he babbled in the hopes that Schultz might reveal something of use. He didn't, but that transcript has been printed at least once as a parody of Gertrude Stein, and William Burroughs wrote a novel and film script based on the gangster's last words, the final four of which were "French Canadian bean soup."

Schuyler, James (1923–1991)

Along with Barbara Guest, Schuyler is the other member of the first generation of the New York School not to go to Harvard. He went to Bethany College in West Virginia, dropped out, served in the navy, and after his discharge came to New York in 1944. He worked for NBC's Voice of America and lived in a cold-water flat at 63 Downing Street in the Village. In the late forties and early fifties he spent a great deal of time in Europe, mostly in Italy, where he worked for a brief period as W. H. Auden's private secretary. In 1952 he roomed with Frank O'Hara in an apartment in the now demolished 326 East Forty-ninth Street. Schuyler lived there off and on for nine years, and it was in this apartment that he wrote his first great poem, "February," in which he sees "the boxy trucks roll up Second Avenue / into the sky." During these years Schuyler followed O'Hara into a job manning the front desk at the Museum of Modern Art, worked as a clerk at the Periscope-Holliday Bookstore on East Fifty-fourth Street, and began in 1955 to write art criticism for *Art News* and other magazines. After a hospital stay in 1961 he went to live with the painter Fairfield Porter and his wife, the poet Anne Porter, and their family in Southampton, Long Island, and on an island off the Maine coast. He stayed for more than ten years. In 1969 his first book of poems, *Freely Espousing*, appeared, to be followed by several others, culminating in his Pulitzer Prize-winning *Morning of the Poem* (1980). Schuyler had moved back to the city in 1971, taking a small and very dark apartment on East Thirty-fifth Street. Here in 1973 he suffered one of the nervous breakdowns that had plagued him since the early sixties. This led to a stay at Payne Whitney, the psychiatric hospital associated with New York Hospital, where he wrote a series of poems that are poignant for the matter-of-fact way they describe his illness and hospital stay. In 1976 he moved into an apartment at 348 West Twentieth Street where his smoking in bed caused a fire that destroyed some of his possessions. He went from there to various rooming houses and hotels until he took Room 625 at the Chelsea Hotel in 1979. There he lived, with the help of several assistants, the poets Eileen Myles and Tom Carey among them, for the rest of his life. There is now a plaque on the Chelsea's facade to commemorate Schuyler's years at the hotel. His *Collected Poems*, edited by his executors (Carey, Raymond Foye, and the painter Darragh Park), appeared in 1993 from Farrar, Straus & Giroux. This book made manifest what those who had long followed Schuyler's work knew: Of all the New York School poets, the city itself shines most brightly in all weathers in his poems. Even more than Frank O'Hara, Schuyler made poetry out of the people and places in his life. In "Dining Out with Doug and Frank" at McFeely's on West Twenty-third and Eleventh Avenue he meditated on the city:

> To be on
> the water in the dark and
> the wonder of electricity—
> the real beauty of Manhattan.
> Oh well. When they tore down
> the Singer Building,
> and when I saw the Bogardus building
> rusting and coming unstitched in
> a battlefield of rubble I deliberately
> withdrew my emotional investments
> in loving old New York. Except
> you can't.

For most of his career Schuyler did not give public readings and he never taught. He was a poet's poet, but then on 15 November 1988, he gave his first public reading at the Dia Foundation in Chelsea. There was a line around the block. Schuyler wrote to a friend that the evening was "a fucking sensation," and no one who was fortunate enough to be there would describe it otherwise.

Schwartz, Delmore (1913–1966)

Schwartz's fall from grace is as spectacular as that of any twentieth-century American writer. He began as a golden boy, the author of a masterpiece, and ended alone, mad, and wretched, never having fulfilled his promise. Born in Brooklyn, Schwartz and his family moved several times: from Eastern Parkway to President Street to Washington Heights before Schwartz crossed the river to college at New York University. In the summer of his junior year, he took an apartment at 813 Greenwich Avenue, determined to work on his poetry. There he wrote "In Dreams Begin Responsibilities." When it appeared two years later, leading off the autumn 1937 issue of *Partisan Review,* it was hailed as an amazing beginning to what surely would be a great career. Although Schwartz wrote some good poems and critical essays, it was his fate to fall short of his own and others' expectations. In some cases this happened out of arrogance. He published an amateurish translation of Rimbaud that many reviewers with better French than his ridiculed for being full of howlers. In other cases—his verse play *Shenandoah* and his long poem *Genesis*—despite flashes of brilliance, he appealed to few readers. From 1943 to 1955 he was an editor at *Partisan Review* and did a variety of literary work. He also began to behave erratically, and put many of his friendships under strain. For a few years he lived in New Jersey and took teaching jobs outside New York when he could get them. During the fifties when he was in the city he drank at the White Horse and could be wonderfully smart and entertaining, but he was also paranoid and increasingly lived in isolation. His book of stories *Summer Knowledge* won the Bollingen Prize in 1960, and he went to teach at Syracuse, where one of his students was the musician Lou Reed. The English department recommended him for tenure but the administration did not move quickly to grant it, and in January 1966 Schwartz simply left the school without telling anyone. He went to the Columbia Hotel at 70 West Forty-sixth Street, one step up from a flophouse, and here he stayed, seeing no one, until he moved on to the Hotel Dixie at 250 West Forty-third Street. On the morning of 11 July, while taking his garbage to the incinerator, he had a heart attack outside his room, 406, and lay there until someone called an ambulance. He was taken to Roosevelt Hospital, where he was pronounced dead. For two days his body lay unclaimed in the morgue. He was saved from a potter's field burial by a reporter who accidentally spotted his name

on the morgue's list. Many of those in the *Partisan Review* days have remembered his brilliance in their memoirs; his friends John Berryman
and Robert Lowell wrote poems to him, and James Atlas wrote his biography. Saul Bellow, whose friendship with Schwartz was more complex and painful than most, portrayed him as Von Humboldt Fleischer
in *Humboldt's Gift*.

Selby, Hubert (b. 1928)

The Brooklyn-born Selby's first literary contact was the poet and novelist Gil Sorrentino. They had both gone to P.S. 102, but didn't meet until
later in the early fifties. Selby remembered that he heard Sorrentino and
his friends talking about Pound and Williams, but "I hadn't read a book
and didn't know from nothing." Eventually, Selby worked on the little
magazine *Neon* with Sorrentino and became friendly with the crowd of
young poets and writers that gathered at LeRoi Jones's apartments in
the Village. In the mid-fifties Selby began writing the stories that he
fused together into his first novel, *Last Exit to Brooklyn*. Grove Press
published it in 1964, and the English put it on trial for obscenity, giving
Grove yet another battle to fight and the novel a great deal of publicity.
Set in Brooklyn's Red Hook section, where Selby lived for some five
years, the novel packs a wallop today. Barney Rosset, Grove's owner,
thought of it as one of the best titles Grove published. The success of the
novel nearly undid Selby. He stayed drunk for almost six years after its
publication and did not publish a second novel until *The Room* in
1971.

Seldes, Gilbert (1893–1970)

As managing editor of the *Dial* Seldes worked with high art while as a
columnist for the *New York Evening Journal,* among many other newspapers and magazines, he wrote on what we have come to call popular
culture: movies, comic strips (George Herriman's "Krazy Kat" was a favorite), advertising, vaudeville, pop music, and so on. In 1924 he published *The 7 Lively Arts*, which made the case that much which had
been considered merely as entertainment now deserved the dignity of
being seen as art. It became an influential book, and Seldes revised it in
1957. By then he had experienced television close up as the first program director for CBS, and he was no longer as gung ho about popular
culture. He now saw that the combination of radio, television, and
movies might bring about the end of the "private art of reading." The
advent of the computer might well have turned Seldes into a Luddite.

Today much of what he thought ought to be given the respect and scrutiny we give high art is routinely afforded such treatment in college classrooms, museums, and books.

Sendak, Maurice (b. 1928)

Benet's Reader's Encyclopedia of American Literature considers only a handful of children's book writers; the Brooklyn-born Maurice Sendak is one of them. Doubtless this is so because his work as a writer and illustrator has appeal, as great works for children almost always do, for everyone. Sendak remembers in his intelligent, delightful, and unabashed *Caldecott & Co.: Notes on Books and Pictures* that when his sister gave him his first book, Mark Twain's *The Prince and the Pauper,* he looked at it for a long time, smelled it, and bit it before finally reading it. "There's so much more to a book than just the reading," he told an interviewer. "I've seen children play with books, fondle books, smell books, and that's every reason why books should be lovingly produced." When he was nine Sendak began writing and illustrating his own stories. As an adult he worked for a time at the F.A.O. Schwartz toy store. After illustrating Ruth Krauss's *A Hole Is to Dig,* he left Schwartz to begin the career that has yielded so many books and illustrations. He is best known for *Where the Wild Things Are* (1963) and *In the Night Kitchen* (1970), but he has illustrated many books and won all the major prizes awarded for children's books. *In the Night Kitchen,* Sendak once said, "is a kind of homage to New York City, the city I loved so much and still love." His *Caldecott & Co.* is a model of forthrightness that demonstrates how an artist can illuminate work and increase the pleasure of his readers without giving anything away. For many years Sendak made his home in Greenwich Village.

Shepard, Sam (b. 1943)

Shepard arrived in the Village in 1963, at about the same time as Bob Dylan. He had dreams of acting, which he would pursue as far as Hollywood, but in New York he began writing plays. For a time he worked as a waiter at the Village Gate and there met Ralph Cook of Theater Genesis at St. Mark's Church. A double bill of his plays *Cowboys* and *The Rock Garden* opened there to a good review in the *Village Voice* and Shepard's career was launched. Over the next several years his plays were produced almost as fast as he could write them and he won Obie awards (the Off-Broadway version of Broadway's Tony) and Rockefeller and Guggenheim grants. At this point his work seems among the most permanent to come out of the Off- and Off-Off Broadway scenes. His best-known plays are *The Tooth of Crime, True West, Cowboy Mouth, Buried Child,* and *Fool for Love.* He is familiar to moviegoers for his performance as the test pilot Chuck Yeager in *The Right Stuff* (1984). In that movie and in others, Shepard carried himself like the son of Gary Cooper.

Simic, Charles (b. 1938)

Born in Belgrade, Yugoslavia, Simic arrived in New York by way of Paris in 1954. He remembers that he spent his first night in the city with his jazz-fan father at the Café Metropole. Simic went to high school in Chicago, but returned to New York in 1958 to begin night school at New York University. During the nine years it took to earn his degree he lived on East Thirteenth Street, at the Hotels Albert and Earle, and in various rooms in the Village. While working to pay for school, Simic held a number of jobs, the longest one being in the NYU payroll department, where he oversaw the checks that went to the school's janitors. After graduation and marriage Simic moved uptown to Ninetieth Street and Second Avenue and worked as the business manager—it was a two-person office and he did a little bit of everything—for the photography magazine *Aperture.* In 1970 he left New York to teach in California. The farther Simic gets from the New York of his young manhood, the more frequently the city appears in his poetry. He sees himself again walking the streets, stopping to read his dog-eared, secondhand copy of Shelley over coffee in a luncheonette. His city is full of wonders and freaks, the down and out and the street-corner ecstatic. He has an eye for much that gets overlooked, as did the artist Joseph Cornell, the subject of Simic's book *Dime-Store Alchemy* (1993).

Simon, Kate (1912–1990)

Born in Poland, Simon emigrated to New York City in 1917. She grew up in the Bronx, graduated from Hunter College and worked for the Book-of-the-Month Club, *Publishers Weekly,* and as a book reviewer before her very successful guidebook, *New York Places and Pleasures,* appeared in 1957. The guide went through several editions and caused Simon to do others on European cities. She returned to writing about New York in her excellent *Fifth Avenue: A Very Social History* (1978). This book is often found in secondhand stores and is worth a look if you are interested in how money is made in the city and what great wealth has made of Manhattan's most famous avenue. In 1982 Simon published the first volume of her autobiography, the forthright and at times very funny *Bronx Primitive*. Four years later she followed it up with the lively and engrossing *A Wider World*. A publisher could do worse than to reissue these two books in one volume. For many years Simon lived at 160 East Twenty-seventh Street.

Singer, Isaac Bashevis (1904–1991)

Singer is the only New York Nobel Prize-winning author who did not write in English. A Polish Jew, Singer wrote in Yiddish and most of his stories appeared in the *Jewish Daily Forward*. Singer was brought to America in 1935 by his brother, the writer I. J. (Israel Joshua) Singer (1893–1944), who had come to America in 1933 under the sponsorship of the *Forward*'s editor, Abraham Cahan. The younger Singer began doing freelance work for Cahan and by 1944 worked his way up to a staff position on the paper. His work began to appear in English in 1950 but did not gain him a wide audience until 1953, when Saul Bellow translated the story that is generally thought of as his masterpiece, "Gimpel the Fool." It appeared in *Partisan Review*. In the late fifties Singer moved to West Eighty-sixth Street, where he lived the rest of his life, spending as many years there as he had in his native Poland. The street is now Isaac Bashevis Singer Boulevard. Not only did Singer write in a language read only by a minority of New Yorkers, he wrote about a world that was gone, the Jewish Poland annihilated by the Nazis. Since there was no Yiddish paper in the world to rival the *Forward*, Singer had come to the right place to do his work. He was awarded a Nobel Prize in 1978. At least he was by the Nobel committee. The stone over his grave in Beth-El Cemetery that was unveiled in 1992 described Singer as a Noble Laureate. The error, made by his wife, Alma, went uncorrected until 1997. There is more to the story. Singer and Alma are buried three gravestones away from Alma's first husband, Walter Wasserman, a cozy arrangement were it not for the fact that Alma left Wasserman for Singer in 1940. At his death Singer had no idea that this was where he would be buried. Alma decided that she wanted to be near her daughter, Inge, from whom she had been estranged since leaving Inge's father. As Inge was buried near Walter, Alma's choice of neighboring plots provides what sounds like the outline of a Singer short story.

Smith, Betty (1904–1972)

Smith's autobiographical novel *A Tree Grows in Brooklyn* (1943) had three lives: as a best-selling book, as a movie, and, in collaboration with George Abbott, as a Broadway musical. Smith was born in Brooklyn's Williamsburg section. The tree she wrote about is the ailanthus, the heavenly tree that grows everywhere, taking root in the tiniest crack in the city's masonry. That is, it did until recently, when throughout New York the ailanthus began to die of a mysterious disease.

Smith, Patti (b. 1947)

Smith is better known as a rock 'n' roll singer and friend of Robert Mapplethorpe than she is as a poet. She will be dealt with in histories of the downtown punk scene, but she published poems before her first record was released and Norton has her in print today: *Early Work 1970–79* and *Coral Sea* (1969). Had she been born a decade earlier . . . well, she is on the cusp where poetry meets rock music. There with her are Lou Reed, Bob Dylan, and Jim Carroll. When she appears in concert today, Smith will often begin by reading a poem.

Sondheim, Stephen (b. 1930)

Perhaps Sondheim became the hope of the American musical theater in 1970 when *Company* opened. Since then Broadway has seen revivals, blockbuster star vehicles based on movies like *Sunset Boulevard* and *Victor, Victoria,* but with a few exceptions such as *Rent* aside, in terms of new musicals it has been Sondheim alone. He debuted on Broadway with the lyrics for Leonard Bernstein's *West Side Story* in 1957, when it was still possible to dream of a career as a writer of musicals. By 1970, for countless reasons, including declining audiences and skyrocketing costs, the Broadway musical, one of America's few homegrown art forms, could no longer sustain dreamers. Why did Sondheim survive? Part of the reason may be that he had hits before the crash. Between 1959 and 1965 he wrote the lyrics for *Gypsy* and *Do I Hear a Waltz?* and the words and music for *A Funny Thing Happened on the Way to the Forum*. Perhaps he just had more talent than anyone else. Whatever the reason, the musical has come down to Sondheim, whose work from *Sweeney Todd* (1979), *Pacific Overtures, Sunday in the Park with George* (1983), to *Passion* (1994) has moved the form into new and darker territory. His abiding theme is the awkwardness, the difficulty if not the impossibility, of love. His most famous song is "Send in the Clowns," but he is less a writer of hit songs than were his peers Rodgers and Hart, Lerner and Lowe, and Cole Porter. His musicals are more of a piece than are theirs. For years Sondheim has lived on East Forty-ninth Street, Turtle Bay, in a house where a recent fire destroyed some of his extensive collection of board games and puzzles.

Sontag, Susan (b. 1933)

"The two pioneering forces of modern sensibility are Jewish moral seriousness and homosexual aesthetics and irony." Susan Sontag wrote this sentence in 1966 in her essay "Notes on Camp." It could have been written nowhere else but in New York, where the two forces were so powerfully active and on display. The essay appeared in *Partisan Review* as did many of the others collected in her first book, *Against Interpretation*. Sontag was the last top-flight writer to get her start in that magazine. She came to New York to teach at Columbia, where she cut a dashing figure in a long black leather overcoat and lived on Riverside Drive. But the academy was not for her. She quickly concluded, in her own words, that "I would pitch my tent outside the seductive, stony safety of the university world." She has done just that in novels, stories, and essays that have covered a wide range of topics from photography to serious illnesses such as cancer and AIDS. Deeply influenced by the movies, she has directed several. She has also been outspoken on any number of political issues from the Vietnam War to the recent war in Bosnia. Her years spent in Paris and mastery of French led her to write on Antonin Artaud, Simone Weil, and Michel Leiris, writers we would know less well were it not for Sontag. In 1992 she published a novel, *The Volcano Lover,* to great fanfare. She has written, "My idea of a writer: someone who is interested in everything." She is the mother of the journalist David Rieff.

Sorrentino, Gilbert (b. 1929)

During the efflorescence of poetry following World War II, whose landmark is Donald Allen's anthology *The New American Poetry,* Sorrentino was active as a poet and editor of the small magazine *Neon.* A Brooklyn native, he went through high school and on to Brooklyn College from which, his time there being broken up by army service, he did not graduate. For many years he was an editor at Grove Press, most notably, among other houses. In his novel *Mulligan Stew* Sorrentino made use of his publishing experience to satiric advantage. His two novels set entirely in New York are *Steelwork* and *Imaginative Qualities.* They are both plotless but tightly structured. The first deals with growing up in Brooklyn in the forties, and the second is a satire of down-town literary bohemia in the late fifties and early sixties. Since the early eighties Sorrentino has lived in California and taught at Stanford.

Stein, Jean (b. 1935)

Before she became the publisher and editor of the magazine *Grand Street,* Stein helped invent a new form, the arrangement of oral histories to create the biography of an individual or chronicle a historical event. This has been called oral biography. In Stein's *Edie* the voices of those who knew the Andy Warhol superstar tell her life story. Stein did the interviews for the book and edited it with George Plimpton of the *Paris Review.* To produce *American Journey: The Times of Robert Kennedy,* Stein interviewed nearly two hundred people and Plimpton did the editing. Her portrait of Kennedy unfolds as the funeral train bearing his remains travels from New York to Arlington National Cemetery in Virginia. The diverse voices give the book a Whitman-like range. To date no one has done more with the form.

Steinbeck, John (1902–1968)

Steinbeck had two New York lives, one before success and one after. He first arrived in the city aboard ship from San Francisco in 1925 and entering the harbor he saw New York as "monstrous." But he had a sister in town, and he soon found an apartment in Fort Greene Place in Brooklyn and a job pushing wheelbarrows of cement on the construction of Madison Square Garden. He followed this with a job as reporter on the *New York American,* an apartment in Gramercy Park, and a girlfriend. The girl dumped him, the paper fired him, and the city, as he wrote in his 1953 essay "The Making of a New Yorker," "had beaten the pants off me." He returned to San Francisco, not to try New York again until 1943, when, *Of Mice and Men* and *The Grapes of Wrath,* his best work, behind him, he came as a renowned and best-selling author. He lived first at 330 East Fifty-first Street and from 1951 until his death at 206 East Seventy-second Street. During the sixties Steinbeck could be seen walking his black standard poodle, Charley, down Seventy-second Street to Central Park. It was Charley with whom he traveled around America, a trip that resulted in his last popular book, *Travels with Charley* (1966). In his 1953 essay, Steinbeck takes a conventional view of New York. It is "an ugly city, a dirty city" whose "competition is murderous" but "all of everything is concentrated here . . . It is tireless and its air is charged with energy." While Manhattan certainly had its

ugly and dirty aspects then, as it does today, it is surprising that Steinbeck overlooked the beauty of New York, its architecture, the electric
wonder of the city at night, the incredible variety of the faces one encounters in the streets, and the city's energy, for that too is beautiful. As
William Blake, whose city was London, knew, "Exuberance is beauty."

Steinem, Gloria (b. 1934)

"Some of us are becoming," Gloria Steinem said at Yale in 1981, "the
men we wanted to marry." For thirty years Steinem has been among the
most articulate, passionate, and humorous spokeswomen for the feminist movement. In 1972 she played a crucial role in that movement by
founding *Ms.* magazine. Steinem had come to New York as a journalist
in the mid-1960s. In 1968 she and Clay Felker founded *New York
Magazine.* Active in the civil rights movement, Steinem began to publish articles on abortion and other feminist issues. Upon publishing "After Black Power, Women's Liberation," she could no longer ignore the
indifference with which her male colleagues met these articles. Steinem
talked Felker into financing what became the preview issue of *Ms.* It
sold out in a week, and the magazine that has published the work of Alice Walker, Erica Jong, Judith Thurman, and Mary Gordon continues
to this day. Steinem gave up the editorship in 1989. She has published
several books, including *Norma Jean,* her rejoinder to Norman Mailer's
book on Marilyn Monroe. When the Milos Forman film *The People vs.
Larry Flynt* opened to rave reviews in 1997, it was Steinem who took to
the *Times* op-ed page to remind us of just what sort of sleaze the admitted pornographer Flynt had peddled in his time.

Stephens, Michael (b. 1946)

Stephens is the only one of sixteen brothers and sisters *not* to be born in
Brooklyn, but he grew up there with the rest of his family before running away from home at fifteen, never to return. He received both a
B.A. and an M.A. from City College, where he studied with the short
story writer and novelist Donald Barthelme. For more than twenty
years he lived at 520 West 110th Street, where he wrote several of his
books, including the novel *The Brooklyn Book of the Dead* and *Green
Dreams: Essays under the Influence of the Irish.* The latter draws on his
boyhood in East New York and covers topics from New York's Irish
gangsters, to alcohol, Brian O'Nolan, Yeats, and Samuel Beckett.

Stettheimer, Florine (1871–1944)

Although she did write poetry, Florine Stettheimer deserves a place in literary New York as a painter and creator of an extraordinary doll-house. She studied at the Art Students League of Manhattan, but spent most of the first two decades of this century in Europe traveling with her sisters, Carrie and Ettie, and their mother, Rosetta. There she saw Nijinsky dance, toured the Prado, discovered the work of Gustav Klimt and Gustave Moreau, and afforded herself an extensive education in the art of painting. The family returned to New York in 1914 to live for many years at 102 West Seventy-second Street. Soon they had established a salon that attracted the novelist Carl Van Vechten, Marcel Duchamp, art critic Henry McBride, playwright Avery Hopwood, the composer Virgil Thomson, and novelist Joseph Hergesheimer. Stettheimer painted portraits of all of them. The salon continued into the thirties at Alwyn Court, 182 West Fifty-eighth Street, where monthly dinners were held. Stetthemier's subjects are notable, but it is her color—acid, commercial, unlike anything in painting at the time—and original sense of composition that put her work in a class by itself. She loved to paint parties, picnics, and dinners, and there is true gaiety in her work. Her "Cathedrals" series, including the *Cathedrals of Art,* radiates an innocent optimism that is American to its core. In 1934 Virgil Thomson brought her in to do the sets for the first production of the opera he wrote with Gertrude Stein, *Four Saints in Three Acts.* When it opened in New York audiences and critics raved about the sets, and Stettheimer went to every performance. Her dollhouse, on view in the toy collection of the Museum of the City of New York on Fifth Avenue at 103rd Street and worth the visit, is a small version of the life she and her sisters made for themselves and their friends. The details, down to the French chef's mustache, are the sort you exclaim over in wonder and appreciation. Duchamp, Van Vechten and his wife, and Thomson, who is seated at the piano, have their roles in what is one of the most eccentric and charming works of art in Manhattan.

Stevens, Wallace (1879–1955)

Upon graduating from Harvard, Stevens came to New York to pursue a career in journalism, but the work quickly bored him and he enrolled in New York Law school. He was admitted to the bar in 1904, spent the next twelve years trying to form a partnership, and, failing to do so, worked at other legal jobs before taking a position with the Hartford (Connecticut) Accident and Indemnity Company in 1916. During his

New York years Stevens, a shy man, stayed pretty much to himself. He liked to take long walks throughout the city and on these may have begun the habit of writing his poems in his head. Stevens did not enter New York literary life until 1914, when his college friend the poet Walter Arensberg moved to the Village and gathered a salon of artists and poets in his home. At the Arensbergs', Stevens met the artist Marcel Duchamp (they spoke French together and Stevens likened the sound to "sparrows round a pool of water"), Alfred Kreymborg, William Carlos Williams, and the composer Edgard Varèse. In his last years in the city Stevens felt his first powerful inspiration as a poet and wrote "Peter Quince at the Clavier," "Disillusionment of Ten O'Clock," and "Sunday Morning." From 1909, the year of his marriage, until he moved to Hartford, Stevens lived in Chelsea at 441 West Twenty-first Street, a house that stands today not more than a stone's throw from where John Ashbery lives. Stevens often returned to Manhattan on business, but played little role in the city's literary life when he did as he was not one to mix his business and writing lives.

Stout, Rex (1886–1975)
In a three-story brownstone house on the north side of West Thirty-fifth Street lives the famed private investigator Nero Wolfe. At least Wolfe lives there in the novels written by Rex Stout. On the actual north side of West Thirty-fifth Street there are no brownstone houses at all. Members of the Wolfepack, fans as devoted to Wolfe as are the Baker Street Irregulars to Sherlock Holmes, believe that Wolfe really lived in Chelsea, perhaps on West Twenty-second Street. Why Stout moved the residence thirteen blocks north is a mystery.

Strong, George Templeton (1820–1875)
Strong follows Philip Hone as the second great diarist of nineteenth-century New York. Put together their diaries cover forty-five years of the city's history, 1830 to 1875, during which the population of Manhattan went from 200,000 to over one million. A graduate of Columbia, Strong followed his father into the law and had a successful practice. He involved himself in a range of civic activities that gave him several different vantage points on the city. As a trustee of Columbia College, Strong was a founder of its law school and a tireless advocate for the School of Mines, which he almost single-handedly persuaded the board to create. He served as a vestryman of Trinity Church and gave a good deal of his time to church affairs. The work that Strong is best

remembered for today is that which he did as treasurer of the Sanitary Commission during the Civil War. The commission had been founded by citizens to improve military hygiene. Faced with an inept War Department, President Lincoln and Secretary of War Simon Cameron gave the commission the responsibility of caring for the wounded and inspecting army camps. Strong's accounts of his meetings with Lincoln, McClellan, Grant, and others in the Union hierarchy were prominent in the Ken Burns television documentary on the Civil War. Few civilians outside the government played a role comparable to Strong's. But his diary is not all public affairs. He was deeply involved in the city's musical life, and there is a thick volume of excerpts that deals with that interest alone. As a member of the city's ruling class, Strong moved in high society, and here too, as everywhere, he kept his eyes and ears open and his pen busy. The historian Allan Nevins edited and published a four-volume version of Strong's diary, but the original is many times that length. It is in the hands of the New-York Historical Society as is that of Hone. The novelist and chronicler of New York, Louis Auchincloss, who edited a coffee-table book devoted to both diaries, reports that while Hone's handwriting is "clear as print" Strong's is "almost illegible." If any New Yorker of stature comparable to Hone or Strong has kept a diary rivaling theirs in this century it has yet to surface.

Styron, William (b. 1925)

After graduating from Duke, Styron came to New York and found work as a junior editor at McGraw-Hill. He did not wear a hat to the office, read the *New York Post,* and otherwise failed to fit in, and finally got himself fired for sailing a paper airplane through the office. At least this is the history he gives the young Southern writer Stingo, the narrator of his novel *Sophie's Choice* (1979). But Styron's New York does not end there. His Duke teacher Bill Blackburn told him to get in touch with the editor Hiram Haydn. In his book *Words and Faces* Haydn describes what happened next: "He signed up at the New School for a fiction course in which he wrote several short stories, and then entered the novel workshop." When he turned in the first twenty pages of *Lie Down in Darkness,* I told him that he was out of place in the class, and took an option on the book for Crown." Over the next three years Styron finished the novel and Haydn saw it through the presses at his new employer, Bobbs-Merrill, in 1951. At twenty-six Styron took his place in a generation of precocious novelists who had been successful their first time out. Norman Mailer had published *The Naked and the Dead* at twenty-five in 1948 and both James Baldwin and James Jones would publish best-selling novels before they reached thirty. The fall his novel appeared Styron lived at 45 Greenwich Avenue. To his door came young women drawn by his sensitive portrait of Peyton Loftis, the heroine of *Lie Down in Darkness*. Styron did not stay in New York but went to Paris, where he helped found the *Paris Review,* and then on to Rome, where he married his wife, Rose. Returning to the States the Styrons moved to rural Connecticut, where presumably he found the solitude he craved to give his subsequent novels the many years, usually seven, each of them has taken to complete.

Swenson, May (1919–1989)

> But then I thought:
> snow in New York is like poetry, or clothes made of roses.
> Who needs it, what can you build with snow, who can you feed?

Swenson, the daughter of Swedish Mormons, came to New York after she finished college. In the fifties she lived on Perry Street in the Village and threw parties that her friend the novelist and journalist Dan Wakefield remembered as featuring "good talk with other good writers." The poet Harvey Shapiro, who became the editor of the *New York Times Book Review,* came to these, as did the art critic Hilton Kramer, the novelist Jane Mayhall, and others. For a time Swenson worked at New Directions going through the slush pile. Her poems keep a sharp eye on the city. In "Snow in New York," she visits a cafeteria: "I went to Riker's to blow my nose / in a napkin and drink coffee for its steam."

Symphony Space
2537 Broadway

This "not-for-profit community-based arts center" invented Selected Shorts, which is now in its fourteenth season. There is no other reading event like it in New York City. There are many different sorts of programs, but in essence Selected Shorts offers short stories read by actors. The 29 January 1996 program is typical. It featured Truman Capote's "A Christmas Memory," William Maxwell's "All the Days and Nights," and Willa Cather's "The Enchanted Bluff" read by John Shea, Tony Roberts, and Stephen Long, respectively. There are also evenings hosted by writers such as Jamaica Kincaid and Paul Auster, who introduce their favorite stories read by, in some cases, actors of their choice. Tickets are on sale for each performance but subscriptions also are available. One does not, however, have to be in the audience to hear Selected Shorts. The programs are aired over National Public Radio before they have a third life on audiocassette, of which there are now ten volumes. The most requested story in the history of the series, Thomas Meehan's "Yma Dream," read by Christine Baranski, is on volume 2. Isaiah Seffer, Symphony Space's artistic director, is a reader, as are Joseph Wiseman, who portrayed the journalist in *Viva Zapata* and Dr. No in the James Bond movie, Celeste Holm, Estelle Parsons, Malachy McCourt, Barbara Barrie, Stockard Channing, Maria Tucci, Frances Sternhagen, Eli Wallach, Ann Jackson, Alex Baldwin—the list is long and distinguished. And so is the list of writers, which ranges from Anton Chekhov, Isaac Babel, Eudora Welty, and Doris Lessing to Jean Rhys, Carson McCullers, Raymond Carver, and Ralph Ellison.

Teachers & Writers Collaborative
5 Union Square West

Now in its thirtieth year, the nonprofit Teachers & Writers Collaborative is active on two main fronts: workshops and publications. The workshops bring teachers and educators together in, as the T & W brochure says, "collaborations that explore the connections between writing and reading literature and that generate new ideas and materials." There are some eighty writers and staff who offer ten workshops covering poetry, fiction, the essay, playwriting, journalism, and children's literature. There are also workshops in memoir and journal writing and in "Whole Language Learning." The organization's publications are many and various. Ron Padgett, T & W's publications director, edited a *Handbook of Poetic Forms* to which nineteen poets contributed seventy-four entries on traditional and modern poetic forms. This is also available in audiocassette. There are books on the list poem, revision, and writing on-line. In *Old Faithful,* eighteen writers present their favorite writing assignments, and in *Blazing Pencils,* Meredith Sue Willis has written a guide to writing fiction and essays. For writing teachers in high school, college, or beyond the T & W catalog is a goldmine. The collaborative's Center for Imaginative Writing, which opened in 1992 at the T & W offices, maintains a full calendar of events that include all sorts of readings, talks by educators such as Herbert Kohl, and presentations by the Society of Children's Book Writers and Illustrators. T & W also publishes a bimonthly magazine. A host of writers have worked for T & W or otherwise participated in its programs, including Peter Elbow, June Jordan, Kenneth Koch, Phillip Lopate, Bill Zavatsky, Grace Paley, Larry Fagin, Tom Carey, Janine Pommy Vega, Wang Ping, Jack Collom, and Wesley Brown. Nancy Lynn Shapiro directs the organization.

Thomas, Dylan (1914–1953)

Drink and death have made the Welsh poet Thomas the most famous literary visitor to New York since World War II. In 1950, 1952, and finally in 1953 Thomas came to America on reading tours. A superb reader, and the very model of a drunken, outrageous poet who left behind at least one memorable anecdote at every college campus he visited, Thomas helped invent the reading tour from which so many poets have profited. When in New York, where he liked to spend as much time as he could, he stayed at the Chelsea Hotel and made his headquarters at the White Horse Tavern on Hudson Street, where there are plaques in his memory. Indeed, the round-faced, impish, and vivid Thomas put the bar on New York's literary map. Although Thomas gave several excellent readings in the city, he is best remembered for the circumstances of his death. On the night of 4 November 1953, the thirty-nine-year-old Thomas returned to his hotel room and said to his young woman companion that he had just drunk eighteen straight whiskeys. He collapsed and was taken to St. Vincent's Hospital at the corner of Eleventh Street and Seventh Avenue, where he lingered for five days, long enough for his wife, Caitlin, to come from Wales and to attract many of his friends and hangers-on, before dying on the ninth. To James Laughlin, his American publisher, fell the duty of identifying the body. Laughlin remembered going to the morgue where a very young woman, who appeared to be no more than a teenager, was in charge. He identified himself as there to view the remains of Dylan Thomas. The young woman asked Laughlin Thomas's profession. "Poet," said the publisher. After a long pause, the young woman asked, "What is a poet?"

Thompson, Dorothy (1894–1961)

Thompson married Sinclair Lewis in 1928, when he was probably America's most famous writer, and they lived at 37 West Tenth Street for the first year of what was to be a rocky marriage. As alcoholism wore down Lewis and his luster dimmed, Thompson went to Europe as a reporter and became known as the first lady of American journalism. In 1936 Hitler, incensed at her reporting, commanded her to leave Berlin. Her column for the *New York Herald* became syndicated in more than two hundred newspapers, and she did a weekly news program on radio. While doing radio coverage of a German-American Bund rally in New York, Thompson laughed derisively over the air about some aspect of the proceedings. The ensuing sensation enhanced her reputation and added to her fame. Following her divorce from Lewis she took an apartment at 237 West Forty-eighth Street in Turtle Bay. She lived there until 1957. Some time afterward Robert Gottlieb, then the editor in chief at Alfred A. Knopf and later to follow William Shawn as editor of the *New Yorker,* moved into Thompson's former apartment.

Thurber, James (1894–1961)

Thurber first came to New York briefly in 1921 to review plays for the Columbus, Ohio, *Dispatch,* his hometown newspaper. He returned in 1926 determined to become a writer. At first he had an apartment on West Thirteenth Street and then moved to Horatio Street. Thurber sent the fledgling *New Yorker,* which had begun publication in 1925, a number of pieces, only to have them rejected. He had thoughts of leaving New York and heading home to Columbus when Franklin P. Adams's newspaper column, "The Conning Tower," accepted a short, humorous item. Thurber went to work for the *New York Evening Post* and in 1927 through his new friend E. B. White met Harold Ross, the *New Yorker*'s editor. Ross hired Thurber on the spot, not as a writer, but as an administrator. Thurber was not, as he put it in his 1959 book, *The Years with Ross,* "the wonder man" Ross imagined him to be. Soon he left administration and began writing "The Talk of the Town" with White. Between then and Ross's death in 1951 the *New Yorker* published, by Thurber's count, 90 percent of his output. Many his stories and cartoons defined the magazine. During the thirties Thurber lived in the Algonquin Hotel when he was in the city, and later he lived in the Grosvenor Hotel and had an apartment on East Fifty-seventh Street. In the 1940s his eyesight began to fail, and during the last twenty years of his life he had little or no vision: He wrote and drew with the aid of a Zeiss loupe, a magnifying glass that had been developed for use in defense plants. He completed his last published drawing, a self-portrait for the cover of *Time* magazine, in 1951. Neither his failing sight nor his heavy drinking and other health problems kept Thurber from his desk. He once claimed that he could write upside down in a boiler room, and he wrote steadily until his last years. Beginning in 1956, with the *New Yorker* now under the editorship of William Shawn, Thurber's relations with the magazine became strained. Thurber did not keep these problems to himself, and his quarrels extended to William Maxwell, as well as to Katherine White and E. B. White, the latter breaking with him over his best-selling memoir on Ross. Regardless of the book's accuracy, Thurber brings Ross vividly alive. In 1960 Thurber appeared on Broadway as himself in the play *A Thurber Carnival,* which ran for eighty-eight performances. He is the first of the New Yorker writers to be recognized by the Library of America, which published his *Writings and Drawings* in the fall of 1996.

Thurman, Wallace (1902–1934)

Thurman came from Salt Lake City by way of Los Angeles and arrived in Harlem on Labor Day in 1925. He was alcoholic, homosexual, very dark skinned, tubercular, and a satirist about whose work no one seems to be able to write without using the word *biting*. He edited the *Messenger* and the single issue that appeared of *Fire!!,* wrote plays, and for a time worked in publishing as, in his words, "the only Negro reader employed by any of the larger publishing firms." His best-known novel, *Infants of the Spring,* is a roman à clef about the boarding house at 267 West 136th Street. Dubbed "Niggerati Manor" by Zora Neale Hurston, who sometimes resided there, the building housed a commune of writers and artists, Langston Hughes among them. Thurman left New York for a brief stint as a Hollywood screenwriter, but returned to the city, where he died of tuberculosis in Bellevue's charity ward. In that same week of December 1934 the Harlem Renaissance novelist Rudolph Fisher also died.

Tibor de Nagy Gallery
724 Fifth Avenue

During the 1950s this gallery did more than any other in New York to encourage the interplay between painting and poetry. The gallery began when John Bernard Myers partnered with the Hungarian refugee and banker Tibor de Nagy. Previously, they had worked together to form a marionette company. Now Myers oversaw the day-to-day operations, and de Nagy, who worked at a midtown bank, looked after the finances. They opened on the second floor of 219 East Fifty-third Street in 1951

and remained together until Myers left to form his own gallery in 1970.
During the gallery's heyday Larry Rivers, Grace Hartigan, Fairfield
Porter, Alfred Leslie, Nell Blaine, and Jane Freilicher, all of whom were
involved with the poets of the New York School, showed there. In 1952
Tibor de Nagy Editions published its first book, Frank O'Hara's *A City
Winter,* which was also his first book, with drawings by Larry Rivers.
Books by Kenneth Koch/Blaine, Hartigan/O'Hara, and Freilicher/John
Ashbery followed. In addition, Myers edited the occasional review *Semi-
colon.* Myers also was a founder of the Artists Theater in 1953. Herbert
Machiz directed most of the theater's productions, which included
plays by Ashbery, Schuyler, Barbara Guest, Tennessee Williams, V. R.
Lang, Lionel Abel, James Merrill, Jane Bowles, and Jean Cocteau. The
sets were largely the work of gallery artists. Myers, who made a great
deal happen from the 1950s until his death in the 1980s, also edited an
anthology of the first and second generations of the New York School.
From 1975 to 1980 he edited the magazine *Parenthese,* which helped
launch the careers of Paul Auster, Alfred Corn, and Douglas Crase. Myers left a memoir of his years in the New York art world, *Tracking the
Marvelous* (1983). Today the gallery, having been at several addresses,
continues its interest in poetry at its current home. Eric Brown and Andrew Arnot are the directors, and they have begun a new publishing
venture with a book that combines the journals poet James Schuyler
and painter Darragh Park kept simultaneously.

Tin Pan Alley

In the late 1890s, when Theodore Dreiser was struggling to complete
Sister Carrie, his brother, the songwriter Paul Dresser, was a success in
Tin Pin Alley. This was the name given to the area where composers,
music publishers, song pluggers, and performers came together to create and sell what became known as popular music. At first located
where Broadway meets Fourteenth Street, Tin Pan Alley gradually
moved uptown until it settled in the early thirties in the Brill Building at
1619 Broadway. Named Tin Pan either because of the tinny upright pi-
anos on which song pluggers pounded out songs or because everyone in
the business was panning for the gold of a hit song, those who worked
the area produced the songs that are now called standards. The rise of
folk music and rock 'n' roll in the late fifties and early sixties gradually
drove Tin Pan Alley out of business, but for more than sixty years thousands of songwriters and composers were active there. Charles K.

Harris's "After the Ball," George M. Cohan's "Give My Regards to Broadway," Dresser's "My Gal Sal," and Harry Von Tilzer's "Wait Till the Sun Shines, Nellie" all appeared as sheet music before World War I. Following the war, the rise of the American musical theater and the dawn of sound recordings brought the golden generation of Jerome Kern, Cole Porter, Irving Berlin, George and Ira Gershwin, Richard Rodgers, Lorenz Hart, and Oscar Hammerstein to Tin Pan Alley. Fats Waller's "Ain't Misbehavin'" and Duke Ellington's "Do Nothin' Till You Hear from Me" were launched there and even Leiber and Stoller, who wrote the Coasters' hits, and Carol King and Gerry Goffin worked in the Brill Building in the early days of the rock 'n' roll revolution. Today there is no place in the country where popular music is as concentrated as it was in Tin Pan Alley.

Trilling, Diana (1905–1996)

A middle-class Jewish girl born in New York and educated at Radcliffe, she met her future husband, Lionel Trilling, in a speakeasy. They were introduced by Clifton Fadiman and his wife, who liked the way the names Lionel and Diana sounded together. The Trillings married in 1929 and remained together until Lionel's death in 1975, an exceptionally durable marriage in their set. Before Diana married Lionel she had been interested in writing, but not in any serious way. In 1941 she began to write unsigned fiction reviews for the *Nation,* which then had a lineup of extraordinary critics: James Agee reviewed movies; Clement Greenberg, art; B. H. Haggin, music; Randall Jarrell, poetry; and Irving Howe, nonfiction. Trilling remained there eight years before moving on to write nonfiction for the *Partisan Review* and other magazines. Her specialty was covering trials, and she wrote about the Profumo sex scandals in England, the Hiss–Chambers case and the J. Robert Oppenheimer security hearings. In 1981 she published *Mrs. Harris: The Death of the Scarsdale Diet Doctor.* The Trillings were part of the *Partisan Review* crowd, and Diana was one of the women known as "the girls," meaning the girls invited to the *Partisan Review* parties. Her cohorts included Elizabeth Hardwick, Mary McCarthy, Lillian Hellman, and Hannah Arendt, who never said so much as hello to her for reasons that remain obscure. In 1993 Diana published a memoir of her marriage, *Beginning the Journey: The Marriage of Diana and Lionel Trilling.*

Trilling, Lionel (1905–1975)

A New York native, Trilling graduated from De Witt Clinton High School and entered Columbia at sixteen years old. He received his B.A. there and then an M.A. and a Ph.D. before becoming the first Jewish faculty member to be given tenure in the school's English department. He was a longtime contributor to the *Partisan Review,* and many of his essays appeared there. Trilling wrote short stories and the novel *The Middle of the Journey,* which is on one level a meditation on the Alger Hiss case, but his influential work was a collection of essays titled *The Liberal Imagination* (1950). As a critic he practiced what his wife called the Talmudic tradition of "significant contention." By this she meant that Trilling and his cohorts on the *Partisan Review* and in the Columbia English department kept doubt as part of their intellectual equipment when considering any book or idea, including their own. *The Liberal Imagination* had the impact it did partly because it questioned all received political ideologies, especially those on the left with which the Trillings had been involved in their youth, and also because it assumed that liberalism, as a philosophy, could best be served by a critical attitude that put "under some degree of pressure the liberal ideas and assumptions of the present time." Throughout their marriage the Trillings were at the heart of what Diana Trilling has called the "critical elite." It was their work that filled the *Partisan Review,* the *Nation,* *Commentary,* the *New Republic,* and many other magazines. This elite was more or less composed of Upper West Side Jewish intellectuals. They are now gone, their place taken by what Mrs. Trilling has named the "scholarly elite."

Trocchi, Alexander (1925–1984)

Trocchi, the self-proclaimed "cosmonaut of inner space," arrived in New York in April 1956. He spent the next five years in the United States, most of it in Manhattan, before fleeing one step ahead of the law, which was after him for supplying drugs to a minor and jumping bail. Trocchi was a heroin addict and the one novel he wrote in New York, *Cain's Book,* is the story of that addiction. Although he had actually begun the book before landing in New York, most of it is set in the Village and on a Hudson River scow on which Trocchi lived. A Scotsman, Trocchi found a home on the scow because a fellow Scot was in charge of hiring captains for the boats. Grove Press published *Cain's Book* in 1960, but not without some difficulty. Like most junkies Trocchi had a chronic and desperate need for cash. He had long since spent his advance for the book, but had not turned in a completed manuscript. His editor, Richard Seaver, Trocchi's friend from their Paris days where they were part of the crowd that put out the magazine *Merlin,* knew he would have to essentially support Trocchi's habit until he could finish his book. He therefore paid him small sums for so many pages done. When the novel appeared Trocchi was too far gone to attend the publication party and he was soon in and out of the Lower Manhattan jail known as the Tombs. George Plimpton, who had also known Trocchi in Paris, helped him, but Trocchi was a determined drug addict. When police arrested his addicted wife and took their child into custody, Trocchi hid out in New York before finally leaving on a bus wearing two of Plimpton's suits. He crossed the U.S.–Canadian border using the passport of one W. Baird Bryant. The Customs officer asked him what the *W* stood for, and for a moment Trocchi could not remember. "Wenzel," he suddenly blurted out. "And if you were called Wenzel you'd say W. Baird Bryant." While cruising the New York streets to score junk, the resourceful Trocchi often carried a portable pulpit. If he saw or felt the presence of the police, he placed this on the pavement, mounted it, and began to preach a sermon. Among those who have admired his book are Norman Mailer, Allen Ginsberg, Terry Southern, and Samuel Beckett.

Twain, Mark (1835–1910)

Twain first came to New York in 1867 riding on the fame of his story "Jim Smiley and His Jumping Frog" (it became famous under the title "The Celebrated Jumping Frog of Calaveras County"), which had been published by the New York magazine *Saturday Press.* He stayed long enough to write a cheeky piece complaining about the city's "torrent of traffic" and its overloaded streetcars, which were, by all accounts, in disgraceful condition. Twain may not have known that they were being run for the benefit of Boss Tweed's political machine. For much of 1894 Twain, now a bona fide famous writer, lived alone in the Player's Club, of which he was a charter member, on Gramercy Park. He had ruined himself financially by investing in the failed Paige typesetting machine. In October 1900 Twain and his family returned to New York from Europe, where they had spent most of the preceding decade because it was cheaper to keep house there. The globe-trotting reading tours that Twain had undertaken to recoup his finances had made him a world figure. The Twains lived that winter at 14 West Tenth Street, where, according to Twain's daughter Clara, "every day was like some great occasion," such was his celebrity and so many were the callers who came to acknowledge it. From there the Twains moved to Riverdale in the Bronx where his wife, Olivia, fell seriously ill. She died in Florence in 1904, and Twain returned to Manhattan to live for the next four years at 21 Fifth Avenue. There he put a billiard table on the third floor as he had at his beloved Hartford, Connecticut, home, Nook Farm. He liked to entertain his guests at the table and often played for hours. In 1906 Twain accepted Alfred Payson Terhune's offer to become his biographer. Terhune moved into the Twain home, beginning a close association that lasted until Twain's death. William Dean Howells, Twain's friend of nearly forty years, lived in New York at this time, and he wrote of his friend's "efflorescence in white serge." For most of his life Twain had habitually worn a black suit, but now he dressed year-round in white and was instantly recognizable when he walked up Fifth Avenue to the Ninety-second Street mansion of his friend Andrew Carnegie. This is the image we have of him today, a head of thick white hair, white suit, and cigar. The actor Hal Holbrook, who has impersonated Twain in a one-man show for many years, has helped keep this alive. Twain died in 1910 at his home in Redding, Connecticut, and was buried out of the Presbyterian Brick Church then at Thirty-seventh Street and Fifth Avenue. His old Hartford friend Joseph Twichell helped conduct the service. Twain left behind a staggering amount of unpublished work, among which was the unfinished story "The Mysterious Stranger," thought by many to be the best of his late writings.

Twain made a famous remark comparing Boston and New York: "In Boston they ask, 'How much does he know?' In New York, 'How much is he worth?'" It is a remark Bostonians love to quote no matter how the times have changed because it underscores their notion that Boston is Athens and New York Sparta. This is so much hometown pride. Few today would agree that Twain's distinction is adequate to either city.

291

291 Fifth Avenue

New York took its first steps to become a capital of modernism in the teens of this century. Some of these occurred at 291 in what had originally been the apartment of the photographer Edward Steichen. There in 1905 a group of photographers calling themselves the Photo-Secession group met for the first time. Alfred Stieglitz became their central figure and spokesman, and it was he that turned the former apartment into a gallery. 291 remained a focal point for the arts until it closed in 1917. Here the work of Rodin, Matisse, Brancusi (his first one-man show anywhere), and Picasso was exhibited side by side with the photographs of Stieglitz, Steichen, Clarence H. White, Paul Strand, Gertrude Käsebier and the paintings of an emerging group of American artists: Charles Demuth, John Marin, Marsden Hartley, Arthur Dove, and Georgia O'Keeffe. There were also shows totally within the modernist spirit of African sculpture and Mexican pottery. After the 1913 Armory show many of the Europeans, Francis Picabia and Marcel Duchamp among them, whose work first appeared there found a home at 291. William Carlos Williams was only one of the writers who found nourishment in the gallery. He saw his first Matisse there and responded with a prose poem; he also forged friendships with Marin, Hartley, and other American painters after first seeing their work at 291. To say "gallery" is to summon up a few quiet rooms in which people look wordlessly at art while the gallery owner and his helpers talk in hushed tones. 291 was more a salon with Stieglitz a fount of information and argument. The Photo-Secession group also published the magazine *Camera Work* to promote their photography. Gertrude Stein and the critic and poet Sadakichi Hartmann were two of the writers who contributed to it. Stieglitz's photographs *The Car Barn* and *Steerage* and Paul Strand's *Wall Street* are among the most memorable images of New York that we have.

Vanderbilt, Gloria (b. 1924)

Vanderbilt was ten and heiress to some 4 million dollars from her father, Reginald's, estate (the money came from the legendary financier Commodore Cornelius Vanderbilt, Gloria's great-great-grandfather) when her aunt Gertrude Whitney sued for custody. She accused Gloria's mother of neglect. In his book *The Vanderbilt Era*, Louis Auchincloss briefly describes what happened next: "A bitter trial ensued in which scandalous evidence of heavy drinking, fornication, and lesbianism was introduced to challenge Mrs. Vanderbilt's parental fitness, and Gertrude at length won a Pyrrhic victory, receiving custody of the child but losing her affection." The trial is notorious to this day. Vanderbilt has been famous ever since, with much of her private life being served up in newspapers, magazines, and books. She has proved to be the opposite of a poor little rich girl and has exhibited a number of talents. She has acted, designed clothes, painted, and written several novels, as well as *A Mother's Story* about the suicide of her son. Her novels have sometimes been reviewed in tones that imply Vanderbilt should stay away from her typewriter and mind her millions. One wonders what critical opinion would have made of them had they been published by Gloria Brown. Over the years Vanderbilt has moved in a great many New York worlds, and she will surely show up in a small library's worth of diaries and biographies.

Van Doren, Mark (1894–1972)

After graduating from Columbia in 1920 with a Ph.D., Van Doren joined the English Department and rose to eminence. Here is how the writer Dan Wakefield describes the Van Doren he was about to meet when he began at Columbia in 1952:

> Van Doren had become a prototype of the American author-scholar-sage as college professor. Winner of the Pulitzer Prize for his *Collected Poems* in 1940, he had influenced such gifted students as John Berryman and Louis Simpson (as well as young renegade poets still to be heard from, like Allen Ginsberg and Lawrence Ferlinghetti), the critics Maxwell Geismar and Lionel Trilling, the editors Robert Giroux and Clifton Fadiman, and the novelist Herbert Gold. He appeared in Whittaker Chambers's political autobiography *Witness,* and in Thomas Merton's spiritual autobiography *The Seven Storey Mountain.* After getting an A in Van Doren's course in Shakespeare, a football player named Jack Kerouac quit the Columbia team to spend more time studying literature. Before his retirement at the end of the decade, Van Doren would be described by *Newsweek* as a living legend.

Van Doren's wife, Dorothy Graffe Van Doren, herself an editor and writer, thought well of him, too. She published their joint autobiography, *The Professor and I,* in 1959. This book appeared after scandal had rocked the Van Dorens. Their son Charles, who was following in his father's footsteps at Columbia, admitted to having cheated while appearing as a contestant on *Twenty-One,* a wildly popular television quiz show of the time. This came after Charles had become a national celebrity for his intelligence, good looks, and charm. The shock his admission created was considerable. The Van Dorens were one of New York's most prominent intellectual families (Mark's brother, Carl, was an esteemed Columbia professor of history and a writer), and many self-righteous voices rose as the scandal progressed to its conclusion. The 1994 movie *Quiz Show* is a recent treatment of these events and personalities. The British actors Paul Scofield and Ralph Fiennes appear as Mark and Charles, respectively, casting that suggests Americans remain unbelievable as eggheads.

During their years in the city the Van Dorens lived at 393 Bleecker Street. With their neighbors on Perry and West Eleventh Streets they did away with fences and outbuildings in the rear of their houses to create what is today Bleecker gardens.

Vanity Fair

The original *Vanity Fair* had its heyday under Frank Crowinshield from 1914 to 1935, when its parent company, Condé Nast, merged it with *Vogue*. Under Crowinshield the magazine hit upon a successful formula of fashion, the arts, literature, and humor. Edmund Wilson, Gertrude Stein, Edna St. Vincent Millay, Aldous Huxley, D. H. Lawrence, Colette, Clare Booth, Donald Ogden Stewart, and John Peale Bishop published in its pages. But its signature style came from the luminous portrait photographs, by Cecil Beaton and others, of movie stars such as Gary Cooper and Greta Garbo, and from the writing of Robert Benchley, Robert E. Sherwood, and Dorothy Parker. Although these three were gone by 1920, their tomfoolery while at the magazine became legend. When the office manager ordered them not to discuss their salaries they responded by writing them on signs that they wore hanging from their necks. After Parker was fired for refusing to tone down her scathing theater reviews, Benchley and Sherwood quit. Parker and Benchley went on to share an office together that was so small Benchley said, "One cubic foot less of space, and it would constitute adultery." The magazine thrived through the twenties but when hard times came in the thirties its sophistication could not keep it afloat. *Vanity Fair*'s offices were at 19 West Forty-fourth Street, which meant that in only a hop, skip, and a jump Parker, Benchley, and Sherwood could be at the Algonquin's Round Table.

In 1983 *Vanity Fair* reappeared as a high-toned gossip sheet. When Tina Brown became editor she knew how to make the focus on movie stars, crime, fashion, and wealth pay off. She had a talent for buffing up the vulgar, and her success catapulted her into the editorship of the *New Yorker*. *Vanity Fair* without her has lost its sheen.

Van Vechten, Carl (1880–1964)

I met Carl Van Vechten in the spring of 1927, at one of Muriel Draper's famous Thursday evenings, in her loft over an old coach house on East Fortieth Street. He looked like a large, blond, faintly Churchillian baby, and he wore a fireman's shirt. I was a freshman at Harvard so I assumed he must be a fireman.

LINCOLN KIRSTEIN

As Kirstein soon discovered, Van Vechten was a sort of fireman, but instead of putting out fires he lit them in literary New York downtown and up in Harlem. Van Vechten arrived in the city in 1906 as the *New York Times* assistant music critic, and through much of his career he wrote about music. His first lived at 39 West Thirty-ninth Street in a single room. Sinclair Lewis had, in Van Vechten's phrase, "an adjoining chamber." During the brief life of Mabel Dodge's salon Van Vechten was a regular. In 1914 he married the actress Fania Marinoff, and although Van Vechten was homosexual their marriage survived for fifty years. They began to give the first of what would become increasingly famous parties in their top floor room at 151 Nineteenth Street. This was in the early 1920s and Van Vechten had published a book on cats as well as his first novel, *Peter Whiffle* (1922). The Van Vechtens soon got a much larger apartment at 150 West Fifty-fifth Street near the Alwyn Court home of the Stettheimer sisters, in whose circle they moved. It was here that Van Vechten, who had begun to explore Harlem and involve himself with black writers and musicians, and his wife gave parties that became legendary. George Gershwin played the piano, Paul Robeson and Bessie Smith sang, and Theodore Dreiser, James Weldon Johnson, Elinor Wylie, and a host of literati, black and white, attended. Langston Hughes, who was often there, remembered that "Van Vechten's parties were so Negro that they were reported as a matter of course in the colored society columns." The apartment became known as the Midtown branch of the NAACP. In 1925 Van Vechten published his most famous novel, *Nigger Heaven*. It became a best-seller and although it divided the black literary community—Wallace Thurman was for it and W. E. B. Du Bois thought it an affront—whites who went up to Harlem used it as a sort of guide to go, in the slang of the times, "van vechtening around." To some it might have seemed that Van Vechten was slumming, but he had been what Zora Neale Hurston termed a "Negrotarian" since writing about the music of Bert Williams and other black singers in the teens. Harlem was hip and ultrafashionable in the 1920s, which Van Vechten certainly enjoyed, but he also worked hard to promote the careers of black writers. He urged the poems of Langston Hughes upon his friend Alfred Knopf, who published Hughes's first book, and he took uptown writers such as Edmund Wilson and the visiting Somerset Maugham. In 1930, having published seven novels, Van Vechten all but gave up writing for photography. He did publish *Sacred and Profane Memories* (1932) and edited the Modern Library's *Selected Works of Gertrude Stein*—a friend of many years—but most of his energy went into photography. Today his portraits of Hurston, Hughes, Ethel Waters, Bessie Smith, Countee Cullen, Richard Wright, and many other black writers and artists are famous even though few who have seen them know the role he played at the time. Van Vechten's interest in black writers did not end in the Harlem Renaissance. He photographed Chester Himes and promoted his work, and he made portraits of James Baldwin and LeRoi Jones (Amiri Baraka), wondering in a letter to Hughes when the two would have a fight. Although Van Vechten's novels are dated and of more interest today to the literary scholar than the general reader, a solid biography is long overdue. He had great style—Kirstein called it "the individual, idiosyncratic authority of elegance as style"—and while this would certainly be hard to bring alive again, Van Vechten saw, and made central to his life and art, an elegance in Harlem that we ought not let get completely buried by the crimes of America's racism. That's the high-minded reason we need such a book. Another reason is that there must have been a lot of fun around Van Vechten.

Vidal, Gore (b. 1925)

"Gifted, brilliant, Luciferian-looking" was the novelist Dawn Powell's description of Gore Vidal when she met him in 1954. Others have also seen the devil in Vidal. Not only has he known everyone from Noël Coward to Jack Kerouac (they had a sexual encounter at the Chelsea Hotel) to Jack Kennedy, but he owns one of the sharpest tongues of his generation and has never been afraid to use it. His association with New York begins after World War II, when he spent six months living in an apartment his father had on Fifth Avenue and worked for the publisher E. P. Dutton, an experience that was not to his taste. From 1950 to 1968, Vidal had a house in Dutchess County and he was often in New York. He recounts some of what went on during those visits in his tell-all memoir, *Palimpsest*. Vidal, like his near-contemporary Norman Mailer, with whom he was friendly for a time, cut across any number of literary circles. Louis Auchincloss has been his close friend, and so were Tennessee Williams and, for a short time, Truman Capote. He championed the work of Dawn Powell, knew both Jane and Paul Bowles, various members of the Beat Generation, Eleanor Roosevelt, Harry S. Truman . . . the list is endless. In *Palimpsest* Vidal writes: "Meanwhile, almost daily, requests arrive from biographers of well—who's at hand?—Carson McCullers, Mary McCarthy, Tennessee Williams, William Faulkner—thank God I never met Hemingway—J. F. Kennedy, Truman Capote, Anthony Tudor, Anaïs Nin—*Rod Serling*!" Vidal had several plays on Broadway, and wrote a number of movie scripts as well as novels, but he may be his naughtiest and most outrageous self in his essays, of which there have been several collections. Powell read an early one, *Messiah* (1954), and wrote in her diary: "More impressed by the writer than the book, which was engaging enough, but the trouble with being a clear, sharply cut, extraordinary individual with a rich articulate gift is that no characters can equal the author himself." Nor can friends, suggests Vidal's memoir.

The Village Voice

In the summer of 1955 Villagers Dan Wolf and Edwin Fancher, who had met at the New School, and Norman Mailer talked about starting a weekly newspaper in Greenwich Village. The talk turned into action with Fancher and Mailer each putting up five thousand dollars start-up money and Wolf becoming the paper's editor. Mailer either gave the paper its name or picked the name from a list drawn up by Fancher and Wolf. The first issue of the *Village Voice* appeared in October 1955—2,500 copies priced at five cents each. In 1962 Fancher and Wolf wrote in their introduction to *The Village Voice Reader* that the paper was created in response to "the vulgarities of McCarthyism" that "had withered the possibilities of true dialogue between people." From the start the *Voice* intended "to demolish the notion that one needs to be a professional to accomplish something in a field as purportedly technical as journalism." While this was, as Fancher and Wolf knew, a "philosophical position," it was based in part on the feeling that there were enough good writers in the Village to sustain this essentially amateur approach. Fancher and Wolf were right. The paper's personal and irreverent tone and the leeway given its writers set it apart not only from other New York papers but from journalism as it had been practiced. Mailer even contributed a short-lived column in which he notably fell on his face in "reviewing" Samuel Beckett's *Waiting for Godot* before he had either read or seen it. (He left the paper in 1956.) Readers picking up the *Voice* never knew exactly what they would find, but they knew they would be amused and hipper for their effort. For twenty years the paper had this kind of verve, which translated into increased circulation so that by 1970 the *Voice* claimed 150,000 readers. At this point wealthy city councilman Carter Burden, who later built a great collection of modern American first editions, bought controlling interest in the paper. The road has gone downhill from then until today, when in a desperate attempt to keep the paper alive it is now given away free in New York City. The *Voice* did not abandon its principles overnight, but it soon became just another paper, a commodity to be owned by Clay Felker of *New York Magazine* and then by Rupert Murdoch. But the paper's glory days were glorious indeed. John Wilcock wrote a column called "The Village Square," Jules Feiffer's cartoons appeared in every issue (Feiffer was the beatnik Peter Arno), Michael Harrington, Stephanie Harrington, and Mary Perot Nichols were on the staff. The roll call could fill pages. These are some of the writers who gave the paper its unique force and vigor: Nat Hentoff, who started out writing on jazz but became the paper's First Amendment watchdog; Jill Johnson; Paul Cowan; Richard Goldstein; Stanley Crouch; Bill Manville, an adman who developed the early column "Saloon Society"; Jean Shepherd; Jerry Tallmer, the managing editor who went on to a long career writing about the arts for various New York City newspapers; filmmaker and film columnist Jonas Mekas; film critics Andrew Sarris and Molly Haskell; dance critic Deborah Jowett; jazz critic and trombonist Michael Zwerin; Joe Flaherty, who managed Norman Mailer's campaign for mayor of New York; art critic John Perrault; Ross Wetzsteon; Don McNeill, who was a participatory journalist on the front line of mid-sixties Village political radicalism before drowning in 1968 at twenty-three; political reporter Jack Newfield; Gary Giddins; Lucian K. Truscott IV; Alexander Cockburn; Pete Hamill; and photographer Fred McDarrah. The *Voice* came along at exactly the right moment to chronicle the last great flowering of Village bohemianism. Between 1955, when the Beat Generation ascended, to 1965 and the beginnings of Bob Dylan's career, the Village was a cheap place to live where artists and writers of all sorts came looking to encounter one another and did. In the late sixties the Village began to shift east and to become what it is today, quiet, residential, and family oriented. When the underground papers of the sixties began they followed in the footsteps of the *Voice*. It is remarkable that the spirit of the original paper survived so long, even flickering in the fat, ad-swollen paper it became in middle age. Today the *New York Observer* has some of the *Voice*'s original irreverence, but its beat is the new high society of wealth and power.

Violet Quill

The novelist Edmund White was among the members of this "casual club" of gay writers who began to meet at one another's apartments in 1979. White remembered that "four of us each time would read our latest pages, then settle down to high tea." The other members were Felice Picano, Andrew Holleran, Robert Ferro, George Whitmore, Christopher Cox, and Michael Crumley. All of these men published at least one novel. An associate member was Vito Russo, who wrote *The Celluloid Closet* about Hollywood's portrayal of gays through the years. White remained in the group until 1983, when he left to live in Paris. When he returned to New York in 1990 AIDS had annihilated Ferro, Whitmore, Cox, Crumley, and Russo. White has written of the Violet Quill in his collection of essays *The Burning Library,* which, given the deaths of many of his contemporaries, will be one of the few books of its kind written by a gay American novelist of White's generation.

Visitors

New York City has never been Paris. Writers have come to the city as visitors but only rarely as expatriates. In the nineteenth century New York lacked the tradition to attract writers, and when, in the 1920s, it began to emerge as a literary and cultural center, Paris was at its zenith. The rise of the Nazis and the outbreak of World War II compelled a mass of writers and artists to seek the safety of New York, but many of these, for example, André Breton, returned home when the war ended. Today writers may come to New York from around the world to do business—successful writers that is—but they do not stay.

ALEXIS DE TOCQUEVILLE (1805–1859), a lawyer, arrived in New York in 1831, commissioned to study America's prison system. He traveled widely in the country and produced both that study and the more famous *Democracy in America.* He gave a picture of the New York City he encountered. At that time more than 200,000 inhabitants lived without a sewer system, and their waste was collected as night soil or allowed to run in the streets. Streets were unpaved, no municipal water supply existed, and manure from horses and cows as well as humans was everywhere. In his book *City Life* Witold Rybczynski writes,

"Garbage simply accumulated outside and was trampled into the streets, which explains why the oldest Manhattan streets are anywhere from six to fifteen feet higher than their original levels."

When CHARLES DICKENS (1812–1870) arrived in 1842 for the first of his two visits, he knew New York principally from Washington Irving's *History of New York,* which went only so far as the "End of the Dutch Dynasty." The New York Dickens saw at first hand he found not "so clean a city as Boston." (His countrywoman Frances Trollope, mother of the novelist Anthony Trollope, had passed through New York in 1827 and praised it as "one of the finest cities I have ever seen.") He liked "sunny Broadway" and found the traffic, and pigs who scavenged in the slum streets, amazing. He had a month in the city during which he gave readings and got around to Five Points, the Tombs, Wall Street, and the Bowery. In his *American Notes* he summed up New York as a city where "a vast amount of good and evil is intermixed and jumbled up together." It was on this visit that the Boz Ball was held in his honor. Three thousand guests came, including Washington Irving and William Cullen Bryant. The diarist Philip Hone attended and called it "the greatest affair in modern times." He observed that the man who catered the oysters got paid two thousand dollars. In 1868 Dickens returned on another reading tour to discover a completely different city, an experience that many infrequent visitors would henceforth share. "Everything in it looks," he wrote, "as if the order of nature were reversed, and everything grew newer everyday, instead of older." Aware that his first impressions of New York had irked some of his fans, Dickens now promised not to denigrate New York again. This apology came at a banquet in his honor at Delmonico's, when he probably did not know he would shortly have a reason to badmouth America if not the city. An early version of the IRS was after Dickens, intent on taking the government's cut from his lecture fees. He sailed for home one step ahead of the law.

The novelist WILLIAM MAKEPEACE THACKERAY (1811–1863) came for the first of his lecture tours in 1852, and the diarist George Templeton Strong attended all of them. Their subject was English humorists of the eighteenth century. Strong found them "spirited and original." Arriving in New York for his first visit in 1882 OSCAR WILDE (1854–1900) is supposed to have replied to a Customs officer's "Have you anything to declare?" "I have nothing to declare except my genius." There were New York writers prepared not to capitulate to Wilde's genius. They had heard about him from his enemies, and they shunned him. His lectures, however, were a smash. He dressed in purple, lavender, and lace, and all eyes were on him from the start. He repaid this attention with a very serious talk titled "The English Renaissance," and the contrast in appearance and manner worked to his advantage, as he expected it might. He spent the next eight months lecturing around the country before returning to spend the final two and a half months of the year in New York. He lived at several hotels before settling at 48 West Eleventh Street. During this stay Wilde's comings and goings were much reported, none more so than his showing up to greet the actress Lily Langtree "dressed as probably no grown man in the world was ever dressed before" and carrying a large bouquet of lilies. Wilde returned in August 1883 for the first production of his play *Vera,* but it met with unenthusiastic notices and closed after two weeks.

Although he never visited New York KARL MARX had a presence in the city through his column on politics and economics that appeared in Horace Greeley's *New York Tribune.* The Russian novelist and playwright MAXIM GORKY (1868–1936) came to New York as an exile after the failed 1905 revolution. Socialists greeted him with a party, but he was shunned by the literati and had a very bleak time, which he recounted in "The City of the Yellow Devil." "This is New York," he wrote. "Twenty-storyed houses, dark soundless skyscrapers, stand on the shore. Square, lacking in any desire to be beautiful, the bulky, the ponderous buildings tower gloomily and drearily." LEON TROTSKY (1879–1940) also lived in exile in New York, in the Bronx, for two and half months before the outbreak of the Russian Revolution. While there he edited *Novy Mir,* which he had printed in the East Village basement of 77 St. Mark's Place, the building where W. H. Auden would live for nineteen years. It was then a neighborhood of Russians, Ukrainians, and Poles, vestiges of which are still evident today.

W. B. YEATS (1865–1939) came three times to New York, in 1903 to lecture and in 1911 and 1914 to visit his father, the painter John Butler Yeats, who had settled in the city in 1908 and lived in Chelsea until his death in 1921. On those visits the younger Yeats stayed with the family friend John Quinn, lawyer and arts patron, at 58 Central Park West. Several times Yeats visited the Irish writers Padraic and Mary Colum, who were then living in temporarily unfashionable Beekman Place.

Frédéric Sauser arrived in New York at the end of 1911 in steerage. He lived in the Bronx and on West Ninety-second Street, spent lots of time at the new Forty-second Street library, met Enrico Caruso, walked the length and breadth of Manhattan, and in April 1912, having changed his name to BLAISE CENDRARS (1887–1961), wrote his first major poem, "Easter in New York." He left New York in May, never to return.

The Russian poet VLADIMIR MAYAKOVSKY (1893–1930) spent time in New York during a three-month-long visit to the States in 1925. Like Hart Crane and others he was inspired by the Brooklyn Bridge. His poem by that name has this wonderful description of the elevated subway trains:

> here trains
> > are crawling and rattling
> like dishes
> > being cleared into a cupboard.

Perhaps the most famous work written in the city by a visitor is FEDERICO GARCÍA LORCA's (1898–1936) *Poet in New York*. García Lorca spent most of nine months, June 1929–March 1930, as a student at Columbia University where he lived in John Jay Hall. While the poems he wrote speak of his depression and isolation, the letters he wrote home suggest that he felt comfortable among his Spanish friends. Lorca learned enough English to collect a few words—*spaghettis* and *shishpil* (sex appeal)—but he never learned the language. García Lorca was inspired by Harlem, the Brooklyn Bridge, Walt Whitman, and the Hudson River. Indeed, in New York his imagination first encountered the city as subject and these are the only poems he wrote that are not related to his native Andalusia. His poems did not appear in his lifetime and did not reach America until 1940. Since then, there have been several translations, the most recent edited by Christopher Maurer.

In the late thirties the novelist MALCOLM LOWRY (1909–1957) landed in New York from England with a trunk that contained a copy of *Moby-Dick* and a single rugby boot. He later composed this mock epitaph:

> Malcolm Lowry
> Late of the Bowery
> His prose was flowery
> And often glowery
> He lived nightly, drank, daily
> And died playing the ukulele.

In the years before World War II, many European Jewish writers and intellectuals fled Hitler and made their way to New York. Some, like HANNAH ARENDT, stayed on after the war. The French surrealists also came, but for the most part, like ANDRE BRÉTON, they returned home after the war. These groups and other émigrés including SIMONE WEIL, who came to New York with her parents while her brother André, the mathematician, was at Princeton, helped make New York for the first time a world intellectual and artistic capital.

In 1941 ANTOINE DE SAINT-EXUPÉRY (1900–1944) took a six-room apartment at 2 Beekman Place. Its previous tenant had been Greta Garbo and her furnishings were left intact. While in residence Saint-Exupéry began work on *Le Petit Prince,* which Americans adopted as one of their favorite children's books.

After the war, with airplane flights still long and expensive, European visitors were rare. JEAN-PAUL SARTRE (1905–1980) made several visits, speaking in Carnegie Hall on one of them. SIMONE DE BEAU-VOIR (1908–1986) also made a number of visits. The French mystery novelist GEORGES SIMENON (1903–1989) stayed in New York long enough in the fifties to soak up the atmosphere for his one novel set in the city, *New York's Underworld.* Simenon's Inspector Maigret finds the city lacking in certain comforts, convenient places to go to the bathroom, and congenial bars. The Japanese novelist and playwright YUKIO MISHIMA (1925–1970) came to New York to see one of his plays produced. When Truman Capote had visited Japan, Mishima had shown him Tokyo, a favor Capote, to Mishima's annoyance, did not return.

In 1964 SAMUEL BECKETT (1906–1989) came to the city for a whirlwind two weeks during a heat wave throughout which he worked on the film *Film,* which starred Buster Keaton, and socialized with his publisher, Barney Rosset. When Beckett went out into the city alone, he insisted on walking and took along maps and notes he had copied down in a minute hand. A lifelong sports fan, he managed to take in a Mets doubleheader at Shea Stadium. On the day he was to leave, the Rossets overslept, causing Beckett to miss his plane. To kill time before the later flight left the Rossets took Beckett to the World's Fair. After this, while waiting in the bar at Idlewild Airport, Beckett turned to Rosset and said, "This is somehow not the right country for me. The people are too strange." Beckett never returned.

Among other foreign visitors who had significant encounters with New York were the Italian journalist Luigi Barzini; Bertolt Brecht; Albert Camus, who visited once in 1946; the Nobel Prize-winner Juan Ramón Jiménez; G. K. Chesterton; Rubén Darío; the novelist Anthony Burgess, who wrote the text for Time-Life's picture book on the city; José Martí, who lived in Manhattan from 1881 to 1895, mostly above

Columbus Circle, and who was Argentina's consul to the city in 1890; Nobel Prize-winner Claude Simon; Nicola Chiaramonte; Jean Cocteau, who was in New York in the thirties and saw Orson Welles's production of *Macbeth*; Léopold Senghor, who wrote the poem "À New York" in 1964; the novelist Brian Moore, who wrote his novel *A Time in Limbo* while living at 150 West Fifteenth Street; Brendan Behan, who followed Dylan Thomas as the Chelsea Hotel's roaring boy; and Maurice Girodias, the publisher of the Olympia Press, who also stayed at the Chelsea while scouring New York for dirty books to publish.

Waldman, Anne (b. 1945)

One of the few New York School poets born in Manhattan, Waldman grew up at 47 MacDougal Street and attended P.S. 8, Grace Church School, and the Friends Seminary. Her mother was the poet Frances LeFevre, and her father, John, wrote *Rapid Reading Made Simple.* Used by her father as a guinea pig, Waldman became a speed reader and once both amazed and slightly irritated a poet friend by reading his one-hundred-page manuscript in a little over ten minutes. Upon graduation from Bennington, she returned to the city and in 1966 became one of three assistant directors to Joel Oppenheimer, the first director of the Poetry Project at St. Mark's Church. In 1968 she took over as director, a position she held for six years. During this time Waldman and her husband, the poet Lewis Warsh, lived at 33 St. Mark's Place, where they kept open house for the poets and artists of the Lower East Side. In 1974 Waldman went west with Allen Ginsberg to begin the Jack Kerouac school of Disembodied Poetics at the Naropa Institute in Boulder, Colorado. She has served as the school's director, taught classes, and coordinated its summer program of visiting writers. A prolific poet from the start, Waldman has published many books, including *Helping the Dreamer: New and Selected Poems, 1966–1988.* Since then she has been at work on the long poem *Iovis,* two volumes of which have appeared. Waldman edited *Out of This World* (1991), an anthology of poems and reminiscences by poets associated with the Poetry Project. Over the past decade she has become a performance poet, which for her means that she will sing, chant, croon, shout, and whisper her poems—anything to get them across as she wants them heard.

Wallant, Edward Lewis (1926–1962)

Wallant worked in advertising, and in the few writing years he had, he published four novels, *The Pawnbroker* being his most acclaimed. It is the story of Sol Nazerman, sole survivor of his Polish-Jewish family, who operates a pawnshop in Harlem and is bedeviled by memories of life in a Nazi concentration camp. There is a brief scene in the book in which a black man pushes a lawnmower into the shop seeking to pawn it. Nazerman can't believe it. A lawnmower in the middle of concrete Harlem! In the exchange between the two men Wallant illustrates and explores the cultural collisions that happen in New York City every day. His novel, which certainly had greater fame as a movie directed by New Yorker Sidney Lumet, is also a reminder of how rarely white writers have ventured into Harlem.

Weinberger, Eliot (b. 1949)

As a translater from the Spanish, primarily the poetry of Nobel Prize-winner Octovio Paz, and the editor of the magazine *Montemora* (1975–1982), Weinberger has been active in New York since the early 1970s. Throughout this time he has written some of the most intelligent and original literary essays produced in the city, and these have been published in three books, *Works on Paper* (1986), *Outside Stories* (1992), and *Written Reaction* (1996), but theirs has been a roundabout journey. Many of these essays first appeared in Mexican and European literary magazines and others in small American magazines like *Sulfur* published far from New York. That Weinberger writes mainly about poetry certainly limits the number of New York magazines in which his work might appear, but it is the city's loss that his work does not appear regularly in some magazine or newspaper. There are few writers of his generation whose minds are so crammed with poetry and whose imagination leads them so easily to original connections with politics and the world at large. Weinberger seems to pay attention in a way that few literary essayists of today do, and he has the advantage of viewing our literary and political culture from knowing, and being active in, several others through his work as a translator. His first two books of essays are published by New Directions and the third by Marsilio, for whom Weinberger now consults as an editor. In 1987 Moyer Bell Limited published *Nineteen Ways of Looking at Wang Wei,* an excellent and concise book about the difficulties and pleasures of translating poets. The book's first sentence is pure Weinberger: "Poetry is that which is worth translating."

Welles, Orson (1915–1985)

Welles came to the city in the late thirties to work in the Federal Theater Project of the Works Progress Administration and quickly threw himself into radio, a medium he loved. His stage productions of *Julius Caesar,* in modern dress, *Macbeth,* with an all-black cast, and Marc Blitzstein's proletarian opera *The Cradle Will Rock* survive only in memoirs, biographies, and still photographs, but their power can be imagined. At a time when the National Endowment for the Arts is under fire, the work Welles and his colleagues did is a shining example of what can happen when public money subsidizes art. Welles's Mercury Theater broadcast H. G. Wells's *The War of the Worlds* on Halloween night 1938 caused a sensation. Welles and his company aired a slew of plays, adaptations of novels, and even of biographies. Although the young Arthur Miller worked with Welles on one of these shows, a biography of Benito Juárez, the networks employed their own staff of writers. Unlike England, where the BBC attracted a host of poets, novelists, and essayists, and gave them more or less a free hand. American radio trained its writers to a specialty such as soap operas or comedy shows. The work Welles and his company did so memorably had little connection with New York's literary life.

Today writers do not appear on radio, except as subjects for interviews. It is not their work radio finds useful but their personalities. This is so much the case that it is all but impossible to imagine what might have been the outcome if, say, Marianne Moore, e. e. cummings, Zora Neale Hurston, Frank O'Hara, James Baldwin, or Charles Ludlum had written, and perhaps even performed, for radio.

West, Nathanael (1903–1940)

Born Nathan Wallenstein Weinstein at 151 East Eighty-fourth Street, West was the son of Max Weinstein, a builder of luxury apartment houses in Harlem, who in 1908 moved the family to the De Peyster, which still stands on Seventh Avenue between 119th and 120th Streets, and after a few years to another of his buildings at 110th Street and Central Park West. As Nathan Weinstein, West attended De Witt Clinton High School and went on to Tufts College, where he flunked out only to wind up a sophomore at Brown University through an error by the Tufts registrar and some chicanery on his part. Like others of his generation West expatriated himself to Paris for a few years. There he began his first novel, *The Dream Life of Balso Snell.* Upon his return to New York, West used his real estate connections to get a job as the night clerk at the Kenmore Hall Hotel at 145 East Twenty-third Street. (Although this hotel still stands, it was taken over by the city in the mid-nineties due to gross neglect by its owners.) West spent three years at the Kenmore, rewriting *Balso Snell* and letting his friends, the writers Quentin Reynolds, Dashiell Hammett, Maxwell Bodenheim, Mike Gold, and S. J. Perelman, who was married to West's sister Laura, stay on the cuff. Hammett came to the hotel after having been thrown out of another. West registered him under the name "Mr. T. Victrola Blueberry," and here Hammett finished *The Maltese Falcon.* In 1930 West moved uptown to the Sutton Club Hotel at 330 East Fifty-sixth Street. As before, he was the night manager and allowed his writer friends to stay free of charge. The novelists Erskine Caldwell and Robert Coates spent time there as did Edmund Wilson, S. J. and Laura Perelman, James T. Farrell, Quentin Reynolds, Lillian Hellman, and Hammett. This time Hammett was on the lam from the Hotel Pierre and was finishing up *The Thin Man,* into which he put Laura Perelman's dog, Asta. The Sutton was, in West's words, "not a place for the successful," and the lonely, aimless suffering he saw there worked its way into his books, especially *Miss Lonelyhearts* (1933) and his great Hollywood novel, *The Day of the Locust* (1939). In the winter of 1935 and the spring of 1936 West lived at the Hotel Brevoort on lower Fifth Avenue. His friend Farrell was also there at the time, and he often came to West's room to read new pages of *Studs Lonigan* as he finished them. In the late thirties West went to Hollywood to write screenplays, and there he married Eileen McKenney, the heroine of Ruth McKenney's *My Sister Eileen.* They died tragically in a car accident returning from a hunting trip in Mexico. West, a notoriously inattentive driver, who somehow once managed to go through eleven straight red lights in New York before hitting a taxi, failed to stop at a stop sign. His four novels are short, bitingly satiric, grim, and brutally funny. He remains an American original.

West End Bar and Grill
2911 Broadway between 113th and 114th Streets
A hangout for Columbia and Barnard students, the West End Bar was also where the Beats drank in the forties, and other literary types followed. For years whenever he heard Kerouac's name a bartender named John pulled out a copy of *The Town and the City,* opened it, and proudly pointed to an inscription and Kerouac's signature. This was impressive because the novel preceded Kerouac's *On The Road* and subsequent fame. John did not know much more about Kerouac and the

others than you could get from the newspapers, but those who talked to him ordered another beer, lit up a Gauloise, and knew they had come to the right place.

Wharton, Edith (1862–1937)

Louis Auchincloss begins his book on Edith Wharton with the provocative sentence, "Somebody once observed that Edith Wharton and Theodore Roosevelt, despite a common background of moneyed Manhattan, were both 'self-made men.'" Auchincloss means to emphasize how thoroughly unconventional Wharton was. Women of her class simply did not become writers. Wharton and Roosevelt rebelled, in Auchincloss's words, "against the complacency of a point of view that found politics too dirty for gentlemen and letters too inky for ladies." Wharton was born Edith Newbold Jones at 14 West Twenty-third Street to a family that belonged to "Old New York." The Joneses were not rich by New York society standards, but they moved comfortably between Europe, where Edith, like her friend Henry James, did much of her growing up, Newport, Rhode Island, and the city. As a child Jones read widely in her father's library and began writing in her early teens when she undertook a novel. In 1879, the year Edith made her debut, her mother published a book of her poems, *Verses,* and William Dean Howells published one of her poems in the *Atlantic.* After her father's death in 1881, Jones lived for a short time at 7 Washington Square North before moving with her mother to 28 West Twenty-fifth Street. In 1885 she married "Teddy" Wharton, a Bostonian and outdoorsman, at Trinity Church, 15 West Twenty-fifth Street, which is now the Serbian Orthodox Cathedral of St. Sava. The Whartons lived in Newport with extended trips to Europe. In 1891 Wharton bought a house at 882 Fourth Avenue, now Park Avenue, on the corner of Seventy-eighth Street and a few years later bought the adjoining house at 884. This became her New York base, but she spent a good deal of time outside the city either in Europe or, after 1901, in her Lenox, Massachusetts, home, "The Mount." All four of New York's great nineteenth-century writers, Whitman, Melville, James, and Wharton, spent significant time away from the city. In Wharton's case this may be ascribed to the natural peregrinations of her class and also to her desire to escape a world that she considered stifling to her ambitions. Beginning in 1896 Wharton began to write about interior decoration, and the book she produced in collaboration with the architect Ogden Codman sold very well. She went on to write stories and historical novels that Henry James found "brilliant and interesting from a literary point of view." But James urged her to take up "the American subject." "*Do New York!*" he exhorted. Wharton took his advice, and when she began to "do" New York she wrote not only her best work and some of the best novels ever written about the city, but some of the most sharply observant and satirical fiction written by an American. In 1905 she published *The House of Mirth,* her first New York book. It is the story of the decline of Lily Burt, a woman "fashioned to adorn and delight," who does not have the "material necessities" to survive in her social world, New York's upper class. An orphan, Lily needs to marry a rich man, but for reasons of convention, and these are subtly and cold-bloodedly revealed by Wharton, she is unable to do so. Lily's ultimate fate smacks of melodrama, but her descent is described with such authority that every step she takes seems inevitable. Throughout the novel Wharton is as precise about the great houses and city in which her story is taking place as she is acute in presenting nuances of feeling. You feel not only that she knows the world she writes about inside and out, but that she has imagined it without letting a drop of sentiment spoil the picture. At times Wharton can seem haughty in her command, as if she is well prepared to play God with her characters. In 1910 Wharton sold her New York home, and in 1911 she sold The Mount. For the last twenty-five years of her life she lived in Europe, mostly in France. There she continued to "Do New York!", producing her masterpiece, *The Age of Innocence,* in 1920. The novel is set in the 1870s, which means that when it appeared it must have seemed like a historical novel, Wharton's "Old New York" having been all but obliterated. On one level, *The Age of Innocence* is the story of how this world came to vanish. Its hero, Newland Archer, is not bold enough to act for love, and in allowing the conventions he disdains to restrict him, he atrophies. As his passions burn down to ash, Wharton shows us that Archer's world too is ash, has become so, in part, of its own accord. "Old New York" became too rigid in its scruples to be violated by vulgar life and survive. *The Age of Innocence* is no elegy, for Wharton did not lament the end of that world. It permeated her imagination, but she regarded it coldly, from the distance she needed to establish herself as a writer. After *Ethan Frome,* her short novel set in New England, *The Age of Innocence* is Wharton's most popular work. It won a Pulitzer Prize and when adapted as a play in the late twenties had a good run on Broadway. In 1993 the director Martin Scorcese, born and raised in New York's Little Italy, turned the novel into a movie. Auchincloss, for one, thought the movie excellent. The

New York Wharton wrote so well about was bounded on the south by Washington Square and on the north by Central Park. Today, you can walk these streets without encountering it, but the city she knew is so replete in her books, such a living and breathing presence, that in a few pages you are there.

White, Edmund (b. 1940)

White came to the city from Cincinnati in 1962 and worked at Time-Life books as a staff writer until 1970, when he left to become a journalist and, eventually, write novels. The Stonewall riots of July 1969 during which gay patrons of the Stonewall Inn on the Village's Sheridan Square stood up to police harassment—the "swish heard round the world," as one drag queen (Ralph Wanda Emerson?) named it—galvanized White. He made speeches at the site and went on to become the foremost gay New York writer of his generation. With the photographer Robert Mapplethorpe, White formed a two-man interviewing team that supplied the magazine *Christopher Street* with interviews of gay writers such as Truman Capote, Christopher Isherwood, and William Burroughs. This led to White's *States of Desire: Travels in Gay America* (1980), by which time he had made his mark as a novelist. But novels had not come easily for him. In his *Paris Review* interview, White remembered, "Part of my problem as a young writer was that I was too much a New Yorker, always second-guessing the 'market.' I became so discouraged that I decided to write something that would please me alone—that became my sole criterion." This helped White produce his first novel, *Forgetting Elena,* which has been followed by four others. His lively, intelligent, and sometimes sensational, at least upon its first publication, journalism is collected in *The Burning Library* (1994). White has also written the National Book Award-winning biography of the French novelist Jean Genet. In 1983 a Guggenheim Fellowship took White to Paris, where he continues to live today. He returns frequently to New York and has taught in American colleges, Brown University most recently. As his generation of gay men has been devastated by AIDS, White has become, by necessity, a eulogist and, at times, a fearless chronicler of the epidemic's progress. There are few writers of his generation as willing to say what they think and let the chips fall where they may.

White, E. B. (1899–1985)

In 1948 White wrote an essay on New York for *Holiday* magazine. The following year Harper and Brothers published it as *Here Is New York,* a very slim book that today can often be found in secondhand book-shops. White wrote it while staying at the Lafayette Hotel, "twenty-two blocks," he wrote, "from where Rudolph Valentino lay in state, eight blocks from where Nathan Hale was executed, five blocks from the publisher's office where Ernest Hemingway hit Max Eastman on the nose, four miles from where Walt Whitman sat sweating out editorials for the *Brooklyn Eagle,* thirty-four blocks from the street Willa Cather lived in when she came to New York to write books about Nebraska..." For some reason this passage appears in almost every reference book written about New York City published since White wrote it. What goes unsaid about White's essay is how little his New York resembles ours. Indeed, his little book reads like a fairy tale. In 1948 there were no drugs, serious crime, or racial problems in the city. There was, however, the fear of nuclear war. "A single flight of planes," White predicted, "can quickly end this island fantasy, burn the towers, crumble the bridges, turn the underground passages into lethal chambers, cremate the millions." Today, of course, we no longer have exactly this fear, and if we imagine the apocalypse it is as coming from within, from over-crowded and ill-equipped schools, from poor housing, from the waste-lands of the South Bronx and Bedford-Stuyvesant, from terrorists based on American soil, or from too much drugs and too many guns. White came to New York after college and lived in an apartment on West Thirteenth Street in a building where James Thurber, his colleague at the *New Yorker,* rented a furnished room. In 1926 White joined the magazine, and he remained there in one capacity or other even after he moved to Maine and became the successful author of the children's books *Charlotte's Web* and *Stuart Little.* He also became famous for his essays, many of which appeared in *Harper's* magazine. While in New York White lived mostly on East Forty-eighth Street, at 239, 245, and from 1945 to 1957 at 229. His wife, Katherine, who joined the *New Yorker* the year before her husband, was one of the magazine's top fic-tion editors. From Maine she contributed a number of elegant essays on gardening.

White Horse Tavern
Hudson and West Eleventh Streets

The White Horse occupies one of the few wood-framed buildings (it was built in 1880) still standing in the city. It had been a speakeasy and sailors' bar before its literary heyday in the fifties and early sixties. After being introduced to the White Horse by the Scottish poet Ruthven

Todd, Dylan Thomas put the bare, comfortably shabby rooms on the literary map. A crowd from the *Village Voice* that included Michael Harrington, whose study of poverty in America, *The Other America,* had political impact during the Kennedy presidency, drank there, as did a group of writers loosely organized by the novelist Vance Bourjaily, who lived nearby, who gathered to talk about writing. Before it petered out Norman Mailer came to these Sunday afternoon gatherings, and so did the critic John Aldridge, the novelist John Clellon Holmes, and, once or twice, two who were decidedly not Village types, Louis Auchincloss and Herman Wouk. The only woman to take part was the wrestler and novelist Roslyn Drexler. In the late fifties Delmore Schwartz, already a ghost of his former self and beset by demons, held court at the bar regaling listeners with stories of having been cuckolded by FDR. It is here that Schwartz is supposed to have pointed out that even paranoids have enemies. Following in the footsteps of Dylan Thomas, Brendan Behan came over from the Chelsea Hotel to make the White Horse his headquarters when he was in town. The bar is frequently mentioned in Jane Jacobs's *The Life and Death of Great American Cities.* Today it has no literary following, but its homely warmth makes an evening or afternoon of drink and talk a pleasure.

Whitman, Walt (1819–1892)

> My city's fit and noble name resumed,
> Choice aboriginal name, with marvellous beauty, meaning,
> *A rocky founded island-shores where ever gayley dash the*
> *coming, going, hurrying sea waves.*
>
> "MANNAHATTA"

"It would be ridiculous to think of *Leaves of Grass* belonging to any one . . . person," Whitman wrote his friend and disciple Horace Trauble. "At the most I am only the mouthpiece . . . I like the feeling of a general partnership—as if the Leaves was anybody's who chooses just as truly as mine." Whitman is New York's great poet because he transformed his experience of anybody and everybody, the man and woman in the street, the mass of humanity he encountered, contemplated and admired into song.

> One's self I sing,
> a simple separate person
> Yet utter the word Democratic,
> the word En-Masse . . .

In the Brooklyn and Manhattan of the 1840s and 1850s, Whitman saw "Modern Man" and this vision was inextricably linked with his experience of the city.

Born on Long Island in what is now Hicksville, Whitman came to New York with his family when he was four years old. His farmer father thought to profit from rural Brooklyn's building boom, and he set to work building houses on speculation. The Whitmans lived on several streets, Front, Cranberry, Johnson, Tillary, Prince, and Adams, in neighborhoods that have long since given way to housing projects and expressways. They had so many addresses because it was the father's plan to build a house, live in it, start another, sell the first, and so on. This plan failed, Whitman noted in *Specimen Days,* because the houses "were mortgaged and we lost them." After years of moving between Brooklyn, various Long Island towns, and Queens, where he taught school for a time, Whitman moved to Lower Manhattan in 1841. He worked as a printer, wrote freelance for papers like *Aurora* and the *Evening Tatler,* edited others, lived in a boarding house at 12 Center Street, among other addresses, and threw himself into the life of the city, the roughneck life of the Bowery 'b'hoys, working men like himself. By the time Whitman returned to Brooklyn in 1845 he had worked for at least ten newspapers. At the time waves of newsprint were breaking over the city. The invention of a tiny cylinder that created printing technology capable of producing daily papers had made this possible, and Whitman, who wrote under the name Walter, was one of many who rode this sea of print. Beginning in 1846, he edited the *Brooklyn Eagle* for two years at 30 Fulton Street. In 1848, after his return from a trip to New Orleans, he built a house at 106 Myrtle Street. This house still stands, but the address is now 99 Ryerson Street, an identification made by Paul Berman, Eli Wilentz, and Sean Wilentz, who have recently worked to preserve existing sites associated with Whitman. In the early fifties, while Whitman was writing the poems that make up the first edition of *Leaves of Grass,* he supplemented his journalism by working as a printer, running a bookstore, and building houses. During these years he lived at a number of addresses: 145 Grand Street, 122 North Portlay Road, and 91½ Classon Avenue. Until 1862, when he went to Washington, D.C., he moved seven times. In many of these houses Whitman lived in a single room, sharing a bed with his crippled and retarded brother Eddy. *Leaves of Grass,* published by Whitman and printed at the shop of James and Alexander Rome at the corner of Fulton and Cranberry Streets, where Cadman Plaza is today, appeared in 1855.

This first edition did not identify the poet by name but had a photograph of Whitman, bearded and wearing his shirt open at the collar, as a frontispiece. He sent the book to Ralph Waldo Emerson, whose letter hailing it as having "the best merits, namely, of fortifying & encouraging," is famous. New York did not greet the book with such enthusiasm. In courting Emerson, Whitman had turned his back on the New York literary establishment, which regarded the Concord sage warily at best. In September of 1855 at the Crystal Palace, in what is now Bryant Park behind the New York Public Library at Forty-second Street, New York publishers gathered and had as their guests William Cullen Bryant, Washington Irving, John Greenleaf Whittier, and Henry Wadsworth Longfellow. Whitman was not invited. Of course, his book had only just appeared, but New York was slow to recognize him. He did try to help his city along by reviewing the book himself and making sure that Emerson's letter found its way into the *New York Herald Tribune*. Sometime in 1849 Whitman had become interested in phrenology, the technique of mapping the contours of the skull to reveal character, and began to frequent Fowler and Wolfe's Phrenological Cabinet at 131 Nassau Street. Fowler and Wolfe had a bookstore at 308 Broadway, which became one of the few to carry *Leaves of Grass,* and they published the much expanded second edition, which appeared in 1856. In that year Henry David Thoreau and Bronson Alcott paid a call on Whitman at his Classon Avenue house. Whitman showed them up to the attic room he shared with Eddy and both visitors noticed the chamber pot in plain sight. Alcott later described Whitman and Thoreau as "two beasts, each wondering what the other would do, whether to snap or run." They neither snapped nor ran, but they did not get along. Thoreau came to love Whitman's work and yet at their one meeting he found the poet egotistical and "strange." Through the late fifties Whitman continued as a journalist, but these were also his bohemian years. He had become a regular at Pfaff's Beer Hall at 653 Broadway above Bleecker Street, the home of New York's literary bohemia and haunt of Henry Clapp Jr., socialist, journalist, and the self-styled Prince of Bohemia. When Emerson visited Pfaff's with Whitman he found it full of "noisy and rowdy firemen." It was during these years that Whitman crossed the East River from Brooklyn nearly every day by ferry, inspiring one of his great New York poems, "Crossing Brooklyn Ferry."

The Civil War put a stop to Whitman's carousing. He began to visit the wounded in New York Hospital and after a trip to the battlefront in Virginia, where his brother George had been wounded, Whitman went to Washington, D.C., to work as a part-time government clerk and volunteer in hospitals as a "Wound-Dresser." This took its toll on Whitman's health, and he came home to Brooklyn in 1864 on sick leave. When he recovered he returned to Washington, never again living in New York for any substantial length of time. Photographs of the period show Whitman, already wearing the familiar full white beard, looking a decade or more older than his forty-six years. The war, as we know from *Specimen Days,* had sapped a good deal of his vitality and drained his spirit. In 1873, at fifty-four, he had a paralytic stroke, and although he lived for another eighteen years his health had been compromised. Through these years he worked on *Leaves of Grass,* true to the motto he kept on his desk, "Make the Works." In 1892, two months before his death, he sent out an announcement about the "Death-Bed" edition that he meant to "supersede all previous ones."

For Whitman, who loved to walk his city and to drive hell-bent down its avenues on the omnibuses whose drivers were his friends, the city offered an endless variety of human types and activities. His poems, optimistic, ecstatic, mournful, intimate but not personal, and unfailingly visionary, love to call the roll, to list in long unscrolling lines all that he encountered. His animating vision of democracy came from New York's busy streets, the streets of the forties and fifties when he was a young "rough," a man who loved the theater and opera, who gloried in his raucous and vibrant city. When he appeared in his first book dressed in the casual manner he favored in those days, he declared that his book was not only the work of a man— "It is I you hold and who holds you, / I spring from the pages into your arms"—but one who was free and easy with the world. Whitman is the great American poet of the city's liberating influence. In one way or another the poets of New York who came after him—from Hart Crane to Charles Reznikoff to Frank O'Hara to Allen Ginsberg, John Ashbery, and James Schuyler—have carried on this vision.

> A million people—manners and free and superb—open voices—
>   hospitality—the most courageous and friendly young men,
> City of hurried and sparkling waters! city of spires and masts!
> City of nested bays! my city!

Williams, Tennessee (1911–1983)

When Williams arrived in New York in 1940 he already had an agent, Audrey Wood, who would be vital to his career. In five years he had his first play on Broadway and his first hit, *The Glass Menagerie*. It has sold more than 800,000 copies and is performed throughout the world today. During the war Williams held on in New York by taking jobs as a waiter in a Greenwich Village bar, an elevator operator in Madison Avenue's San Jacinto Hotel, and an usher at the Strand Theater on Broadway and Forty-seventh Street. During these years James Laughlin spied the shabbily dressed Williams at one of Lincoln Kirstein's parties and engaged him in conversation. Laughlin became not only Williams's publisher, first of his poetry and then his fiction and plays, but his friend for life. Following the success of *The Glass Menagerie*, Williams remained one of America's most celebrated and, because of the sex in his plays, notorious Broadway playwrights until the late 1960s, when Broadway began to move away from the legitimate theater and into extravaganzas. He had such celebrated hits as the Pulitzer Prize-winning *Streetcar Named Desire* (1947), in which Marlon Brando starred. He also had flops. *Camino Real* (1953) was one. Between the late 1940s and early 1950s Williams lived in an apartment at 235 East Fifty-eighth Street. It was here that his friends Gore Vidal and Truman Capote managed to break in one night. Williams came home to be met by his "guests" and the police who had been called by a neighbor. During Williams's glory years he was praised mightily for one play only to be damned when the next was produced. *Cat on a Hot Tin Roof* (1955) was a hit and so was *The Night of the Iguana* (1961). As these plays appeared they were quickly made into movies, which gave Williams a public far beyond Broadway. Beginning in the 1950s because of his world travels and frequent nervous breakdowns he was more often in the gossip columns than literary journals. In the 1960s, which Williams described as his "stoned age" and said he "slept through," he lived at 15 West Seventy-second Street and at 14 West Fifty-fifth Street. Late in the 1970s he had an apartment at 400 West Forty-third Street. The last plays Williams wrote, *In the Bar of a Tokyo Hotel* (1968), *Vieux Carré* (1972), and *Clothes for a Summer Hotel* (1980), did not fare well when they were first produced and are not nearly as well known today as his work of the 1950s. While New Directions puts the collected plays into print, Broadway is no longer able nor willing to give us a full look at Williams's career. *A Streetcar Named Desire* stands as an essential American play, but it is impossible to do more than guess at what

Williams's large body of work adds up to. And a large body of work it is. For all the drama in Williams's private life and his use of alcohol and drugs *and* his traveling, he never stayed too long away from his desk. Suffice it to say that for over a decade his lyrical Southern voice held more playgoers than any other on Broadway. It is sad to report the facts of this flamboyant man's wretched end in New York. This came in the Hotel Elysée at 54–60 East Fifty-fourth Street when Williams somehow inhaled the top of a medicine bottle while taking pills and choked to death. To date the first volume of Lyle Leverich's excellent biography of Williams has been published.

Williams, William Carlos (1883–1963)

> I wanted to write a poem
> that you would understand.
> For what good is it to me
> if you can't understand it?
>   But you got to try hard—
> But—
>   Well, you know how
> the young girls run giggling
> on Park Avenue after dark
> when they ought to be home in bed?
> Well,
> that's the way it is with me somehow

Thus ends Williams's "January Morning," perhaps the first American poem to follow the rhythm of commuting as the doctor-poet crosses the Hudson River on a ferry from New Jersey to see his patient, an old woman, in uptown Manhattan. In his poem Williams gathers images from his journey as if to present them to her as a bouquet. Although he never lived in New York he began his long association with the city when his father sent him to the Horace Mann School, then in Morningside Heights at 120th Street. After graduating from medical school in 1906, Williams interned at the French Hospital, which stood at what is now the Lincoln Tunnel exit at West Thirty-fourth Street, and then at Nurse's and Children's Hospital at Sixty-first Street and Tenth Avenue. Williams did not want a New York practice, preferring to remain in his native Rutherford, New Jersey, where he could, in his words, "be myself, and find out what was what." Following the Armory Show in 1913, at which he "gaped," Williams joined the poets and artists around Alfred Kreymborg and Walter Arensberg's magazine *Others*.

When he could get away from his practice he came into the gatherings at Kreymborg's on Fourteenth Street and at the nearby apartment of the poet Lola Ridge, also an *Others* author. Here and at Walter Arensberg's studio Williams met the poet Mina Loy, Marcel Duchamp, John Reed, Louise Bryant, Kay Boyle, and later the poet Louise Bogan. He was able to make it in from Rutherford to appear opposite Loy in Kreymborg's play *Lima Beans*. Williams continued commuting both for advanced training in pediatrics and to be part of the city's poetry and art whirl. In his autobiography he tells of meeting the painter Marsden Hartley, Djuna Barnes, Marianne Moore, Malcolm Cowley, Hart Crane, the *Dial*'s Scofield Thayer, Margaret Anderson and Jane Heap of the *Little Review*, and most of the cast of characters then active in the Village. He devotes a chapter to one of the more exotic Villagers of the time, Baroness Elsa von Freytag-Loringhoven. She was German, a sculptor, a poet, and an exhibitionist who once shaved her head and glued postage stamps on her skull, wore a coal scuttle for a hat, and for a dress, in Williams's description, "a black Mother Hubbard with moons cut out front and back for ready reference." She offered to sleep with Williams so he could contact syphilis from her and thus free his mind for serious art and achieve true greatness. He declined. Williams certainly had other adventures in New York, but his autobiography does not pause over these. His work, with its attention to urban detail and emphasis on the rhythms of twentieth-century American life, has been decisive for several generations of poets who have lived and worked in New York. Clark Coolidge has called Williams "our Cézanne" and in "Personism: A Manifesto," Frank O'Hara allows that "only Whitman and Crane and Williams, of the American poets, are better than the movies."

Wilson, Edmund (1895–1972)

Wilson came to the city in 1916 after graduating from Princeton, where F. Scott Fitzgerald and John Peale Bishop had been his classmates. He got a job as a reporter on the *New York Evening Sun* and lived with three friends on Eighth Street between Fifth and Sixth Avenues. They employed a Chinese servant and entertained frequently. Wilson would never again live so high in New York. After World War I he returned to the city to work as an editor at *Vanity Fair*. Wilson, who habitually dressed in brown suits, looked older than his years, and was nicknamed "Bunny" for his white-and-pink complexion, was at the center of Village literary life until the late thirties. During these years he wrote poems, plays, and a novel, but it was his critical writing, essays, and reporting that brought him renown. From 1926 to 1931 his work as literary editor of the *New Republic* raised that magazine to prominence. In the late thirties Wilson married Mary McCarthy, seventeen years his junior and one of the brightest young literary lights in New York. They lived on Cape Cod until returning to New York in 1944 to live at 14 Henderson Place off Eighty-sixth Street on the Upper East Side. They divorced in 1946, and McCarthy put several unflattering portraits of Wilson into her subsequent novels. Wilson continued to live in various apartments on the Upper East Side through the forties and into the fifties, but he mostly wintered in them as his home base remained Wellfleet on Cape Cod. For many years he contributed book reviews to the *New Yorker,* but after the early forties Wilson pursued his own intellectual interests and wrote a number of books whose subjects ranged from the Dead Sea Scrolls to the Civil War to Canadian literature. He was often called the country's foremost man of letters, but that description is inadequate. Wilson was too much his own man to belong to any establishment or follow the conventional path. Throughout his life Wilson kept a diary that was organized by decade and published in several volumes following his death. They provide an intimate record of his years in New York and show him mixing in a number of literary worlds. One aspect of his personality that comes across in these books is how much he liked to socialize, to talk about writing and writers with other writers and intellectuals. He surely held forth at great length, but he also liked a good time, excitement, and in this regard called himself a "man of the twenties." Surely his Village was a lively place as it would be through the fifties. While much of Wilson's literary journalism has faded somewhat with time, there is a core of work, essays, journals, and journalism, that has to do with the American character as Wilson observed it that may well be rediscovered by another generation.

Wolfe, Thomas (1900–1938)

Wolfe came to New York in 1923 as a playwright. Over the next fifteen years he lived at numerous addresses and wrote, wrote, wrote (he delivered manuscripts to his publishers in trunks and packing crates). He also taught, off and on between 1924 and 1930, at New York University, where he shared an office with William Charvat, the historian of American book publishing. Wolfe began his first novel, *Look Homeward, Angel* (1929), while living with the set designer Aline Bernstein at 13 East Eighth Street. They later lived at 263 West Eleventh Street, which is described in the posthumously published, *You Can't Go Home*

Again (1940). In the early thirties Wolfe lived in Brooklyn at four different addresses, all in Brooklyn Heights: 40 Verandah Place, 111 Columbia Heights, 101 Columbia Heights, and 5 Montague Terrace. Here he produced a gargantuan manuscript that he titled *October Fair*. With the help of Maxwell Perkins, his editor at Scribner's, Wolfe published this as *Of Time and the River* (1935). The Hotel Leopold in this novel is based on the Hotel Albert on University Place near Eleventh Street. To work closely with Perkins, Wolfe took an apartment at 865 Third Avenue, two blocks from where the editor lived. As Wolfe seemed incapable of trimming or even controlling his writing, there is no question that Perkins did more editing and shaping than editors usually do. Wolfe came to resent this and before he died he broke with Scribner's and Perkins, only to place his work in the hands of another "creative" editor, Edward C. Aswell of Harper and Brothers. It is said that Wolfe delivered to Aswell a manuscript that stood nearly eight feet tall. After Wolfe's sudden death, Aswell excavated from this mass of pages *The Web and the Rock* (1939), *You Can't Go Home Again,* and a collection of fragments, *The Hills Beyond* (1941). Recently, scholars have accused Aswell of taking liberties with Wolfe's manuscripts. It seems obvious that he, and Perkins before him, were as much collaborators as editors.

Wolfe, Tom (b. 1931)

A Virginian and Yale graduate, Wolfe came to New York in the early sixties and worked as a reporter on the *New York Herald-Tribune* before becoming an editor at *New York Magazine* and *Esquire*. He is one of the two inventors of New Journalism (Norman Mailer is the other), and his flamboyant and satiric prose style has indelibly stamped a generation of writers. Wolfe came to prominence with long pieces that made pop heroes of figures like stock car racer Junior Johnson, heretofore unknown to New Yorkers. He had an anthropologist's or folklorist's interest in all aspects of American culture and a reporter's instincts for the way to play up a story. For a few years in the late sixties readers could not wait for the next Tom Wolfe article. In 1968 he published a book on the novelist Ken Kesey and the Merry Pranksters, *The Electric Kool Aid Acid Test,* and after this he concentrated on New York. His piece on Leonard and Felicia Bernstein's fund-raising party for the Black Panthers and his profile of William Shawn, editor of the *New Yorker,* were the talk of the town. But journalism ages quickly. Today much of Wolfe's work is embalmed in the period detail that once gave it life and you need a scorecard to identify the players. Wolfe's best-selling novel *The Bonfire of the Vanities* (1987) was also of its time, the height of Reagan-era Yuppie greed. While it aims for satire, no novel that so loves to get details exactly right, the make of cars, the cut of clothes, *the* store where attaché cases must be bought, can really outrage and educate. The love undermines the satire. Wolfe went, as an Englishman claims all Americans do, "deeply into the surface of things." Since his days as a journalist, the courtly Wolfe has been a literary light in Manhattan. He is the antithesis of all that is bohemian, especially in his dress. Walking the streets of his Upper East Side neighborhood in his sugar white suits, high-collared shirts, and magnificent neckwear, Wolfe looks like he stepped out of a bandbox. The other American writer to conspicuously favor white suits was Mark Twain, of whom Wolfe is, in his journalism at least, a descendant.

Woodlawn Cemetery
233rd Street and Webster Avenue

At four hundred acres Woodlawn is so large that Judi Culbertson and Tom Randall, the authors of the invaluable guide to where the bodies are buried in New York City's cemeteries, *Permanent New Yorkers,* lay out several possible tours. Among the writers buried at Woodlawn are the Yankee Doodle Dandy, George M. Cohan; the poet Countee Cullen; Clarence Day, author of *Life with Father;* Damon Runyon, whose stories of Broadway characters became *Guys and Dolls;* Joseph Pulitzer, the newspaper magnate after whom the Pulitzer Prize is named; the "stunt journalist" Nellie Bly (under her married name Elizabeth Cochrane Seaman); and Herman Melville. Other New Yorkers of interest buried in Woodlawn are the financier Jay Gould; the "Little Flower," Mayor Fiorello La Guardia, who once worked as an interpreter on Ellis Island; Edward Kennedy "Duke" Ellington; and Miles Davis.

Wright, James (1927–1980)

Wright would probably be amused to know that his one New York listing in a standard reference book other than this tells only that he was buried out of the Riverside Church on Riverside Drive between 120th and 122nd Streets. The Ohio-born Wright wrote two books in the high-toned Audenesque voice fashionable after World War II, and then discovered the flat accents of his youth in which he wrote the poems he is known for today. Although he taught at Hunter College for some years, he set the bulk of his poems in the Midwest and Europe and thus is rarely associated with New York. Farrar, Straus & Giroux published his complete poems, *Above the River,* in 1990.

Wright, Richard (1908–1960)

At the time Wright came to Greenwich Village in 1927 from the Midwest, he had worked at a number of jobs, joined the Communist Party, been a member of the Federal Writers' Project, and turned down a permanent position in the post office that would have paid him nearly two thousand dollars a year. He wanted to give himself to writing, and in New York he did. He wrote for the Communist *Daily Worker* and contributed the Harlem section to the Federal Writers' Project *New York Panorama,* but most important Wright wrote the novel that made him famous, *Native Son.* He began the book at the 175 Carleton Avenue, Brooklyn, home of his Chicago friends Herbert and Jane Newton, often working mornings outdoors in nearby Fort Greene Park. He finished a first draft of the novel while living with the Newtons, whom he felt necessary for his writing, at 522 Gates Avenue in Brooklyn and then completed the book while still with the Newtons at 87 Lefferts Place. Published in 1940, *Native Son* sold over 215,000 copies in three weeks. Orson Welles and John Houseman signed Wright to adapt the novel into a play, which opened, with Canada Lee in the title role, at the St. James Theater in 1941. The following year Wright and his wife, Ellen, lived briefly at 7 Middagh Street in Brooklyn, but in another part of the house separate from the George Davis-W. H. Auden-Carson McCullers ménage. While continuing to live in Brooklyn, the Wrights found a house to buy in the Village at 13 Charles Street. To make sure his race did not rule them out as buyers, they started "Richelieu Realty Co.," in whose name they bought the house in 1945. That March Wright published *Black Boy,* which became number one on the best-seller list and stayed there for six weeks. Two years later Wright left New York for Paris where he spent the rest of his life as, in effect, a self-exile.

After the writers of the Harlem Renaissance, Wright was the most prominent black writer not only in New York City but in the country and the first whose books were immediate best-sellers. This did not divide him from his fellow black writers, to whom by all accounts he was a generous friend and mentor. During the brief time he lived in Harlem at the Douglas Hotel at 809 St. Nicholas Avenue Wright befriended Ralph Ellison, who stood up as his best man in 1939. Wright knew and liked Langston Hughes, served as a pallbearer for Countee Cullen, and helped the Chicago poet Gwendolyn Brooks get her first book published. In 1945 he met the twenty-year-old James Baldwin and helped him get a Saxton Foundation Fellowship. Wright was the first black American novelist to gain a reputation in Europe, and he was a friend of Jean-Paul Sartre's and Simone de Beauvoir's before he got to France.

But Wright's celebrity did not make living in America a piece of cake. As a former Communist he was denounced by the party faithful even as the State Department gave him trouble when he applied for a passport. Perhaps one anecdote will dramatize the oddity of Wright's position as a famous black novelist. In 1947 a Hollywood producer wanted to film *Native Son* on the condition that the novel's hero, Bigger Thomas, become a white man. Wright refused.

The Writers Room, Inc.
10 Astor Place, Sixth Floor

The Writers Room is a "literary retreat" *in* the city. Founded eighteen years ago by a group of writers, among whom were David Garrard Lewis, Lucinda Franks, and Nancy Mitford, the Room is now in its third, and largest, space. Susan Brownmiller, Joseph Lash, Robert Caro, and Joan K. Davidson helped get the original four-desk space at 41 East Forty-first Street started. From there the Room moved to a much bigger space at 153 Waverly Place. In March 1995 the move was made to Astor Place where as many as 260 writers a year can be accommodated. The Room is open twenty-four hours a day, seven days a week, and thirty-five desks are assigned on a first-come, first-served basis. There are also residencies subsidized by grants and contributions. One hundred and ninety per quarter year are available, and all writers may apply. The Room has a separate room for typing, a library of 1,000 volumes, storage for computers, a kitchen—all the comforts of an office *plus* the vibes put into the air by a beehive of working writers.

Yau, John (b. 1950)

Yau came to New York by way of Boston and Bard College. In the early seventies he studied with John Ashbery at Brooklyn College and began writing the art criticism by which he earns his living today. Yau's indefatigable gallery and museum going coincided with the late seventies-early eighties explosion of the New York art world. He put himself in the middle of things, writing reviews, catalogs, essays for periodicals here and abroad, and, like many of the New York School poets, collaborating with painters. He has published work with an impressive lineup that includes Norman Bluhm, Bill Jensen, Trevor Winkfield, Jake

Berthot, and Archie Rand. Throughout, Yau has written and published a great deal of poetry—*Forbidden Entries* is his most recent collection— and his short stories have been collected in *Hawaiian Cowboys*. He has also published books on Andy Warhol and Jasper Johns, who is for Yau the most important painter of his generation. During these years Yau has lived all over lower Manhattan in apartments on Crosby and Mott Streets, at 140 Sullivan Street for many years, and then on Spring Street in SoHo and on to Brooklyn and now TriBeCa. In 1991 he collaborated with the photographer Bill Barette to produce *Big City Primer*, one of the most original visions of New York to appear in this decade.

Yiddish Poets

Of the seventeen million immigrants who entered the United States through New York City between 1880 and 1919, two million of them were Jewish and of these the majority were Russian Jews. Enough of these Jews settled on New York's Lower East Side so that beginning in the 1880s a great Jewish city, by far the largest concentration of Jews in the world, a Yiddish-speaking city, occupied that neighborhood. Many who settled there were literate tradesmen with political convictions, and Yiddish newspapers flourished. Soon poetry began to appear in these papers, a poetry addressed to the conditions of Jewish life as it was lived in slum and sweatshop. The first group of Yiddish poets active in New York were the "sweatshop poets": Morris Winchevsky, who never worked in a sweatshop, and David Edelstadt and Morris Rosenfeld, both of whom knew firsthand the experiences they wrote about. Rosenfeld, a tailor, is generally regarded as the most gifted of these poets. The opening line of his poem "The Sweatshop" is typical of the bluntness of these poets: "Corner of Pain and Anguish, there's a worn old house." In 1907 another, and quite different, group of Yiddish poets emerged in the small magazine *Yugend* (Youth). They were less interested in ideology than the sweatshop poets and aspired to a "purer" poetry. These poets were derisively called *Di Yunge,* a name they took as their own. The leading figures of *Di Yunge,* Joseph Rolnick, Mani Leib, Moshe Leib Halpern, and Zisha Landau, rank among the master Yiddish poets of this century. They came from Poland, Austria, Russia, and Germany and arrived on the Lower East Side between 1906 and 1914. There, for the most part, they spent the rest of their lives. After World War I a third group of poets, the "Introspectives," modernist in their outlook, came to the fore. Jacob Glatstein, who earned a law degree at New York University, is the most renowned of these. English-speaking literary New York knew next to nothing about these poets, and the Yiddish poets operated in total independence from literary New York. The Yiddish poets could do this because, as Irving Howe has written, "the Yiddish subculture of New York was so vital and encompassing that they could readily live out their imaginative lives entirely with it." For a glimpse into this subculture and the poetry that arose in it the book to get is *The Penguin Book of Modern Yiddish Verse*, edited by Irving Howe, Ruth R. Wisse, and Khone Shmeruk.

Young, Marguerite (1909–1995)

The Indiana-born Young arrived in New York in the early forties and settled in the Village, where she became one of its better-known literary eccentrics. For many years she taught fiction writing at the New School for Social Research while working on her huge novel, *Miss MacIntosh, My Darling*. At 1,198 pages—said to be the longest novel ever published in a single volume—and three-quarters of a million words, it appeared in 1965 and was met with loud snores and a few shouts of praise. Through the nearly twenty years that it took her to write the book, Young attracted a cult following that included Anaïs Nin and Djuna Barnes. Because of the novel's length and dreamlike narrative it has probably gone largely unread, but there are those who profess to love it. The hero of Anne Tyler's novel *The Accidental Tourist* carries a copy and reads it to refresh his spirit. After *Miss MacIntosh* Young worked on a biography of Eugene V. Debs under the title *Harp Songs for a Radical*. She delivered a manuscript of over 2,500 pages to her publisher Alfred A. Knopf Jr. The book has yet to appear. Young, it is clear, was determined to follow her imagination wherever it led. Several times she startled her New School students by announcing the arrival in class of Henry James or Emily Dickinson or Virginia Woolf. Edgar Allan Poe, with whom she was, she acknowledged, "on very close terms," came as well.

Zenger, John Peter (1697–1746)

At thirteen Zenger immigrated from his native Germany and within the year became apprentice to New York's official printer, William Bradford. He worked with Bradford on the city's first newspaper, the

Gazette, but soon left to set up his own print shop. Here he printed in both Dutch and English. Although New York had been a British colony since 1664, many of its citizens still read and spoke Dutch. Zenger's shop was not a success, and he faced bankruptcy when several leaders of a party opposed to the British governor decided to back him in publishing a newspaper. The first issue of the *Weekly Journal* appeared on 5 November 1733, and although it was a sloppily produced small folio sheet it was lively and satirical—lively enough that its contents found their way by word of mouth to many illiterate New Yorkers. From the outset the *Journal* attacked New York's governor Cosby. The paper used logical arguments where it could while lampooning him and his staff at every turn. After several weeks of this the paper got under Cosby's skin and he acted to suppress it. He had issues confiscated and burned, but he wanted Zenger prosecuted. In November 1734 his attorney general charged Zenger with seditious libel. Upon his arrest Zenger was locked in a cell where he was to spend an entire year. At this time there was no such thing as freedom of the press. In England printer-publishers were routinely thrown in jail, and had Zenger's case ended with his imprisonment, there would have been nothing remarkable about it. But Zenger's backers, who hoped to embarrass if not bring down Cosby, had something up their sleeve. While Zenger remained in prison his lawyers argued that the administration's chief justice, De Lancey, should not preside over the case. This led to the lawyers being disbarred, and Zenger's trial began with a court-appointed attorney, one John Chambers, speaking for the defense. In reaction to the charge of publishing "false, scandalous and seditious" items Chambers responded meekly. At this point Zenger's backers played their card and another attorney rose to speak for him. He was Andrew Hamilton of Philadelphia, the most famous lawyer in the colonies. Throughout the summer of 1735 Hamilton argued his case, which he summed up in this way: "It is not the bare printing and publishing of a paper that will make it libel. The words themselves must be libelous—that is false, scandalous and seditious—or else my client is not guilty." Hamilton knew well that common law of his day held that the greater the truth, the greater the libel. He set himself the task of overturning this. In effect, Hamilton argued that the truth about a public figure could not be libel. The jury agreed with him and in freeing Zenger affirmed the principle, revolutionary at the time, that citizens had the right to criticize government officials publicly. Charges of libel could not be used to muzzle the press. After Hamilton carried the day, the backers of the

Journal celebrated their victory at a banquet the unfortunate Zenger could not attend because he remained in jail on a technicality.

Fifty years after Zenger's acquittal the British government made law of the precedent established in his trial. In 1821 the State of New York incorporated this principle basic to freedom of the press into the state's constitution. Zenger's trial had become a landmark in the struggle to guarantee a free press. The trial also gave America a figure of speech that we use to this day. Such was Hamilton's command and eloquence and so intelligent his advocacy that the phrase "as sharp as a Philadelphia lawyer" entered the language.

Zukofsky, Louis (1904–1978)

Born on the Lower East Side to Yiddish-speaking parents and educated at Columbia University, Zukofsky lived most of his life in New York City. In the twenties he befriended Ezra Pound and Pound introduced him to *Poetry* magazine's Harriet Monroe, resulting in the 1931 "Objectivist" issue of *Poetry* edited by Zukofsky. He did not, as is sometimes attributed to him, invent the term *objectivist*. This was forced on him by Monroe, and it stuck both to his work and that of Charles Reznikoff, George Oppen, and Carl Rakosi. Although Zukofsky remained a valued friend and editor of Pound and William Carlos Williams, he published, in his own words, "barely and widely" into the 1960s. From 1947 until his retirement in 1966 he taught English at the Brooklyn Polytechnic Institute, and he lived for many years at 135 Willow Street on Brooklyn Heights. Zukofsky's long poem, his masterwork, *A*, begins on 5 April 1928, at a Carnegie Hall concert of St. Matthew's Passion with the lines

> "A
> Round of fiddles playing Bach."

He published one of everything; one long poem, one book of shorter poems (*All*), one book of criticism, one book of translations—Catullus in collaboration with his wife, Celia—and one novel. The critic Hugh Kenner believes that, because of the demands it makes, the grandeur of Zukofsky's poetry will go unrecognized until sometime in the twenty-first century when it will still appear as fresh and new.

IN THE CITY THAT NEVER SLEEPS, there are good and worthy writers who are not included in *New York Literary Lights*. Such is life in New York City that no book of this nature can claim to be inclusive. A number of writers and other literary figures came to this writer's attention too late to have a place in this volume. God willing, a second edition will see those listed below, and others not yet known, join the present company: the novelist and anthologist Jessica Hagedorn, poet Alfred Corn, poet and essayist Katha Pollitt, poet Rachel Hadas, publisher Michael Nauman who came from Germany to run Henry Holt, the essayist Hilton Als, the poet Tim Dlugos, the novelists Christopher Cox and David Markson, poet Audre Lorde, poet Ned O'Gorman, the poet and cook Frank Lima, and the poet and autobiographer Paul Zweig, who, a note tells me, lived for a time at 310 Riverside Drive.

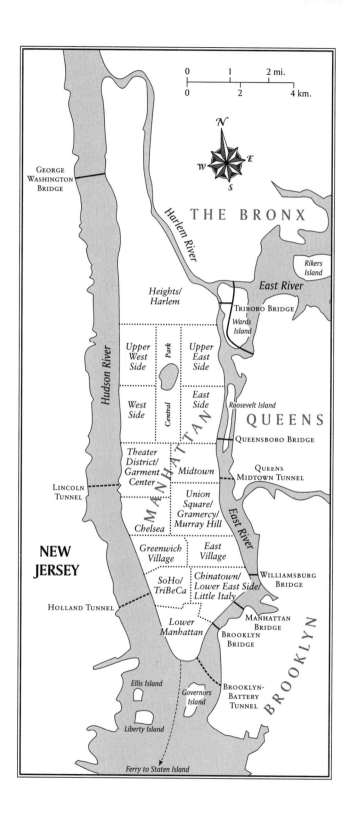

0   1   2 mi.

0   2   4 km.

N

W   E

S

GEORGE
WASHINGTON
BRIDGE

THE BRONX

Harlem River

*Rikers
Island*

*Heights/
Harlem*

East River

TRIBORO BRIDGE

*Wards
Island*

*Upper
West
Side*

Park

*Upper
East
Side*

*West
Side*

Central

*East
Side*

Roosevelt Island

Hudson River

QUEENS

QUEENSBORO BRIDGE

*Theater
District/
Garment
Center*

Midtown

QUEENS
MIDTOWN TUNNEL

MANHATTAN

LINCOLN
TUNNEL

*Union
Square/
Gramercy/
Murray Hill*

Chelsea

**NEW
JERSEY**

*Greenwich
Village*

*East
Village*

East River

*SoHo/
TriBeCa*

*Chinatown/
Lower East Side/
Little Italy*

WILLIAMSBURG
BRIDGE

HOLLAND TUNNEL

*Lower
Manhattan*

MANHATTAN
BRIDGE

BROOKLYN
BRIDGE

BROOKLYN

Ellis Island

*Governors
Island*

BROOKLYN-
BATTERY
TUNNEL

Liberty Island

Ferry to Staten Island

Neighborhoods

New York's literary lights never dim, but they do flicker on and off as businesses, people, and neighborhoods move or change. So, incomplete by its very nature, here is an honest, however flawed attempt to associate names with New York neighborhoods.

Brooklyn /
Brooklyn Heights
Agoos, Julie
Alfred, William
Allen, Woody
Anastasia, Albert
Asekoff, Louis
Ashbery, John
Auden, W. H.
Auster, Paul
Banks, Russell
Bares, David
Barrett, Edward
Bennett, James Gordon
Bernstein, Leonard
Blackburn, Paul
Bowles, Jane
Bowles, Paul
Britten, Benjamin
Brodsky, Joseph
Brooklyn College
Broyard, Anatole
Capote, Truman
Community Bookstore
Crane, Hart
Dalí, Salvadore
Davis, George
di Prima, Diane
Donleavy, J. P.
Du Bois, W. E. B.
Dugan, Alan
Emerson, Ralph Waldo
Erasmus Hall High
    School

Fadiman, Clifton
Fields, Jennie
Fields, Kathryn
Frazier, Ian
Gallo, Joey
Gardner, Isabella
    Stewart
Gottschalk, Louis
    Moreau
Greeley, Horace
Green-Wood Cemetery
Guare, John
Hamill, Pete
Harris, Frank
Heller, Joseph
Hochman, Gail
Horton, Philip
Hustvedt, Siri
Ignatow, David
Kalman, Chester
Kazin, Alfred
Kirstein, Lincoln
Lee, Gypsy Rose
MacNeice, Louis
Mailer, Norman
Malamud, Bernard
Mann, Golo
McCullers, Carson
McElroy, Joseph
McMillan, Terry
Middagh Street
Miller, Arthur
Miller, Henry
Montague, John

Montez, Lola
Moore, Marianne
Morris, Mary
Morse, Samuel F.B.
Nin, Anaïs
Nkiru Books
Nurkse, Dennis
Pears, Peter
Podhoretz, Norman
Powers, Alice Leccese
Reznikoff, Charles
Rittenberg, Ann
Roebling, John
Roebling, Washington
Rosten, Norman
Sante, Luc
Sapphire
Schaeffer, Susan
    Fromberg
Schwartz, Delmore
Selby, Hubert
Sendak, Maurice
Sexton, Andrea Wyatt
Simon, Neil
Smith, Betty
Smith, Lillian
Smith, Oliver
Sorrentino, Gilbert
Steinbeck, John
Stephens, Michael
Thoreau, Henry David
Tweed, William M.
    "Boss"
Warsh, Lewis

307

Whitman, Walt
Wolfe, Thomas
Wright, Ellen
Wright, Richard
Yau, John
Zukofsky, Louis

Chelsea
 Boundaries:
   West 34th Street,
   Sixth Avenue,
   West 14th Street,
   Hudson River
Anderson, Margaret
Arensberg, Walter
Ashbery, John
Bard, Stanley
Behan, Brendan
Blackburn, Paul
Books of Wonder
Bryant, William Cullen
Burckhardt, Rudy
Caledonia
Calisher, Hortense
Carey, Tom
Chelsea Hotel
Christopher Street
Coleman, Ornette
Crane, Hart
Denby, Edwin
Dia Center for the Arts
Different Light
Dylan, Bob
Farrell, James T.
Girodias, Maurice
Grateful Dead
Harnack, Curtis
Heap, Jane
Henry, O.
Howells, William Dean
Huncke, Herbert
Jones, Hettie

Jones, LeRoi/Baraka,
 Amiri
Kerouac, Jack
Little Review, The
Marty Hotel
Masters, Edgar Lee
McCarthy, Mary
McFeeley's
Miller, Arthur
Moore, Clement
 Clarke
Myles, Eileen
O'Hara, John
Olympia Press
Publishers Weekly
Rex Foundation
Reznikoff, Charles
Robinson, Edwin
 Arlington
Rorem, Ned
Saroyan, William
Schuyler, James
Sex Pistols
Sid Vicious
Sloan, John
Spungeon, Nancy
Stevens, Wallace
Stout, Rex
Thomas, Dylan
Thomson, Virgil
Totem Press
Twain, Mark
Warhol, Andy
Wolfe, Thomas

Chinatown /
Little Italy
 Boundaries:
   Canal Street
   Lafayette Street,
   East Houston,
   the Bowery

Burroughs, William
Foster, Stephen
Mulberry Street
Riis, Jacob
Scorsese, Martin
Yau, John

East Side
 Boundaries:
   East 59th Street,
   East 86th Street,
   Fifth Avenue,
   East River
Argosy
Auchincloss, Louis
Barbizon Hotel
Blackwood, Lady
 Caroline
Books & Co.
Crawford & Doyle
 Booksellers
Frick, Henry Clay
Grolier Club
Gunther, John
Hellman, Lillian
Hemingway, Ernest
Hurst, Fannie
Hurston, Zora Neale
Jones, Evan & Judith
Lenox Hill Hospital
Luce, Henry
Madison Avenue
 Bookshop
Mayfair Hotel
Merrill, James
O'Hara, John
O'Neill, Eugene
Paris Review
Payne Whitney at New
 York Hospital
Plath, Sylvia
Plimpton, George

Grant's Tomb
Halleck, Fitz-Greene
Harlem Renaissance
Harlem Suitcase
    Theater
Harmon, William E.
Hecht, Anthony,
Himes, Chester
Hollander, John
Horace Mann School
Horowitz, James
Howe, Irving
Hughes, Langston
Hurston, Zora Neale
Johnson, James
    Weldon
Kerouac, Jack
Kleinzahler, August
Koch, Kenneth
Krim, Seymour
Labyrinth
Lehrer, Tom
Levin, Ira
Lewis, Anthony
Lewis, David Levering
Locke, Alain
Lumet, Sidney
Malcolm X
Martí, José
Mason, Mrs. R. Osgood
McKay, Claude
Melville, Herman
Miller, Arthur
Miller, Warren
Moore, Clement
    Clarke
Murray, Albert
Nemerov, Howard
Odets, Clifford
Ozick, Cynthia
Payton, Philip A.
Poe, Edgar Allan
Poets Corner

Posmans at Barnard
Pulitzer, Joseph
Rosenwald, Julius
Rukeyser, Muriel
Runyon, Damon
Salter, James
Schomburg Center for
    Research in Black
    Culture
Schultz, Dutch
Schwartz, Delmore
Simon, Kate
Spingarn, Amy
Temple 7
Thurman, Wallace
Trinity Cemetery
Trotsky, Leon
Twain, Mark
Van Vechten, Carl
Vollmer, Joan
Walker, A'Lelia
Wallant, Edward Lewis
Watson, Steven
West End Bar and Grill
Williams, William
    Carlos
Woodlawn Cemetery
Wouk, Herman
Wright, James
Wright, Richard

Lower East Side
    Boundaries:
    Below East
    Houston from
    the Bowery to the
    East River
Berlin, Irving
Berrigan, Ted
Blackburn, Paul
Cage, John
Cahan, Abraham

Clark, Tom
Cruz, Victor Hernández
Dahlberg, Edward
Dawson, Fielding
di Prima, Diane
Di Yunge
Edelstadt, David
Feldman, Morton
Fuchs, Daniel
Ginsberg, Allen
Glatstein, Jacob
Gold, Mike
Goldman, Emma
Halpern, Moshe Leib
Howe, Irving
Jones, LeRoi
Kazin, Alfred
Kerouac, Jan
Kinnell, Galway
Landau, Zisha
Leib, Mani
Mailer, Norman
Mayer, Bernadette
Padgett, Ron
Riis, Jacob
Rolnick, Joseph
Rosenfeld, Morris
Roth, Henry
Roth, Philip
Shmeruk, Khone
Waldman, Anne
Winchevsky, Morris
Wisse, Ruth R.
Yiddish Poets
Yugend
Zukofsky, Louis

Lower Manhattan
    Boundaries:
    Chambers Street,
    East River,
    Hudson River

Bradford, William
Brown, Charles
    Brockden
Charles Wiley's Shop
da Verrazano, Giovanni
Fraunces Tavern
Freneau, Philip
Gelber, Jack
Gómez, Esteban
Greeley, Horace
Hudson, Henry
Irving, Washington
Jarvis, John Wesley
Melville, Herman
Millenium Hotel
O'Neill, Eugene
Paine, Thomas
Pfaff's Beer Hall
St. Paul's Chapel
Trinity Church
Whitman, Walt

Midtown
    Boundaries:
        Grand Central
            Terminal,
        Rockefeller Center,
        United Nations,
        Central Park,
        Avenue of the
            Americas,
        59th Street,
        39th Street,
        East River
Algonquin Hotel
Algonquin Round
    Table
Bankhead, Tallulah
Barclay Hotel
Brownmiller, Susan
Caldwell, Erskine
Capote, Truman

Caro, Robert
Case, Frank
Coates, Robert
Commodore Hotel
Davidson, Joan K.
de Saint-Exupéry,
    Antoine
DeVries, Peter
Draper, Muriel
Fairbanks, Douglas
Farrell, James T.
Faulkner, William
Fitzgerald, F. Scott
Franks, Lucinda
Garbo, Greta
Gotham Book Mart
Gottlieb, Robert
Greeley, Horace
Hacker
Hammett, Dashiell
Harriman, Margaret
    Case
Hellman, Lillian
Hemingway, Ernest
Kirstein, Lincoln
Kirkus Reviews
Lash, Joseph
LeSueur, Joe
Lewis, David, Garrard
Liveright, Horace
Luce, Henry
Lunts, the
Marshall Club
Marx, Harpo
McCarthy, Mary
McMein, Neysa
Mencken, H.L.
Miller, Arthur
Mitford, Nancy
New York Public
    Library
New Yorker, The
O'Hara, Frank

O'Hara, John
Parker, Dorothy
Perelman, S. J.
Plaza, the
Random House
Reynolds, Quentin
Ross, Harold
Schuyler, James
Scribner's
Sondheim, Stephen
St. Patrick's Cathedral
Stein, Gertrude
Steinbeck, John
Stettheimer, Florine
Sutton Club Hotel
Thompson, Dorothy
Thurber, James
Tibor de Nagy Gallery
Toklas, Alice B.
Updike, John
Van Vechten, Carl
Vanity Fair
Vidal, Gore
West, Nathanael
White, E. B.
Wilder, Thornton
Williams, Tennessee
Wilson, Edmund
Writers Room

Queens
Creedmore State
    Hospital
Guare, John
Guthrie, Woody
Kerouac, Jack
Malcolm X
Marquis, Don
Merman, Ethel
Mumford, Lewis
Riis, Jacob
Whitman, Walt

Simon, Kate
Smith, Patti
Steichen, Edward
Steinbeck, John
Teachers & Writers
  Collaborative
Twain, Mark
Velvet Underground
Waldman, Anne
Warhol, Andy
Warsh, Lewis
West, Nathanael "Pep"
Wharton, Edith
Williams, William
  Carlos

Upper East Side
  Boundaries:
    East 86th Street,
    East 110th Street,
    Fifth Avenue,
    East River
92nd Street Y
Auchincloss, Louis
Barr, Alfred H., Jr.
Berkson, Bill
Berlin, Irving
Elaine's
Hijuelos, Oscar
Kaufman, Elaine
Kitchen Arts and
  Letters
Macdonald, Dwight
McCarthy, Mary
Roth, Philip
Simic, Charles
Straus, Roger

Unterberg Poetry
  Center
West, Nathanael
Wilson, Edmund
Wolfe, Tom

Upper West Side
  Boundaries:
    Central Park,
    Hudson River,
    West 86th Street,
    Cathedral Parkway,
    West 110th Street
Adelman, Stanley
Arendt, Hannah
Barthelme, Donald
Bellow, Saul
Blücher, Heinrich
Capote, Truman
Cendrars, Blaise
Delaney, Samuel R.
Heller, Joseph
Hellman, Lillian
Living Theater
Mailer, Norman
Podhoretz, Norman
Rudman, Mark
Salinger, J. D.
Singer, Isaac Bashevis
Stephens, Michael
Trilling, Diana
Trilling, Lionel
Zweig, Paul

West Side
  Boundaries:
    Hudson River,
    Central Park,
    West 59th Street,
    West 86th Street
Allen, Woody
Ansonia Hotel
Baldwin, James
Bellow, Saul
Crosby, Harry
Dreiser, Theodore
Duchamp, Marcel
Epstein, Barbara
Epstein, Jason
Fitzgerald, F. Scott
Fitzgerald, Zelda
Hardwick, Elizabeth
Heller, Joseph
Hergesheimer, Joseph
Hopwood, Avery
Hotel des Artistes
Lowell, Robert
McBride, Henry
New York Review of
  Books
Nin, Anaïs
Parker, Dorothy
Poe, Edgar Allan
Quinn, John
Reznikoff, Charles
Rorem, Ned
Stettheimer, Florine
Thomson, Virgil
Van Vechten, Carl
Volney Hotel
Williams, Tennessee

Continued from page 33: More bookstores of note include Shakespeare & Co. (716 Broadway), Posman Books (1 University Place), Tower Books (383 Lafayette Street), N.Y.U. Book Center (18 Washington Place), Spring Street Books (169 Spring Street), Different Light (151 West 19th Street), Crawford & Doyle Booksellers (1082 Madison Avenue), Madison Avenue Bookshop (833 Madison Avenue), Coliseum Books (1771 Broadway), Labyrinth (536 West 112th Street), and Posman's at Barnard (2955 Broadway).

Index

Rodgers and Hart, 24, 252–253
Rodgers, Richard, 265
Roebling, John Augustus, 69, 236
Roebling, Washington, 40, 69, 236
Rogers, W. G., 108
Rohatyn, Felix, xxv
Rolling Stones, 86
Rolnick, Joseph, 301
Roosevelt, Theodore, 58, 138, 170, 234, 235, 285
Roosevelt Hospital, 247
Rorem, Ned, 61, 93, 94, 211, 236
Rosenberg, Harold, 57, 65
Rosenfeld, Morris, 301
Rosenfeld, Paul, 151
Rosenthal, Bob, 192
Rosenthal, M. L., 192
Rosenwald, Julius, 121
Ross, Harold, xxiii, 7, 51, 60, 180, 193, 262, 263
Ross, Lillian, 125, 181, 193
Rosset, Barney, 115, 248, 280
Rosten, Norman, 236–237
Roth, Henry, 100, 105, 237–238
Roth, Philip, 3, 8, 58, 65, 100, 164, 202, 208, 238
Rothenberg, Jerome, 55, 75, 187, 216
Rothko, Mark, xviii, 151

Rudman, Mark, 192, 238–239
Rukeyser, Muriel, 55, 239–240
Runyon, Damon, 39, 240, 298
Rushdie, Salman, 4, 108
Ruskin, Mickey, 166
Russell, Bertrand, 156
Russell, Diarmuid, 5
Russell, John, 244
Russo, Vito, 276
Ryan, D. D., 52, 94
Rybczynski, Witold, 276–277

S

Sacks, Oliver, 13
Said, Edward, 64
Saint-Gaudens, Augustus, 9, 138
Salinger, J. D., xviii, 194, 240–241
Salle, David, xx
Salter, James, 129, 196, 211, 217, 242
Sandburg, Carl, 87
Sanders, Ed, 216, 242–243
San Remo, 13, 176, 243
Santayana, George, 79, 218
Sante, Luc, 41, 64
Sapphire, 42, 197
Sargent, John Singer, 138
Saroyan, William, 63, 243–244
Sarris, Andrew, 275

Sartre, Jean-Paul, 34, 224, 280, 299
Sawyer-Lauçanno, Christopher, 34
Schaeffer, Susan Fromberg, 42
Schama, Simon, 64
Schapiro, Meyer, 63, 188, 244–245
Schell, Jonathan, 194
Scherman, Harry, 28
Schisgal, Murray, 3
Schlesinger, Arthur M. Jr., 65, 208
Schnabel, Julian, xx, 167
Schneeman, George, 25, 203
Schoenberg, Arnold, 48, 49, 74
Scholnick, Michael, 192
Schomburg Center for Research in Black Culture, 189–190
Schomburg, Arthur, 189–190
Schulberg, Budd, 142
Schultz, Dutch, 245
Schuyler, James, 13, 34, 35, 57, 61, 78, 94, 95, 117, 149, 166, 191, 199, 216, 229, 236, 245–247, 264, 292
Schwartz, Delmore, 22, 50, 90, 108, 187, 192, 208, 247–248, 289
Schwartz, Lynne Sharon, 65
Scofield, Paul, 271
Scorsese, Martin, 286

Wilentz, Eli, 90, 290
Wilentz, Sean, 91, 290
Wilentz, Ted, 90
Wiley, Charles, 30, 32, 66
Will, George F., 45
Willen, Drenka, 89
Williams, Bert, 272
Williams, Jonathan, 74
Williams, Tennessee, xviii, xxiii, 5, 8, 33, 34, 37, 61, 108, 142, 179, 187, 188, 264, 274, 293–294
Williams, William Carlos, xviii, 12, 18, 27, 55, 63, 79, 87, 129, 150, 154, 157, 182, 186, 196, 207, 227, 239, 248, 257, 269, 294–295, 304
Willis, Meredith Sue, 260
Willis, Nathaniel Parker, 160
Willkie, Wendell, 168, 239
Wills, Gary, 45, 191
Wilson, August, 196
Wilson, Earl, 8
Wilson, Edmund, xvi, xvii, 113, 143, 168, 178, 190, 194, 195, 196, 210, 219, 271, 273, 284, 295–296
Wilson, Lanford, 198, 199

Wilson, Robert, 25, 33
Winchevsky, Morris, 301
Winger, Debra, 33
Winkfield, Trevor, 203, 300
Wiseman, Frederic, 180
Wiseman, Joseph, 260
Wisse, Ruth R., 302
Wolf, Blanche, 148
Wolf, Dan, 162, 274
Wolfe, Theodore F., 160
Wolfe, Thomas, xvii, 5, 41, 60, 61, 210, 224, 296–297
Wolfe, Tom, xxv, 95, 96, 297–298
Wolff, Christian, 49
Wolff, Geoffrey, 71
Wood, Audrey, 5, 293
Wood, Michael, 64, 191
Woodlawn Cemetery, 39, 175, 298
Woolf, Virginia, 6, 302
Woollcott, Alexander, 2, 7, 195
Woolrich, Cornell, 64
World, The, 192, 216, 221
Wouk, Herman, 39, 289
Wright, Frank Lloyd, xxiv
Wright, James, 298
Wright, Richard, 91, 171, 173, 177, 190, 273, 299–300

Writers Room, 300
Wylie, Andrew, 4, 5
Wylie, Elinor, 87, 272
Wyn, A. A., 1

Y

Yanovsky, V. S., 13
Yau, John, xx, 42, 216, 300–301
Yeats, John Butler, 222, 278
Yeats, William Butler, 79, 255, 278
Yiddish Poets, 301–302
Young, Andrew, 184
Young, Art, 87
Young, Kevin, 110
Young, Marguerite, 302
Yugen, 90, 139, 140
Yugend, 301

Z

Z Press, 93
Zaturenska, Marya, 114
Zavatsky, Bill, 18, 64, 216, 261
Zenger, John Peter, xii, xxi, 35, 302–304
Zukofsky, Louis, ix, 64, 108, 233, 304
Zweig, Paul, 305
Zwerin, Michael, 275

Source Notes

We gratefully acknowledge the cooperation of publishers, agents, and the authors for their permission to reprint excerpts from the following works. In some cases, best efforts were made on the author's behalf to gain permission to reprint excerpts, but we acknowledge these below in good faith.

Ashbery, John. "The Instruction Manual" from *Some Trees* by John Ashbery (New Haven: Yale University Press, 1956). Copyright © 1956 by John Ashbery. Reprinted by permission of Georges Borchardt, Inc. for the author.

Auden, W.H. "September 1, 1939" from *W. H. Auden: Collected Poems* by W. H. Auden, edited by Edward Mendelson. Copyright © 1940 by W. H. Auden. Reprinted by permission of Random House, Inc.

Berrigan, Ted. Excerpts from *Selected Poems* by Ted Berrigan, published by Penguin Books, copyright © 1994 by Alice Notley and the Estate of Ted Berrigan.

Bishop, Elizabeth. Excerpts from "Letter to N.Y." and "Invitation to Miss Marianne Moore" from *The Complete Poems 1927–1979* by Elizabeth Bishop. Copyright © 1979, 1983 by Alice Helen Methfessel. Reprinted by permission of Farrar, Straus & Giroux, Inc.

Cheever, John. Preface excerpt from *The Stories of John Cheever* by John Cheever, published by Alfred A. Knopf, Inc. Copyright © 1978 by John Cheever.

Corso, Gregory. "Marriage" by Gregory Corso from the book, *Mindfield*. Copyright © 1989 by Gregory Corso. Used by permission of the Publisher, Thunder's Mouth Press.

Cruz, Victor Hernández. "Essay on William Carlos Williams" copyright © 1991 by Victor Hernández Cruz. Reprinted from *Red Beans,* published by Coffee House Press.

Ginsberg, Allen. Four lines from "America" from *Collected Poems 1947–1980* by Allen Ginsberg. Copyright © 1956, 1959 by Allen Ginsberg. Copyright Renewed. Reprinted by permission of HarperCollins Publishers, Inc.

Ginsberg, Allen. Five lines from "Kaddish" from *Collected Poems 1947–1980* by Allen Ginsberg. Copyright © 1959 by Allen Ginsberg. Copyright Renewed. Reprinted by permission of HarperCollins Publishers, Inc.

Guest, Barbara. "Santa Fe Trail," copyright © 1960, 1995 by Barbara Guest. Reprinted from *Selected Poems* by Barbara Guest with the permission of Sun & Moon Press.

Hughes, Langston. "Harlem" and other excerpts from *Selected Poems of Langston Hughes* by Langston Hughes, published by Alfred A. Knopf, Inc. Copyright © 1987 by George Houston Bass and the Estate of Langston Hughes.

Kirstein, Lincoln. Excerpt from "Carl Van Vechten: 1880–1964" from *By With To & From: A Lincoln Kirstein Reader* by Lincoln Kirstein, edited by Nicholas

Jenkins. Copyright © 1991 by Lincoln Kirstein. Reprinted by permission of Farrar, Straus & Giroux, Inc.

Leiber, Stoller, Mann, and Weil. "On Broadway" lyrics by Jerry Leiber, Mike Stoller, Barry Mann, and Cynthia Weil. Copyright © 1993 Warner Bros. Publications, Inc.

Lorde, Audre. "When the Saints Come Marching In" copyright © 1976 by Audre Lorde, from *The Collected Poems of Audre Lorde* by Audre Lorde. Reprinted by permission of W.W. Norton & Company, Inc.

Merrill, James. *Lines on Books & Co.* by James Merrill. Reprinted with the permission of the Estate of James Merrill.

Montague, John. "A Muddy Cup" from *Born in Brooklyn: John Montague's America.* Copyright © 1991 by John Montague. Reprinted by permission of White Pine Press.

Moore, Marianne. "New York" by Marianne Moore reprinted with the permission of Simon & Schuster from *The Collected Poems of Marianne Moore.* Copyright © 1935 by Marianne Moore; copyright renewed © 1963 by Marianne Moore and T. S. Eliot.

Obenzinger, Hilton. "Triangle Shirtwaist Company" from Hilton Obenzinger, *New York on Fire,* copyright © 1989 Hilton Obenzinger, The Real Comet Press, Seattle, WA.

O'Hara, Frank. "The Day Lady Died" and other excerpts from *The Collected Poems of Frank O'Hara* by Frank O'Hara, edited by Donald Allen and published by Alfred A. Knopf, Inc. Copyright © 1971 by Maureen Granville-Smith and the Estate of Frank O'Hara.

Porter, Cole. "I Happen to Like New York" lyrics by Cole Porter. Copyright © 1931 Warner Bros. Publications, Inc.

Reznikoff, Charles. Three lines by Charles Reznikoff, from *By the Waters of Manhattan.* Copyright © 1959 by Charles Reznikoff. Reprinted by permission of New Directions Publishing Corp.

Schuyler, James. Excerpt from "Dining Out with Doug and Frank" from *Collected Poems* by James Schuyler. Copyright © 1993 by the Estate of James Schuyler. Reprinted by permission of Farrar, Straus & Giroux, Inc.

Swenson, May. "Snow in New York," copyright © 1978 by May Swenson. Used with permission of the Literary Estate of May Swenson.

Wakefield, Dan. Excerpt from *New York in the Fifties* by Dan Wakefield and published by Houghton Mifflin Company. Copyright © 1993 by Dan Wakefield.

Williams, William Carlos. "January Morning" by William Carlos Williams, from *Collected Poems: 1909–1939, Volume I.* Copyright © 1938 by New Directions Publishing Corp. Reprinted by permission of New Directions Publishing Corp.

Acknowledgments ─────────

A book of this scope needs friends. This one has been fortunate enough to have many who gave generously of their time and attention. They are Paul Auster, Siri Hustvedt, Jane Gunther, Ed Friedman, Kenward Elmslie, Ron Padgett, Marni Corbett, Fred C. Moten, Tamara McKenna, Steven Watson, Christopher Sawyer-Lauçanno, Darragh Park, Nathan Kernan, Ed Barrett, Sue Miller, Steve Hull, Mike County, Judith Watkins, Ben E. Watkins, Roland F. Pease Jr., Spurgeon Keeny, Charles Peck, Jonathan Aaron, Dionisio Arñas, Arden Corbett, Deborah Treisman, Mark Rudman, Jane Shore, Jane Hammond, James Laughlin, August Kleinzahler, Jaime Manrique, and Michael Moore.

I salute Jessica Davis, who first suggested I write about literary New York City. Had she not put the bee in my bonnet I almost certainly would never have written in this way about a city I have loved since my first childhood visits.

More than thanks are owed to Robert Frumkin. This book is lucky beyond measure that he married our daughter Marni in May 1996. A lifelong New Yorker, Robert has been indefatigable in doing my legwork as I wrote this book in Boston and Greensboro, Vermont. This alone earns my heartfeld gratitude, but he did more, painstakingly reading this book in manuscript, suggesting corrections, and demanding the best I had. His work on, and support of, my efforts has made all the difference, and I am one grateful father-in-law.

The text of *New York Literary Lights* is set in Sabon, a typeface based on letters cut by Claude Garamond and named for his pupil Jacques Sabon. Sabon was designed in the 1960s by Jan Tschichold. Entry headings are set in Gerard Unger's Amerigo typeface; the script is Isadora, by Kris Holmes. Stanton Publication Services, Inc., set the type and the book was manufactured by Edwards Bros., Ann Arbor on acid-free paper.